Lecture Notes in Computer Scie

T0259899

Commenced Publication in 1973
Founding and Former Series Editors:
Gerhard Goos, Juris Hartmanis, and Jan van Leeuwen

Editorial Board

David Hutchison
Lancaster University, UK

Takeo Kanade
Carnegie Mellon University, Pittsburgh, PA, USA

Josef Kittler
University of Surrey, Guildford, UK

Jon M. Kleinberg
Cornell University, Ithaca, NY, USA

Alfred Kobsa
University of California, Irvine, CA, USA

Friedemann Mattern
ETH Zurich, Switzerland

John C. Mitchell
Stanford University, CA, USA

Moni Naor
Weizmann Institute of Science, Rehovot, Israel

Oscar Nierstrasz
University of Bern, Switzerland

C. Pandu Rangan
Indian Institute of Technology, Madras, India

Bernhard Steffen
TU Dortmund University, Germany

Madhu Sudan
Microsoft Research, Cambridge, MA, USA

Demetri Terzopoulos
University of California, Los Angeles, CA, USA

Doug Tygar
University of California, Berkeley, CA, USA

Gerhard Weikum
Max Planck Institute for Informatics, Saarbruecken, Germany

Yang Xiang Mukaddim Pathan Xiaohui Tao
Hua Wang (Eds.)

Data and Knowledge Engineering

Third International Conference, ICDKE 2012
Wuyishan, Fujian, China, November 21-23, 2012
Proceedings

 Springer

Volume Editors

Yang Xiang
Deakin University
School of Information Technology
Burwood, VIC, Australia
E-mail: yang@deakin.edu.au

Mukaddim Pathan
Media Distribution
Telstra Corporation Limited
Melbourne, VIC, Australia
E-mail: mukaddim.pathan@team.telstra.com

Xiaohui Tao
The University of Southern Queensland
Department of Mathematics and Computing
Toowoomba, QLD, Australia
E-mail: xtao@usq.edu.au

Hua Wang
The University of Southern Queensland
Department of Mathematics and Computing
Toowoomba, QLD, Australia
E-mail: hua.wang@usq.edu.au

ISSN 0302-9743   e-ISSN 1611-3349
ISBN 978-3-642-34678-1   e-ISBN 978-3-642-34679-8
DOI 10.1007/978-3-642-34679-8
Springer Heidelberg Dordrecht London New York

Library of Congress Control Number: 2012951317

CR Subject Classification (1998): I.2, H.3-5, C.2, J.1, K.6.5

LNCS Sublibrary: SL 3 – Information Systems and Application, incl. Internet/Web
and HCI

© Springer-Verlag Berlin Heidelberg 2012
This work is subject to copyright. All rights are reserved, whether the whole or part of the material is
concerned, specifically the rights of translation, reprinting, re-use of illustrations, recitation, broadcasting,
reproduction on microfilms or in any other way, and storage in data banks. Duplication of this publication
or parts thereof is permitted only under the provisions of the German Copyright Law of September 9, 1965,
in its current version, and permission for use must always be obtained from Springer. Violations are liable
to prosecution under the German Copyright Law.
The use of general descriptive names, registered names, trademarks, etc. in this publication does not imply,
even in the absence of a specific statement, that such names are exempt from the relevant protective laws
and regulations and therefore free for general use.

Typesetting: Camera-ready by author, data conversion by Scientific Publishing Services, Chennai, India

Printed on acid-free paper

Springer is part of Springer Science+Business Media (www.springer.com)

Preface

The International Conference on Data and Knowledge Engineering (ICDKE) 2012 was held in WuyiShan, Fujian, China, during November 21–23, 2012, jointly with the 6th International Conference on Network and System Security (NSS 2012) and the 5th International Conference on Internet and Distributed Computing Systems (IDCS 2012). ICDKE 2012 was organized and supported by the School of Mathematics and Computer Science, Fujian Normal University, China, and the Faculty of Sciences, University of Southern Queensland, Australia.

ICDKE is a leading international forum for researchers, developers, and end-users to explore cutting-edge ideas and results for the problems in the data and knowledge fields, and to exchange related techniques and methodologies. The missions of ICDKE are to share novel research solutions to problems of today's information society that fulfill the needs of heterogeneous applications and environments, as well to identify new issues and directions for future research and development.

The First International Conference on Data and Knowledge Engineering (ICDKE 2010) was held in Melbourne, Australia, during September 1–3, 2010; the Second International Conference on Data and Knowledge Engineering (ICDKE 2011) was held in Milan, Italy, during September 6–8, 2011. Following the great success of ICDKE 2010 and 2011, the Third International Conference on Data and Knowledge Engineering (ICDKE 2012) was held in Wuyishan, China, providing a forum for academics and industry practitioners to present research on all practical and theoretical aspects of advanced data-intensive applications, data and knowledge engineering as well as case studies and implementation experiences. ICDKE 2012 gave researchers and practitioners a unique opportunity to share their perspectives with others interested in the various aspects of engineering.

ICDKE 2012 attracted 53 submissions from 11 countries and regions: Australia, Brazil, China, Egypt, France, Germany, Hong Kong, Iran, Ireland, Pakistan, and Tunisia. The review process was rigorous. Each paper was reviewed by at least two reviewers, and most of them reviewed by three to four reviewers. The Program Committee accepted 13 submissions as full papers (giving an approximate acceptance rate of 25%) and seven short papers for inclusions in the proceedings.

We would like to thank the members of the Program Committee and Organizing Committee who contributed to the success of the conference. Last, but certainly not least, our thanks go to all authors and attendees. We hope you enjoy the conference proceedings!

November 2012

Yang Xiang
Mukaddim Pathan
Xiaohui Tao
Hua Wang

ICDKE 2012 Organization

General Co-chairs

Hua Wang · University of Southern Queensland, Australia
Xinyi Huang · Fujian Normal University, China

Program Co-chairs

Xiaohui Tao · University of Southern Queensland, Australia
Hongmin Cai · South China University of Technology, China

Publicity Co-chairs

S. Ramasamy · Computer Society of India, India
Ji Zhang · University of Southern Queensland, Australia
Xiaodong Zhu · Nanjing University of Information Science and Technology, China
Lei Zou · Peking University, China

Program Committee

Abdulmohsen Algarni · Queensland University of Technology, Australia
James Bailey · University of Melbourne, Australia
Irena Bojanova · University of Maryland University College, USA
Karima Boudaoud · University of Nice, Sophia Antipolis, France
Jin Chen · Michigan State University, USA
Zhong Chen · Peking University, China
Flavius Frasincar · Erasmus University Rotterdam, The Netherlands
Naoki Fukuta · Shizuoka University, Japan
Qigang Gao · Dalhousie University, Canada
Jihong Guan · Tongji University, China
Jingzhi Guo · University of Macau, China
Abdul Hafeez-Baig · University of Southern Queensland, Australia
Jan Hidders · TUDelft, The Netherlands
Stephen Huang · The University of Houston, USA
Shaoquan Jiang · University of Calgary, Canada
Yuhua Jiao · Michigan State University, USA
Raymond Y.K. Lau · City University of Hong Kong, China
Jiuyong Li · University of Southern Australia, Australia

Tianrui Li	Southwest Jiaotong University, China
Yidong Li	Beijing Jiaotong University, China
Zhengrong Li	Ergon Energy, Australia
Xiaodong Lin	University of Ontario Institute of Technology, Canada
Qing Liu	CSIRO ICT Centre, Australia
Xuezheng Liu	Google Inc., Beijing, China
Yezheng Liu	Hefei University of Technology, China
Yuee Liu	Queensland University of Technology, Australia
Sofian Maabout	University of Bordeaux, France
Nils Muellner	University of Oldenburg, Germany
Niu Nan	Mississippi State University, USA
Sanaullah Nazir	AOL Global Operations Limited, Ireland
Sudsanguan Ngamsuriyaroj	Mahidol University, Thailand
Kok-Leong Ong	Deakin University, Australia
Kanagasabai Rajaraman	Institute for Infocomm Research (I2R), Singapore
Chunming Rong	University of Stavanger, Norway
Julian Schutte	Fraunhofer Institute for Secure Information Technology, Germany
Yanfeng Shu	CSIRO ICT Centre, Australia
Paulo de Souza	CSIRO ICT Centre, Australia
Hai Wang	Saint Mary's University, Canada
Ying-Hong Wang	Tamkang University, Taiwan
Ian Welch	Victoria University of Wellington, New Zealand
Guandong Xu	Victoria University, Australia
Shin-Jer Yang	Soochow University, Taipei, Taiwan
Chunxia Zhang	Beijing Institute of Technology, China
Yi Zhang	Sichuan University, China
Laiping Zhao	Kyushu university, Japan
Yanchang Zhao	RDataMining, Australia
Emily X. Zhou	CSIRO ICT Centre, Australia
Xujuan Zhou	Queensland University of Technology, Australia

Table of Contents

ICDKE: Artificial Intelligence and Data Engineering

ICDKE: Knowledge Discovery and Data Management

OR-Tree: An Optimized Spatial Tree Index
for Flash-Memory Storage Systems

Na Wang[1], Peiquan Jin[1], Shouhong Wan[1], Yinghui Zhang[2,3], and Lihua Yue[1]

[1] School of Computer Science and Technology,
University of Science and Technology of China, 230027, Hefei, China
wangna@mail.ustc.edu.cn, {jpq,wansh,llyue}@ustc.edu.cn
[2] Beihang University, 100085, Beijing, China
[3] Beijing Institute of Remote Sensing, 100011, Beijing, China

Abstract. Nowadays, flash memory is widely used in various portable devices such as PDAs (personal digital assistants) and HPCs (handheld PCs). With the development of location-based services (LBS) provided by those portable devices, how to provide efficient spatial data management over flash-equipped LBS devices has become a critical issue in recent years. In this paper, we aim to propose an efficient flash-optimized spatial tree index, called OR-tree, to improve the queries and updates on flash-resident spatial data. The OR-tree is based on R-tree and introduces two new techniques to make the R-tree suitable for flash memory storage system. First, we employ a lazy node splitting policy by introducing overflow nodes for the leaf nodes in R-tree. Next, we redesign the algorithms of update operations to adapt the unbalanced OR-tree structure. To evaluate the performance of the OR-tree, we conduct experiments on a spatial data set gathered from the R-tree portal. We run different workloads and compare the OR-tree with other competitors on the basis of different metrics including flash page usage, flash write count, erasure count, and runtime. The experimental results show that the OR-tree outperforms the competitors considering both space efficiency and time performance.

Keywords: Spatial tree index, Flash memory, Algorithm, R-tree.

1   Introduction

Nowadays, flash memory as well as flash-based solid state drives (SSDs) becomes more and more popular as it has several superior characteristics compared with magnetic disks, such as smaller size, lighter weight, lower power consumption, shock resistance, lower noise and faster read performance [19-21]. In particular, flash memory greatly gained acceptance in various portable devices such as PDAs (person-al digital assistants) and HPCs (handheld PCs). At present, many types of PDAs and HPCs provide location-based services (LBS) [23]. Therefore, how to provide efficient spatial data management over flash-equipped LBS devices has become a critical issue in recent years [6].

In this paper, we focus on optimizing spatial tree index for flash memory. Spatial tree index structures, among which the R-tree [8-9] is the most representative, are

Y. Xiang et al. (Eds.): ICDKE 2012, LNCS 7696, pp. 1–14, 2012.
© Springer-Verlag Berlin Heidelberg 2012

necessary to boost up spatial query performance. However, flash memory has many properties differing from magnetic disk, e.g. write-once, block erasure, asymmetric read/write speed and limited block erase count. Traditional spatial tree indexes do not consider the asymmetric I/O properties of flash memory (as shown in Table 1). Yet, reducing the write/erase count for indexing approaches is not only useful to improve the runtime, but also helpful to extend the life cycle of flash memory.

Table 1. The characteristics of NAND Flash memory [17].

Operation	Access time	Access granularity
Read	25μs/page	Page(2KB)
Write	200μs/page	Page(2KB)
Erase	1500μs/block	Block(256KB=128pages)

There are also some previous studies focusing on flash-based spatial tree indexes [1, 5, 24]. Most of them are based on the B-tree and employ a lazy update policy to reduce the high-cost random writes and erase operations on flash memory, in which all the node updates are buffered in main memory and the node with the most updates is written into flash memory in case of buffer replacement. However, little attention has been paid on the improvement of the high-cost node splitting operation in R-tree.

In this paper, we propose an optimization approach to solve the problem existing in previous flash-aware R-tree. The main idea and contributions of the paper can be summarized as follows:

(1) We propose a flash-optimized spatial tree index called OR-tree. The OR-tree employs the idea of deferring node splitting when updating R-tree by using overflow nodes. This will result in an unbalanced tree structure but can reduce the random writes and further erasures on flash memory (see Section 3.1). We propose the merge back operation of overflow nodes, which efficiently avoid the gains of unbalanced OR-tree to be counterweighed by read overhead of overflow nodes (see Section 3.2).
(2) We redesign the algorithms of update operations to adapt the unbalanced OR-tree structure. The revised *OR_Insert* algorithm choose to add the new element into the overflow node instead of invoking node splitting if the primary node is full, while the OR_*Search* algorithm needs to check both the primary node and the overflow node during lookup of the OR-tree. Compared with previous flash-aware R-tree algorithms, our approach can reduce more flash random writes especially under skewed access patterns (see Section 4).
(3) We conduct simulated experiments on a spatial dataset and run one million transactions to evaluate the efficiency of the OR-tree by using different workloads and different metrics. The experimental results show that the OR-tree outperforms the competitors considering both space efficiency and time performance. (see Section 5).

2   Related Work

Due to the characteristics that random writes are much slower than sequential writes and random reads on flash memory, it is common to reduce the number of random writes so as to obtain high update performance. Some flash-aware indexes sacrifice sequential writes and random reads to avoid random write operations, such as write-optimized B-tree [13] and dynamic hash [14].

Generally, the update performance on flash memory can be improved by buffering updates in memory and flushing them to flash memory in batches. Wu et al. proposed BFTL [15] and RFTL [1] respectively for B-Tree and R-tree that handle fine-grained updates in a layer over FTL for flash-memory-based disks. They allowed modification entries of different nodes to be stored sequentially in memory, and then packaged them into sectors to write to flash memory when in-memory storage is full. As the number of updates delayed is in proportion to memory size, Kang et al. proposed μ-Tree [25] to put all the nodes along the path from the root to the leaf together into a single NAND flash memory page for raw flash memory at the absence of FTL. However, it can't adapt to large amount of data because it only used small-sized nodes in the index structure. Agrawal et al. proposed LA-Tree [4] that used to buffer updates in flash resident cascaded buffers which are corresponded to each two-level subtree, it consequently reduced the traditional use of memory for caching. LA-Tree focused on raw, small-capacity and byte addressable flash memory. Li et al. proposed FD-Tree [2, 3] for off-the-shelf large flash SSDs, which improved update performance by allowing main memory resident head tree and organizing elements of remaining levels in an ascending order, while improved search performance by stored fence pointer in each level. However, FD-Tree needs to reorganize all its entries when the merge operation generates a new level.

LCR-tree [24] as an efficient spatial index for SSDs was designed to combine newly arrival log with origin ones on the same node, which renders great decrement of random writes with at most one additional read for each node access. However, it needs to read all origin logs and rewrite them for each modification. Sarwat proposed FAST-Rtree [5] that used an external upper-layer framework which encapsulates the original algorithms. In FAST-Rtree, updates are buffered in main memory and hashed by node identifier so as to be flushed to flash memory in batches. However, it has not considered node splitting techniques.

Srinivasan et al. presented an adaptive overflow technique to defer node splitting in B-Trees to improve the storage utilization [7], however it didn't consider to merge back the overflow node until it was full. Manousaka et al. proposed lazy parent split to achieve better concurrency [26] while it didn't reduce the number of random write operations. Bozanis et al. proposed a logarithmic decomposable spatial index method named as LR-tree [27] based on R*-tree [22] to avoid performance tuning with forced reinsertion, each component sub-structures called blocks is organized as a weak R-tree. Whenever an insertion operation must be served, a set of blocks are chosen to first destroy and then reconstruct using bulk-loading. However, the invalid space in nodes of sub-structures due to the deletion-only principle and the additional bulk-loading cost in LR-tree reconstruction phrase cannot be neglected. Koltsidas et al. presented desiderata for improved I/O performance of spatial tree index over flash memory and gave a brief analysis of the unbalanced structure of spatial tree index [6]. It can be easily seen the superiority of the unbalanced structure of spatial tree index, which is also adopted in our improved version of R-tree.

3   Deferring Node Splitting on OR-Tree

To address the problems of RFTL and FAST-Rtree mentioned in Section 2, we propose an improved spatial index tree structure for flash memory storage system, which
is called *OR-tree (Overflow R-tree)*. Our goal is to achieve high update performance
while maintaining acceptable search performance. The general idea of OR-tree is to
improve R-tree by deferring node splitting on R-tree. This is done by using overflow-
ing nodes, which in turn results in an unbalanced tree structure.

3.1   Unbalanced OR-Tree Structure

R-tree and its variations [22] are all balanced trees. If a newly added element causes
the designated node to exceed the maximum capacity, a node splitting operation in R-
tree will be invoked. A node splitting operation generally brings three write operations, while only one write operation happens if no splitting occurs. This distinction is
never mind in hard disk memory where the read and write costs have no significant
difference. Given the unique characteristics of flash memory, we should pay special
attention to reduce the number of node splitting operations in spatial tree index.

In OR-tree, we defer node splitting operation and then execute more than one node
splitting at the same time. The unbalanced spatial tree index structure is the result of
deferring splitting. The unbalanced structure for B+-tree has been demonstrated to be
useful in improving space utilization [7], but we will show that the unbalanced OR-
tree can also improve updating and searching performance. Figure.1 shows the unbalanced tree structure of OR-tree after inserting an element e to a full node P. P and its
parent node R is not updated, a new node Q is created, and the new element is inserted
into Q. We call Q as an *Overflow Node* (denoted as O-node in the following text), and
the attached node P is a *Primary Node* (denoted as P-node).

According to the structure illustrated in Fig.1, there is only one random write to Q,
when inserting a new element into the OR-tree, even if the targeted leaf node is full.

OR-tree utilizes a hash table named as *Overflow Node Table* to keep track of the
correspondence of P-node and O-nodes that have not been merged back yet. Assuming there is no hashing collision, each entry in the hash table represents all the O-
nodes that attached to a unique P-node identifier, and has the former of (k, *TSC*, *list*)
where k is O-nodes count, *TSC* is the total count of search operations for elements in

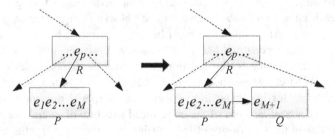

Fig. 1. Unbalanced OR-tree after Inserting Element e

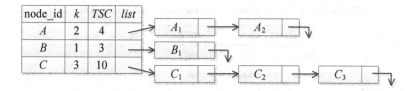

Fig. 2. Overflow Node Table

O-nodes attached to the P-node identifier, while list is a list of O-node identifier that was attached to the same P-node identifier. Figure.2 gives an example of the *Overflow Node Table*. Namely, there are two O-nodes A_1, A_2 attached to P-node A, and there have been four search operations for elements in A_1, A_2 aggregately.

3.2 Merge Back of the Overflow Nodes

OR-tree aims to reduce the count of random writes by inserting new elements into O-nodes instead of node splitting. However, this solution will introduce a new problem. As each overflow node (O-node) is associated with a primary node (P-node), access to O-node needs additional read operations. Although read is faster than write on flash memory, gains of unbalanced OR-tree would be counterweighed by read overhead caused by overflow nodes.

In order to solve this problem, we introduce the merge back operation to the OR-tree. The merge back operation is designed to merge a P-node with its associated O-nodes. This operation is able to reduce the read operations when accessing the elements in the original O-nodes, because they have been merged into P-nodes and no additional read operations are required. Based on the merge back operation, the count of the O-nodes associated with each P-node will remain a small number, which ensures that less read operations are needed when an O-node is accessed.

As the objective of deferring node splitting is to reduce random writes on flash memory, more deferred node splitting operations generally will result in less random writes to flash memory but more reads to the O-nodes. Therefore, we have to find a best solution to maintain the chain of O-nodes, so that we can gain the best I/O performance over flash memory.

Table 2 shows the symbols used to analyze the merge back operations. Suppose that there are k O-nodes which are attached to a specific P-node P in OR-tree, the total count of elements in P-node and O-nodes is $N \in [k \times M+1, (k+1) \times M]$, in which M is the maximum node capacity. When we determine whether a merge back operation should be performed, we employ a cost-based scheme to find the right answer. Let $TG(P)$ denotes the total gains of the deferring node splitting for the P-node P, $TC(P)$ is the total costs of performing a merge back operation for the P-node P, we have to ensure $TG(P) > TC(P)$. Next, we will analyze the details of $TG(P)$ and $TC(P)$.

First we assume the average cost of read on flash memory is x, and the average cost of write on flash memory is y. If the unbalanced OR-tree has deferred t node splitting operations, we can find that $t \in [k, 2 \times k+1]$. As every node splitting operation brings three writes to flash memory, namely two writes to the child nodes and one to

Table 2. Symbols used to analyze the merge back operation

Symbol	Meaning
x	Average cost of reading a flash page
y	Average cost of writing a flash page
M	Capacity of an OR-tree node
k	Count of the associated O-nodes for a given P-node
$TG(P)$	Gained benefits of deferring node splitting for the P-node P
$TC(P)$	Total costs of merge back for the P-node P
$TSC(P)$	the total count of accesses to the O-nodes associated with the P-node P

the parent node, the total gains of k O-nodes in OR-tree is $3 \times t \times y$. Therefore, the average value of TG can be determined as the following formula (1), where t is assigned its average value $(3 \times k+1) / 2$.

$$TG(P) = \left\lfloor \frac{3}{2} \times (3 \times k + 1) \right\rfloor \times y \tag{1}$$

Next, we give the analysis on $TC(P)$. If k O-nodes are needed to be merged back, it would bring $k+2$ writes. Besides, one random write is required when creating an O-node. As a result, k O-nodes consumes totally $(2k+2) \times y$ write costs after merging back. Apart from this, each access to O-node brings x additional read cost. Therefore, the total costs of merge back k O-nodes can be formulated as follows:

$$TC(P) = (2 \times k + 2) \times y + TSC(P) \tag{2}$$

Here $TSC(P)$ refers to the total count of accesses to the O-nodes associated with the P-node P. In order to ensure $TG(P) > TC(P)$, we can deduce formula (3) from (1) and (2):

$$TSC(P) < \left\lfloor \frac{5 \times k - 1}{2} \right\rfloor \times \frac{y}{x} \tag{3}$$

Table 3. The count of overflow nodes vs. the access count threshold

O-node count	Total access count threshold
1	$2 \times \dfrac{y}{x}$
2	$4 \times \dfrac{y}{x}$
...	...
k	$\left\lfloor \dfrac{5 \times k - 1}{2} \right\rfloor \times \dfrac{y}{x}$

As long as the total count of accesses to k O-nodes does not exceed $\left\lfloor \frac{5 \times k - 1}{2} \right\rfloor \times \frac{y}{x}$, the unbalanced OR-Tree structure is still preferable. For example, if there is only one

O-node associated with the P-node, i.e., $k=1$, the threshold of total access count to decide when to merge back the O-node must be less than $\frac{2y}{x}$. According to formula (3), we can get the quantitative relation of O-node count k and total access count threshold TSC (as shown in Table 3).

The merge back operation is performed when a new element is inserted into the OR-tree, which is shown in Algorithm.1 *AddElement*. The algorithm first checks if the leaf node P is full. If P is not full, the new element e is inserted into P directly. Otherwise, we find the entry for the node P in the *Overflow Node Table*, and insert the new element into one of the found O-nodes in the *Overflow Node Table*. Then it determines whether to merge back the O-nodes.

Algorithm.1. *AddElement*(Node P, Element e)
1. **If** P is non-full node, insert e into P as a child node.
2. **If** P is full, let *HashEntry* = P entry in the *Overflow Node Table*
3.   **If** *HashEntry* is not NULL, find a non-full O-node in *HashEntry.list* and insert an element e into it. **If** $HashEntry.TSC = \left\lfloor \dfrac{5 \times HashEntry.k + 1}{2} \right\rfloor \times \dfrac{y}{x}$, merge back the O-nodes of P to obtain P and a node set S; delete *HashEntry* in the *Overflow Node Table*.
4.   **Else**, create a new entry for node P in the *Overflow Node Table*. Then insert an O-node with only one element e into *list* of the new entry.

End *AddElement*

It is interesting to see that the merge back operation has an impact on the flash memory space overhead of the OR-tree. As shown in Algorithm.1, *AddElement* merges back the O-nodes of P to return P and a node set S. P and the nodes in S contain the element e, the old elements in P, and the old elements in all its O-nodes. If we abandon the original O-nodes and create new nodes during the merge back operation, OR-tree will consume one more flash page than R-tree for each O-node, and in turn result in a large space overhead. Another way is to reuse the existed O-nodes to store the new nodes in S, since the O-nodes are free to use after being merged back. In this case, OR-tree consumes the same amount of flash memory space as traditional R-tree, or even less. Our experiments demonstrate that OR-tree has a comparable space overhead with the traditional R-tree. Details will be discussed in Section 5.

4   Operations on OR-Tree

The update operations of OR-tree can be classified into insertion, deletion and modification. The modification is accomplished by first insertion and then deletion, while the deletion focuses on searching for the element.

4.1   Insertion of OR-Tree

The insertion operation in OR-tree is described in the *OR_Insert* algorithm (as shown in Algorithm.2). It consists of the following two stages.

(1) Firstly, it executes the insertion in main memory and records all the modified nodes in list *List* (line 1 to 4 in Algorithm.2). It first invokes *ChooseLeaf* (as shown in Algorithm.3) to select the optimal leaf node to place the element *e*; then invokes *AddElement(L, e)* to insert the element *e* into the leaf node *L*. After that, it invokes *AdjustTree(L)* (as shown in Algorithm.4) to adjust MBBs and propagate node merging operation from the leaf node to the root. If necessary, a new root will be created.

(2) Secondly (line 5 to 6 in Algorithm.2), for each node *N* in the list *List*, the *OR_Insert* algorithm caches updates occurred in *N* in the main memory buffer. Due to the high cost of random write on flash memory, we employ a buffering scheme proposed by Sarwat in [5] for OR-tree, which first buffers the node updates to *P*-nodes and *O*-nodes in main memory, and then flushes them to flash memory in batch before in-memory buffer overflows. Previous work has proved that on raw flash devices, e.g. TC58DVG02A1FT00 [10], the optimal flushing unit size is similar to one block [11], while for SSDs a flushing unit size of 16KB is a good choice. Due to the rule that pages which have continuous logical page-id are used to reside adjacent to each other [12], we will gather nodes with continual node-id into the same flushing unit, and then select the flushing unit with the highest number of in-memory updates to flush into flash memory according to the flushing algorithm described in the literature [5].

Algorithm.2. *OR_Insert*(Root *R*, Element *e*)

1. Invoke ***ChooseLeaf***(*R, e*)   to find a leaf node *L* to place element *e*.
2. Invoke ***AddElement***(*L, e*) to insert the element *e* into the leaf node *L*.
3. Invoke ***AdjustTree*** (*L*) to adjust MBBs and propagate node merging operation up the tree.
4. If the propagation caused *O*-nodes of the root *R* to merge back and produced a node set *S*, then create a new root whose children are *R* and nodes in *S*.
5. Let *List*= the list of the modified nodes during the insertion of the element *e*.
6. **For** each node *N* in *List*, cache updates of *N* in the main memory buffer.

End *OR_Insert*

Algorithm.3. *ChooseLeaf*(Node *N*, Element *e*)

1. **If** *N* is a leaf node, **Return** *N*.
2. **Else** find the element *f* in *N* or its *O*-nodes whose MBB *f.mbb* needs least enlargement to include *e.mbb*, and increase the *TSC* of *N* entry in the *Overflow Node Table*.
3. Set *N* to be the child node pointed to by *f.ptr* and go to Step 1.

End *ChooseLeaf*

Algorithm.4. *AdjustTree*(Node *N*)

1. **If** *N* is the root, **Return**.
2. Let *P* be the parent node of *N*, and e_N be *N*'s element in *P*, adjust $e_N.mbb$ so that it tightly includes all element MBBs in *N* and its *O*-nodes.
3. **If** *P* is a *O*-node and P_1 is the *P*-node of *P*, let *P* to be P_1.
4. **If** *N* has a node set *S* resulting from earlier merging back operation, **for** each node *NN* in *S*, create a new element e_{NN} with $e_{NN}.ptr$ pointing to *NN* and $e_{NN}.mbb$ enclosing all MBBs in *NN*; Invoke ***AddElement***(*P*, e_{NN}).
5. Set *N*=*P* and repeat from Step 1.

End *AdjustTree*

4.2   Searching and Deletion in OR-Tree

Given an OR-tree whose root node is R, when it receives a lookup request, *OR_Search* searches the tree up-to-bottom and finds all satisfied records whose MBBs overlap a searching MBB m. A main distinction from an R-Tree is that if a node on the root-to-leaf path has several attached *O*-nodes, the OR-tree also scans attached *O*-nodes to find elements that satisfy the lookup request. A unique feature of our work is that while performing a scan to an *O*-node of the *P*-node, the *OR_Search* algorithm increases the *TSC* of R's entry in the *Overflow Node Table* by one. In *AddElement*, it determines whether to merge back the *O*-node according to the *TSC* value of entry in the *Overflow Node Table*.

In a similar manner to *OR_Insert*, the deletion of OR-tree *OR_Delete* firstly locates leaf node L containing the element e to be deleted; Secondly, element e is removed from node L and check if L is underflow; Thirdly, it invokes *AdjustTree(L)* to adjust MBBs and propagate elimination or node merging operation up the tree; Finally, it determines whether to remove the original root node if the root node has only one child and no *O*-nodes at all. A main distinction from *OR_Insert* is that in the second stage, when L is underflow, it further checks if L has any *O*-nodes. If it is, it merges back *O*-nodes of L; Else, it just eliminates node L and reinserts all L's elements at the end of the function.

5   Performance Evaluation

5.1   Experimental Setup and Datasets

In this section, we compare the OR-tree with the standard R-tree, and two flash-aware spatial indexes, RFTL and FAST-Rtree. As discussed in [5], FAST-Rtree is proved to be superior to RFTL. Therefore, in our experiment we only implement the standard R-tree, the FAST-Rtree and the OR-tree. While our work primarily focuses on flash memory, we empirically evaluate the OR-tree's performance over commercial flash disks such as flash-based Solid State Drives (SSDs). These devices are designed using raw NAND flash memory, but have an on-board hardware controller that hides flash complexity and provides a disk-like abstraction to the operating system.

The experiments are conducted based on our flash memory simulation framework Flash-DBSim [16]. Flash-DBSim is a reusable and reconfigurable framework for the simulation-based evaluation of algorithms on flash disks. In our experiment, we simulate a 512MB NAND flash-based SSD, which has 128 pages per block and 2KB per page. The I/O characteristics of the flash-based SSD are shown in Table 1.

The dataset used in the experiments is downloaded from the R-tree portal website (*http://www.rtreeportal.org*) [18], which contains the MBRs of 2,249,727 roads and streets (polylines) of California. Our experiments consist of two parts. First, we use the previous 1,449,727 records of the dataset to complete the index construction and compare the index construction cost. The metrics measured are mainly the count of read/write/erase operations over flash memory, the average response time per transaction. Besides, we also record the count of flash pages consumed by the index to reflect the usage of flash memory space. Second, we evaluate the maintenance performance of spatial indexes and use two synthetic workloads:

(1) **Workload1**: that includes 80% search operations and 20% update operations (i.e., insert, delete and update).
(2) **Workload2**: that includes 20% search operations and 80% update operations.

In this stage, we use a 256KB write buffer to maintain the node updates. As in real applications this buffer is maintained inside SSDs, it typically has a small size. In the implementation of R-tree over flash memory, the write buffer is only used to maintain recently updated nodes. There are total one million transactions used in the experiment. The *TSC* threshold is calculated by the formula (3).

5.2   Index Construction Costs

In this stage, we record the number of read, write and erase operations for the construction of R-tree, FAST-Rtree and OR-tree with the buffer memory size varying from 128KB to 512KB (as shown in Table 4). As Table 4 shows, the construction of R-tree consumes the unbearable number of operations, suggesting that standard R-tree cannot be directly explanted to flash memory storage. The read count of OR-tree is slightly more than that of FAST-Rtree, because OR-tree needs an additional read when inserting element into the *O*-node. However, OR-tree still performs better than FAST-Rtree, with only one fifth to one sixth of the number of erase operations encountered in FAST-Rtree. This is mainly due the overflow policy used in OR-tree that amortizes the block erase operations over a large number of insertions.

Table 4. Flash read/write/erase count during the construction of index structures

buffer size (KB) / # of operations	R-tree			FAST-Rtree			OR-tree		
	128	256	512	128	256	512	128	256	512
read	8975352	6418307	5756432	4677234	4443621	4185284	4797679	4576275	4292249
write	7783451	6440566	5872663	105906	81849	68311	81203	60387	47083
erase	123782	99611	91256	632	251	77	243	40	0

Figure 3(a) shows the count of flash page usage respectively for the construction of R-tree, FAST-Rtree and OR-tree with the buffer memory size varying from 128KB to 512KB. It is evident that the amount of flash pages consumed by OR-tree in this stage is less than that of R-tree for all buffer sizes. This is because OR-tree doesn't create a new page physically while merging back *O*-nodes and the overflow node technique make nodes of OR-tree tighter than that of R-tree, which thus improve the flash memory storage utilization. Besides, the amount of flash page consumed by FAST-Rtree is the same as that of R-tree, which remains unchanged for all buffer sizes. This is because FAST-Rtree is an external upper-layer framework which does not alter the original algorithms of R-tree, and the implementation result of FAST-Rtree is immune to the buffering schema. However, the flash memory utilization of OR-tree shows a slightly ascending trend with the buffer size increases, as larger buffer memory can reduce the total access count *TSC* of *O*-node, which thus defer the merging back operation of *O*-node, and bring tighter OR-tree nodes while merging back.

Figure 3(b) shows the average runtime per insertion with the buffer memory size varying from 128KB to512KB for FAST-Rtree and OR-tree. For all buffer sizes, OR-tree performs better than FAST-Rtree during the initiation of OR-tree.

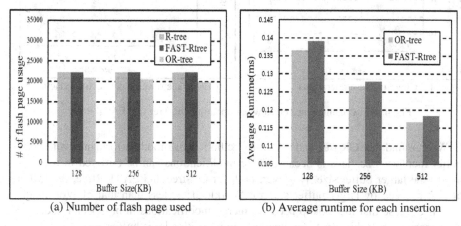

(a) Number of flash page used   (b) Average runtime for each insertion

Fig. 3. Index Construction Costs of OR-tree and FAST-Rtree

5.3   Maintenance Costs

Figure 4(a) gives the number of erase operations encountered in FAST-Rtree and OR-tree for Workload1 and Workload2 with the buffer memory size varying from 128KB to 512KB. For brevity, we only show the number of erase operations as we got a similar trend for the measure of write operations number. For both workloads and all buffer sizes, OR-tree consistently has much lower erase operations than FAST-Rtree. More specifically, OR-tree results in having half to one third of the erase operations encountered by FAST-Rtree, which is mainly due to the smart overflow policy used in OR-tree.

For a fixed buffer size, the extent of cost reduced by OR-tree in this stage is less than that in the initiation stage, because the insertion can benefit from our overflow policy, while the search performance may be decreased due to additional read operations. This can also explain that for a fixed memory size the extent of cost reduced by OR-tree for Workload1 is less than that of Workload2. OR-tree adapts to update-intensive workload rather than lookup-intensive workload.

Figure 4(b) gives the average runtime per transaction when updating FAST-Rtree and OR-tree. It is obvious that OR-tree shows faster average response speed rather than FAST-Rtree for Workload2 while it gives slightly slower average response speed rather than FAST-Rtree for Workload1. This can ensure that OR-tree results in high update performance while maintaining acceptable search performance.

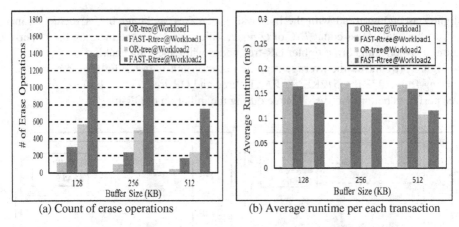

(a) Count of erase operations   (b) Average runtime per each transaction

Fig. 4. Index maintenance costs when updating OR-Tree and FAST-Rtree

We can find that OR-tree and FAST-Rtree both show good performance with large buffer memory size. This is because more modifications can be buffered in memory due to the larger buffer size. However, both for OR-tree and FAST-Rtree, the extent of cost reduced by larger buffer size for Workload1 is less than that of Workload2. This is because that the lookup needs to merge modifications in buffer and nodes on flash memory, and this would be time-consuming with a large buffer.

5.4   Effect of the TSC Threshold

The optimal *TSC* threshold is calculated to determine when to merge back *O*-node (as shown in formula (3)). Our experiment verifies that OR-tree index system shows good performance with this optimal *TSC* threshold. Figure 5 shows the number of erase operations encountered in OR-tree under different *TSC* threshold (as depicted in 3.2).

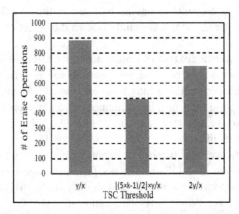

Fig. 5. Effect of *TSC* Threshold (*x* and *y* denotes the average cost of reading and writing a flash page, respectively. *k* is the number of *O*-nodes)

It can be easily seen that our smart choice of *TSC* threshold (as formula (3)) shows better performance rather than intermediate value y/x and bound value $2y/x$.

6 Conclusion

The rapid development of flash memory has spurred the increasing research of flash-aware index tree. In this paper, we concentrated on the design, analysis and implementation of OR-tree, a flash-optimized spatial index tree. In particular, we render two key techniques to improve the performance of OR-tree, namely deferring node splitting operations and merging back the overflow node. Several experiments were conducted on the real dataset and synthetic datasets respectively and results showed that the algorithms of our OR-tree has better performance than the standard R-tree and the recently proposed FAST-Rtree over flash memory.

In future research, we plan to spread the OR-tree as a generic framework which can adapt a wide variety of spatial index structures. Secondly, we will improve OR-tree with lazy deletion mechanism so as to avoid node merging operation in case of node underflows. Finally, we will consider the implementation of OR-tree on the hybrid storage of magnetic hard disk and flash-based SSDs.

Acknowledgement. This paper is supported by the National Science Foundation of China (No. 60833005 and No. 61073039).

References

1. Wu, C.H., Chang, L.P., Kuo, T.W.: An Efficient R-tree Implementation over Flash-Memory Storage Systems. In: Proceedings of the 11th ACM International Symposium on Advances in Geographic Information Systems (GIS), pp.17–24 (2003)
2. Li, Y., He, B., Yi, K.: Tree Indexing on Flash Disks. In: Proc. ICDE (2009)
3. Li, Y., He, B., Luo, Q., Ke, Y.: Tree Indexing on Solid State Drivers. In: Proceedings of VLDB Endowment (2010)
4. Agrawal, D., Ganesan, D., Sitaraman, R., Diao, Y., Singh, S.: Lazy-adaptive tree: An Optimized Index Structure for Flash Devices. PVLDB 2(1), 361–372 (2009)
5. Sarwat, M., Mokbel, M.F., Zhou, X., Nath, S.: FAST: A Generic Framework for Flash-Aware Spatial Trees. In: Pfoser, D., Tao, Y., Mouratidis, K., Nascimento, M.A., Mokbel, M., Shekhar, S., Huang, Y. (eds.) SSTD 2011. LNCS, vol. 6849, pp. 149–167. Springer, Heidelberg (2011)
6. Koltsidas, I., Viglas, S.D.: Spatial Data Management over Flash Memory. In: Pfoser, D., Tao, Y., Mouratidis, K., Nascimento, M.A., Mokbel, M., Shekhar, S., Huang, Y. (eds.) SSTD 2011. LNCS, vol. 6849, pp. 449–453. Springer, Heidelberg (2011)
7. Srinivasan, B.: An Adaptive Overflow Technique to Defer Splitting in B-trees. Comp. J. 34, 416–425 (1991)
8. Guttman, A.: R-tree: A Dynamic Index Structure for Spatial Searching. In: Proc. ACM SIGMOD Intl. Symp. on the Management of Data, pp. 45–57 (1984)

9. Theodoridis, Y., Sellis, T.: A Model for The Prediction of R-tree Performance. In: Proceedings of the Fifteenth ACM SIGACT-SIGMOD-SIGART Symposium on Principles of Database Systems, Montreal, Canada, June 3-5 (1996)

10. Toshiba TC58DVG02A1FT00 NAND flash chip datasheet, http://toshiba.com/taec (accessed in March 2012)

11. Bouganim, L., Jónsson, B., Bonnet, P.: uFLIP: Understanding Flash IO Patterns. In: CIDR (2009)

12. Kang, J.-U., Jo, H., Kim, J.-S., Lee, J.: A Superblock-based Flash Translation Layer for NAND Flashes Memory. In: EMSOFT 2006: Proceedings of the 6th ACM & IEEE International Conference on Embedded Software, pp. 161–170. ACM, New York (2006)

13. Graefe, G.: Write-optimized B-trees. In: Proc. of VLDB, pp. 672–683 (2004)

14. Xiang, L., Zhou, D., Meng, X.F.: A New Dynamic Hash Index for Flash-based Storage. In: Proc. of WAIM (2008)

15. Wu, C.-H., Chang, L.-P., Kuo, T.-W.: An Efficient B-Tree Layer for Flash-Memory Storage Systems. In: Chen, J., Hong, S. (eds.) RTCSA 2003. LNCS, vol. 2968, pp. 409–430. Springer, Heidelberg (2004)

16. Jin, P.Q., Su, X., Li, Z., Yue, L.H.: A Flexible Simulation Environment for Flash-aware Algorithms. In: Proc. of CIKM 2009, Demo. ACM Press (2009)

17. Samsung Electronics. K9XXG08UXA 1G x 8 Bit / 2G x 8 Bit / 4G x 8 Bit NAND Flash Memory Data Sheet (2006)

18. Car.tar.gz, http://www.rtreeportal.org (accessed in March 2012)

19. Wu, C.H., Kuo, T.W.: An Adaptive Two-Level Management for The Flash Translation Layer in Embedded Systems. In: Proc. of IEEE/ACM ICCAD 2006, pp. 601–606 (2006)

20. Chang, L.P., Kuo, T.W.: Efficient Management for Large-Scale Flash-Memory Storage Systems with Resource Conservation. ACM Trans. on Storage (TOS) 1(4), 381–418 (2005)

21. Xiang, X.Y., Yue, L.H., Liu, Z.Z.: A Reliable B-Tree Implementation over Flash Memory. In: Proc. of ACM SAC 2008, pp. 1487-1491 (2008)

22. Beckmann, N., Kriegel, H.P., Schneider, R., Seeger, B.: The R*tree: An Efficient and Robust Access Method for Points and Rectangles. In: Proc. ACM SIGMOD Intl. Symp. on the Management of Data, pp. 322–331 (1990)

23. Del Corso, D., Passerone, C., Reyneri, L.M., Sansoe, C., Borri, M., Speretta, S., Tranchero, M.: Architecture of a Small Low-Cost Satellite. In: 10th Euromicro Conference on Digital System Design, pp. 428–431 (2007)

24. Lv, Y., Li, J., Cui, B., Chen, X.: Log-Compact R-Tree: An Efficient Spatial Index for SSD. In: Xu, J., Yu, G., Zhou, S., Unland, R. (eds.) DASFAA Workshops 2011. LNCS, vol. 6637, pp. 202–213. Springer, Heidelberg (2011)

25. Kang, D., Jung, D.: $^{\mu}$-tree: An Ordered Index Structure for NAND Flash Memory. In: EMSOFT, pp. 144–153 (2007)

26. Manousaka, A., Manolopoulos, Y.: Fringle Analysis of 2-3 Trees with Lazy Parent Split. The Computer Journal 43(5), 420–429 (2000)

27. Bozanis, P., Nanopoulos, A., Manolopoulos, Y.: LR-tree: a Logarithmic Decomposable Spatial Index Method. Comput. J. 46(3), 319–331 (2003)

Directional Skyline Queries

Eman El-Dawy, Hoda M.O. Mokhtar, and Ali El-Bastawissy

Faculty of Computers and Information, Cairo University, Cairo, Egypt
{emiomar2000,hmokhtar}@gmail.com, alibasta@hotmail.com

Abstract. Continuous monitoring of queries over moving objects has become an important topic as it supports a wide range of useful mobile applications. A continuous skyline query involves both static and dynamic dimensions. In the dynamic dimension, the data object not only has a distance from the query object, but it also has a direction with respect to the query object motion. In this paper, we propose a direction-oriented continuous skyline query algorithm to compute the skyline objects with respect to the current position of the user. The goal of the proposed algorithm is to help the user to retrieve the best objects that satisfy his/her constraints and fall either in any direction around the query object, or is aligned along the object's direction of motion. We also create a pre-computed skyline data set that facilitates skyline update, and enhances query running time and performance. Finally, we present experimental results to demonstrate the performance and efficiency of our proposed algorithms.

Keywords: Skyline queries, continuous query processing, moving object databases, direction-based skyline queries.

1 Introduction

With the rapid advances in wireless communications and technologies for tracking the positions of continuously moving objects, algorithms for efficiently answering queries about large numbers of moving objects are increasingly needed [2, 6]. This meets the requirements for location based services (LBS) [2, 14]. A moving object is simply defined as an object whose location and/or geometry changes continuously over time [13]. Consequently, a moving object database is a database that is designed to efficiently handle the huge amount of location data, and also to efficiently manage, and query location information. The main difference between moving object databases and traditional databases is that traditional databases are best suited for static data while moving object databases were designed for dynamic data (i.e. data continuously changing over time). Furthermore, moving object databases are tailored for high frequency of updates that is a common consequence of the rapidly changing location information [13]. These new types of data (i.e. location data) generated new types of queries that query the spatial and/or temporal properties of moving objects. Skyline queries are an important class of queries that target applications involving multi-criteria decision making. In general, a skyline query is defined as: Given a set of multi-dimensional data points, a skyline query retrieves a set of data points that are not

Y. Xiang et al. (Eds.): ICDKE 2012, LNCS 7696, pp. 15–28, 2012.
© Springer-Verlag Berlin Heidelberg 2012

dominated by any other points in all dimensions. A skyline query finds a set of interesting objects, satisfying a set of possibly conflicting conditions.

In our proposed algorithms we evaluate the skyline objects based on both distance and direction with respect to the query point "QP". The basic idea is as follows: for a given query point QP, we propose two approaches, the first one is an *all directional continuous skyline query algorithm* to find the interesting objects around the user in all directions, the second one is a *my direction continuous skyline query* that finds the interesting objects to the user that **only** fall along his motion direction.

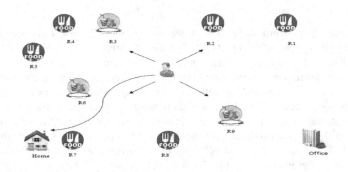

Fig. 1. Motivation example

Example 1: Consider the example illustrated in Fig. 1. Suppose a person wants to take lunch before going home, and he searches for the best restaurant in terms of price, rank, and distance. In this example there are 2 static attributes (price, rank), and a dynamic attribute (distance). And in his way he found that he forgot an important thing in his office and decided to go back to his office.

Considering first the static skyline as shown in Fig. 2, the person wants to take his lunch and he searches for the preference restaurants in terms of price and rank and he found that restaurants R2, R4 and R6 are interesting and can be retrieved by a skyline query. Thus, if we have a point "p" we can see if it dominates another point "q", then, "p" dominates "q" if it is better or as good as "q" on all considered directions.

Suppose now we also consider the dynamic attributes, in this example we have two types of dynamic attributes: *distance and motion direction* of the query object. Consider the example shown in Fig. 3, in this example we have 6 nearest neighbor objects (R7,R8,R9,R10,R11,R12) around the query object "QP" located at (0, 0) and sorted by the distance with respect to QP.

In this example we have vectors $\vec{R}7$,..., $\vec{R}12$ originating from QP.

We assume that two vectors are in the same direction if the included angle between the two objects is smaller than a predefined threshold $\theta_{threshold}$. In this paper we fix the value of $\theta_{threshold}$ to be $\pi/3$. Consequently, the object R7 is in the same direction as R8 as the included angle between the two vectors R7 and R8 is equal to $26°$. In addition, R7 is closer to QP than R8, thus R7 dominates the other objects in the same direction (i.e. object R8) and will be one of the recommended objects to the user.

Similarly, we can say that R9 dominates R11, and R10 dominates R12, and thus R7, R9, R10 are not dominated by other objects. Hence, the result of the dynamic skyline part is {R7, R9, and R10} w.r.t. the query object QP, and it forms the result for the candidate objects located all around the query object (i.e. in all directions). However, when we consider only the objects that QP meets along its motion (as he moves towards the East direction), we can find that the point R7 is the only candidate for the dynamic skyline query (i.e. in one direction, the East). In the remaining of the paper we show the details of our proposed direction-based skyline evaluation algorithms.

Restaurant	Price	Rank
1	6	4
2	5	1
3	5	6
4	3	2
5	2	6
6	1	3

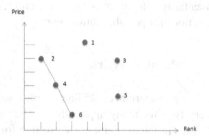

Fig. 2. Example of static skyline

Restaurant®	D®	Dir®
R7	22	27°
R8	5	53°
R9	54	158°
R10	6	270°
R11	67	117°
R12	72	236°

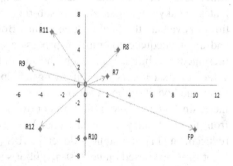

Fig. 3. Example of dynamic skyline

Generally, the crucial questions in skyline queries are: How to retrieve the best results to the user with respect to both the static attributes and the dynamic attributes in all directions, and/or in his direction? Also, it is interesting to know how to update the results of the query in the most efficient way. In summary, the contributions of this work can be enumerated as follows:

1. We propose two algorithms: the *all directional-based continuous skyline query* (All_Skyline), and *the my direction continuous skyline query* (My_Dir_Skyline) algorithms which not only retrieve the objects satisfying the user requirement criteria, but also consider the direction of motion of the user in order to return to the user the objects that are both satisfying his requirements and are along his route.

2. We enhanced the computation of the directional skyline technique proposed in [5] by using an additional filter based on the furthest point (FP) introduced in [4].
3. We efficiently update the query result by creating a pre-computed set of candidate objects to facilitate updating the result and consequently enhancing query running time and performance following a similar approach to the one proposed in [4].
4. We compare our work to the directional spatial skyline (DSS) algorithm presented in [5]. To have a fair comparison we changed the DSS algorithm to query the static attributes as well rather than considering the dynamic attributes only.

The rest of this paper is organized as follows: In section 2, we describe the related work. In section 3, we propose our solutions for directional skyline queries. The experimental results are presented in section 4. Finally, section 5 concludes and proposes directions for possible future work.

2   Related Work

For their importance, skyline queries were targeted in many works as an essential query type for many applications. The authors in [1] propose two algorithms for the skyline problem namely, a straightforward non-progressive Block-Nested-Loop (BNL), and a Divide-and-Conquer (DC) algorithm. In the BNL approach they recursively compares each data point with the current set of candidate skyline points, which might be dominated later. The DC approach divides the search space and evaluates the skyline points from its sub-regions, respectively, followed by merge operations to evaluate the final skyline points. Both algorithms may incur several iterations, and are inadequate for on-line processing. In [10], two progressive algorithms are presented: the bitmap approach and the index method. Bitmap encodes dimensional values of data points into bit strings to speed up the dominance comparisons. The index method classifies a set of d-dimensional points into d-lists, which are sorted in increasing order of the minimum coordinate. The index scans the lists synchronously from the first entry to the last one. With the pruning strategies, the search space is reduced. In [11], the authors develop BBS (branch-and-bound skyline), a progressive algorithm also based on nearest neighbor search, which is I/O optimal. The authors in [9] introduce the concept of Spatial Skyline Queries (SSQ). Where, given a set of data points P and a set of query points Q, SSQ retrieves those points of P which are not dominated by any other point in P considering their derived spatial attributes with respect to query points in Q. The authors in [12] expand the skyline query concept and propose continuous skyline query which involves not only static dimensions but also the dynamic ones. In this paper the authors use spatio-temporal coherence to refer to those spatial properties that do not change abruptly between continuous temporal scenes. The positions and velocities of moving points do not change by leaps between continuous temporal scenes, which enable them to maintain the changing skyline incrementally. In [7], the authors propose the ESC algorithm, an Efficient update approach for Skyline Computations, where objects with dynamic dimensions move in an unrestricted manner, which creates a pre-computed second skyline set that facilitates an efficient and incremental skyline update strategy and results in a quicker response time. In [3], the authors present a framework for processing predictive skyline queries for moving objects. The authors present two schemes, namely RBBS (BBS with Rescanning and Repacking) and TPBBS (time-parameterized R-tree with Non- Spatial dimensions), to answer predictive skyline queries. In [5], the authors propose a direction-based spatial skyline(DSS) queries to retrieve nearest objects around the user from different directions and they don't take into account non-spatial attributes. In [14] they extend the work in paper [5] by augmenting road networks. Finally, in [4] the authors present a Multi-level Continuous Skyline Query algorithm(MCSQ), which basically creates a pre-computed skyline data set that facilitates skyline update, and enhances query running time and performance.

Inspired by the importance of skyline queries, in this work with follow the same update approach presented in [4] and augment it with an additional selection criteria that is based on the use of direction of motion of the query object as in [5].

3   Directional Skyline Query

3.1   Problem Definition

In Location Based Services (LBS) most queries are continuous queries. Unlike snapshot queries (instantaneous queries) that are evaluated only once, continuous queries require continuous evaluation as the query results vary with the change of location and/or time. In the same sense, continuous skyline query processing has to recompute the skyline when the query object and/or the databases objects change their locations. However, updating the skyline of the previous moment is more efficient than conducting a snapshot query at each moment.

In this paper we consider 2-dimensional data (both the data points which are static data points, and the query point that is a moving point), and the direction of the dynamic points in skyline query w.r.t. the query point QP, as we need to get the nearest objects around QP from different directions, as well as the objects in the direction of QP. We focus on moving query points, where the query point changes its location over time. We assume we are given a threshold angle $\theta_{threshold}$ (that represents the accepted deviation angle between the query point and the data point) specified at query time. We treat time as a third dimension for the moving point. In table 1, we summarize the symbols used in this paper.

Table 1. Symbols and description

Symbol	Description
$\overrightarrow{p}_i$	Vector between QP and p_i
$\theta_{threshold}$	Acceptable angle of deviation around QP
$D(p_i)$	Distance between QP and p_i
FP	Furthest point in the static skyline

Table 1. (*continued*)

Dir_{pi}	Direction of $\vec{P}_i$:the angle between $\vec{P}_i$ and $(1,0)$
$\lambda_{ij}(\lambda_{pipj})$	Included angle between $\vec{P}_i$ and $\vec{P}_j$
$\varphi_{ij}(\varphi_{pipj})$	Partition angle between $\vec{P}_i$ and $\vec{P}_j$
S_{static}	Static part in the skyline query result
$S_{dynamic}$	Dynamic part in the skyline query result

The included angle between $\vec{p}_i$ and $\vec{p}_j$ is denoted by λ_{pipj} (λ_{ij} for short). λ_{ij} should be in the range $0 \leq \lambda_{ij} \leq \pi$, and is defined by the following equation as proposed in [5]:

$$\lambda_{ij} = \arccos \frac{\vec{p}_i \cdot \vec{p}_j}{|\vec{p}_i| \cdot |\vec{p}_j|} \tag{1}$$

We use Equation (1) to define objects alignment (in same direction) as follows.

Definition 1 (Same Direction). Given two data objects p_i and p_j, and a moving query point QP. p_i and p_j are in the same direction w.r.t QP if $0 \leq \lambda_{ij} \leq \theta_{threshold}$.

Thus, in Fig. 3, if $\theta_{threshold}$ is given as $\pi/3$, object R8 is in the same direction as object R7 w.r.t QP since the included angle λ_{R7R8} between their vectors is less than $\theta_{threshold}$ ($\lambda_{R7R8} = 27°$). On the other hand object R7 is on a different direction than object R9 w.r.t QP as $\lambda_{R7R9} > \theta_{threshold}$.

Since in this work we deal with moving query points, we consider the distance function to be the traditional *Euclidean* distance for its simplicity and applicability to our work. Thus the distance between any 2 points $p_1(x_1, y_1)$, $p_2(x_2, y_2)$ at time instant t_i is given by:

$$D(p_1, p_2) = \sqrt{(x_1(t_i) - x_2(t_i))^2 + (y_1(t_i) - y_2(t_i))^2} \tag{2}$$

Definition 2 (Dominate). Given a query point QP, a threshold angle $\theta_{threshold}$, and two data points p_1, p_2. If the distance $D(Qp, p_1) \leq D(Qp, p_2)$ and p_1, p_2 are in the same direction w.r.t QP, this implies that p_1 *dominates* p_2.

In this paper we consider the evaluation of continuous skyline queries while moving, and hence the queries involve distance, direction, along with other static dimensions. Consequently, such queries are dynamic due to the change in the spatial variables. In our solution, we only compute the initial skyline at the start time t_0. Subsequently, continuous query processing is conducted for each user by updating the skyline instead of computing a new one from scratch each time. Without loss of generality, we restrict our discussion to what follows the MIN skyline annotation, in which smaller values of distance are preferred in our comparison to determine the dominance between two points, and we assume that our data set points are static and the query object is the only moving object.

3.2   Directional Multi-level Continuous Skyline Query (DCSQ)

In this section we discuss our proposed directional continuous skyline update algorithms. Our algorithms distinguish the data points that are permanently in the skyline and use them to derive a search bound as we compute the static skyline points (S_{static}). To proceed in our algorithm we first need to distinguish the data point which is the furthest point (FP) in the S_{static} points, we use the same approach presented in [4]. In general, the FP point is the static data point in the skyline which has the maximum distance to the query point; assume we have a point "P", its predecessor is "P'", and it's successor is"P''"; so to enter the point P in a dynamic skyline ($S_{dynamic}$) it must have an advantage over FP in their distance function value. We used λ as the included angle between two points and $θ_{threshold}$ as an acceptable angle; if the angle between the predecessor of the point P and the angle between the successors of P is greater than $θ_{threshold}$ then P will be entered into the $S_{dynamic}$ part of the skyline.

Fig. 12 shows how we can compute All_Skyline in all directions with respect to QP, and Fig. 13 shows how we can compute My_Dir_Skyline only in the direction of QP. This characteristic of the FP point and the acceptable angle $θ_{threshold}$ enables us to use them as a filter for $S_{dynamic}$ points before entering to the continuous skyline query(i.e. before considering the full skyline = $S_{static}+ S_{dynamic}$).

Definition 3 (*Directional Multi-level Continuous Skyline Query (DCSQ).* A DCSQ *with M levels* is a continuous skyline query that creates a pre-defined data set for the dynamic part in the skyline such that the number of the pre-defined data sets depends on the value of M, and then uses these data sets to update the pervious skyline set and consequently updating the first skyline.

In brief, our algorithm proceeds as follows: Initially, we classify skyline into static skyline (S_{static}), and dynamic skyline ($S_{dynamic}$). Then, we compute static skyline only once at the beginning, and at every time instance we basically update the distance function "D" and the direction "dir_R" with respect to the new location of the query point and the given deviation tolerance $θ_{threshold}$. Next, after we compute the static skyline (S_{static}) we create a view for the data set with the data except the pre-considered static points in the skyline, so the dynamic skyline part will not rescan static skyline points and consequently returns the new result in faster response time as justified in [4]. Finally, the DCSQ computation depends on pre-computation of the set of dynamic data points which will be used to update the previous result set and yields faster response time.

In the remaining of this section we technically present our proposed algorithm in more details. We basically propose two algorithms:

First: All_Skyline Algorithm

- First we compute the dominating points with respect to the non-spatial attributes. Then, we use the resulting set (S_{static}) to compute the furthest point (FP).
- Using the FP as a filter for the data points, we compare the distance between QP and each data point, if less than the distance to FP, then this data point might be in

the 1st level of the dynamic skyline denoted by "$S1_{dynamic}$". Thus, at any time if we find that there exist a data point whose distance to the query object is greater than the distance of the furthest point (i.e. D (FP) < D (p)), we can just terminate checking the remaining points as we keep them sorted by distance.

- We keep checked points in a list denoted by "eval_obj", then, we compute for each point (p) in "eval_obj" the angle between it and its predecessor (p⁻) point and the angle with its successor point (p⁺) as points are put in a circular list. If the angle between p- and p+ (denoted by the partition angle φ) is greater than the given acceptable deviation angle $θ_{threshold}$, then we add the point 'p' to $S1_{dynamic}$.

- We save the difference between the points in eval_obj(is a list of visited points) and its successor point in a list of angles Φ and if we find that all the angels in Φ are less than $2θ_{threshold}$ then we terminate checking the remaining point as in [5].

- Next, we merge $S1_{dynamic}$ along with S_{static} to obtain the result for the first skyline.

- To update the results of the skyline query we use the same approach in [4].

  Fig. 12 shows how we can compute the All_Skyline algorithm.

Example 2: Continuing with Example 1, assume we want to compute the All_Skyline algorithm. First, if we consider the non-spatial attributes to compute the dominating points we get S_{static}={R2,R4,R6} as the preferred restaurant in the non-spatial dimensions. Next, we compute the furthest point (FP) using the S_{static} set and we find that R6 is the FP point.

Then, for the points in the 6-NN in Fig. 2. If the distance of any point to QP is greater than the distance of the furthest point (i.e. D (FP) < D (p)), we can just terminate checking the remaining points in the 6-NN as we already have them sorted by distance as shown in Fig. 3 where the D (FP) =112.

Thus, as shown in Fig. 3 we can see that D(R7)<D(FP) so we save R7 in "eval_obj", and also in $S1_{dynamic}$. Assume we checked R7,R8,R9,R10 as shown in Fig. 3, the vectors of those objects partition the $2π$ angle into four partition angles $φ_{R7R8}$ =26°, $φ_{R8R9}$=105°,$φ_{R9R10}$ =112°, and $φ_{R10R7}$=117°, and also the distance of the checked objects are smaller than FP so we can terminate our process and $S1_{dynamic}$ ={R7,R9,R10}. Finally, we merge $S1_{dynamic}$ along with S_{static} to obtain the result for the first skyline = {R7, R9, R10, R2, R4, R6} sorted by distance to QP.

Second: My_Dir_Skyline Algorithm

- As the previous algorithm we first compute S_{static} and the FP point.

- If a point 'p' is closer than FP and the angle between the QP and p is smaller than $θ_{threshold}$, then p is in the direction of the QP and is entered into $S1_{dynamic}$.

- Next, we merge $S1_{dynamic}$ along with S_{static} to obtain the result for the first skyline.

- To update the results of the skyline query we use the same approach in [4].

Fig. 13 shows how we can compute the My_Dir_Skyline algorithm.

We also make some changes in the directional spatial skyline (DSS) to make them consider both spatial and static attributes as we describe in Fig. 14.

Example 3: Assume we want to compute the My_Dir_Skyline for the example presented in Example 1 and 2. If the point p in our 6-NN example has a smaller distance than FP and the angle between the QP and p is smaller than $\theta_{threshold}$, then p is in the direction of the QP and entered to $S1_{dynamic}$. As shown in Fig. 3 we can find that R7 is the dynamic skyline point as it is in the direction of QP (East); so $S1_{dynamic} = \{R7\}$. Next, we merge $S1_{dynamic}$ along with S_{static} to obtain the result for the first skyline= {R7, R2, R4, R6}.

4   Experimental Evaluations

In this section we present our experiments for evaluating the proposed algorithms. We evaluated the performance by comparing it with the MCSQ algorithm [4] and DSS algorithm [5]. For the accuracy, our proposed algorithm retrieves that same skyline result as the result obtained by both algorithms proposed in [4, 5]. For our moving query point we use the Brinkhoff generator for moving object trajectories [8]. As for the data points, we use a real data set about residential building from Aswan town in Egypt. We assumed that our data set points are static and the query object is a dynamic object which changes its location with respect to time. Since our data set is reasonable in size, we do not use index structure in our experiments and all the data points are stored in memory. We used 1000 record and $\theta_{threshold}$=60° as a default value on most of our experiments. We used SQL server 2005 and visual studio 2008 (C#) in our experiment. Experiments are implemented on a 3GHz Pentium 4 PC with 1.0GB memory, running Windows XP service pack 3.

In the first experiment we used two dimensional non-spatial attributes and we vary the size of the data set (200, 400, 600, 800, and 1000) and observe the effect of increasing the number of records on the CPU time and on update time. Fig. 4 shows the effects of varying the number of records on both the All_Skyline and the My_Dir_Skyline algorithms, and compares it to the MCSQ and DSS algorithms. We can observe that the proposed algorithms enhance the CPU time, however the MCSQ algorithm has a smaller response time as it does not need to compute the direction. Fig. 5 shows that our algorithms and the MCSQ algorithm are better than the DSS algorithm in terms of the time needed to update the results of skyline query result as both approaches use a candidate set for updating the skyline results. So our algorithms improve the update time, however, the CPU time is increased due to the use of the additional directional filter that acts as an additional dimension in our computation.

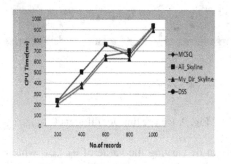   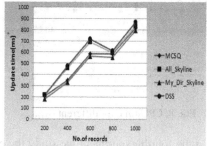

Fig. 4. CPU time for different no. of records   **Fig. 5.** Update time for different no. of records

In the second set of experiments we study the effect of varying the number of levels (2, 3, 4, and 5) on the CPU time and update time. In the first experiment we compare the All_Skyline and the My_Dir_Skyline algorithms with the MCSQ algorithm. As shown in Fig. 6, My_Dir_Skyline algorithm requires less CPU time compared to All_Skyline algorithm as it needs fewer computations to compute the points in the same direction of the user. We also observe that MCSQ algorithm requires less CPU time than All_Skyline algorithm. The reason behind this observation is that both All_Skyline and the My_Dir_Skyline algorithms require more computations to compute the direction of the objects. In Fig. 7 we show the update time of both the All_Skyline and the My_Dir_Skyline algorithms and the MCSQ algorithm. As shown as number of levels increases, the update time decrease as we need less time to update our skyline query result using the previous candidate sets of the skyline.

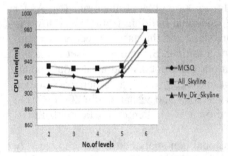
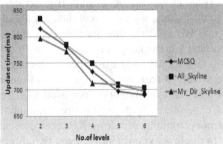

Fig. 6. CPU time for different no. of levels   **Fig. 7.** Update time for different no. of levels

The third experiment examines the effect of varying the value of the angle $\theta_{threshold}$ on both the number of examined objects to get our skyline points, and on the output result size (skyline points). In these experiments we vary the angle in the range [15, 85] and study the effect on both CPU time and update time. Fig. 8 and Fig. 9 show that CPU and update time decrease when the value of $\theta_{threshold}$ increases. The reason behind this observation is that more objects can dominate larger angle ranges given a larger value of θ.

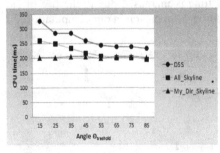
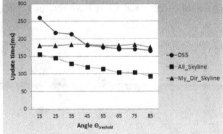

Fig. 8. CPU time for different $\theta_{threshold}$ **Fig. 9.** Update time for different $\theta_{threshold}$

In the fourth experiment we study the effect of varying the value of $\theta_{threshold}$ which varies in the range of [15, 85] on the number of checked nearest neighbor objects until we get the skyline points and on the objects in the skyline result. Fig. 10 shows that both the number of checked nearest neighbor objects and the objects in the skyline query decreases by increasing the value of $\theta_{threshold}$ as an object can dominate larger angle ranges given a larger value of $\theta_{threshold}$. In the last experiment we examine the effect of varying the value of $\theta_{threshold}$ on the number of objects in the skyline. In fig. 11 we can see that when we increase the value of $\theta_{threshold}$ the number of points in the skyline query results decreases in the All_Skyline algorithm. The reason behind this observation is that more objects can dominate larger angle ranges given a larger value of $\theta_{threshold}$, however in the My_Dir_Skyline algorithm the number of points in the skyline increases when the value of $\theta_{threshold}$ increases because when the value of θ increases the range of directions around the query object increases so the number of candidates increases and consequently it has more points in the skyline results.

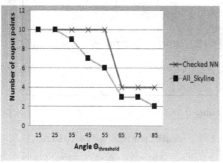 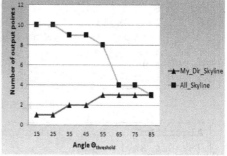

Fig. 10. Effects of varying $\theta_{threshold}$ on the No. of output results

Fig. 11. Effects of varying value of $\theta_{threshold}$ on All_Skyline & My_Dir_Skyline

---

Algorithm 1 All directional continuous skyline (All_Skyline)

1. <u>Input:</u> data set points $p = (p_1, p_2, ..., p_m)$,
   Query point: QP, $\theta_{threshold}$, Query point trajectory time instances $\tau_{QP}[t]$
2. <u>Output:</u> All_Skyline // continuous skyline query result
3. Compute S_{static} at time $\tau_{QP}[1]$
4. FP = Find(FP)   // compute FP
5. IF (D(p) <D(FP)) THEN {
6. $S_{dynamic}=\{p\}$ ELSE terminate   // result set
7. $\Phi=\{\varphi_{pp}\}$ //initialize the partition angle set
8.   REPEAT
9.   p = get_next_ nn
10.   p-,p+   // pred and succ of P
11.   eval_obj=eval_obj $\cup\{p\}$
12.   IF (D(P)<D(FP)) THEN   {
13.   IF ($\lambda_{pp-} \geq \theta_{threshold} \wedge \lambda_{pp+} \geq \theta_{threshold}$) THEN
14. $S_{dynamic} = S_{dynamic} \cup\{p\}$ // p in dynamic skyline

Fig. 12. All_Skyline Procedure

```
15.                                          }
16.       ELSE terminate
17.    Φ = (Φ - {φ_p-p+ })∪{φ_p-p ,φ_pp+ }; // update  angle
18. UNTIL FALSE or all the objects are processed
19. Get S_dynamic                            }
20. All_Skyline= S_satatic+S_dynamic; //update All_Skyline.
21. Compute FP at time τ_QP[2] and Compute S_Mdynamic at
    time τ_QP[2]
22. FOR (2≤ t ≤ |τ_QP[t]| ) DO FOR (every point p in S_stat-
    ic)
23.        Update D (p, QP)
24.    END FOR
25.    S_dynamic= S_Mdynamic  ;             // update S_dynamic
26.    All_Skyline= S_satatic + S_dynamic
27.    Compute FP at time τ_QP[t+1] and  Compute  S_Mdynamic
    at time τ_QP[t+1]
28. END FOR
29. END
```

Fig. 12. (*continued*)

```
Algorithm2   My   directional   continuous   skyline
(My_Dir_Skyline)
1. Input:
      Data set points p = (p_1, p_2,..., p_m),
      Query point: QP, θ_threshold, Query point trajectory
   time instances τ_QP[t]
2. Output: All_Skyline   // continuous skyline query
   result
3. Compute S_static at time τ_QP[1]
4. FP = Find FP          // compute FP
5. S_dynamic=∅ ;
6. Init_NN_query(q) ;    // initialize the NN query
7. IF(D(p)<D(FP))  THEN
8.    S_dynamic ={p};  ELSE terminate  // result set
9. REPEAT
10.  p = get_next_ NN
11.   IF(D(P)<D(FP) ∧ dir_p < θ_threshold) THEN
12.    S_dynamic = S_dynamic ∪{p}; // p in dynamic skyline
13.   ELSE terminate
14.   UNTIL all the objects are processed
15. get S_dynamic at time τ_QP[1]
16.   My_Dir_Skyline= S_satatic + S_dynamic ;    // update
   My_Dir_Skyline
```

Fig. 13. My_Dir_Skyline Procedure

```
17.     Compute FP at time τ_QP[2] and Compute S_Mdynamic at
   time τ_QP[2]
18.     FOR (2≤t≤|τ_QP[t]| ) DO
19.         FOR( every point p in S_static)
20.             Update D (p, QP)
21.         END FOR
22.     S_dynamic= S_Mdynamic;              // update S_dynamic
23.     All_Skyline= S_satatic + S_dynamic
24.     Compute FP at time τ_QP[t+1] and Compute  S_Mdynam-
   ic at time τ_QP[t+1]
25.     END FOR
26.     END
```

Fig. 13. (*continued*)

```
Algorithm 3 Directional continuous skyline (DSS) with
static attributes
1. Input: data set points  p = (p_1, p_2, ..., p_m) ,
         Query point: QP and acceptable angle θ_threshold

         Query point trajectory time instances τQP[t]
2. Output: DSS      // continuous skyline query result
3. Compute S_static at time τQP[1]
4. S_dynamic=∅ ;
5. Init_NN_query(q) ;      // initilize the NN query
6. eval_obj=p ;            // get the first NN object
7. S={p};                  // result set
8. Φ={ φ_pp};      //initialize the partition angle set
9. REPEAT
10.      p = get_next_ nn
11.      p⁻,p⁺;                    // pred and succ of P
12.      eval_obj=eval_objU{p}
13.      IF(λ_pp- ≥ θ_threshold ∧ λ_pp+ ≥ θ_threshold ) THEN
14.          S=SU{p};   // p in dynamic skyline
15.          Φ = (Φ − {φ_p-p+ }) U{φ_p-p, φ_pp+ };
// update the part_angle set
16. UNTIL FLASE or all the objects are processed
17. get S_dynamic; DSS= S_static + S_dynamic ;
18. FOR (2≤t≤| τQP[t]| ) DO
19.    FOR( every point p in S_static)
20.        UPDATE D (p, QP)
21.    END FOR
22.      Compute S_dynamic time τQP[t] //  update S_dynamic
23.      DSS= S_satatic + DS_dynamic
24. END FOR
25. END
```

Fig. 14. DSS Procedure

5   Conclusions and Future Work

In this paper, we propose 2 algorithms which efficiently update Skyline query results through limiting the search space when updating skyline results, and by considering only the objects around the user from different directions and also the points in the same direction as the user. Experimental studies are conducted using a real data. The experiments show that the proposed methods are robust and efficient. For future work we aim to increase our data set size and use an index structure to study the effect of an index structure on the performance of our algorithm. We also plan to investigate the performance of our proposed algorithms in the case of moving data objects.

References

1. Borzsony, S., et al.: The Skyline Operator. In: Proceedings of the 17th Intl. Conf. on Data Engineering, pp. 421–430 (2001)
2. Benetis, R., et al.: Nearest and Reverse Nearest Neighbor Queries for Moving Objects. The VLDB Journal 3(15), 229–249 (2006)
3. Chen, N., Shou, L., Chen, G., Gao, Y., Dong, J.: Predictive Skyline Queries for Moving Objects. In: Zhou, X., Yokota, H., Deng, K., Liu, Q. (eds.) DASFAA 2009. LNCS, vol. 5463, pp. 278–282. Springer, Heidelberg (2009)
4. El-Dawy, E., Mokhtar, H.M.O., El-Bastawissy, A.: Multi-level Continuous Skyline Queries (MCSQ). In: Zhang, J., Livraga, G. (eds.) Intl. Conf. on Data and Knowledge Engineering (ICDKE), pp. 36–40. IEEE, Milan (2011)
5. Guo, X., Ishikawa, Y., Gao, Y.: Direction-based spatial skylines. In: Proceedings of the Ninth ACM Intl. Workshop on Data Engineering for Wireless and Mobile Access, pp. 73–80. ACM, Indianapolis (2010)
6. Güting, R.H., Schneider, M.: Moving objects databases, 1st edn. Diane D. Cerra, San Francisco (2005)
7. Hsueh, Y.-L., Zimmermann, R., Ku, W.-S.: Efficient Updates for Continuous Skyline Computations. In: Bhowmick, S.S., Küng, J., Wagner, R. (eds.) DEXA 2008. LNCS, vol. 5181, pp. 419–433. Springer, Heidelberg (2008)
8. Library, S.I.,
   http://www.research.att.com/~marioh/spatialindex/index.html
9. Sharifzadeh, M., Shahabi, C.: The spatial skyline queries. In: Proceedings of the 32nd Intl. Conf. on Very Large Data Bases, Seoul, Korea, pp. 751–762 (2006)
10. Sistla, A.P., et al.: Modeling and Querying Moving Objects. In: Proceedings of the 3rd Intl. Conf. on Data Engineering, pp. 422–432 (1997)
11. Tan, K.-L., Eng, P.-K., Ooi, B.C.: Efficient Progressive Skyline Computation. In: Proceedings of the 27th Intl. Conf. on Very Large Data Bases, pp. 301–310 (2001)
12. Tung, A.K.H.: Continuous Skyline Queries for Moving Objects. IEEE Trans. on Knowledge and Data Eng., 1645–1658 (2006)
13. Xiong, X., et al.: Scalable Spatio-temporal Continuous Query Processing for Location-aware Services. In: Proceedings of the 16th Intl. Conf. on Scientific and Statistical Database Management, p. 317 (2004)
14. Guo, X., et al.: Direction-based surrounder queries for mobile recommendations. The VLDB Journal, 743–766 (2011)

Transforming Nescient Activity into Intelligent Activity

Rafiqul Haque, Nenad Krdzavac, and Tom Butler

Department of Accounting and Information Systems College of Business and Law,
University College Cork, Cork City, Ireland
{ARHaque,N.Krdzavac,Tom.Butler}@ucc.ie

Abstract. A nescient activity within financial service process is prone to risk of producing inconsistent outcome that results severe legal consequence for a financial institute e.g., bank. Financial service process activities must be intelligent to understand and comply financial regulations. Intelligent process activities will assist to prevent producing outcomes that are inconsistent to financial regulations. Existing process technologies support defining only nescient activities. Currently, there is no solution that underpins transforming a nescient activity into intelligent activity. In this paper, we offer a solution that supports transformation of a nescient activity into intelligent activity.

Keywords: Process, Activity, Financial Regulation, Knowledge Base, Reasoning.

1 Introduction

A process in a simple word, is a set of ordered activities [12]. Activities carry out *operations* while a process is running and producing outcomes. In a financial service process (FSP), the operations must be performed complying *financial regulations* that are essentially financial rules. An operation produces an inconsistent outcome if it does not comply with relevant regulations. Inconsistent compliance outcomes bring severe consequences for an organization regardless of whether it is a financial or business organization. The *Enron-Scandal* [9] is a practical example. Therefore, compliance is a highly significant issue in FSP.

Activities within FSPs are *regulation-intensive* which means that they underlie financial regulations (e.g., Basel III accords [2]). However, some activities within an FSP may not be regulation-intensive. A regulation-intensive activity within an FSP is called *nescient* if it lacks explicit knowledge about the underlying regulations, it lacks correlation with financial regulations, and the activity cannot produce consistent outcomes. A nescient activity is not able to perform operations that comply with financial regulations. This promotes the need for activities that are able to perform operations in compliance with regulations.

Existing process technologies (e.g., BPEL [3]) lacks the constructs to support defining (modeling) intelligent activities in a financial service process. Some approaches (e.g., Business Process Model and Notation (BPMN) [4])facilitate annotating meta-data for process activity. However, these approaches cannot be

Y. Xiang et al. (Eds.): ICDKE 2012, LNCS 7696, pp. 29–37, 2012.
© Springer-Verlag Berlin Heidelberg 2012

used due to complexity and ambiguity in financial regulations. A solution that supports transforming a nescient activity into an intelligent one is strongly required for *smart* financial service processes.

In this research, we offer a solution that underpins transforming nescient activities into intelligent activities within the FSP space. It is important to mention that the transformation happens *indirectly* i.e., the solution supports the nescient activities by providing the exact meaning of regulations and also assists to perform operations complying with financial regulation. In order to do so, the proposed solution uses the notion of the *knowledge base*. The knowledge base is developed using an ontology approach.

The remainder of this paper is organized as follows. In section 2, the preliminaries are described. Then we present a financial service process in section 3. The financial regulation knowledge base is described in section 4. Section 5 discusses reasoning with financial regulations. In section 6, we discuss the implementation of our proposed solution. We describe related works in subsequent section. Finally, section 8 outlines conclusion and future works.

2 Preliminary

2.1 Intelligent Activity

In this paper, we introduce intelligent activities for FSP. An intuitive definition of intelligent activity is given below,

Definition 1. *Each regulation-intensive an activity is an intelligent activity if and only if*

- *semantics of regulations are interpreted to the activity,*
- *it has explicit correlation with the regulations,*
- *it cannot produce outcomes that are non-compliant to regulations.*

Any activity that does not satisfy these conditions will not be considered as intelligent activity within FSP.

2.2 Ontologies and Description Graph

The Ontology Web Language (OWL2) [5] is used for modeling ontologies. The $\mathcal{SROIQ}$ DL [11] provides reasoning services for ontologies based on tableau algorithm. The basic OWL2 concepts are classes, object properties, data-type properties, and individuals. Additionally, an ontology contains class axioms, property assertions as well as individual assertions. Semantic Web Rule Language (SWRL) [10] is used to model rules in an ontology.

A Description Graph (DG) [15] is a directed labeled graph that contains set of vertices, edges as well as a labeling function that assigns each node to an atomic concept, and each vertex to an atomic role. According to [15], a graph-extended knowledge base is a 4-tuple $\mathcal{K} = (\mathcal{T}; \mathcal{P}; \mathcal{G}; \mathcal{A})$ where $\mathcal{T}$ is a TBox, $\mathcal{P}$ is a program, $\mathcal{G}$ is a GBox, and $\mathcal{A}$ is an ABox. The $\mathcal{P}$ consists of a finite number of connected rules. The $\mathcal{G}$ contains graphs roles i.e. roles one can use in a DG [14].

3 Tier 1 Capital Adequacy Calculation Process

This sections sets out *Tier 1 Capital Ratio Calculation Process* model. We have developed this model based on the description provided in [2]. Fig. 1 shows the process model.

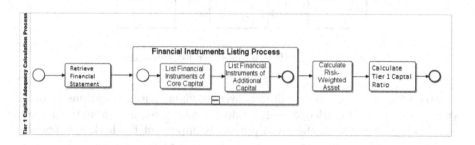

Fig. 1. Tier 1 Capital Ratio Calculation Process Model

The process starts with performance of the *Retrieve Financial Statement* activity that gives financial instruments of a financial institute. The sub-process (is a special type of activity nested in a process) *Financial Instrument Listing Process* contains *List of Financial Instruments of Core Capital* and *List of Financial Instruments of Additional Capital* activities. The activity 'List of Financial Instruments of Additional Capital' *succeeds* 'List of Financial Instruments of Core Capital' implies that they execute *sequentially*. The other activities within the process are *Calculate Risk-Weighted Assets* and *Calculate Tier 1 Capital Ratio*. After executing these activities successfully, the *end* event signals the *completion* of the process.

The Tier 1 capital ratio calculation process is driven by a large number of regulations defined by regulatory standards particularly, Basel. The *List Financial Instruments of Core Capital* and *List Financial Instruments of Additional Capital* are regulation-intensive activities. The actions performed by these activities must comply with Basel III regulations.

The current status of activities within 'Tier 1 Capital Ratio Calculation' is nescient. The proposed solution transforms these activities into intelligent activities. The solution leads financial service process execution complying corresponding Basel III regulations and prevents unwanted consequence for financial institutes.

4 Graph-Extended Knowledge Base for Financial Regulations

This section outlines how to encode regulation corresponding to the Tier 1 capital ratio calculation process (shown on Fig. 1) into a graph-extended knowledge base [15] and check satisfiability of the knowledge base using hyper-tableau algorithm

[14]. Modeling FSPs using graphs is not new idea [16]. A problem arises, however, when one needs to apply automated reasoning on the processes which must satisfy certain regulations. The execution of each activity in Tier 1 capital ratio calculation process relies on regulations i.e. Basel III. Reasoning with the process

Fig. 2. Encoding FSP to graph-extended knowledge base

(shown on Fig. 2) is provided indirectly over reasoning with regulations encoded as a graph-extended knowledge base. We do not specify regulations in the process itself. The reasoning with the given process is important to check whether the activity of financial service processes is compliant wit the Basel regulations upon execution. It means that activity has been executed successfully and is consistent to regulations from where it is taken [2]. To consume regulations encoded as graph-extended knowledge base, the reasoner must check satisfiability (see Fig. 2). To encode financial regulations underlying the activities within an FSP space, we use graph-extended knowledge base, as follows:

– Elements related to each activity are encoded as nodes in DG,
– The interconnection between elements is represented by graph roles,
– DG rules and SWRL implement regulations related to activity,
– Restrictions on the graphs implements control flows between elements.

We encode the regulations into graph-extended knowledge base because of the following reasons:

– OWL2 is not expressive enough to encode financial regulations as non-tree structures [14],
– Hyper-tableau algorithm is practically efficient in reasoning with more than one DG. Also it is possible to encode process regulations into more than one DG.
– In order to establish if formalization processes comply with regulations a reasoner such as, Hermit [17], checks consistency of the regulations.

Execution of the *List of Financial Instruments of Core Capital* and the *List of Financial Instruments of Additional Capital* (see Fig. 1) must comply with the following regulations, taken from [2]:

(R1) If a financial institute has financial instrument as common stock and the common stock can be converted to a currency, then the given currency is principal amount for the financial institute.

(R2) If a financial institute has a currency as a principal amount and the currency is represented by as common stock, then the financial institute has a financial instrument as given common stock.

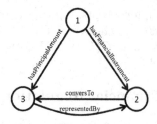

Fig. 3. DGs for Tier 1 Capital Ratio Calculation Process shown on Fig. 1

The regulations (R1), (R2) are encoded into the following first order logic formulas:

$$(\forall x, y, z)(FinancialInstitute(x) \wedge hasFinancialInstrument(x, y) \wedge$$
$$convertsTo(y, z) \Rightarrow hasPrincipalAmount(x, z)) \quad (1)$$

$$(\forall x, y, z)(FinancialInstitute(x) \wedge hasPrincipalAmount(x, y) \wedge$$
$$representedBy(y, z) \Rightarrow hasFinancialInstrument(x, z)) \quad (2)$$

$$(\forall x, y)(FinancialInstitute(x) \wedge convertsTo(x, y) \Rightarrow representedBy(y, x)) \quad (3)$$

Formula (1) encodes regulation (R1) while formula (2) encodes regulation (R2). The formula (3) specifies relationship between common stock and currency. Formulas (1), (2) can be expressed as property chains that are not allowed in OWL2. Instead, we use formalism based on DGs. Fig. (3) shows DG which corresponds to regulations (R1) and (R2). Formal definition of the DG shown on Fig. 3 is: $G = (V, E, \lambda)$, where $V = \{1, 2, 3\}$, $E = \{(1, 2), (1, 3), (2, 3)\}$. Concept names are represented as nodes in graph (see Fig. 3) as shown in formulation (4) [15]:

$$\lambda \langle 1 \rangle = FinancialInstitute; \lambda \langle 2 \rangle = CommonStock; \lambda \langle 3 \rangle = Currency; \quad (4)$$

Concept *FinancialInstitute* is the main concept. Each node in the graph (see Fig. 3) is related to a concept name. The graph roles are defined as follows:

$$\lambda \langle 1, 2 \rangle = hasFinancialInstrument; \lambda \langle 1, 3 \rangle = hasPrincipalAmount;$$
$$\lambda \langle 2, 3 \rangle = convertsTo; \quad (5)$$

The extended signature of the graph (see Fig. 3) is:

$$N_C = \{FinancialInstitute, CommonStock, Currency\},$$
$$N_{Rt} = \emptyset, \quad (6)$$
$$N_{Rg} = \{hasFinancialInstrument, convertTo,$$
$$represnetedBy, hasPrincipalAmount\},$$
$$N_I = \{bankOfIrelan, stock1, euro\}$$

N_C represents the set of graph concepts, N_{Rg} is the set of graph roles, and N_I represents the set of individuals. The set of Tbox roles is empty and all roles are graph roles [15]. The formula $G(BankOfIreland, stock1, euro)$ represents an instantiation of the graph.

5   Reasoning with Financial Regulations

Reasoning with financial regulations involved in Tier 1 capital ratio calculation process (see Fig. 2) includes:

- Preprocessing the DG which implements regulations consumed by Tier 1 adequacy calculation process,
- Application derivation rules to the graph-extended knowledge base.

The preprocessing step includes the process of encoding rules for the given DG. It includes rules in program $\mathcal{P}$, equality rules and disjointness rules. In our case, we encode the DG (shown on Fig. 3) into rules according to specification in [15]. Rules in program $\mathcal{P}$ can propagate constraints within DG. The following rules in program $\mathcal{P}$ corresponds to given DG (shown in Fig. 3):

$$hasFinancialInstrument(?x, ?y) \land conversTo(?y, ?z) \rightarrow$$
$$hasPrincipalAmount(?x, ?z) \tag{7}$$
$$hasPrincipalAmount(?x, ?y) \land representedBy(?y, ?z) \rightarrow$$
$$hasFinacialInstrument(?x, ?z)$$

The DG shown on Fig. 3, contains an inverse role i.e. $conversTo$ is inverse role of $representedBy$ role, so the inverse role can be formalized using the following DG rules:

$$conversTo(?x, ?y) \rightarrow representedBy(?y, ?x) \tag{8}$$
$$representedBy(?x, ?y) \rightarrow conversTo(?y, ?x) \tag{9}$$

Formula (10) specifies one equality rule, while the formula (11) specifies one disjointness rule.

$$G(x_1, y_1, z_1) \land G(x_1, y_2, z_2) \rightarrow y_1 = y_2 \tag{10}$$
$$G(x_1, y_1, z_1) \land G(x_2, x_1, z_2) \rightarrow \bot \tag{11}$$

Finaly, the following semantic web rules must be defined:

$$hasFinancialInstrument(?x, ?y) \land hasFinancialInstrument(?x, ?z) \rightarrow$$
$$SameAs(?y, ?z) \tag{12}$$
$$convertsTo(?x, ?y) \land convertsTo(?x, ?z) \rightarrow$$
$$SameAs(?y, ?z) \tag{13}$$
$$hasPrincipalAmount(?x, ?y) \land hasPrincipalAmount(?x, ?z) \rightarrow$$
$$SameAs(?y, ?z)$$
$$representedBy(?x, ?y) \land representedBy(?x, ?z) \rightarrow$$
$$SameAs(?y, ?z) \tag{14}$$

Applying derivation rules the hyper-tableau algorithm checks the satisfiability of $(\mathcal{R}, \mathcal{A})$ where $\mathcal{R} = [\sim](\mathcal{G}) \cup \mathcal{P}$, where $\mathcal{A}$ is defined Abox [14]. To prove satisfiability of given graph-extended knowledge base, the hyper-tableau algorithm tries to construct a model of a $(\mathcal{R}, \mathcal{A})$ by applying different derivation rules to $\mathcal{R}$, $\mathcal{A}$. Before applying the rules, it is important to define at least one Abox $\mathcal{A}$. If $\perp \in \mathcal{A}$ then there is a clash and the algorithm will detect inconsistency of the knowledge base.

6   Implementation

In this section, we sketch out the ongoing implementation of the Tier 1 capital adequacy process and required service components.

First, we implement the service components. For implementing components, we use the hermit-reasoner API [17] as well as OWL API [20]. To create graph concepts and roles we use *AtomicConcept* and *AtomicRole* classes respectively imported from Hermit API packages [17]. For the creation of graph roles we allocate memory using *AtomicRole* class. We use *OWLOntologyManager* class to load ontology. To check satisfiability of the knowledge base, the Hermit reasoner takes ontology and DG as input. In order to do that, we use the *Reasoner* class imported from the Hermit API.

Next, we wrap the components as services using web service description language (WSDL)[22] and stored in University College Cork Financial Service (UCCFS) repository. In addition, the repository contains calculate risk-weighted assets and calculate capital adequacy ratio services.

Finally, we define the process that will use these services. To implement process, we use BPEL (version 2.0) - an eXtensible Markup Language (XML) based *de facto* language for developing business processes. We start with specifying the `process name` and `target namespace` then import the services in the `capital adequacy` process. Next, we define `partnerLinks` that are characterised using `partnerLinkType`, which defines interactions between the partners involved in this process. Note that, these interactions are then defined in `wsdl` specifications of corresponding service components. The variables for inputs and outputs are defined. Finally, the sequence is defined for ordering the operations performed by the FSP activities. After implementing the FSP, we deploy it on process engine.

7   Related Works

In this section, we discuss the related solutions revolving around the financial regulation knowledge base, reasoning, and process. To the best of our knowledge, financial regulation has been scoped in a very small number of researches. Thus, the actual need (e.g., machine readable definition of Basel-based regulations) of financial service industry has been addressed very little in current solutions. Some very recent researches including [18], [19], and [1] focus on investigating the issues and challenges, and defining roadmap for governance, risk and compliance within business processes. Nonetheless, no concrete solution has been discussed in these works. Additionally, a language to capture the compliance requirements of business processes is proposed in [21] and [6]. The language is promising, but offers a very limited number of constructs that do not facilitate defining financial regulations in FSB. Solutions entailing [7] and [13] are offered to perform reasoning on business processes to verify the correctness of business process. However, these solutions do not address the problem of this research.

8 Conclusion and Future Work

In this paper, we have shown how to transform a nescient activity within an FSP into an intelligent activity. In order to support the transformation, we have shown how to encode financial regulations into a graph-extended knowledge base that assists process activities to perform operations intelligently. Additionally, we have shown how to perform reasoning with financial regulations. We have also described the current state of implementation.

We plan to extend the solution in order to enable a system to decide actions for the conditions that are evolved at runtime. In future, we plan to cover more complex financial regulations. In addition, our intention is to cover financial regulations from various standard bodies. We also plan to extend to enable these systems to do fuzzy reasoning. Keeping completeness for incomplete ontology reasoner is a challenge [8] which we have experienced in this research. We will try to tackle this challenge in future extension.

Acknowledgments. This research is done within the scope of the Governance Risk Compliance Technology Centre project funded by the Enterprise Ireland.

References

1. Syed Abdullah, N., Sadiq, S., Indulska, M.: Emerging Challenges in Information Systems Research for Regulatory Compliance Management. In: Pernici, B. (ed.) CAiSE 2010. LNCS, vol. 6051, pp. 251–265. Springer, Heidelberg (2010)
2. Basel III: A Global Regulatory Framework. Bank for International Settlement (December 2010)
3. Business Process Execution Language. Organization for the Advancement of Structured Information Standards, OASIS (2007),
   http://docs.oasis-open.org/wsbpel/2.0/wsbpel-v2.0.pdf
4. Business Process Modeling Notation. Object Management Group (OMG),
   http://www.omg.org/spec/BPMN/2.0/
5. Cuenca Grau, B., Horrocks, I., Motik, B., Parsia, P., Patel-Schneider, P.F., Sattler, U.: OWL 2: The next step for OWL. Journal of Web Semantics 6(4), 309–322 (2008)
6. Elgammal, E., Türetken, O., Heuvel, W.J.V.D.: Using Patterns for the Analysis and Resolution of Compliance Violations. International Jounrnal of Cooperative Information System 21(1), 31–54 (2012)
7. Di Francescomarino, C., Ghidini, C., Rospocher, M., Serafini, L., Tonella, P.: Reasoning on Semantically Annotated Processes. In: Bouguettaya, A., Krueger, I., Margaria, T. (eds.) ICSOC 2008. LNCS, vol. 5364, pp. 132–146. Springer, Heidelberg (2008)

8. Grau, B.C., Motik, B., Stoilos, G., Horrocks, I.: Completeness Guarantees for Incomplete Ontology Reasoners: Theory and Practice. Journal of Artificial Intelligence Research 43, 419–476 (2012)
9. Healy, M.P., Palepu, G.K.: The Fall of Enron. Journal of Economic Perspectives 17(2), 3–26 (2003)
10. Horrocks, I., Patel-Schneider, P.F., Boley, H., Tabet, S., Grosof, B., Dean, M.: SWRL: A Semantic Web Rule Language Combining OWL and RuleML. W3C Member Submission (May 21, 2004)
11. Horrocks, I., Kutz, O., Sattler, U.: The Even More Irresistible SROIQ. In: Proc. of the 10th Int. Conf. on Principles of Knowledge Representation and Reasoning (KR 2006), pp. 57–67. AAAI Press (2006)
12. Leymann, F., Roller, D.: Production Workflow: Concepts and Techniques, 1st edn., September 18. Prentice Hall (1999) ISBN-10: 0130217530
13. Missikoff, M., Proietti, M., Smith, F.: Reasoning on Business Processes and Ontologies in a Logic Programming Environment. In: The Proceedings of 3rd Interop-Vlab.It Workshop, CEUR-WS, 653 (2010)
14. Motik, B., Shearer, R., Horrocks, I.: Hypertableau Reasoning for Description Logics. It Journal of Artificial Intelligence Research 36, 165–228 (2009)
15. Motik, B., Cuenca Grau, B., Horrocks, I., Sattler, U.: Representing Structured Objects using Description Graphs. In: Brewka, G., Lang, J. (eds.) Proc. of the 11th Int. Joint Conf. on Principles of Knowledge Representation and Reasoning (KR 2008), pp. 296–306. AAAI Press, Sydney (2008)
16. Polyvyanyy, A., Weske, M.: Hypergraph-Based Modeling of Ad-Hoc Business Processes. In: Ardagna, D., Mecella, M., Yang, J. (eds.) BPM 2008 Workshops. LNBIP, vol. 17, pp. 278–289. Springer, Heidelberg (2009)
17. Shearer, R., Motik, B., Horrocks, I.: HermiT: A Highly-Efficient OWL Reasoner. In: Ruttenberg, A., Sattler, U., Dolbear, C. (eds.) Proc. of the 5th Int. Workshop on OWL: Experiences and Directions (OWLED 2008 EU), Karlsruhe, Germany, October 26-27 (2008), http://hermit-reasoner.com/
18. Sadiq, W.S., Muehlen, Z.M., Indulska, M.: Governance, risk and compliance: Applications in information systems. Information Systems Frontiers 14(2), 123–124 (2012)
19. Sadiq, S.: A Roadmap for Research in Business Process Compliance. In: Abramowicz, W., Maciaszek, L., Węcel, K. (eds.) BIS Workshops 2011 and BIS 2011. LNBIP, vol. 97, pp. 1–4. Springer, Heidelberg (2011)
20. The OWL API, http://owlapi.sourceforge.net/ (last visited May 2012)
21. Türetken, O., Elgammal, A., Heuvel, W.J.V.D., Papazoglou, P.M.: Capturing Compliance Requirements: A Pattern-Based Approach. IEEE Software 29(3), 28–36 (2012)
22. Web Service Description Language (WSDL) (March 2001), http://www.w3.org/TR/wsdl

Self-adaptive Non-stationary Parallel Multisplitting Two-Stage Iterative Methods for Linear Systems*

Guo-Yan Meng[1], Chuan-Long Wang[2], and Xi-Hong Yan[2]

[1] Department of Compute Science, Xinzhou teacher University,
Xinzhou 034000,Shanxi Province, P.R. China
[2] Department of Mathematics, Taiyuan Normal University,
Taiyuan 030012, Shanxi Province, P.R. China
clwang218@126.com

Abstract. In this paper,the new non-stationary parallel multisplitting two-stage iterative methods with self-adaptive weighting matrices are presented for the linear system of equations when the coefficient matrix is nonsingular. Self-adaptive weighting matrices are given, especially, the nonnegativity is eliminated. The convergence theories are established for the self-adaptive non-stationary parallel multisplitting two-stage iterative methods. Finally, the numerical comparisons of several self-adaptive non-stationary parallel multisplitting two-stage iterative methods are shown.

Keywords: Self-adaptive weighting matrices, non-stationary, multisplitting, two-stage, linear systems.

1 Introduction and Preliminaries

To solve large sparse linear system of equations on multiprocessor systems,

$$Ax = b, \ A = (a_{ij}) \in R^{n \times n} \text{ nonsingular and } b \in R^n \ . \tag{1}$$

O'Leary and White [12] first proposed parallel methods based on multisplitting of matrices in 1985, after this, combing with two-stage iterative methods (see [2,4]), the multisplitting two-stage iterative methods [13] were proposed, where several basic convergence results were found. The scheme was proposed as following

$$A = B_i - C_i, \quad B_i = M_i - N_i, \quad i = 1, 2, \cdots, m \ , \tag{2}$$

$$M_i x_i^{(k,l)} = N_i x_i^{(k,l-1)} + C_i x^{(k)} + b \ , \tag{3}$$

$$x^{(k+1)} = \sum_{i=1}^{m} E_i x_i^{(k,q(i,k))} \ , \tag{4}$$

---

* This work is supported by NSF of China (11071184) and NSF of Shanxi Province (201001006, 2012011015-6).

Y. Xiang et al. (Eds.): ICDKE 2012, LNCS 7696, pp. 38–47, 2012.
© Springer-Verlag Berlin Heidelberg 2012

where $E_i \geq 0$, diagonal, and $\sum\limits_{i=1}^{m} E_i = I$. $(M_i, N_i, C_i, E_i)_{i=1}^{m}$ will be unchanged and independent of the iterative number k.

Later, many authors studied the methods for the case A is an M-matrix, an H-matrix or a symmetric positive definite matrix. When A is an M-matrix or an H-matrix, many parallel multisplitting two-stage iterative methods (see [3,5,6,13,15]) were presented, and the weighting matrices $E_i, i = 1, 2, \cdots, m$ were generalized (see [1,10])

$$\sum_{i=1}^{m} E_i^{(k)} = I(\text{or} \neq I), \quad E_i^{(k)} \geq 0, \quad \text{diagonal } i = 1, 2, \cdots, m, \ k = 1, 2, \cdots \ ,$$

but these weighting matrices were preset as multi-parameter.

When A is a symmetric positive definite matrix, generally, which require that assumption that the weighting matrices are multiples of the identity, that is $E_i = \alpha_i I$, $i = 1, 2, \cdots, m$ (see [12]), but these results have little applicability for analysis of parallel processing. In order to improve the weighting matrices, White [17] and Wen [16] presented the multisplitting which had a very special structure, Cao [7] gave a nonstandard multisplitting, Migallón [11] proposed the non-stationary multisplittings, Wang and Bai [15] discussed the non-stationary two-stage multisplitting, but the non-stationary multisplitting usually had a block splitting for parallel processing. Furthermore, As we know, the weighting matrices have important role in parallel multisplitting methods, but the weighting matrices in all above-mentioned methods are determined previously,they are not known to be good or bad, this influences the efficiency of parallel methods. In fact, none has ever studied that how to choose optimal weighting matrices for the two-stage multisplitting parallel iterative algorithms, we will discuss this problem in the paper.

Here, we still use the scalar weighting matrices $E_i^{(k)} = \alpha_i^{(k)} I$ $(i = 1, 2, \cdots, m,$ $k = 1, 2, \cdots)$ for the nonsingular matrix A , but $\alpha_i^{(k)}$ $(i = 1, 2, \cdots, m, \ k = 1, 2, \cdots)$ are chosen by finding the optimal point in the hyperplane H_k, where

$$H_k = \left\{ x | x = \sum_{i=1}^{m} \alpha_i^{(k)} x_i^{(k)}, \ \sum_{i=1}^{m} \alpha_i^{(k)} = 1 \right\}, \quad k = 1, 2, \cdots \ , \tag{5}$$

Thus, $\alpha_i^{(k)}(i = 1, 2, \cdots, m, \ k = 1, 2, \cdots)$ are the optimal parameters in k-th iteration. In other words, the point $x^{(k)} = \sum\limits_{i=1}^{m} \alpha_i^{(k)} x_i^{(k)}$ generated by the optimal weighting matrices $E_i^{(k)} = \alpha_i^{(k)} I$, $(i = 1, 2, \cdots, m, \ k = 1, 2, \cdots)$ may be the optimal point to the solution of linear systems (1) in H_k. Thus, we search the optimal weighting matrices without nonnegative condition. In fact, numerical examples (will be seen in section 4) show that the methods which the weighting matrices $E_i^{(k)} = \alpha_i^{(k)} I$ $(i = 1, 2, \cdots, m, \ k = 1, 2, \cdots)$are effective.

In this study, we first give some notations and preliminaries in Section 1, and then the self-adaptive non-stationary parallel multisplitting two-stage iterative methods are put forward in Section 2, the convergence of these self-adaptive non-stationary parallel multisplitting two-stage iterative methods are established in Section 3. Finally, we give the comparisons by the numerical example.

Here are some essential notations and preliminaries. $R^{n \times n}$ is used to denote the $n \times n$ real matrix set, A^T denotes the transpose of the matrix A. A matrix $A \in R^{n \times n}$ is called symmetric positive definite(or semidefinite), if it is symmetric and for all $x \in R^n, x \neq 0$, it holds that $x^T A x > 0$(or $x^T A x \geq 0$). $A = M - N$ is called a splitting of the matrix A if $M \in R^{n \times n}$ is non-singular; this splitting is called a convergent splitting if $\rho(M^{-1}N) < 1$; a P-regular splitting of the symmetric positive definite matrix A if $M^T + N$ is positive definite, a symmetric positive definite splitting if N is symmetric positive semi-definite (see [6,14]).

2   Algorithms

In this section, we give the self-adaptive non-stationary parallel multisplitting two-stage iterative methods.

Let

$$E_i^{(k)} = \alpha_i^{(k)} I, \ i = 1, 2, \cdots, m, \ \sum_{i=1}^{m} \alpha_i^{(k)} = 1, \ \ k = 1, 2, \cdots \quad (6)$$

It is denoted $\alpha^{(k)} = (\alpha_1^{(k)}, \alpha_2^{(k)}, \cdots, \alpha_m^{(k)})^T$.

Algorithm 1. (SMTS) The self-adaptive non-stationary parallel multisplitting two-stage iterative methods

Step 0. Given the precision $\epsilon > 0$, the initial point $x^{(0)}$ and set $k := 0$; For $k = 0, 1, \cdots$, until convergence.

Step 1. For all processors

$$x_i^{(k,0)} = x^{(k)} \ ,$$

Step 2. For processor i, for $l = 0, 1, \cdots, q(i, k) - 1$

$$M_i x_i^{(k,l+1)} = N_i x^{(k,l)} + C_i x^{(k)} + b, \quad i = 1, 2, \cdots, m \ ; \quad (7)$$

Step 3. Computing $\alpha_i^{(k)} (i = 1, 2, \cdots, m)$ by the following quadratic programming models. Let $x = \sum\limits_{i=1}^{m} \alpha_i x_i^{(k,q(i,k))}$,

$$\min_{\alpha} \frac{1}{2} x^T A x - x^T b$$

$$s.t. \ \sum_{i=1}^{m} \alpha_i = 1 \ . \quad (8)$$

Step 4.

$$x^{(k+1)} = \sum_{i=1}^{m} \alpha_i^{(k)} x_i^{(k,q(i,k))} \ . \quad (9)$$

Step 5. If $\|Ax^{(k+1)} - b\| < \varepsilon$, stop; Otherwise, set $k:=k+1$;   Go to Step 1.

By introducing matrices

$$G(i,k) = \sum_{l=0}^{q(i,k)-1} (M_i^{-1}N_i)^l M_i^{-1} , \tag{10}$$

$$H(i,k) = (M_i^{-1}N_i)^{q(i,k)} + \sum_{l=0}^{q(i,k)-1} (M_i^{-1}N_i)^l M_i^{-1}C_i . \tag{11}$$

We can rewrite the **SMTS** as the following iteration

$$x^{(k+1)} = \sum_{i=1}^{m} E_i^{(k)}(H(i,k)x^{(k)} + G(i,k)b) = H(k)x^{(k)} + G(k)b , \tag{12}$$

where

$$H(k) = \sum_{i=1}^{m} E_i^{(k)} H(i,k), \quad G(k) = \sum_{i=1}^{m} E_i^{(k)} G(i,k) . \tag{13}$$

It follows from straightforward derivation that

$$H(i,k) = I - G(i,k)A, \quad i = 1, 2, \cdots, m, \quad k = 0, 1, \ldots \tag{14}$$

and the iteration matrix

$$H(k) = I - G(k)A, \quad k = 0, 1, 2, \cdots \tag{15}$$

For the quadratic programming, we have following results (see [9]).
Let

$$X(k) = (x_1^{(k,q(1,k))}, \cdots, x_m^{(k,q(m,k))}), \quad \alpha = (\alpha_1, \cdots, \alpha_m)^T, \quad e = (1, \cdots, 1)^T .$$

Theorem 1. *Let $\{x_1^{(k,q(1,k))}, \cdots, x_m^{(k,q(m,k))}\}$ be linear independent, the solution of the quadratic programming (8) is as following*

$$\alpha = (X(k)^T AX(k))^{-1}(X(k)^T b + \mu e) , \tag{16}$$

where $\mu = \frac{1-e^T(X(k)^T AX(k))^{-1}X(k)^T b}{e^T(X(k)^T AX(k))^{-1}e}$.

3   Convergence Analysis

In this section, we study the convergence theories for algorithm 1 with self-adaptive weighting matrices.

Lemma 1. *[10] Assume that A is a symmetric positive definite matrix, let $A = M - N$ be P-regular splitting. Then there exists a positive number r such that*

$$\|A^{\frac{1}{2}}(M^{-1}N)A^{-\frac{1}{2}}\|_2 \leq r < 1 . \tag{17}$$

Lemma 2. *[8] Assume that A is a symmetric positive definite matrix, let $A = F - G$ is a P-regular splitting. Then there exists a unique splitting $A = P - Q$ such that $P^{-1}Q = (F^{-1}G)^m$ and $A = P - Q$ is also a regular splitting.*

Lemma 3. *Assume that A is a symmetric positive definite matrix. Let $A = B_i - C_i, i = 1, 2, \cdots, m$ be symmetric positive definite splittings, and let $B_i = M_i - N_i$ be P-regular splittings. If there exists a positive integer q such that the non-stationary iteration number $q(i, k) \leq q,\ k = 1, 2, \cdots$. Then there exists a positive number r such that*

$$\|A^{\frac{1}{2}}H(i, k)A^{-\frac{1}{2}}\|_2 \leq r < 1, \quad i = 1, 2, \cdots, m,\ k = 1, 2, \cdots \tag{18}$$

Proof. We compute $G(i, k)$ directly

$$G(i, k) = \sum_{l=0}^{q(i,k)-1} (M_i^{-1}N_i)^l M_i^{-1} = (I - (M_i^{-1}N_i)^{q(i,k)})(I - M_i^{-1}N_i)^{-1}M_i^{-1}$$

$$= (I - (M_i^{-1}N_i)^{q(i,k)})B_i^{-1} \tag{19}$$

From Lemma 2, there exists a unique P-regular splitting $B_i = P_i(k) - Q_i(k),\ i = 1, 2, \cdots, m, k = 1, 2, \cdots$, such that $P_i^{-1}(k)Q_i(k) = (M_i^{-1}N_i)^{q(i,k)}$. Hence, it is derived that

$$G(i, k) = (I - P_i^{-1}(k)Q_i(k))B_i^{-1} = P_i^{-1}(k), i = 1, 2, \cdots, m,\ k = 1, 2, \cdots.$$

and thereby,

$$\begin{aligned} H(i, k) &= I - P_i^{-1}(k)A = P_i^{-1}(k)(P_i(k) - A) \\ &= P_i^{-1}(k)(B_i + Q_i(k) - (B_i - C_i)) \\ &= P_i^{-1}(k)(Q_i(k) + C_i), \quad i = 1, 2, \cdots, m,\ k = 1, 2, \cdots. \end{aligned} \tag{20}$$

From the assumptions of Lemma 3, the splitting

$$A = P_i(k) - (Q_i(k) + C_i), \quad i = 1, 2, \cdots, m,\ k = 1, 2, \cdots \tag{21}$$

are P-regular splittings. Thus, there exist the positive numbers $r(i, k),\ i = 1, 2, \cdots, m,\ k = 1, 2, \cdots$, such that

$$\|A^{\frac{1}{2}}H(i, k)A^{-\frac{1}{2}}\|_2 \leq r(i, k) < 1, \quad i = 1, 2, \cdots, m,\ k = 1, 2, \cdots.$$

Because of the $q(i, k) \leq q,\ q(i, k) = 1, 2, \cdots, q$ has q different values. Thus, the splittings (21) have at most q different splittings, so are the positive numbers $r(i, k), i = 1, 2, \cdots, m,\ k = 1, 2, \cdots$. Hence, there exists a positive number r such that (18) holds. ☐

Theorem 2. *Assume that A is a symmetric positive definite matrix. Let $A = B_i - C_i, i = 1, 2, \cdots, m$ be symmetric positive definite splitting, and let $B_i = M_i - N_i$ be P-regular splittings. Suppose that weighting matrices $E_i^{(k)} = \alpha_i^{(k)}I,\ k = 1, 2, \cdots$ are given by (8). If there exists a positive integer q such that the non-stationary iteration number $q(i, k) \leq q$. Then $\{x^{(k)}\}$ generated by algorithm 1 converges to the unique solution of the linear system of equations (1).*

Proof. Let x^* be the unique solution of linear system of equations (1), and let $\varepsilon^{(k)} = x^{(k)} - x^*, \quad k = 1, 2, \cdots$. From the algorithm 1, we have

$$\varepsilon^{(k)} = H(k)\varepsilon^{(k-1)}, \quad k = 1, 2, \cdots \qquad (22)$$

where

$$H(k) = \sum_{i=1}^{m} \alpha_i^{(k)} ((M_i^{-1} N_i)^{q(i,k)} + \sum_{l=0}^{q(i,k)-1} (M_i^{-1} N_i)^l M_i^{-1} C_i), \; k = 1, 2, \cdots \quad (23)$$

On the other hand, model (8) is equivalent to the following quadratic programming model,

$$\min_{\alpha} \frac{1}{2}(x - x^*)^T A(x - x^*)$$

$$s.t. \sum_{i=1}^{m} \alpha_i = 1. \qquad (24)$$

From (24), we have

$$\varepsilon^{(k)^T} A\varepsilon^{(k)} \leq \tilde{\varepsilon}_i^{(k)^T} A\tilde{\varepsilon}_i^{(k)}, i = 1, 2, \cdots, m, \quad k = 1, 2, \cdots \qquad (25)$$

where

$$\tilde{\varepsilon}_i^{(k)} = H(i,k)\varepsilon^{(k-1)}, \; i = 1, 2, \cdots, m, \; k = 1, 2, \cdots \qquad (26)$$

(22) and (23) combine (25) and (26), for $k = 1, 2, \cdots$, it holds that

$$\begin{aligned}
\|A^{\frac{1}{2}}\varepsilon^{(k)}\|_2 &= \|A^{\frac{1}{2}} H(k)\varepsilon^{(k-1)}\|_2 \leq \|A^{\frac{1}{2}} H(i,k)\varepsilon^{(k-1)}\|_2 \\
&= \|A^{\frac{1}{2}} H(i,k) A^{-\frac{1}{2}} A^{\frac{1}{2}} \varepsilon^{(k-1)}\|_2 \\
&\leq \|A^{\frac{1}{2}} H(i,k) A^{-\frac{1}{2}}\|_2 \|A^{\frac{1}{2}} \varepsilon^{(k-1)}\|_2 \\
&\leq \cdots \\
&\leq \Pi_{k=0}^{\infty} \|A^{\frac{1}{2}} (H(i,k)) A^{-\frac{1}{2}}\|_2 \|A^{\frac{1}{2}} \varepsilon^{(0)}\|_2, \; i = 1, 2, \cdots, m .
\end{aligned}$$

From Lemma 3, we have

$$\|A^{\frac{1}{2}} H(i,k) A^{-\frac{1}{2}}\|_2 \leq r < 1, \; i = 1, 2, \cdots, m .$$

Thus,

$$\lim_{k \to \infty} \varepsilon^{(k)^T} A\varepsilon^{(k)} = 0 ,$$

which is equivalent to $\lim_{k \to \infty} \varepsilon^{(k)} = 0$. $\qquad \square$

Remark 1. The choice the optimization model of weighting matrices in k-th iteration can be various. Here, we only consider one schemes of optimizing weighting matrices for a linear system. In order to obtain self-adaptive weighting matrices, we need to solve the quadratic programming, but it may decrease the iterations largely because of the inequality implied in Theorem 2. Furthermore, we can parallel compute α as (16).

4   Numerical Experiments

In this section, we give some preliminary computational results. We implement our Algorithm 1 with three splittings (Gauss-Seidel splitting, Relaxation splitting and upper Gauss-Seidel splitting) to solve the linear system (1).

All our tests are started from zero vector, and terminated when the current iteration satisfied $\|r^{(k)}\| < 10^{-5}$, where $r^{(k)}$ is the residual of the current, say k-th iteration or the number of IT is up to 5000. For the latter the iteration is failing. The computation times and iteration of these methods for problem with different sizes are given in the following table.

Example 1. Consider another linear system of equations,that is Discrete Poisson equations of nine-point $Ax = b$, with $A =$

$$\begin{pmatrix} D_p & G_p & & & \\ G_p & D_p & G_p & & \\ & \ddots & \ddots & \ddots & \\ & & G_p & D_p & G_p \\ & & & G_p & D_p \end{pmatrix}_{q \times q},$$

$$D_p = \begin{pmatrix} 20 & -4 & & & \\ -4 & 20 & -4 & & \\ & \ddots & \ddots & \ddots & \\ & & -4 & 20 & -4 \\ & & & -4 & 20 \end{pmatrix}_{p \times p}, \; G_p = \begin{pmatrix} -4 & -1 & & & \\ -1 & -4 & -1 & & \\ & \ddots & \ddots & \ddots & \\ & & -1 & -4 & -1 \\ & & & -1 & -4 \end{pmatrix},$$

the right-hand side vector $b = (1, 2, 3, \cdots, n)^T$.

Three splittings are proposed as following

Let $A = B_i - C_i$, $i = 1, 2, 3$ with $B_i = \begin{pmatrix} D_{ip} & G_{ip} & & & \\ G_{ip} & D_{ip} & G_{ip} & & \\ & \ddots & \ddots & \ddots & \\ & & G_{ip} & D_{ip} & G_{ip} \\ & & & G_{ip} & D_{ip} \end{pmatrix}$, where

$$D_{1p} = \begin{pmatrix} 24 & -4 & & & \\ -4 & 24 & -4 & & \\ & \ddots & \ddots & \ddots & \\ & & -4 & 24 & -4 \\ & & & -4 & 24 \end{pmatrix}, \; G_{1p} = \begin{pmatrix} -2 & -1 & & & \\ -1 & -2 & -1 & & \\ & \ddots & \ddots & \ddots & \\ & & -1 & -2 & -1 \\ & & & -1 & -2 \end{pmatrix},$$

$$D_{2p} = \begin{pmatrix} 22 & -4 & & & \\ -4 & 22 & -4 & & \\ & \ddots & \ddots & \ddots & \\ & & -4 & 22 & -4 \\ & & & -4 & 22 \end{pmatrix}, G_{2p} = \begin{pmatrix} -3 & -1 & & & \\ -1 & -3 & -1 & & \\ & \ddots & \ddots & \ddots & \\ & & -1 & -3 & -1 \\ & & & -1 & -3 \end{pmatrix},$$

$$D_{3p} = \begin{pmatrix} 26 & -3 & & & \\ -3 & 26 & -3 & & \\ & \ddots & \ddots & \ddots & \\ & & -3 & 26 & -3 \\ & & & -3 & 26 \end{pmatrix}, G_{3p} = \begin{pmatrix} -4 & & & \\ & -4 & & \\ & & \ddots & \\ & & & -4 \end{pmatrix}.$$

Let

$$B_i = D_i - L_i - L_i^T, i = 1, 2, 3 , \tag{27}$$

where $D_i = diag(D_{i,p}, \cdots, D_{i,p}), i = 1, 2, 3.$ and corresponding to the D_i block, L_i is strictly block lower triangular matrix. M_i and N_i of algorithm 1 are determined by the following three splitting methods.

The Gauss-Seidel splitting method

$$M_1 = D_1 - L_1, \quad N_1 = L_1^T ; \tag{28}$$

The SOR splitting method

$$M_2 = \frac{1}{\omega}(D_2 - \omega L_2), \quad N_2 = \frac{1}{\omega}((1 - \omega)D_2 + \omega L_2^T) ; \tag{29}$$

The upper Gauss-Seidel splitting method

$$M_3 = D_3 - L_3^T, \quad N_3 = L_3 . \tag{30}$$

Here, the weighting matrices $E_i^{(k)} = \alpha_i^{(k)} I, \quad i = 1, 2, 3, \quad k = 1, 2, \cdots.$

In order to compare old algorithm with the fixed weighting matrices, we propose the fixed weighting matrices as following,

(1) $E_i = \alpha_i I, \ i = 1, 2, 3,$ with $\alpha_1 = 0.2, \ \alpha_2 = 0.2 \ \alpha_3 = 0.6;$
(2) $E_i = \alpha_i I, \ i = 1, 2, 3,$ with $\alpha_1 = 0.4, \ \alpha_2 = 0.3, \ \alpha_3 = 0.3;$
(3) $E_1 = diag(\alpha_1 I_p, \alpha_2 I_p, \cdots, \alpha_q I_p), E_2 = diag(\beta_1 I_p, \beta_2 I_p, \cdots, \beta_q I_p),$
$E_3 = diag(\gamma_1 I_p, \gamma_2 I_p, \cdots, \gamma_q I_p),$ where α_i and $\beta_i (i = 1, 2 \cdots q)$ are generated **randomly** in (0,1), and $\gamma_i = 1 - \alpha_i - \beta_i.$

The following table shows the computational result.

From above example, we can see that the iteration number and the CPU times of SMTS are much less than the usual algorithm with fixed weighting matrices. the reason is that the nonnegativity of weighting matrices are deleted, the range for finding the optimal weighting matrices is extended. The results confirm that the self-adaptive strategy for weighting matrices is effective.

Table 1. Comparison of computational results ($\omega = 1.5$, $q(i,k) = 5$)

p, q		SMTS	old Alg with(1)	old Alg with (2)	old Alg with (3)
10,10	IT	25	174	137	125
	CPU(s)	0.0312	0.0624	0.0468	0.0780
20,20	IT	84	669	525	463
	CPU(s)	0.4368	2.6364	2.4024	1.8252
30,30	IT	188	1528	1199	991
	CPU(s)	3.8376	28.8914	23.8730	19.5781
40,40	IT	334	2770	2172	1628
	CPU(s)	21.8089	169.2923	148.9030	109.6843
50,50	IT	534	4407	3455	2585
	CPU(s)	94.3806	756.6829	578.8573	468.7986

References

1. Bai, Z.-Z., Sun, J.-C., Wang, D.-R.: A unified framework for the construction of various matrix multisplitting iterative methods for large sparse system of linear equations. Comput. Math. Appl. 32, 51–76 (1996)
2. Bai, Z.-Z.: A class of two-stage iterative methods for systems of weakly nonlinear equations. Numer. Alg. 14, 295–319 (1997)
3. Bai, Z.-Z.: Parallel multisplitting two-stage iterative methods for large sparse systems of weakly nonlinear equations. Numer. Alg. 15, 347–372 (1997)
4. Bai, Z.-Z.: The convergence of the two-stage iterative method for hermitian positive definite linear systems. Appl. Math. Lett. 11, 1–5 (1998)
5. Bai, Z.-Z.: Convergence analysis of two-stage multisplitting method. Calcolo 36, 63–74 (1999)
6. Bai, Z.-Z., Wang, C.L.: Convergence theorems for parallel multisplitting two-stage iterative methods for mildly nonlinear systems. Lin. Alg. Appl. 362, 237–250 (2003)
7. Cao, Z.-H., Liu, Z.-Y.: Symmetric multisplitting of a symmetric positive definite matrix. Lin. Alg. Appl. 285, 309–319 (1998)
8. Castel, M.J., Migallón, V., Penadés, J.: Convergence of non-stationary parallel multisplitting methods for Hermitian positive definite matrices. Math. Comput. 67, 209–220 (1998)
9. Fletcher, R.: Practical Methods of Optimization, 2nd edn. John Wiley and Sons, Chichester (1987)
10. Frommer, A., Syzld, D.B.: Weighted max norms, splittings, and overlapping additive Schwarz iterations. Numer. Math. 83, 259–278 (1999)
11. Migallón, V., Penadés, J., Szyld, D.B.: Nonstationary multisplittings with general weighting matrices. SIAM J. Matrix Ana. Appl. 22, 1089–1094 (2001)
12. O'Leary, D.P., White, R.E.: Multi-splittings of matrices and parallel solutions of linear systems. SIAM J. Alg. Disc. Meth. 6, 630–640 (1985)
13. Szyld, D.B., Jones, M.T.: Two-stage and multisplitting methods for the parallel solution of linear systems. SIAM J. Matrix Anal. Appl. 13, 671–679 (1992)
14. Varga, R.S.: Matrix Iterative Analysis. Prentice-Hall, Englewood Cliffs (1962)

15. Wang, C.-L., Bai, Z.-Z.: On the convergence of nonstationary multisplitting two-stage iteration methods for Hermitian positive definite linear systems. J. Comput. Appl. Math. 138, 287–296 (2002)
16. Wen, R.-P., Wang, C.-L., Meng, G.-Y.: Convergence theorems for block splitting iterative methods for linear systems. J. Comput. Appl. Math. 202, 540–547 (2007)
17. White, R.E.: Multisplitting of a symmetric positive definite matrix. SIAM J. Matrix Anal. Appl. 11, 69–82 (1990)

Towards a Case-Based Reasoning Approach Based on Ontologies Application to Railroad Accidents

Ahmed Maalel[1,*], Lassad Mejri[1], Habib Hadj-Mabrouk[2], and Henda Ben Ghézela[1]

[1] RIADI Labs., ENSI, National School of Computer Sciences,
University of Manouba, 2010, Tunisia
ahmed.maalel@ensi.rnu.tn,
mejrilassad@yahoo.fr,
hhbg.hhbg@gmail.com
[2] French Institute of Science and Technology of Transport, Planning and Networking,
IFSTTAR, 23 Rue Alfred Nobel, 77420 CHAMPS-SUR-MARNE, France
habib.hadj-mabrouk@ifsttar.fr

Abstract. The work presented in the context of this paper is to develop a system of Case-Based Reasoning (CBR) to help capitalize and exploit the knowledge on railroad accidents from our field of application. To streamline and strengthen the acquisition process, representation and exploitation of this domain knowledge, initially, it is necessary to harmonize and standardize the terminology used by the domain actors. In this context, we have agreed to call on building ontologies. Far from being just an effect of "fashion" or a goal in itself, ontology finds its place in resolving problems. For this purpose, ontologies can play an important role in the CBR systems, because they can greatly reduce the effort of acquiring knowledge in various stages of reasoning. In this paper, we will present the first realized works in our approach.

Keywords: Knowledge Management, Case-based Reasoning, Ontologies, Railroad Accident.

1 Introduction

In our daily lives, we often use our experience to solve some problems we had before. Case based-reasoning CBR copies this human behavior and solves problems by searching for similar cases already resolved in the past. CBR is a type of reasoning in Artificial Intelligence AI in the field of automatic learning. Case based reasoning means remembering past situations similar to the current situation and by these situations to help resolve the current situation. CBR is a form of reasoning by analogy the analogy searches for cause and effect relation in past situations and transfer to the current situation the similarities between the past situations as well as the current situation.

Our approach to CBR is based on ontologies to model the knowledge of cases and the knowledge of the reasoning cycle. The challenge of such a research is

---

* Corresponding author.

Y. Xiang et al. (Eds.): ICDKE 2012, LNCS 7696, pp. 48–55, 2012.
© Springer-Verlag Berlin Heidelberg 2012

twofold: (1) addressing the issue of reusing the domain knowledge of the railroad accident, while (2) contributing to advances in the knowledge engineering discipline by proposing a model based on the coupling between CBR and ontologies.

The organization of this paper is as follows. Section 2 presents the notion of an accident scenario. Section 3 presents our approach, through the description of the functional architecture of the proposed CBR system, the presentation of the developed knowledge model and the tool implemented for querying-it.

2   Notion of an Accident Scenario

An accident scenario is a logical and chronological combination of values taken by the operating parameters or component failures (equipment, procedures, environment or human actions) leading to the hazardous event (the accident) and the danger materialization [1].

We adopt in our approach a static characterization of an accident scenario, through a description comprising a set of parameters with several attributes. Each accident scenario is characterized by a membership class.

2.1   Descriptive Parameters of an Accident Scenario

We base our work on a set of descriptors of an accident scenario; these descriptors have been structured into three families of descriptors: [2].

— *The type descriptors "symptoms"* (the context of the accident) define the context of the scenario of an accident and are the framework within which it takes place. They concern descriptors such as: event = dreaded collision, accident area = terminus and hazardous elements = operator roaming.
— *The type descriptors "causes"* represent the failures and causes related to three factors (human, system and environment) causing the accident. They concern, for instance, these descriptors: cause-related system= failure automatic steering board, cause related to the human = non compliance with regulatory requirements, and cause related to the environment = loss of visibility due to fog.
— *The type descriptors "solutions"* represent the solutions that can maintain or restore the operation of a transport system and therefore inhibit the consequences of failures. The solutions adopted have been : the prevention and / or protection, for example, solution = prohibit mode switching I / O, so that a mode is in progress.

2.2   Operationalization of an Accident Scenario

We present here a concrete example of an accident scenario (loss of an element after penetrating an occupied block) [3] through a textual description and a diagram (Figure 1):

A train enters an occupied block due to a defect in its emergency brake (permanent pull). The AP (autopilot) intersects the fixed FS / HT (frequency of security / high voltage). The CCP (control and checkpoint post) examines the situation, and does not see that there are two trains on the same block and restores the FS / HT. The train will not restart downstream but the upstream train leaves with a maximum tensile stress which causes a collision remedial [3].

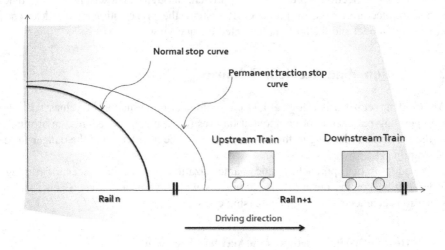

Fig. 1. Accident synoptic : Loss of an element after penetrating an occupied block

We now present our approach.

3   Proposed CBR Approach

Our goal is to design a system of case-based reasoning CBR to help build and operate all the historical accidents from the railroad, our current application domain. We present in this section, the general description of our system and in particular the first part of the embodied approach, the knowledge model.

4   General Description of the Approach

Several approaches of CBR systems have been proposed in the literature. These archi-tectures share more or less the same components. Inspired by these works and archi-tectures, our system [4] has two parts: an offline process, and an on-line process (Figure 2):

- *The offline process* includes the real field knowledge and those extracted from the domain experts, the formalization of knowledge related to reasoning, the construc-tion of a knowledge model based on ontologies (domain ontology and operational ontology) and finally the preparation of the case base.

- *The on-line process* includes an interface dedicated to the interaction between the expert / user and the system along CBR reasoning cycle.

We resume CBR cycle of Cordier [5], composed of five stages: (1) preparation, (2) memory retrieval, (3) reuse (adaptation), (4) revision and (5) memorization (learning). A set of cases is capitalized in the knowledge base (base case). The created cases will be indexed according to their class membership during the instantiation. A case is an instantiation of the domain ontology represented by the triplet composed of a problem and a solution of a membership class.

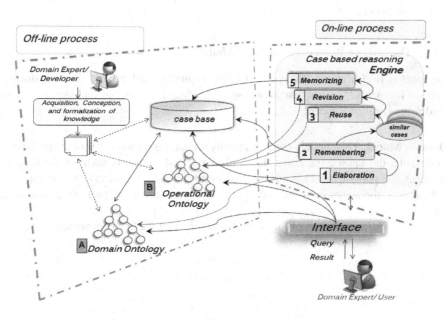

Fig. 2. Functional architecture of the proposed CBR approach

We trigger the process by the first CBR stage, (1) preparation, which is the development of a target case; the domain ontology will be instantiated and will be viewed as a form to be completed by the user who in turn selects the main concepts of the problem part to which it can characterize its target case [6]. The validation of its formulation will be the input of the next stage; (2) which is remembering that allows you to search for similar cases. The user can also enrich the ontology with new concepts or new relationships if it is a necessity to do so (Figure 2). During this second phase, the system infers with the operational ontology to restrict the search space of the source case to the sole cases of the identified class starting from the decision rules and key concepts of the target case. The selection of similar cases is based on a similarity measure. If similar cases exist in the base case, the solutions brought from this base case are displayed to the user. The next phase, which is (3) adaptation, refers also to the adaptation rules extracted from the operational ontology to take advantage of the rememorized source case and in light of clearing the solution to the new problem represented by the new target case. During the fourth phase, (4) which is using revision, the proposed solution may not appeal to the user from who, in turn, may modify or reject it completely. The identification of possible causes of this failure can help improve the adaptation knowledge. If successful, the system (5) stores the target case adapted and revised in the case base, hence allowing its enrichment. Each new leaned case allows the evolution of the system knowledge base.

Taking into account that our work is ongoing, the rest of this article will focus only on the first part of our approach materialized; the knowledge model include the domain model and operational model and the tool implemented for querying ontology and acquisition case.

4.1   The Offline Process (*Knowledge Model*)

Our goal is to design a CBR system to help capitalize and exploit all the historical railroad accidents. We base our work on a knowledge model that includes a domain model an operational model.

Domain Model. This model is represented by an ontology that contain the vocabulary to describe the knowledge about the field of railroad accidents such as: the type of accident, the geographical area (zone of occurrence of the accident), the principle of railway line, the actors involved and their failure, preventive and protective measures, etc. ..

Figure 3 shows a portion of the domain ontology that we have developed:

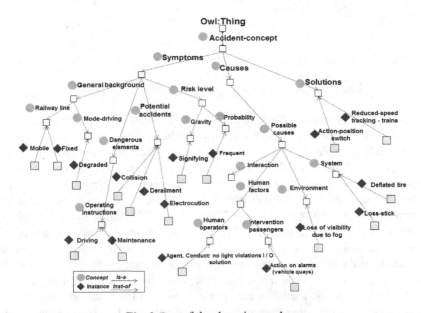

Fig. 3. Part of the domain ontology

The conceptual vocabulary that we have used in the domain model consists of a set of concepts and a set of relations [7]. We mention here:

— The *is-a* relationship between two proven concepts or two relations (also called Subsumption relationship or specialization / generalization) is used to build taxonomies (tree or mesh of concepts and relations);
— The ownership of abstraction of a concept or exhaustive-decomposition in [8]. A concept is considered abstract if it does not allow a direct instance: all instances are necessarily instances of its son concepts ;
— The property of disjunction between two concepts. Note that it is possible to define a partition [8] using both the abstraction and disjunction. For example, the decomposition of the risk level into the damage gravity and the occurrence probability is a partition because the risk level is an abstract concept and the damage gravity and the occurrence probability are disjoint;
— The relationship inst-*of* is used to associate one or more instances of a concept.

Operational Model. We have agreed to develop an operational model based on the domain model. We know that the domain model in the occurrence of the domain ontology is considered as an effective way to unify the terminology and share knowledge in a domain.

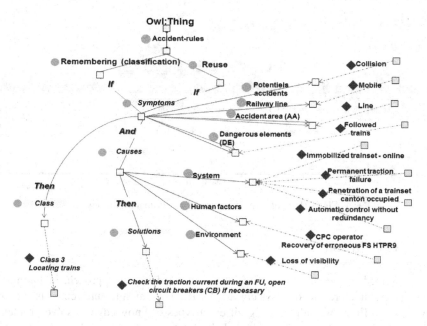

Fig. 4. Part of the operational ontology

However, an ontology should not only consider what the terminological component of a domain can do as a thesaurus, but also must integrate all the knowledge of the latter. To meet this goal, we have evolved the domain ontology described as "light" to a "heavier" ontology to cover a maximum level of semantics we need. The proposed operational model in figure 4 serves as a conceptual basis for the operational ontology that we use as part of our approach.

4.2   Online Process (First Steps)

Query Tool of the Ontology Implemented. Although it is interesting to implement tools to interact with ontologies, we must certainly develop these tools for reasoning mechanisms to allow the representation of different types of knowledge (knowledge of terminology, facts, rules and constraints). The goal is to make operational the ontology in order to manipulate knowledge represented through mechanisms tailored to the target system already defined (Figure 5).

Fig. 5. Tool of acquisition case from domain ontology

5   Conclusion

We presented in this article the first works realized in our approach, including the general architecture of our system of CBR. This architecture consists of two processes, offline and online, using different types of knowledge to solve problems. We have described the model of knowledge, in particular, the field and case relied upon by our system. We presented also the tool used to interrogate and develop the case base. Although the scope of this work is in itself an original, we can also extend the application given the generic and open model of knowledge we have proposed, to other fields of application such as the road sector, sea sector or even in other sectors.

We are currently working on the acquisition of reasoning knowledge to improve developed knowledge model in particular ontology, so as to show the direct impact of this improvement on the process of Case Based Reasoning If we are going to graft in the system.

References

1. Mejri, L., Hadj-Mabrouk, H., Caulier, P.: Un modèle générique unifié de représentation et de résolution de problèmes pour la réutilisation des connaissances. Application à l'analyse de sécurité des systèmes de transport automatisés, Recherche Transports Sécurité 26/103, 131–148 (2009) 0761-8980
2. Mejri, L.: Une démarche basée sur l'apprentissage automatique pour l'aide à l'évaluation et à la génération de scenarios d'accidents. Application à l'analyse de sécurité des systèmes de transport automatises. Université de valenciennes, 210p base de cas d'accidents (INRETS) (Décembre 6, 1995)
3. Hadj-Mabrouk, H.: Acquisition et évaluation des connaissances de sécurité des systèmes industriels. Application au domaine de la certification des systèmes de transport guidés, Thèse d'Habilitation à Diriger des Recherches, Université de Technologie de Compiègne (1998)
4. Maalel, A., Mejri, L., Hadj Mabrouk, H., Ben Ghezela, H.: Toward a Knowledge Management Approach Based on an Ontology and Case-based Reasoning (CBR). In: IEEE RCIS 2012, Sixth International Conference on Research Challenges in Information Science, Valencia, Spain, May 16-18 (2012)
5. Cordier A., Fuchs B., Lieber J., et Mille, A.: Acquisition interactive des connaissances d'adaptation intégrée aux sessions de raisonnement à partir de cas - Principes, architecture IAKA et prototype KAYAK. In: Actes du 15ème atelier de Raisonnement à Partir de Cas (RàPC 2007), Grenoble, France, pp. 71–84 (2007).
6. Maalel, A., Hadj Mabrouk, H., Mejri, L., Ben Ghezela, H.: Development of an Ontology to Assist the Modeling of an Accident Scenario: Application on Railroad Transport. Journal of Computing 3(7) (July 2011)
7. Abou-Assali, A.: Acquisition des connaissances d'adaptation et Traitement de l'hétérogénéité dans un système de RàPC basé sur une Ontologie. Application au diagnostic de la défaillance de détecteurs de gaz. Thèse de doctorat (2010)
8. Gomez-Perez, A., Fernandez-Lopez, M., Corcho, O.: Ontological Engineering. Advanced Information and Knowledge Processing. Springer (2003)

An Agile Knowledge Discovery in Databases Software Process

Givanildo Santana do Nascimento[1,2] and Adicinéia Aparecida de Oliveira[1]

[1] Federal University of Sergipe, São Cristóvão, Brazil
[2] Petrobras, Aracaju, Brazil
gsnascimento@petrobras.com.br, adicineia@ufs.br

Abstract. In a knowledge society, transforming data into information and knowledge to support the decision-making process is a crucial success factor for all organizations. In this sense, the mission of Software Engineering is to build systems able to process large volumes of data, transform them into relevant knowledge and deliver them to customers, so they can make the right decisions at the right time. However, companies still fail in determining the process model used in their Knowledge Discovery in Databases projects. This article introduces the AgileKDD, an agile and disciplined software process for developing systems capable of discovering the knowledge hidden in databases, which was built on top of the Open Unified Process. A case study shows that AgileKDD can increase the success factor of projects whose goal is to develop Knowledge Discovery in Databases applications.

Keywords: Knowledge Discovery in Databases, Agile Software Development, Software Process.

1 Introduction

Data, information and knowledge constitute key assets for all organizations working in knowledge-based economies. The global competition is becoming increasingly based on the ability to transform data into information and knowledge in an effective way. Knowledge is equated with the traditional factors of production – land, capital, raw materials, energy and manpower – in the process of wealth creation. Knowledge management, Data Mining, Knowledge Discovery in Databases (KDD) and, more generally, Business Intelligence (BI) are key concepts in a knowledge-based economy [1]. KDD applications have vital importance for many organizations and can help them manage, develop and communicate their intangible assets such as information and knowledge, improving their performance [2].

However, companies still face problems in determining the process model used to develop KDD applications. As business requirements become more dynamic and uncertain, the traditional static, bureaucratic and heavy processes may not be able to deal with them. Recent researches have demonstrated that waterfall lifecycles and traditional software processes are not successful in KDD because they are unable to

Y. Xiang et al. (Eds.): ICDKE 2012, LNCS 7696, pp. 56–64, 2012.
© Springer-Verlag Berlin Heidelberg 2012

follow dynamic requirement changes in a rapidly evolving environment [3]. As a software process is mandatory for KDD development, one possible solution is to use an agile process, which is typically characterized by flexibility, adaptability, face-to-face communication and knowledge sharing.

This article discusses the importance of using an agile software process in KDD applications development. Thus, the main objective of this paper is to present Agi-leKDD, an agile process able to guide the KDD applications development in a manner compatible with the current ever-changing requirement environments. The next sections of this article are organized as follows: section 2 describes KDD as a technique for transforming raw data into information and knowledge. The section 3 presents the agile software processes. Section 4 presents the AgileKDD, an agile KDD process model built on top of the Open Unified Process. Section 5 presents related work and, finally, section 6 presents the conclusion and future work.

2   Knowledge Discovery in Databases

The raw data evolve into information and knowledge as they receive degrees of association and meaning [4]. KDD is a nontrivial process of identifying valid, novel, potentially useful and understandable patterns in data [5]. Data Mining (DM) is the main activity of KDD and consists of applying algorithms to extract models or patterns from data [5]. KDD applications are characterized by the ability to deal with the explosion of business data and accelerated market changes. These characteristics provide powerful tools for decision makers. Such tools can be used by business users to analyze huge amount of data for patterns and discover trends [1].

The KDD systematization effort has resulted in a variety of process models, including the KDD Process [5] and the Cross-Industry Standard Process for Data Mining (CRISP-DM) [6], which are the most widely used in KDD projects, the most frequently cited and supported by tools. These two processes are considered the *de facto* standards in the KDD area. Several other process models were derived from KDD Process and CRISP-DM. Fig. 1 shows the evolution of 14 DM process models and methodologies. KDD Process can be pointed out as the initial approach, and CRISP-DM as the central approach of the evolution diagram [7]. Most of the approaches are based on these process models.

The KDD process models created between 1993 and 2008 were discussed in detail in a survey by [8] and then categorized by [7] into three groups:

- KDD related approaches – KDD Process (1993); Human-Centered (1996); 5A's (1996); 6-σ (1996); Cabena et al. (1997); Two Crowns (1998); and Anand & Buchner (1998).
- CRISP-DM related approaches – CRISP-DM (2000); Cios et al. (2000); RAMSYS (2001); DIME (2002); Marbán et al. (2007); and the CRISP-DM 2.0 initiative (2008, not concluded).
- Other approaches – KDD Roadmap (2001).

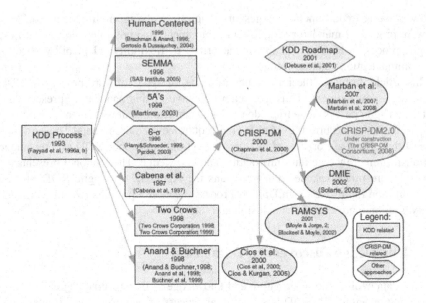

Fig. 1. Evolution of data mining process models (Source: [7])

Sometime later [9] continued the older surveys done by [7] and [8], and proposed a different categorization to the KDD process models:

- Traditional approach – Starting with KDD Process, many other process models used the same sequential steps: business understanding, data understanding, data processing, data mining, model evaluation, and deployment.
- Ontology-based approach – This approach is the combination of ontology engineering and traditional approach.
- Web-based approach – This approach is similar to the traditional approach, but it has some steps to deal with web log data analysis.
- Agile-based approach – Integrates agile processes and methodologies with traditional approaches. The unique model in this category is Adaptive Software Development – Data Mining (ASD-DM) Process Model [10].

Thus, the knowledge discovery process models are evolving from traditional to agile processes, becoming more adaptive, flexible and human-centered. However these processes still lack software engineering capabilities such as requirements management, project management and changes management. Many companies still develop KDD applications without the guidance of a software process, but, as any software project, KDD projects need a software process to succeed [11]. Also, the dynamic business requirements, the needs of quick ROI and fluid communication between stakeholders and the team led to agile process as one possible solution [3].

3   Agile Software Engineering Processes

A software process provides an ordered sequence of activities related to the specification, design and implementation as well as validation and deployment of software products, transforming user expectations into software solutions [12]. According to [13], the software processes set the context in which technical methods are applied, the work artifacts (data, models, documents, reports, forms) are produced, the milestones are established, quality is assured and changes are managed.

The traditional software development processes are characterized by rigid mechanisms with a heavy documentation process, which make it difficult to adapt to a high-speed, ever-changing environments [14]. Researchers have suggested that the complex, uncertain and unstable environment is pushing developers to adopt agile processes rather than traditional software processes. They claim that agile approach is the answer to the software engineering chaotic situation, in which projects are exceeding their time and budget limits, requirements are not fulfilled and, consequently, leading to unsatisfied customers [15].

The Manifesto for Agile Software Development [16] defines the values introduced by the agile software processes: individuals and interactions over processes and tools; working software over comprehensive documentation; customer collaboration over contract negotiation; and responding to change over following a plan. Ultimately, by following these values, software development becomes less formal, more dynamic, and more customer-focused. Based on these values, agile processes are people-oriented and have the customer satisfaction as the highest priority through the early and continuous delivery of functioning software [15]. Also, the response to all types of changes and fluid communication between all projects participants become top priorities. In agile development, the main work product is the increment of functioning software, delivered to the customer within fixed timeframes. Agile approaches are best fit when requirements are uncertain or volatile; this can happen due to business dynamics and rapidly evolving markets. It is too difficult to practice traditional plan-oriented software development in such unstable environments [14].

3.1   Unified Process and Open Unified Process

The Unified Process (UP) [17] is based on the Incremental Model [13], focuses on architecture and is use cases driven. Based on the use cases model, the analysis, design and implementation models are created to realize the use cases. The UP is focused on architecture, so it starts by the definition of an application skeleton (the architecture), which evolves gradually over development. The UP is also an iterative and incremental process because it offers an approach of partitioning the work into smaller portions or mini-projects. In UP, the architecture provides the framework to guide the system development into iterations, while the use cases define the targets and lead the work of each iteration.

Open Unified Process (OpenUP) is a variation of the UP that applies agile, iterative and incremental approaches within a structured lifecycle. OpenUP embraces a pragmatic, agile philosophy that focuses on the collaborative nature of software development. It is a low-ceremony process that can be extended to address a broad variety of project types [18]. OpenUP has compliance with the Manifesto for Agile Software Development, is minimal, complete and extensible. Moreover, it increases collaboration and continuous communication between project participants, more than formalities and comprehensive documentation [19].

The OpenUP process is divided into three layers, has four phases and six disciplines. The process applies intensive collaboration as the system is incrementally developed by a committed, self-organized team. OpenUP layers are illustrated by Fig. 2. They are [18]:

- Project Lifecycle – structures the software project into four phases: Inception, Elaboration, Construction and Transition. A project plan defines the lifecycle and results in a released application.
- Iteration Lifecycle – OpenUP divides the project into iterations: planned, time-boxed intervals typically measured in weeks. Iterations focus the team on delivering incremental value to stakeholders in a predictable manner.
- Micro-increment – personal effort in an OpenUP project is organized in micro-increments. These micro-increments provide an extremely short feedback loop that drives adaptive decisions within each iteration.

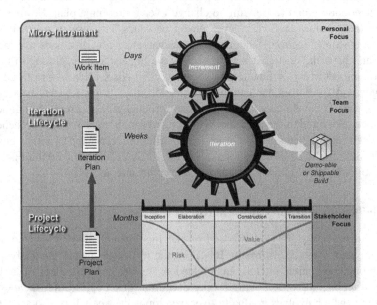

Fig. 2. OpenUP layers and lifecycle (Source: [18])

The OpenUP phases are inception, elaboration, construction and transition. In inception phase the product vision is specified. The product architecture is defined in elaboration phase. The result of construction is a demonstrable or deliverable product version, deployed to the customer at the end of the transition phase. The OpenUP disciplines are requirements, architecture, development, testing, project management, and configuration and change management.

The development of KDD applications must be guided by a software process. Waterfall lifecycles and traditional processes are not successful in KDD because they are unable to follow requirements in ever-changing environments [3]. Hence, one possible solution is to use an agile process, which is typically characterized by flexibility, adaptability, fluid communication and knowledge sharing.

4   AgileKDD

AgileKDD is an agile and disciplined process for the development of KDD and BI applications. CRISP-DM and KDD Process provide the capabilities related to knowledge discovering. OpenUP provides to AgileKDD the lifecycle, phases and disciplines, which are requirements, architecture, development, test, project management and changes management. OpenUP also adds the agile software development core values and principles, without giving up the management disciplines. The process applies intensive collaboration between the actors as the system is built incrementally.

AgileKDD divides the projects in iterations with fixed time boxes, usually measured in weeks. The iterations drive the team to deliver incremental value to stakeholders in a predictable manner. Iteration plan defines what must be delivered during the iteration and the result is a demonstrable or deliverable piece of the KDD or BI solution. The AgileKDD lifecycle provides stakeholders and project team visibility and decision points at various milestones, until a working application is fully delivered to stakeholders. Fig. 3 presents an overview of AgileKDD, highlighting its phases and activities.

The Inception phase has the aim of developing an understanding of the application domain and the relevant prior knowledge and identifying the goal of the KDD project from the customer's viewpoint. In this phase the project vision and plans are defined and agreed by all project participants. Also, in inception the target data set, or subset of variables or data samples, is selected. The knowledge discovery processes will be performed on the selected target data set.

The Elaboration phase is responsible by the system's architecture, the data preprocessing and modeling. Data cleaning removes noise, collects the necessary information to model and decides on strategies for handling missing data fields. The data quality is a critical success factor for any KDD or BI project, so it is verified prior to the DW and data marts modeling.

Once DW and data marts are modeled, ETL processes are built to extract, integrate, transform and load the selected target data into DW and data marts. Thus, the DM techniques that best fit to the data are selected and applied to the information stored in data marts. Data mining tools search for meaningful patterns in data, including association rules, decision trees and clusters. The team can significantly aid the DM method by correctly performing the preceding steps. The OLAP reports and charts as well as the dashboards are built to allow user data exploration. The verification and validation activities guarantee that the data was extracted, loaded and processed correctly, according to business objectives.

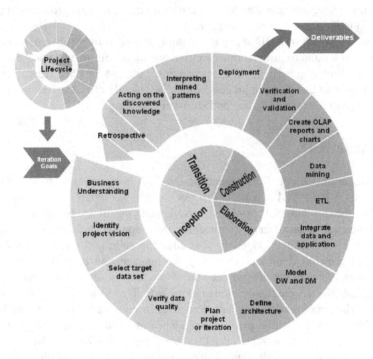

Fig. 3. AgileKDD lifecycle

In Transition phase the deployment of both software and knowledge takes place, the knowledge is interpreted, actions are created and the retrospective discusses lessons learnt during the project to promote continuous process improvement. Interpreting mined patterns involve visualization and storage of the extracted knowledge into knowledge bases, or simply documenting and reporting it to interested parties. This activity also includes checking for and resolving potential conflicts with previously believed knowledge. The AgileKDD process can involve significant iteration, interaction and can contain loops between any two phases.

AgileKDD has been validated by a case study in oil and gas field. The process was applied to a KDD project that dealt with Reservoir Evaluation data and afforded the early and continuous delivery of results to the costumers. The first iteration was entirely dedicated to the Inception phase. DM results were delivered in the second iteration, two months after the project kickoff. The third iteration delivered the performance indicators as a dashboard and the fourth iteration deployed the OLAP reports, graphs, and *ad hoc* exploration of the DW.

The case study showed that AgileKDD was able to guide a KDD application development and helped to anticipate the project ROI. Moreover, the process was refined after the project retrospective. Requirements changes directly affected the project planning, but did not harm the product objectives achievement because they were discovered early, between project iterations.

5 Related Work

The main work that applies agile methodologies to KDD is [1]. [14] discusses KDD, BI and Agile Methodologies for knowledge-based organizations in a cross-disciplinary approach. [10] introduces Adaptive Software Development – Data Mining (ASD-DM) Process Model. The main difference between this work and these is the fact that AgileKDD is a process, not a methodology. As a process, AgileKDD defines what to do instead of how to do KDD development. Also, the process proposed by this work defines lifecycle, roles, activities, inputs and outputs regarding agile KDD application development. Moreover, AgileKDD contains management disciplines like project, changes and requirements management, which were inherited from OpenUP. Even in an agile process like AgileKDD, management is a crucial success factor for any software projects.

6 Conclusion and Future Work

A software process is mandatory for KDD applications development, but traditional software development processes are not successful in KDD because they are unable to follow dynamic requirement changes in an ever-changing environment. Agile processes fit in KDD better than traditional processes because they are iterative, inter-active and characterized by flexibility, adaptability, communication and knowledge sharing.

This work presented AgileKDD, a KDD process based on KDD Process, CRISP-DM and Open Unified Process. AgileKDD has been validated by a case study and results indicate that the process is able to guide KDD applications projects. AgileKDD bring benefits such as more customer satisfaction through early and continuous delivery of functioning software, better communication between team members and reducing projects failures risks. Future work can validate AgileKDD by case studies in different areas and investigate the need of storing the knowledge discovered into ontology bases or knowledge bases.

References

1. El Sheikh, A., Alnoukari, M.: Business Intelligence and Agile Methodologies for Know-ledge-Based Organizations: Cross-Disciplinary Applications, pp. 1–370. IGI Global (2012)
2. Alnoukari, M., Alhawasli, H., Alnafea, H., Zamreek, A.: Business Intelligence: Body of Knowledge. In: Business Intelligence and Agile Methodologies for Knowledge-Based Or-ganizations: Cross-Disciplinary Applications, pp. 1–13. IGI Global (2012)
3. Larson, D.: Agile Methodologies for Business Intelligence. In: Business Intelligence and Agile Methodologies for Knowledge-Based Organizations: Cross-Disciplinary Applica-tions, pp. 101–119. IGI Global (2012)
4. Elmasri, R., Navathe, S.B.: Fundamentals of Database Systems, 6th edn. Pearson (2010)

5. Fayyad, U.M., Piatetsky-Shapiro, G., Smyth, P.: From datamining to knowledge discovery: an overview. In: Proc. Advances in Knowledge Discovery and Data Mining, pp. 1–34 (1996)
6. Chapman, P., Clinton, J., Kerber, R., Khabaza, T., Reinartz, T., Shearer, C., Wirth, R.: CRISP-DM 1.0: Step-by-step data mining guide (2000)
7. Mariscal, G., Marbán, O., Fernández, C.: A survey of data mining and knowledge discovery process models and methodologies. The Knowledge Engineering Review 25, 137–166 (2010)
8. Kurgan, L., Musilek, P.: A survey of Knowledge Discovery and Data Mining process models. The Knowledge Engineering Review 21, 1–24 (2006)
9. Alnoukari, M., El Sheikh, A.: Knowledge Discovery Process Models: From Traditional to Agile Modeling. In: Business Intelligence and Agile Methodologies for Knowledge-Based Organizations: Cross-Disciplinary Applications, pp. 72–100. IGI Global (2012)
10. Alnoukari, M., Alzoabi, Z., Hanna, S.: Applying adaptive software development (ASD) agile modeling on predictive data mining applications: ASD-DM Methodology. In: IEEE Proceedings of International Symposium of Information Technology, pp. 1083–1087 (2008)
11. Marbán, O., et al.: Towards data mining engineering: a software engineering approach. Information Systems Journal 34(1) (March 2009),
    http://dl.acm.org/citation.cfm?id=1458745 (October 1, 2011)
12. Sommerville, I.: Software Engineering, p. 864. Addison Wesley (2006)
13. Pressman, R.: Software Engineering: A Practioner's Approach. McGraw-Hill (2005)
14. Alnoukari, M.: Business Intelligence and Agile Methodologies for Knowledge-Based Organizations: Cross-Disciplinary Applications. In: CEPIS UPGRADE: The European Journal for the Informatics Professional (2011),
    http://www.cepis.org/upgrade/media/III_2011_alnoukari1.pdf (April 20, 2012)
15. Alzoabi, Z.: Agile Software: Body of Knowledge. In: Business Intelligence and Agile Methodologies for Knowledge-Based Organizations: Cross-Disciplinary Applications, pp. 14–34. IGI Global (2012)
16. Beck, K., et al.: Manifesto for Agile Software Development (2001),
    http://agilemanifesto.org (April 20, 2012)
17. Booch, G., Rumbaugh, J., Jacobson, I.: The Unified Modeling Language User Guide. Addison Wesley (1999)
18. Hristov, H.: Introduction to OpenUP (2011),
    http://epf.eclipse.org/wikis/openup/index.htm (October 1, 2011)
19. Santos, S.: OpenUP: Um processo ágil (2009),
    http://www.ibm.com/developerworks/br/rational/local/open_up/index.html (October 8, 2011)

An Innovative Outlier Detection Method Using Localized Thresholds

Ji Zhang[1], Jie Cao[2], and Xiaodong Zhu[2]

[1] Department of Mathematics and Computing &
Centre for Systems Biology (CSBi)
University of Southern Queensland, Australia
ji.zhang@usq.edu.au
[2] School of Economics and Management
Nanjing University of Information Science and Technology
Nanjing, Jiangsu, China
cj@nuist.edu.cn, zxdnuist@126.com

Abstract. In this paper, we investigate the research problem of specifying the thresholds to effectively detect outliers and propose an innovative technique that leverages multiple localized thresholds for detecting outliers. Our technique is able to overcome a major limitation of the existing outlier detection approaches that use a single universal threshold to distinguish outliers from normal data. The experiments conducted demonstrate that our technique is able to achieve a better detection effectiveness than the traditional approaches.

1 Introduction

Outlier detection, which aims to detect abnormal or inconsistent instances from the given data sources, has been a long-standing research problem in the domains of data mining and data management which is still attracting significant research attentions at present. Its long-term research popularity is mainly due to its important application in a wide range of areas in business, security, health and engineering, to name a few.

Numerous research work on outlier detection, primarily dealing with a centralized database, has been proposed which can broadly categorized as the distribution-based methods, the distance-based methods, the density-based methods and the clustering-based methods, etc. Distribution-based methods [3][8], also known as statistical methods, rely on the statistical approaches that assume a distribution or probability model to fit the given dataset. Outliers are those data that do not agree with or conform to the underlying model of the data. Distance-based methods [11] [12] [17] use distance-based metrics to quantify the proximity between the data point and its neighborhood. Most existing metrics are defined based upon the concepts of local neighborhood or k nearest neighbors (kNN). Those data points that are far from their respective neighbors are considered as outliers. Density-based methods [2] [10][20][22][24] use more

Y. Xiang et al. (Eds.): ICDKE 2012, LNCS 7696, pp. 65–73, 2012.
© Springer-Verlag Berlin Heidelberg 2012

complex mechanisms to model the outlier-ness of data points than distance-based methods. They usually involve investigating not only the local density of the data being studied but also the local densities of its nearest neighbors. Thus, the outlier-ness metric of a data point is relative in the sense that it is normally a ratio of density of this data against the averaged densities around its nearest neighbors. The clustering-based methods regard outliers as a by-product of clustering algorithms [1][7][9][15][23][25] themselves and define outliers as data that do not lie in or located far apart from any clusters. Thus, the clustering techniques implicitly define outliers as the background noise of clusters which are filtered out when clustering is performed.

There have been other recent developments of outlier detection. For instance, research work has been carried out to deal with other formats of data other than relational datasets such as dynamic data and data streams[27][28]. Also, there has been research work on outlier detection from distributed data sources[21][29]. Interested readers can refer to [30] for a survey of recent outlier detection methods.

The traditional distance-based and clustering-based outlier detection methods invariably need to use one or more distant thresholds for specifying either the scope of neighborhood where the local density is calculated or the cut-off distance to the nearby dense regions. The long-standing difficulty in applying these methods in practice is that the distance threshold is typically specified based on users experiences, which turns out to be quite difficult especially when the data distribution/characteristics is not clear prior to outlier detection. This will usually result in a high false positive rate or false negative rate in outlier detection when the distance threshold is inappropriately chosen. For the density-based approaches, the problem of setting the value for the distance threshold is not as important as the distance-based and clustering-based approaches discussed above. Nevertheless, density-based-approaches achieve this by implementing much more expensive calculation to measure the ratio between the density of the target point and that of its neighbors. This significantly hampers the scalability of this methods to deal with large datasets.

To overcome the key limitations of existing outlier detection methods, we devised the idea of multiple thresholding in an attempt to better take into account the different data distribution in different areas/regions in the data space, without involving a high computational overhead. The technical contributions of this work are summarized as follows:

- Firstly and most importantly, we proposed a novel outlier detection that uses multiple localized thresholds to identify outliers. The specification of the value of these localized thresholds closely reflects the local data distribution, which is key to the accurate detection of outliers in different regions;
- We also developed a pruning strategy to boost the efficiency of our technique by intelligently exclude the areas where the calculation of localized threshold are unnecessary;
- We experimentally evaluate our proposal technique and compare it with the existing outlier detection approaches, which demonstrate the better performance achieved by our method.

The remainder of this paper is organized as follows. In Section 2, we discuss in details on our outlier detection technique that utilizes multiple localized thresholds. The experimental evaluation of the proposed technique is presented in Section 3. The final section concludes the whole paper.

2 The Basic Outlier Detection Algorithm

In this section, we present a grid-based outlier detection method. Referred to as the basic outlier detection method, it serves a basis for our new multiple localized thresholding method that is to be introduced in the next section. The method is a highly efficient and well scalable towards large datasets.

As a data pre-processing step, the data space is undergone an equal-width partition which involves superimposing a grid structure into the data space under study. This results in a number of cells existing in the grid that feature the same cell width for each dimension. Outlier detection is ready to perform when the data partition is performed. More specifically, this outlier detection method works in the following steps:

1. For each data in the input dataset, assign it to one and only one cell in the grid. Cell density is calculated and book kept for all the populated cells. That is, when a data point is assigned to a cell, then the density of this cell will be incremented by 1;

2. After all the data has been assigned into the grid and the density of populated cells have been recorded, we will rank the populated cells based on their density in a descending order and select a specific number of most dense cells whose total number of data points have exceeded $q\%$ (for example 80%) of the number of data in the whole data set. These cells are called dense cells. The centroids of these dense cells are called representative points. The data points that do not fall into the dense cells are called outlier candidates that require further evaluation in order to detect true outliers from them;

3. When representative data have been selected, then the outlier score of each outlier candidate will be calculated which is defined as the distance between each data and its nearest representative data;

4. The outlier candidates whose outlier score is higher than a user-specified distance threshold T_{dis} are detected as outliers and returned to users.

Based upon the above discussion, it is clear that the distance between each outlier candidate to its nearest representative point is an important indicator used to decide whether this candidate is really an outlier or not. A straightforward way to distinguish outliers from the dense data regions is to apply a single cut off distance threshold to identify outliers, as presented in the above description of the algorithm. Yet, this fails to take into account the data distribution/characters in different regions, which may lead to inaccuracy of the detection.

3   Incorporating Localized Thresholding in Outlier Detection

3.1   Multiple Localized Thresholding

In this paper, we propose an innovative technique to leverage multiple thresholds for detecting outliers spanned in different regions in the data space. These thresholds are localized in the sense that their values are specified based upon the distribution and characteristics of data located in different regions. We develop an algorithm to automatically determine the appropriate values for different thresholds that are to be used. The basic idea for specifying localized thresholds is that we take into account the data statistics (including the mean and standard deviation) of each dense cell whereby an appropriate threshold value is quantified such that it can effectively distinguish nearby outliers from the normal data located in the cell.

The first step in deciding the value of the localized threshold associated with a dense cell is to quantify the mean and then standard deviation of the data inside the cell. These statistical measurements are able to cast a light on the distribution of the normal data in the local region delimited by the cell. Mathematically speaking, let's denote $SD(c)$ be the standard deviation of a dense cell c. According to Chebyshev's inequality, it is known that for any data sample, the possibility of observations that deviate from the sample mean by more than p sample standard deviation is no higher than $\frac{1}{p^2}$. For the purpose of detecting outliers, p normally falls into the range of $[1.5, 3]$ such as in the Boxplot approach. As per Chebyshev's inequality, the ratio of observations that deviate from the mean of the data in a given cell by more than 3 times as the standard deviation of the data in this cell is no more than 11% irrespective of the data distribution.

For each outlier candidate (the data that does not fall into any dense cells), denoted as oc, we need to first identify the nearest dense cell of oc, denoted as $NDC(oc)$, and decide whether oc is an outlier or not based on the localized threshold associated with $NDC(oc)$. More specifically, the following rule is used to evaluate outlier candidate

$$oc \text{ is an outlier iff } dist(oc, Mean(NDC(oc))) \geq LT(NDC(oc))$$

oc is labeled as a normal data if the above rule is not satisfied. In the event of the rare, but possible, cases that an outlier candidate has more than one nearest dense cell, a situation that happens when there is a tie for the distances between this outlier candidate and the centroid of a few dense cells, then an adjusted localized threshold, denoted as LT', is generated based upon the localized thresholds associated with these dense cells in the following way:

$$LT' = min(LT_1, LT_2, \ldots, LT_n)$$

where n is the number of dense cells whose centroids have a tie distance in relation to the outlier candidate. In other words, when a distance tie occurs, an outlier candidate is considered to be an outlier should its distance to the nearest cell centroid exceed the minimum localized threshold of the dense cells involved in the tie.

3.2 Pruning Strategy

In the algorithm discussed in subsection 3.1, the localized threshold for each dense cell needs to be calculated. To speed up the algorithm, we develop a fast pruning technique to reduce the number of dense cells whose localized thresholds need to be calculated. The basic idea for this pruning technique is that if a dense cell is surrounded by other dense cells in all directions then it is safe to exclude this dense cell from calculating its localized threshold. The underlying rationale is that once a dense cell is surrounded completely by other dense cells, then it is sufficient to use the localized thresholds associated with its neighbors to identify nearby outliers. The problem of checking whether a dense cell is surrounded entirely by other dense cells is straightforward for low dimensional datasets with for example 2-3 dimensions. However, in those datasets with a high dimensionality, this problem becomes nontrivial as its computational overhead grows exponentially with respect to the dimensionality of the data. For a given cell c, its complete neighborhood contains $3^d - 1$ neighbors, where d represents the dimension of the data, which renders the problem totally intractable in high-dimensional data space. In case of this, we only consider the adjacent neighborhood as an approximate alternative, which is able to reduced the number of neighbors from an exponential order to a linear order (i.e., from the complexity of $3^d - 1$ down to $2d$) and make the neighborhood checking much more efficient for high-dimensional datasets. This pruning strategy is able to speed up the algorithm because the neighborhood checking is generally much faster than the calculation of localized threshold for each dense cell.

4   Experimental Results

In this section, we report the evaluation results of our proposed technique in terms of efficiency and effectiveness. For the purpose of experimental evaluation, we devise the following measurement to qualitatively measure the quality of the outliers that are detected. This measurement reflects the difference between the data compactness before and after the outliers are detected and removed from the original dataset. Intuitively, when outliers are detected and removed, the remainder of the data set, presumably consisting of only normal data, should exhibit a better compactness with respect to different data clusters. Given this, the better the compactness of data are achieved after outliers are removed, the better quality of outliers that are detected. More specifically, the quality score of a set of outliers S_{out} is defined as follows:

$$Quality\_score(S_{out}) = \frac{|Compact(D) - Compact(D - S_{out})|}{Compact(D)}$$

where

$$Compact(D) = \frac{\sum_{i=1}^{k} SD_i}{k}$$

SD_i is the standard deviation of the ith cluster in D. Similarly, we can calculate $Compact(D - S_{out})$ based on the dataset D after S_{out} is removed. A higher value of $Quality\_score(S_{out})$ indicates a better set of outliers detected.

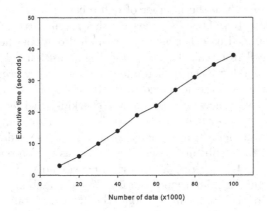

Fig. 1. Efficiency under varying number of instances

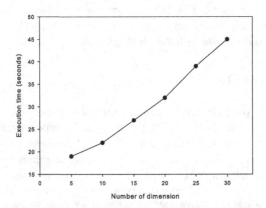

Fig. 2. Efficiency under varying dimensionality

To calculate the outlier quality score, we need to obtain data clusters first. Given the representative points that are readily available in our approach, clustering can be efficiently performed by first clustering the representative points and then label the data that belongs to the same cluster of representative points as being in the same cluster. This is obviously much faster than using other existing clustering method to cluster data from scratch. In terms of computational complexity, this fast clustering method only requires a single scan of the whole data set in the worst the case while in a much more ideal scenario it only requires a logarithmic complexity if the data membership of each dense cell has been maintained beforehand which removes the need to scan the data again.

4.1   Efficiency Evaluation

The efficiency evaluation involves the investigation of the speed of our technique under varying number of data instances and dimensionality of the given dataset. This evaluation will help to establish the scalability of our proposed technique when the number of instances and dimensionality of the given dataset grows. We use our data generator for this purpose to produce different datasets featuring varying numbers of instances and dimensionality. The experiment results are presented in Figure 1 and 2. As Figure 1 shows that, the execution time of our technique features a linear curve with regard to the number of instances in the dataset. The dimension of the data is fixed to 5 for this experiment. This linear behavior is due to that only two scans of the given dataset is required in the whole process of outlier detection. We can also see from Figure 2 that our technique enjoys an approximately linear scalability when the dimensionality of the dataset goes up. The numbers of data is fixed to 50,000 for this experiment. Even though the number of the cell in the grid structure will grow exponentially with regard to the data dimensionality, the actual number of occupied cells will only grow in most cases, if not all, in an approximate linear complexity. This result establishes that our technique is fairly efficient when dealing with multiple or high dimensional datasets without suffering the problem of curse of dimensionality.

4.2   Effectiveness Evaluation

We also carry out experiments for evaluating the effectiveness of outlier detection by using multiple localized thresholds. The outlier quality score is used to provide a quantitative indication in the effectiveness evaluation. In this experiment, we first compare our proposed technique using multiple thresholds with the same technique using a single universal threshold which is specified as 2 times of the standard deviation of all the data located in the dense cells. Then, we compare our technique using multiple thresholds with some of the major existing outlier detection methods. All the comparison results using different real-life datasets are presented in Table 1. Rather than using a 'relative' distance threshold that is defined based on the distribution of the dense regions, all the existing methods use the some kind of 'absolute' distance value. Therefore, we try 10 different possible and reasonable distance threshold values and produce the averaged value based on these 10 runs for the outlier quality score. We can see that our proposed technique is able to achieve an outlier quality score that is approximately 13-30% better than the existing methods without tedious parameter tuning. This experiment demonstrates that our proposed method, by using localized multiple thresholds, is able to deliver a better detection performance of the outliers located in different regions than the existing methods.

Table 1. A comparison of outlier quality scores for different methods

Methods	Multiple thresholding	Single thesholding	distance-based	clustering-based
Relative quality score	1.0	0.82	0.71	0.87

5 Conclusions

In this paper, we propose a novel technique for detecting outliers using multiple localized thresholds. These localized thresholds reflect the local data distribution and characteristics, providing a more accurate means to distinguish outliers from normal data. Experimental results demonstrate that our method is more accurate than the traditional methods that leverage a single universal threshold.

Acknowledgment. This research work is partially supported by NSFC, China (60804047) and the Priority Academic Program Development of Jiangsu Higher Education Institutions (PAPD), China.

References

1. Agrawal, R., Gehrke, J., Gunopulos, D., Raghavan, P.: Automatic subspace clustering of high dimensional data for data mining applications. In: SIGMOD 1998, pp. 94–105 (1998)
2. Breuning, M., Kriegel, H.-P., Ng, R., Sander, J.: LOF: Identifying Density-Based Local Outliers. In: SIGMOD 2000, Dallas, Texas, pp. 93–104 (2000)
3. Barnett, V., Lewis, T.: Outliers in Statistical Data, 3rd edn. John Wiley (1994)
4. Branch, J.W., Szymanski, B.K., Giannella, C., Wolff, R., Kargupta, H.: In-Network Outlier Detection in Wireless Sensor Networks. In: ICDCS 2006, p. 51 (2006)
5. Chhabra, P., Scott, C., Kolaczyk, E.D., Crovella, M.: Distributed Spatial Anomaly Detection. In: INFOCOM 2008, pp. 1705–1713 (2008)
6. Dutta, H., Giannella, C., Borne, K.D., Kargupta, H.: Distributed Top-K Outlier Detection from Astronomy Catalogs using the DEMAC System. In: SDM 2007 (2007)
7. Ester, M., Kriegel, H.-P., Sander, J., Xu, X.: A Density-based Algorithm for Discovering Clusters in Large Spatial Databases with Noise. In: SIGKDD 1996, Portland, Oregon, USA, pp. 226–231 (1996)
8. Hawkins, D.: Identification of Outliers. Chapman and Hall, London (1980)
9. Hinneburg, A., Keim, D.A.: An Efficient Approach to Cluster in Large Multimedia Databases with Noise. In: SIGKDD 1998, New York, NY, pp. 58–65 (1998)
10. Jin, W., Tung, A.K.H., Han, J.: Finding Top n Local Outliers in Large Database. In: SIGKDD 2001, San Francisco, CA, pp. 293–298 (2001)
11. Knorr, E.M., Ng, R.T.: Algorithms for Mining Distance-based Outliers in Large Dataset. In: VLDB 1998, New York, NY, pp. 392–403 (1998)

12. Knorr, E.M., Ng, R.T.: Finding Intentional Knowledge of Distance-based Outliers. In: VLDB 1999, Edinburgh, Scotland, pp. 211–222 (1999)
13. Koufakou, A., Georgiopoulos, M.: A fast outlier detection strategy for distributed high-dimensional data sets with mixed attributes. Data Mining and Knowledge Discovery 20(2), 259–289 (2010)
14. Kaosar, M.G., Xu, Z., Yi, X.: Distributed Association rule mining with minimum communication overhead. In: AusDM 2009 (2009)
15. Ng, R., Han, J.: Efficient and Effective Clustering Methods for Spatial Data Mining. In: VLDB 1994, Santiago, Chile, pp. 144–155 (1994)
16. Otey, M., Ghoting, A., Parthasarathy, S.: Fast distributed outlier detection in mixed attribute data sets. Data Mining and Knowledge Discovery 12(2), 203–228 (2006)
17. Ramaswamy, S., Rastogi, R., Shim, K.: Efficient Algorithms for Mining Outliers from Large Data Sets. In: SIGMOD 2000, Dallas, Texas, pp. 427–438 (2000)
18. Sheng, B., Li, Q., Mao, W., Jin, W.: Outlier detection in sensor networks. In: MobiHoc 2007, pp. 219–228 (2007)
19. Su, L., Han, W.-H., Yang, S.-Q., Zou, P., Jia, Y.: Continuous Adaptive Outlier Detection on Distributed Data Streams. In: Perrott, R., Chapman, B.M., Subhlok, J., de Mello, R.F., Yang, L.T. (eds.) HPCC 2007. LNCS, vol. 4782, pp. 74–85. Springer, Heidelberg (2007)
20. Tang, J., Chen, Z., Fu, A.W.-c., Cheung, D.W.: Enhancing Effectiveness of Outlier Detections for Low Density Patterns. In: Chen, M.-S., Yu, P.S., Liu, B. (eds.) PAKDD 2002. LNCS (LNAI), vol. 2336, pp. 535–548. Springer, Heidelberg (2002)
21. Zhou, J., et al.: A novel outlier detection algorithm for distributed databases. In: FSKD 2005 (2005)
22. Zhang, J., Wang, H.: Detecting Outlying Subspaces for High-dimensional Data: the New Task, Algorithms and Performance. In: Knowledge and Information Systems (KAIS). Springer (2006)
23. Zhang, J., Hsu, W., Lee, M.L.: Clustering in Dynamic Spatial Databases. Journal of Intelligent Information Systems (JIIS) 24(1), 5–27 (2005)
24. Zhang, J., Lou, M., Ling, T.W., Wang, H.: HOS-Miner: A System for Detecting Outlying Subspaces of High-dimensional Data. In: VLDB 2004, Toronto, Canada, pp. 1265–1268 (2004)
25. Zhang, T., Ramakrishnan, R., Livny, M.: BIRCH: An Efficient Data Clustering Method for Very Large Databases. In: SIGMOD 1996, Montreal, Canada, pp. 103–114 (1996)
26. Zhang, J., Ling, T.-W., Bruckner, R.M., Liu, H.: PC-Filter: A Robust Filtering Technique for Duplicate Record Detection in Large Databases. In: Galindo, F., Takizawa, M., Traunmüller, R. (eds.) DEXA 2004. LNCS, vol. 3180, pp. 486–496. Springer, Heidelberg (2004)
27. Zhang, J., Dekeyser, S., Wang, H., Shu, Y.: DISTRO: A System for Detecting Global Outliers from Distributed Data Streams with Privacy Protection. In: Kitagawa, H., Ishikawa, Y., Li, Q., Watanabe, C. (eds.) DASFAA 2010. LNCS, vol. 5982, pp. 477–481. Springer, Heidelberg (2010)
28. Zhang, J., Gao, Q., Wang, H., Liu, Q., Xu, K.: Detecting Projected Outliers in High-Dimensional Data Streams. In: Bhowmick, S.S., Küng, J., Wagner, R. (eds.) DEXA 2009. LNCS, vol. 5690, pp. 629–644. Springer, Heidelberg (2009)
29. Zhang, J., Cao, J., Zhu, X.: Detecting Global Outliers from Large Distributed Databases. In: 9th International Conference on Fuzzy Systems and Knowledge Discovery (FSKD), Chongqing, China, pp. 1646–1650 (May 2012)
30. Zhang, J.: Recent Advancement of Outlier Detection: A Survey. ICST Transaction on Scalable Information Systems (accepted in press, 2012)

A Self-stabilizing Algorithm for Finding a Minimal K-Dominating Set in General Networks

Guangyuan Wang, Hua Wang, Xiaohui Tao, and Ji Zhang

Department of Maths and Computing
University of Southern Queensland, QLD, 4350, Australia
{guangyuan.wang,hua.wang,xiaohui.tao,ji.zhang}@usq.edu.au

Abstract. Since the publication of Dijkstra's pioneering paper, a lot of self-stabilizing algorithms for computing dominating sets have been proposed in the literature. However, there is no self-stabilizing algorithm for the minimal k-dominating set (MKDS) in arbitrary graphs that works under a distributed daemon. The proposed algorithms for the minimal k-dominating set (MKDS) either work for trees (Kamei and Kakugawa [16]) or find a minimal 2-dominating set (Huang et al. [14,15]). In this paper, we propose a self-stabilizing algorithm for the minimal k-dominating set (MKDS) under a central daemon model when operating in any general network. We further prove that the worst case convergence time of the algorithm from any arbitrary initial state is $O(n^2)$ steps where n is the number of nodes in the network.

Keywords: Self-stabilizing algorithm, Minimal k-dominating set, Central daemon model, General network, Convergence.

1 Introduction

A distributed system consists of a set of loosely connected processes that do not share a common or global memory. Each process has one or more shared registers and possibly some non-shared local variables, the contents of which specify the local state of the process. Local states of all processes in the system at a certain time constitute the global configuration (or, simply, configuration) of the system at that time. The main restriction of a distributed system is that each process in the system can only access the data (i.e., read the shared data) of its neighbors. Since a distributed algorithm is an algorithm that works in a distributed system, it cannot violate this main restriction. Depending on the purpose of a distributed system, a global criterion for the global configuration is defined. Those global configurations satisfying the criterion are called *legitimate configurations*, whereas other global configurations are called *illegitimate configurations*. When the system is in a legitimate configuration, the purpose of the system is fulfilled.

Y. Xiang et al. (Eds.): ICDKE 2012, LNCS 7696, pp. 74–85, 2012.
© Springer-Verlag Berlin Heidelberg 2012

1.1 Dijkstra's Central Daemon Model

Self-stabilization is an optimistic fault tolerance approach for distributed systems. It was introduced by Dijkstra in [2,3]. According to his work, a distributed system is self-stabilizing if it can start at any possible global configuration and regain consistency in a finite number of steps by itself without any external intervention and remains in a consistent state [4]. Recently, some self-stabilizing algorithms for dominating sets, independent sets, colorings, and matchings in graphs have been developed [12,8,13,17].

A fundamental idea of self-stabilizing algorithms is that the distributed system may be started from an arbitrary global state. After finite time the system reaches a correct global state, called a *legitimate* or *stable* state. An algorithm is *self-stabilizing* if, when the system executes the algorithm,

(i) for any initial illegitimate state it reaches a legitimate state after a finite number of node moves, and

(ii) for any legitimate state and for any move allowed by that state, the next state is a legitimate state.

In a self-stabilizing algorithm, each process maintains its local variables, and can make decisions based on the knowledge of its neighbors' states. A process changes its local state by making a *move* (a change of local state). The algorithm is a set of rules of the form "*if condition part (or guard)*" then "*action part*". The condition part (or guard) is a Boolean function over the states of the process and its neighbors; the action part is an assignment of values to some of the process's shared registers. A process i becomes *privileged* if it's condition is true. When a process becomes privileged, it may execute the corresponding move. A *central daemon* selects, among all privileged processes, the next process to move or to write. We assume a serial model in which no two processes move simultaneously. If two or more processes are privileged, one cannot predict which one will move next. Multiple protocols exist [1,7,18] that provide such a scheduler.

The topology of a distributed system can be represented as an undirected graph $G = (V, E)$ (called the system's communication graph), where the nodes represent the processes and the edges represent the interconnections between the processes. As remarked earlier, throughout this paper, we denote by n the number of nodes ($|V| = n$), and by m the number of edges ($|E| = m$) in the graph G. Let $i \in V$ be a node; then $N(i)$, its *open neighborhood*, denotes the set of nodes to which i is adjacent. Every node $j \in N(i)$ is called a neighbor of node i. We denote by $d(i)$ the number of neighbors of node i, or its degree ($d(i) = |N(i)|$). Throughout this paper we assume G is connected and $n > 1$.

1.2 Minimal K-Dominating Set Problem

Let $G = (V, E)$ be a simple connected undirected graph that models a distributed system, with each node $i \in V$ representing a process in the system and each edge $(i, j) \in E$ representing the bidirectional link connecting processes i and j. Let k be an arbitrary positive integer. A subset D of V is a k-dominating set in

G if each node not in D has at least k neighbors in D. A k-dominating set D in G is minimal if any proper subset of D is not a k-dominating set in G. The so-called minimal k-dominating set problem is to find a minimal k-dominating set (MKDS) in G. A k-dominating set for $k = 1$, i.e., a 1-dominating set, is just an ordinary dominating set. Recently, Kamei and Kakugawa [16] considered the k-dominating set problem for general k (i.e., for k being an arbitrary positive integer) in a tree. Huang et al. [14,15] developed two self-stabilizing algorithms to find a minimal 2-dominating set in an arbitrary network. However, there is no self-stabilizing algorithm for the minimal k-dominating set (MKDS) in arbitrary graphs that works under a distributed daemon.

1.3   Main Results and the Organization of the Rest of the Paper

In this paper, we are interested in a minimal k-dominating set (MKDS) in any general network. We believe the following to be our contributions in this paper.

1. We present a self-stabilizing algorithm for finding a minimal k-dominating set (MKDS) under a central daemon in an arbitrary simple connected undirected network graph.
2. We further prove that the worst case convergence time of the algorithm from any arbitrary initial state is $O(n^2)$ steps where n is the number of nodes in the network.

The rest of this paper is organized as follows. Section 2 presents related work. Section 3 presents a self-stabilization algorithm and an illustration for finding a minimal k-dominating set (MKDS). Section 4 proves the convergence and the time complexity of the algorithm. Section 5 discusses the algorithm comparison. Section 6 concludes the paper and discusses the future work.

2   Related Work

Graph algorithms have natural applications in networks and distributed systems, since a distributed system can be modeled with an undirected graph. Due to the publication of Dijkstra's pioneering paper, some self-stabilizing algorithms for graph problems have been proposed in the literature, such as the self-stabilizing algorithms for dominating sets [5], independent sets and matchings in graphs [8,12]. Dominating Set and related problems are considered to be of central importance in combinatorial optimization and have been the object of much research. Due to the NP-complete of domination problems [6], researchers have developed some self-stabilizing algorithms for finding minimal dominating sets.

Since any maximal independent set in a graph is a minimal dominating set in that graph, a self-stabilizing algorithm for the maximal independent set problem can be viewed as a self-stabilizing algorithm for the minimal dominating set problem. Hedetniemi et al. [12] presented two *uniform* algorithms (a distributed algorithm is said to be *uniform* if all of the individual processes run the same code) for the dominating set (DS) and the minimal dominating set (MDS) problems. The algorithms all work for any connected graph and assume a *central daemon* (only one process can execute an atomic step at one time). Goddard et al. [8] proposed another uniform algorithm for finding a minimal dominating set (MDS) in an arbitrary graph under a *distributed daemon*, which selects a subset of the system processes to execute an atomic step at the same time.

On the other hand, some self-stabilized algorithms have been proposed in the multiple domination case. Kamei and Kakugawa [16] presented two self-stabilizing algorithms for the minimal k-dominating set (MKDS) problem in a tree. The first uniform algorithm works under a central daemon and the second algorithm works under a distributed daemon. Huang et al. [14,15] presented two self-stabilizing algorithms to find a minimal 2-dominating set (M2DS) in an arbitrary graph. The first algorithm works under a central daemon with liner time complexity [14] and the second algorithm works under a distributed daemon [15] respectively. For a more detailed discussion of self-stabilizing algorithms for dominating sets, see a survey [9].

However, there is no algorithm for the minimal k-dominating set (MKDS) problem in arbitrary graphs that works under a distributed daemon. The proposed algorithms for the minimal k-dominating set (MKDS) either work for trees (Kamei and Kakugawa [16]) or find a minimal 2-dominating set (Huang et al. [14,15]). In this paper, we are considering the extension problem of minimal 2-dominating set (M2DS) just mentioned in [14,15]. We will solve that extension problem for general k (i.e., for k being an arbitrary positive integer) in general networks. We firstly develop a new self-stabilization algorithm for finding a minimal k-dominating set (MKDS) in a general network and analyze the time complexity of the proposed algorithm.

3 Self-stabilizing K-Dominating Set Algorithm

3.1 Formal Definition of the Problem

Let $G = (V, E)$ be a simple connected undirected graph. The number of nodes is denoted by n. Assume now that for each node $i \in V$, the set $N(i)$ represents its *open neighborhood*, denotes the set of nodes to which i is adjacent. $d(i)$ represents the number of neighbors of node i, or its degree $(d(i) = |N(i)|)$. Assume further that each node i in the G has a boolean flag $x(i)$, whose value is either 0 or 1. At any given time, we will denote with D the current set of nodes i with $x(i) = 1$. That is,

$$x(i) = \begin{cases} 0 & \text{if } i \notin D \\ 1 & \text{if } \in D. \end{cases} \tag{1}$$

Definition 1. *$X(i)$ denotes the set $\{j \in N(i) | x(j) = 1\}$, and $|X(i)|$ denotes the cardinality of $X(i)$.*

Note $X(i)$ is the set of $i's$ neighbor nodes in D, that is $N(i) \cap D$.

3.2 Proposed Algorithm

The Algorithm 1 consists of two rules (R1 and R2) is shown below. Assume k being an arbitrary positive integer. In Algorithm 1 each node i has a boolean variable $x(i)$ indicating membership in the set D that we are trying to construct. The value $x(i) = 1$ indicates that $i \in D$, while the value $x(i) = 0$ indicates that $i \notin D$ as the equation (1) describes. The set $X(i)$ is the set of $i's$ neighbor nodes in D and $|X(i)|$ denotes the cardinality of $X(i)$. The variable $|X(i)|$ is designed to count $N(i) \cap D$. Thus, a node i is privileged if it holds R1 or R2, and then executes the corresponding move. An example to illustrate the execution of Algorithm 1 is shown in Fig. 1 and Fig. 2.

Algorithm 1. Finding Minimal K-Dominating Set

> **Input:** A graph $G = (V, E)$, $\forall i \in V$, a boolean flag $x(i)$
> **Output:** $D = \{i \in V | x(i) = 1\}$
> **R1:** $x(i) = 0 \wedge |X(i)| \leq k - 1 \rightarrow x(i) = 1$
> **R2:** $x(i) = 1 \wedge |X(i)| \geq k \rightarrow x(i) = 0$

R1 says that a node i should enter D if it has fewer than k neighbors in D. R2 says that a node i should leave D if it is dominated by more than k nodes in D. The legitimate configurations are defined to be all those configurations in which

$$\forall i \in V[(x(i) = 0 \wedge |X(i)| \geq k) \vee (x(i) = 1 \wedge |X(i)| \leq k - 1)].$$

It is obvious that the system is in a legitimate configuration if and only if no node in the system is privileged. The following lemma clarifies that in any legitimate configuration, a minimal k-dominating set (MKDS) $D = \{i \in V | x(i) = 1\}$ can be identified.

Lemma 1. *If Algorithm 1 stabilizes (no node in the system is privileged), then the set $D = \{i \in V | x(i) = 1\}$ is a minimal k-dominating set (MKDS).*

Proof: Suppose no node in G is privileged. For any $i \notin D$, since $x(i) = 0$ and i is not privileged by R1, we have $|X(i)| \geq k$. Thus i has at least k neighbors in D and thus, D is a k-dominating set in G. We now claim D is minimal as well. If D is not minimal, then there is a proper subset D'?of D such that D' is also a k-dominating set (KDS). Let $j \in D - D'$, then $x(j) = 1$. Since D' is also a k-dominating set and $j \notin D'$, j has at least k neighbors in D' in view of the definition of KDS. It follows that j has at least k neighbors in D, i.e., $|X(j)| \geq k$. With $x(j) = 1$ and $|X(j)| \geq k$, j is privileged by R2, which causes a contradiction. Therefore D is a minimal k-dominating set.   □

3.3 An Illustration of a Minimal 3-Dominating Set

The example in Fig. 1 and Fig. 2 is to illustrate the execution of Algorithm 1. Without loss of generality, we consider the case $k = 3$ and use a minimal 3-dominating set example to illustrate the execution of Algorithm 1. Note that in each configuration, the shaded nodes represent privileged nodes, whereas the shaded node with a darkened circle represents the privileged node selected by the central daemon to make a move.

In the last configuration (Fig. 3), which is a legitimate configuration of Fig. 1 and Fig. 2, we can see a minimal 3-dominating set $D = \{a, c, d, g, h\}$ can be identified (the shaded nodes).

4   The Stabilization Time of Algorithm 1

In this section, we show the convergence of Algorithm 1. We will provide some preliminaries and a correctness proof of convergence for Algorithm 1. We consider a distributed system whose topology is represented as a simple connected undirected graph $G = (V; E)$, where the nodes represent the processes and the edges represent the interconnections between the processes. We denote by $d(i)$ the number of neighbors of node i, or its degree $(d(i) = |N(i)|)$, and we denote by δ the minimum degree of G $(\delta = min\{d(i)|i \in V\})$ and Δ the maximum degree of G $(\Delta = max\{d(i)|i \in V\})$ respectively.

In a distributed system, under a central daemon model, the behavior of the system under the action of the algorithm can be described by an execution sequence $\Gamma = (\gamma_1, \gamma_2, ...)$ in which for any $i \geq 1$, γ_i represents a global configuration. For any configuration γ_i, let γ_{i+1} be any configuration that follows γ_i which is obtained after exactly one process in the system makes the ith move. Then, we denote this transition relation by $\gamma_{i+1} \to \gamma_i$.

Definition 2. *Let a sequence $\Gamma = (\gamma_1, \gamma_2, ...)$ be a set of all configurations, and an algorithm E is self-stabilizing with respect to $\Lambda \subseteq \Gamma$ if and only if the following two conditions hold:*

a) Convergence: Starting from any arbitrary configuration, configuration eventually becomes one in Λ, and

b) Closure: For any configuration $\lambda \in \Lambda$, any configuration γ that follows λ is also in Γ.

Each $\lambda \in \Lambda$ is called a legitimate configuration. And Λ is called a set of legitimate configurations.

We now show the convergence of Algorithm 1.

Theorem 1. *Algorithm 1 always stabilizes, and finds a minimal k-dominating set (MKDS).*

Proof: In light of Lemma 1 we see that if Algorithm 1 is stabilizing it always finds a minimal k-dominating set (MKDS), which satisfies the closure. We need only prove stabilization (convergence). We divide the distributed system (graph) into two cases: $\delta < k$ and $\delta \geq k$.

Case 1: $\delta < k$. Suppose that there exists an infinite computation E starting from γ_0 that does not reach a legitimate configuration. First, we consider the process $i \in V$ (P_i) with the degree δ. Because of $\delta < k$, a guarded command that i may

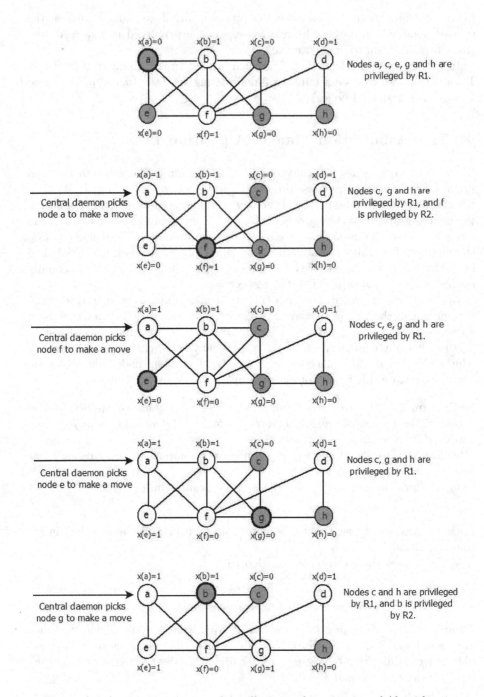

Fig. 1. A 3-dominating set example to illustrate the execution of Algorithm 1

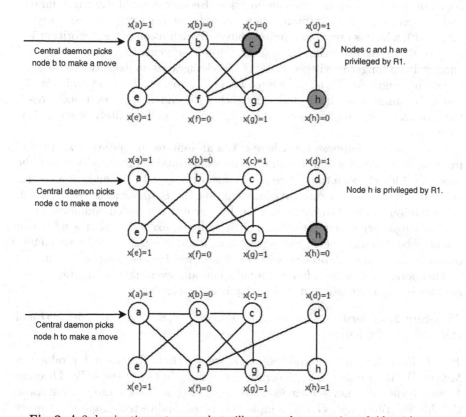

Fig. 2. A 3-dominating set example to illustrate the execution of Algorithm 1

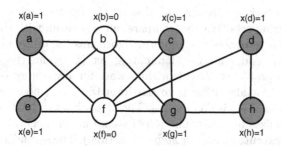

Fig. 3. A minimal 3-dominating set $D = \{a, c, d, g, h\}$ of Fig. 1 and Fig. 2

execute is only R1. By definitions of R1 and k-dominating set, the P_i can execute R1 at most once in an infinite computation. Because computation E is infinite and the processes in G is finite, there must be at least one process , say P_j $(d(j) \geq k)$, which is executed infinitely often. By definition of the Algorithm 1, a process alternates executing R1 and R2. After P_j executes a guarded command once, it is no longer privileged until $|X(j)|$ changes by an execution of at least one of the neighbors. Thus, there must be a neighbor, say P_k, of P_j which is also executed infinitely often. By following such a dependency, we eventually reach the process i. This implies that the P_i must be executed infinitely often. This is a contradiction.

Case 2: $\delta \geq k$. Suppose that there exists an infinite computation E starting from γ_0 that does not reach a legitimate configuration. First, we consider the process $i \in V$ (P_i) with the degree Δ. Because of $\Delta \geq k$, by definitions of R1, R2 and k-dominating set, a guarded command that the P_i may execute is R1 or R2. By definition of the Algorithm 1, after P_i executes a guarded command once, it is no longer privileged until $|X(i)|$ changes by an execution of at least one of the neighbors. Thus, the P_i execute R1 and R2 at most Δ times in an infinite computation. Since the processes in G is finite (n). This is a contradiction.

Therefore, there is no infinite computation, and eventually computation terminates in a configuration in which no process is privileged   □

Theorem 2. *Algorithm 1 produces a minimal k-dominating set (MKDS) and stabilizes in $O(n^2)$ steps.*

Proof: From Lemma 1 and Theorem 1, we see that Algorithm 1 produces a MKDS. We need only prove Algorithm 1 stabilizes in $O(n^2)$ steps. By Theorem 1, each node will change its x-value at most Δ times in a finite computation. Considering the graph G is a simple connected undirected graph, the upper bound of the Δ is $(n-1)$, therefore, the stabilization time of Algorithm 1 is $O(n^2)$ steps.   □

5   Algorithm Comparison

In this section we respectively present and discuss the existing self-stabilizing algorithms for dominating sets. We also compare our algorithm with them.

Hedetniemi et al. [12] presented two uniform algorithms (all of the individual processes run the same code) for the dominating set (DS) and the minimal dominating set (MDS) problems. The algorithms work for any connected graph. The main idea of the first algorithm is to partition the set of nodes into two disjoint sets, such that each set is dominating. The algorithm for the dominating set (DS) problem stabilizes in linear time ($O(n)$ steps) under a central daemon (only one process can execute an atomic step at one time). The second algorithm calculates a MDS. The main idea of this algorithm is that it allows a node to join the set S, if it has no neighbor in S. On the other hand, a node that is already a member of S, and has a neighbor that is also a member of S, will leave the set if all its neighbors are not pointing to it. Thus, after stabilization the set S

will be a MDS. The algorithm for the minimal dominating set (MDS) problem stabilizes in $O(n^2)$ steps under a central daemon.

Recently, Goddard et al. [8] proposed another uniform self-stabilizing algorithm for finding a minimal dominating set (MDS) in an arbitrary graph under a distributed daemon (a distributed daemon selects a subset of the system processes to execute an atomic step at the same time). The main idea of their algorithm is that it uses a boolean variable to determine whether a node is a member of the MDS or not, and an integer to count a node's neighbors that are members of the MDS. The algorithm allows an undominated node that has smaller identifier than any undominated neighbor to join the set under construction. On the other hand, a node leaves this latter set if it is not the unique dominator of itself nor any of its neighbors. The algorithm stabilizes in $O(n)$ steps.

On the other hand, some self-stabilizing algorithms have been proposed in the k-domination case. Kamei and Kakugawa [16] presented two uniform algorithms for the minimal k-dominating set (MKDS) problem in a tree. The first algorithm allows a node to join the set under construction S if it has fewer than k neighbors in S, and to leave the set S if it has more than k neighbors in S. The first algorithm works for a central daemon. Based on this idea, in the second algorithm, a node having more than k neighbors in the set under construction S will first make a request to leave S, and then leaves the set S only if its identifier is the smallest among all the neighbors requesting to leave S. So, after stabilization the set S will become a minimal k-dominating set (MKDS). The second algorithm works under a distribute daemon. The time complexity of the two algorithms are both $O(n^2)$ steps.

Huang et al. [14] presented a self-stabilizing algorithm to find a minimal 2-dominating set (M2DS) in an arbitrary graph. The algorithm allows a node to join the set under construction S if it has fewer than 2 neighbors in S, and to leave the set S if it has more than 2 neighbors in S. The algorithm works under a central daemon, with liner time complexity.

Huang et al. [15] presented another self-stabilizing algorithm to find a minimal 2-dominating set (M2DS) in an arbitrary graph. The algorithm assumes globally unique identifiers for the nodes and works under a distributed daemon. The algorithm allows a node to join the set under construction if it is dominated by fewer than two nodes and none of its neighbors having smaller identifier is in the same situation. Also, a node may leave the set under construction if it is dominated by more than two nodes, and all of its neighbors are either in the set under construction or dominated by more than two nodes.

In order to select a small size of k-dominating set (KDS) in large networks, we present a uniform algorithm for finding a minimal KDS (MKDS) that works in arbitrary graphs. We use a boolean flag x and an integer variable X and the proposed algorithm works under a central daemon. The algorithm allows a node i to join the set D (the value $x(i) = 1$) under construction if it is dominated by fewer than k nodes in D (R1). Also, a node i may leave the set under construction the set D if it is dominated by more than k nodes (R2). The time complexity of our algorithm in any arbitrary graphs is $O(n^2)$ steps.

The algorithms we compared in this section are summarized in Table 1. As we can see, the first three self-stabilizing algorithms are for single domination; and the algorithms for k-dominating set by Kamei et al [16] are just considering in a tree graph; the algorithms by Huang et al. [14,15] are for 2-dominating set. Our algorithm is the first work using a self-stabilizing approach to discuss the MKDS problem in general networks.

Table 1. Algorithms for dominating set

Reference	Output	Required topology	Self-stabilizing	Daemon	Complexity
Hedetniemi et al. [12]-1	DS	Arbitrary	Yes	Central	$O(n)$ steps
Hedetniemi et al. [12]-2	MDS	Arbitrary	Yes	Central	$O(n^2)$ steps
Goddard et al. [8]	MDS	Arbitrary	Yes	Distributed	$O(n)$ steps
Kamei et al. [16]-1	MKDS	Tree	Yes	Central	$O(n^2)$ steps
Kamei et al. [16]-2	MKDS	Tree	Yes	Distributed	$O(n^2)$ steps
Huang et al. [14]	M2DS	Arbitrary	Yes	Central	$O(n)$ steps
Huang et al. [15]	M2DS	Arbitrary	Yes	Distributed	
This paper	MKDS	Arbitrary	Yes	Central	$O(n^2)$ steps

6 Conclusions and Future Work

In the above, we have successfully solved the extension problem, "To find a self-stabilizing algorithm for the minimal k-dominating set problem in general networks, under the central daemon model", for the general k. Since the minimal k-dominating set problem is more general than the 2-dominating set problem, it is much complicated to handle. Kamei and Kakugawa have been the first to attack the above extension problem, although their results in [16] are restricted to tree networks only. Huang et al. [14,15] discussed the case $k = 2$, 2-dominating set in any general network. In the future, we still further study the exact stabilization time of our algorithm. Another research direction is to develop some self-stabilizing algorithms for k-dominating set under a distributed daemon in arbitrary network.

References

1. Beauquier, J., Datta, A.K., Gradinariu, M., Magniette, F.: Self-Stabilizing Local Mutual Exclusion and Daemon Refinement. In: Herlihy, M.P. (ed.) DISC 2000. LNCS, vol. 1914, pp. 223–237. Springer, Heidelberg (2000)
2. Dijkstra, E.W.: Self-stabilizing Systems in Spite of Distributed Control. ACM. Commun. 17(11), 643–644 (1974)
3. Dijkstra, E.W.: A Simple Fixpoint Argument Without the Restriction to Continuity. J. Acta. Inf. 23(1), 1–7 (1986)
4. Dolev, S.: Self-Stabilization. MIT Press, Cambridge (2000)

5. Gairing, M., Hedetniemi, S.T., Kristiansen, P., McRae, A.A.: Self-Stabilizing Algorithms for {k}-Domination. In: Huang, S.-T., Herman, T. (eds.) SSS 2003. LNCS, vol. 2704, pp. 49–60. Springer, Heidelberg (2003)
6. Garey, M.R., Johnson, D.S.: Computers and Intractability: A Guide to the Theory of NP-Completeness. W. H. Freeman, New York (1979)
7. Goddard, W., Hedetniemi, S.T., Jacobs, D.P., Srimani, P.K.: A self-stabilizing distributed algorithm for minimal total domination in an arbitrary system grap. In: 17th International Symposium on Parallel and Distributed Processing, pp. 485–488. IEEE Press, Nice (2003)
8. Goddard, W., Hedetniemi, S.T., Jacobs, D.P., Srimani, P.K., Xu, Z.: Self-stabilizing graph protocols. Parallel Processing Letters 18(1), 189–199 (2008)
9. Guellati, N., Kheddouci, H.: A survey on self-stabilizing algorithms for independence, domination, coloring, and matching in graphs. Journal of Parallel and Distributed Computing 70(4), 406–415 (2010)
10. Haynes, T.W., Hedetniemi, S.T., Slater, P.J.: Domination in Graphs: Advanced Topics. Marcel Dekker, New York (1998)
11. Haynes, T.W., Hedetniemi, S.T., Slater, P.J.: Fundamentals of Domination in Graphs. Marcel Dekker, New York (1998)
12. Hedetniemi, S.M., Hedetniemi, S.T., Jacobs, D.P., Srimani, P.K.: Self-stabilizing algorithms for minimal dominating sets and maximal independent sets. Computer Mathematics and Applications 46(5-6), 805–811 (2003)
13. Hedetniemi, S.T., Jacobs, D.P., Srimani, P.K.: Linear time self-stabilizing colorings. Information Processing Letters 87(5), 251–255 (2003)
14. Huang, T.C., Chen, C.Y., Wang, C.P.: A Linear-Time Self-Stabilizing Algorithm for the Minimal 2-Dominating Set Problem in General Networks. Inf. Sci. Eng. 24(1), 175–187 (2008)
15. Huang, T.C., Lin, J.C., Chen, C.Y., Wang, C.P.: A self-stabilizing algorithm for finding a minimal 2-dominating set assuming the distributed demon model. Computers and Mathematics with Applications 54(3), 350–356 (2007)
16. Kamei, S., Kakugawa, H.: A self-stabilizing algorithm for the distributed minimal k-redundant dominating set problem in tree network. In: 4th International Conference on Parallel and Distributed Computing, Applications and Technologies, pp. 720–724. IEEE Press, Chengdu (2003)
17. Manne, F., Mjelde, M., Pilard, L., Tixeuil, S.: A New Self-Stabilizing Maximal Matching Algorithm. Theoretical Computer Science. 410(14), 1336–1345 (2008)
18. Nesterenko, M., Arora, A.: Stabilization-Preserving Atomicity Refinement. Journal of Parallel and Distributed Computing 62(5), 766–791 (2002)

Optimal Combination of Feature Weight Learning and Classification Based on Local Approximation

Hongmin Cai[1,*] and Michael Ng[2]

[1] South China University of Technology, Guangdong, P.R. China
hmcai@scut.edu.cn
[2] Department of Mathematics, Hong Kong Baptist University, Hong Kong

Abstract. Currently, most feature weights estimation methods are independent on the classification algorithms. The combination of discriminant analysis and classifiers for effective pattern classification remains heuristic. The present study address the topics of learning of feature weights by using a recently reported classification algorithm, *K-Local Hyperplane Distance Nearest Neighbor (HKNN)* [18], in which the data is modeled as embedded in a linear hyperplane. Motivated by the encouraging performance of the Learning Discriminative Projections and Prototypes, the feature weights are estimated by minimizing the classifier leave-one-out cross validation error of HKNN. Approximated explicit solution is obtained to give feature estimation. Therefore, the feature weighting and classification are perfectly matched. The performance of the combinational model is extensively assessed via experiments on both synthetic and benchmark datasets. The superior results demonstrate that the method is competitive compared with some state-of-art models.

Keywords: Feature weighting, local hyperplane, discriminant analysis, classification, Nearest Neighbor.

1 Introduction

Discriminant analysis methods have been widely used in pattern recognition problems. Among the most well-known is Fisher linear discriminant analysis (FLDA) [5], which aims to find a projection axis such that the Fisher criterion (i.e. the ratio of the between-class scatter to the within-class scatter) is maximized after the projection of samples. FLDA receives intense attention in the past decade and numerous variants were designed to cast for empirical needs. By using the kernel tricks, nonlinear version of FLDA, the kernel Fisher Discriminant (KFD), was also proposed for dealing with the data with nonlinear

* This work was supported in part by NSFC under award number 60902076, NSF of Guangdong Province under award number 9451027501002551, and the Fundamental Research Funds for the Central Universities under award number 11$lgpy$33.

Y. Xiang et al. (Eds.): ICDKE 2012, LNCS 7696, pp. 86–94, 2012.
© Springer-Verlag Berlin Heidelberg 2012

structures [2,21,8]. Both the FLDA and KFD pay much attentions to the global structures of the data. Recently, it has been found that local structures are more appealing for applications than traditional global analysis based ones. For example, Locally Linear Discriminant Analysis was presented based on the idea that global nonlinear data structures are locally linear [7]. A family of locality characterization based discriminant analysis techniques, such as Locality Preserving Projections (LPP) [6], Local Discriminant Embedding (LDE) [4], Locality Sensitive Discriminant Analysis (LSDA) [3], Marginal Fisher Analysis (MFA) [20], have been recently reported. Feature weights estimation via exploiting local structure have also been reported. For example, [12] breaks a nonlinear problem into a set of locally linear ones through local learning, and then learns the feature relevance within the classical RELIEF framework [14,11]. A local Fisher discriminant analysis by combining the ideas of LFDA and LPP is reported in [9,10]. In [23], the authors extended the feature selection for unsupervised clustering within the well-known framework of Local Learning-Based Clustering (LLC) [19]

The existing discriminant analysis methods, however, are generally independent of selection of the classifier. Generally, a discriminant analysis is performed before pattern classification. The connection between the discriminant analysis methods and the classifiers is very loose. Exhaustive searching may be expected to find a well-matched pair of the discriminant analysis and the classifier. Recently, [22] reports a way to design discriminant analysis method bounded with Nearest-Neighbor (NN) classifiers. A local mean based classification rule (called LM-NNDA) is used to design a criteria similar to the Fisher's ratio. Therefore, the LM-NNDA based feature extractor and the local mean based classifier is perfected integrated. However, it is well-known that NN based classifiers are sensitive to the noise degenerations. Advanced pattern recognition model combining disclaimant analysis and classification simultaneously is largely anticipated in both theory and applications.

In the present paper, we begin with a local hyperplane based classifier, which consider each data sample lying on a local hyperplane, thus preserving the topological properties of the input space [18]. Then by minimization of its leave-one-out-cross-validation (LOOCV) error, a feature weighting scheme is derived explicitly. Therefore, the derived discriminator, called local hyperplane based discriminant analysis (LHDA), matches to the HKNN classifier optimally in theory. The proposed LHDA method is evaluated on both synthetic and real-time datasets. The experimental results demonstrate the performance advantage of LLDA over other feature weighting methods with respect to the HKNN classifier.

This paper is organized as follows. Section 2 introduces the background of the local hyperplane based classification model. A local discriminant feature extractor is reported by minimization of the LOOCV error of the HKNN classifier. Section 3 demonstrates the performance of the proposed model. Extensive experiments have been conducted to compare with the classical methods on benchmark data sets. Conclusion is presented in Section 4.

2   The Proposed Method

2.1   Problem Formulation

Let $x_i \in R_d$ $(i = 1, 2, \ldots, n)$ be d-dimensional samples and $y_i \in \{1, 2, \ldots, c\}$ be associated class labels, where n is the number of samples and c is the number of classes. Let X be the matrix of all samples: $X = (x_1, x_2, \ldots, x_n)$. The purpose of this draft is to have an efficient classification model which combines the feature weights and local structure learning simultaneously.

2.2   Pattern Classification by Feature Weighted Local Hyperplane

In the classification model of K-Local Hyperplane Distance Nearest Neighbor (HKNN) [18], each class was modeled as a smooth low-dimensional plane embedded in the high-dimensional data space by assuming that the plane was locally linear. Mathematically, for an observed sample x, it can be represented by a local hyperplane of class c by:

$$LH_c(x) = \{s \mid s = H\alpha\}, \tag{1}$$

where H is a $d \times n$ matrix composed by n NNs of the sample x: $H = \{h_1, h_2, \cdots, h_n\}$, with h_i being the i-th nearest neighbor of class c. The parameter of $\alpha = (\alpha_1, \ldots, \alpha_n)^T$ is the weights of the prototypes $\{h_i, \ i = 1, 2, \ldots, n\}$. It can be viewed as spanning coefficients of the subspace $LH_c(x)$. Therefore, the hyperplane can be represented as: $\{\cdot \mid H\alpha = \alpha_1 h_1 + \alpha_2 h_2 + \ldots + \alpha_n h_n\}$. When the feature weights are given via prior estimation, one can accurate represent the data in a feature weighted space. Therefore, the value of α is solved by minimizing the distance between the sample x and its local hyperplane of $LH_c(x)$ in feature space

$$
\begin{aligned}
J_c(\alpha) &= arg \min \frac{1}{2} \sum_{i=1}^{I} \omega(i)(x_i - s_i)^2 \\
&= \frac{1}{2}(x - H\alpha)^T W(x - H\alpha)
\end{aligned}
$$

$$
\textit{Subject to :} \\
\sum_{i=1}^{k} \alpha_i = 1, \alpha \geq 0.
$$

where W is a diagonal matrix with diagonal elements w_i being the weight of the i-th feature, and $s = (s_1, s_2, \ldots, s_I) = H\alpha \in LH_c(x)$. For an observed new sample, its labeling is decided by the class in which the distance between the sample and its hyperplanes is minimized.

A simple yet effective way of estimation of the feature weight W was obtained through LFDA in [15]. This approach, however, is heuristic and less accurate in multi-classification problems. Moreover, what discriminant analysis optimally matches the classier is generally unknown to us.

2.3 Local Hyperplane Based Discriminant Analysis (LHDA)

In order to have a feature weighting scheme which is perfectly matched to the HKNN classifier, we propose to minimize a cost functional on the classification error of LOOCV. Other than estimating the distance between a sample and its nearest neighbors, we use the distance between the sample and its local hyperplane instead. For a binary classification problem, one can firstly construct its two nearest neighboring hyperplanes, wherein one is from its same class (called *the nearest hit* or NH) and the other is from a different class (called *the nearest miss* or NM) [13]. Therefore, the classification error of LOOCV is given by:

$$J(W) = \frac{1}{N} \sum_{i=1}^{n} S[\frac{d_W(x, NH(x))}{d_W(x, NM(x))} - 1]$$ (2)

where the function $S(\cdot)$ is step function defined by

$$S(x) = \begin{cases} 1 : x \geq 0 \\ 0 : x < 0 \end{cases}$$

The distance $d_W(\cdot, \cdot)$ will be the Euclidean distance between a sample to its local hyperplane, both in the feature weighted space. Therefore, this distance is given by:

$$d_W(x_1, x_2) = \sqrt{\sum_{i=1}^{d} [w(i)(x_1(i) - x_2(i))^2]}$$ (3)

where the sub-index i denotes the i-th component. Since the step function $S(\cdot)$ is not differentiable at discontinuous points, one may approximate it by Sigmoid function,

$$S_\beta(x) = \frac{1}{1 + e^{\beta(1-x)}}$$ (4)

where the parameter of β is the slope for the Sigmoid function. Through this modification, the error functional turns to be differentiable and the corresponding minimization problem can be solved by gradient descent algorithm.

In summary, the error functional Eq. (2) is now rewritten by,

$$J(W) = \frac{1}{N} \sum_{i=1}^{n} S_\beta(\frac{d_W(x, NH(x))}{d_W(x, NM(x))} - 1)$$

$$subject\ to: \quad \|W\|_2 = 1$$ (5)

The Lagrangian of Eq. (5) is

$$L = \frac{1}{N} \sum_{i=1}^{n} S_\beta(\frac{d_W(x, NH(x))}{d_W(x, NM(x))}) + \lambda(\|W\|_2 - 1)$$ (6)

where λ is Lagrangian multipliers. Taking the derivative of L with respect to W and setting it to zero yields, one has

$$\frac{\partial L}{\partial W} = \frac{1}{N} \sum_{i=1}^{n} S_\beta'(y - 1)y(\frac{\nabla_W d_W^{NH}}{d_W^{NH}} - \frac{\nabla_W d_W^{NM}}{d_W^{NM}}) + 2\lambda W$$ (7)

where $d_{\mathbf{W}}^{NH} = d_{\mathbf{W}}(\mathbf{x}, NH(\mathbf{x}))$, $d_{\mathbf{W}}^{NM} = d_{\mathbf{W}}(\mathbf{x}, NM(\mathbf{x}))$, and $\mathbf{y}$ is the ratio of distances to the nearest hitting hyperplane and nearest missing hyperplane, given by $\mathbf{y} = \frac{d_{\mathbf{W}}(\mathbf{x}, NH(\mathbf{x}))}{d_{\mathbf{W}}(\mathbf{x}, NM(\mathbf{x}))}$). The function $S'_\beta(x)$ is the derivative of the Sigmoid function with respect to x

$$S'_\beta(x) = \frac{\beta e^{\beta(1-x)}}{(1 + e^{\beta(1-x)})^2} \tag{8}$$

In particulary, the gradient of the squared distance with respect to the weight $\mathbf{W}$ is given by:

$$\begin{aligned}
\nabla_{\mathbf{W}} d_{\mathbf{W}}^{NH} &= (\mathbf{x} - NH(\mathbf{x}))(\mathbf{x} - NH(\mathbf{x}))^T \mathbf{W} \\
&= < \mathbf{W}(\mathbf{x} - NH(\mathbf{x})), \mathbf{x} - NH(\mathbf{x}) > \\
&= d_1 \tag{9} \\
\nabla_{\mathbf{W}} d_{\mathbf{W}}^{NM} &= (\mathbf{x} - NM(\mathbf{x}))(\mathbf{x} - NM(\mathbf{x}))^T \mathbf{W} \\
&= < \mathbf{W}(\mathbf{x} - NM(\mathbf{x})), \mathbf{x} - NM(\mathbf{x}) > \\
&= d_2 \tag{10}
\end{aligned}$$

Therefore, Eq. (7) can be reformulated as

$$\frac{\partial L}{\partial \mathbf{W}} = \frac{2}{N} \sum_{i=1}^{n} S'_\beta(\mathbf{y} - 1)\mathbf{y}R(\mathbf{x})\mathbf{W} + 2\lambda\mathbf{W} \tag{11}$$

where

$$R(\mathbf{x}) = \frac{d_1}{d_{\mathbf{W}}^{NH}} - \frac{d_2}{d_{\mathbf{W}}^{NM}} \tag{12}$$

In summary, one can solve the minimization problem of Eq. (5) by the gradient descent update equations

$$w_i^{(r+1)} = w_i^{(r+1)} - \gamma \frac{\partial L}{\partial w_i} \tag{13}$$

where γ controls the size of each iteration steps.

3   Experimental Results

We shall demonstrate the performance of the proposed scheme through evaluation of the classification effect on both synthetic and empirical problems. We conducted experiments of classification on the UCI datasets with different data type, number of classes, and dimensionality [1]. We mainly interest in the combinational performance of the feature weighting scheme and classification algorithm.

The proposed approach was compared with similar techniques including, namely LM-NNDA [22], LSDA [3], I-RELIEF [12] and LDPP [16,17], use the classifier of KNNs. We pay special attention to the method of LDPP, which shares the same merits with our approach, except that the underline base classifier is 1-NN.

3.1   UCI Data Sets

In the first experiment, we tested the proposed technique on benchmark data sets, downloaded from the UCI Machine Learning Repository [1], and they have been widely tested by various classification benchmark models.

For each dataset, various discriminant analysis were firstly carried out to have the projection matrices, which were used to scale the raw datasets into the feature space, where classification experiments were conducted. Twenty times repeated 10-fold cross-validation experiments on each dataset were performed independently and the classification errors were averaged to evaluate the performance of the feature weighting scheme. For most of the DA schemes, the classifier of KNN was served as base classifier to test the combinational performance. In particular to the proposed LHPP, the HKNN is selected to achieve the task. Due to the proximity of LDPP to LHPP, both the classifier of KNN and HKNN were used to carry experiments on various datasets.

The results are summarized in Table 1. The performance of classification after LHPP is better than its peers in 6 among 11 experiments. Although various strategy perform differently, the proposed LHPP shows more robust by producing consistent performance than other combinations did.

Table 1. Error rates (%) on eleven real data sets. The best results are highlighted in bold. The combination of the feature weighting and classification based on hyperplane outperforms its peers in 6 among 11 experiments.

Dataset	LDPP HKNN	LDPP KNN	LM-NNDA KNN	I-RELIEF KNN	LSDA KNN	LHPP HKNN
Heart	0.185	**0.148**	0.233	0.339	0.293	0.181
Iris	**0.035**	0.107	0.044	0.040	0.037	0.036
Glass	0.303	0.440	0.352	0.344	0.333	**0.297**
Vote	0.090	0.082	0.092	0.032	**0.031**	0.053
Sonar	0.171	0.274	0.193	0.207	**0.099**	0.103
Cancer	0.228	0.328	0.248	0.302	0.274	**0.200**
Pro	0.103	0.232	0.149	0.129	0.117	**0.095**
Euk	0.172	0.502	0.222	0.268	0.229	**0.160**
Ionosphere	0.146	0.145	**0.107**	0.154	0.155	0.111
Pima	0.263	0.246	0.274	0.291	0.289	**0.257**
Spambase	0.078	0.091	0.077	0.287	0.087	**0.072**

3.2   Artificial Example

To test the robustness of the proposed scheme on noise degenerations, the famous Fermat's Spiral was selected for further experiments. The tested Spiral consists of two classes with 200 samples for each class. The labels of the Spiral are completely determined by its first two features. The shape of the Fermat's Spiral distribution is shown in Fig. 1. In the experiment, irrelevant features are

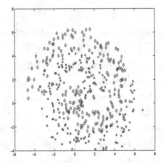

Fig. 1. Distribution of binary Fermat's Spiral problem. Each class has 200 samples and is labeled by different colors.

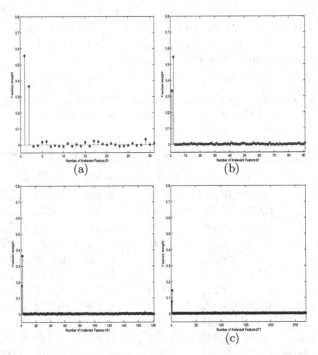

Fig. 2. Experiments on feature weights estimation of the Fermat's Spiral problem by adding irrelevant features in verified dimension, extending from 0 to 300. The first two features completely determine the labels of the synthetic samples, while other features are redundant noises. The estimated feature weight are plotted when the dimension of the noisy features is: (a) 30; (b) 90; (c) 180; (d) 270. The example results show that the first two features are vital when compared with other ones. This observation is coincide with the data setting scheme.

added to the clean Spiral. The irrelevant features are independently sampled from zero-mean and unit-variance Gaussian distribution. Their dimensions are ranged from $\{0, 30, 60, 90, 120, 150, 180, 210, 240, 270, 300\}$. The LHPP was used firstly to estimate the feature weights within the noisy settings. We plotted the learned feature weights under various noise dimensions of $30, 90, 180, 270$ in Fig. 2(a-d), respectively. Ideally, the first two features are vital since they completely determine the labels of the Spiral. Other features are presumably useless and low weights should be assigned. The experimental results coincided with the assumption in that the weights for the first features are significantly larger than those from noisy features. It implies that the LHPP not only produce accurate weight estimation but also is robust to the noise variations.

4   Discussion

Feature selection (or weighting) method is the key step of data processing. It is highly related with discriminant analysis and dimensionality reduction. Accurate feature selection method can efficiently facilitate the data analysis and reflect the intrinsic structure. Specifically, the performance of data classification can be greatly improved by incorporating suitable feature weighting scheme. However, most of the current classification models are independent on the feature selection method. Motivated by the encouraging performance of LDPP, this paper propose to learn feature weight through minimization of LOOCV errors of HKNN instead of the classical KNN model, which is notoriously known for its sensitivity to noise degenerations. Therefore, the classifier is perfectly matched with the feature weighting scheme to achieve optimal classification. Experimental results on both synthetic and real-world dataset validate our findings. The proposed weighting scheme performs superior on most test datas with respect to classification error.

We also observed that the proposed scheme is convergent in most cases and performs comparable for different number of NNs. However, rigorous formulation and extensive experiments need to be conducted to have a subject evaluation of the proposed model.

References

1. Asuncion, A., Newman, D.: UCI machine learning repository (2007),
   http://www.ics.uci.edu/~mlearn/MLRepository.html
2. Baudat, G., Anouar, F.: Generalized discriminant analysis using a kernel approach. Neural Comput. 12(10), 2385–2404 (2000)
3. Cai, D., He, X., Zhou, K., Han, J., Bao, H.: Locality sensitive discriminant analysis. In: International Joint Conference on Artificial Intelligence, IJCAI 2007 (2007)
4. Chen, H.T., Chang, H.W., Liu, T.L.: Local discriminant embedding and its variants. In: Proceedings of the 2005 IEEE Computer Society Conference on Computer Vision and Pattern Recognition (CVPR 2005), vol. 2, pp. 846–853. IEEE Computer Society, Washington, DC (2005)
5. Fukunaga, K.: Introduction to statistical pattern recognition, 2nd edn. Academic Press Professional, Inc., San Diego (1990)

6. He, X., Yan, S., Hu, Y., Niyogi, P., Zhang, H.J.: Face recognition using laplacian-faces. IEEE Trans. Pattern Anal. Mach. Intell. 27(3), 328–340 (2005)
7. Kim, T.K., Kittler, J.: Locally linear discriminant analysis for multimodally distributed classes for face recognition with a single model image. IEEE Trans. Pattern Anal. Mach. Intell. 27(3), 318–327 (2005)
8. Mika, S., Ratsch, G., Weston, J., Scholkopf, B., Mullers, K.R.: Fisher discriminant analysis with kernels. In: Proceedings of the 1999 IEEE Signal Processing Society Workshop on Neural Networks for Signal Processing IX, pp. 41–48 (August 1999)
9. Sugiyama, M.: Dimensionality reduction of multimodal labeled data by local fisher discriminant analysis. Journal of Machine Learning Research 8, 1027–1061 (2007)
10. Sugiyama, M., Idé, T., Nakajima, S., Sese, J.: Semi-supervised local fisher discriminant analysis for dimensionality reduction. Machine Learning 78(1-2), 35–61 (2010)
11. Sun, Y.: Iterative relief for feature weighting: Algorithms, theories, and applications. IEEE Trans. Pattern Anal. Mach. Intell. 29(6), 1035–1051 (2007)
12. Sun, Y., Todorovic, S., Goodison, S.: Local-learning-based feature selection for high-dimensional data analysis. IEEE Trans. Pattern Anal. Mach. Intell. 32(9), 1610–1626 (2010)
13. Sun, Y., Todorovic, S., Goodison, S.: Local-learning-based feature selection for high-dimensional data analysis. IEEE Trans. Pattern Anal. Mach. Intell. 32(9), 1610–1626 (2010)
14. Sun, Y., Wu, D.: A relief based feature extraction algorithm. In: SDM, pp. 188–195 (2008)
15. Tao, Y., Vojislav, K.: Adaptive local hyperplane classification. Neurocomputing 71(13-15), 3001–3004 (2008)
16. Villegas, M., Paredes, R.: Simultaneous learning of a discriminative projection and prototypes for nearest-neighbor classification. In: CVPR (2008)
17. Villegas, M., Paredes, R.: Dimensionality reduction by minimizing nearest-neighbor classification error. Pattern Recognition Letters 32(4), 633–639 (2011)
18. Vincent, P., Bengio, Y.: K-local hyperplane and convex distance nearest neighbor algorithms. In: Advances in Neural Information Processing Systems, pp. 985–992. The MIT Press (2001)
19. Wu, M., Schölkopf, B.: A local learning approach for clustering. In: NIPS, pp. 1529–1536 (2006)
20. Yan, S., Xu, D., Zhang, B., Zhang, H.J., Yang, Q., Lin, S.: Graph embedding and extensions: A general framework for dimensionality reduction. IEEE Trans. Pattern Anal. Mach. Intell. 29(1), 40–51 (2007)
21. Yang, J., Frangi, A.F., Yang, J.Y., Zhang, D., Jin, Z.: Kpca plus lda: A complete kernel fisher discriminant framework for feature extraction and recognition. IEEE Trans. Pattern Anal. Mach. Intell. 27(2), 230–244 (2005)
22. Yang, J., Zhang, L., Yang, J.Y., Zhang, D.: From classifiers to discriminators: A nearest neighbor rule induced discriminant analysis. Pattern Recognition 44(7), 1387–1402 (2011)
23. Zeng, H., Cheung, Y.M.: Feature selection and kernel learning for local learning-based clustering. IEEE Trans. Pattern Anal. Mach. Intell. 33(8), 1532–1547 (2011)

A Model of User-Oriented Reduct Construction Based on Minimal Set Cover

Suqing Han* and Guimei Yin

Computer Science and Technology Department
Taiyuan Normal University TYNU
Shanxi Taiyuan, China

Abstract. An implicit assumption of many learning algorithm is that all attributes in the attribute set are of the same importance. However, this assumption is unreasonable or practical. If attributes in the attribute set are considered of non-equal importance with respect to their own situation, then the model obtained from those attributes would be more realistic. This paper designed a user oriented reduction model based on the minimal set cover by seamlessly combining an order of attributes that describes user preferences. The accessibility and efficiency of this algorithm is shown by an example.

Keywords: attribute reduction, minimal attribute reduction, set cover, minimal set cover, order of attributes.

1 Introduction

Reduct construction is a special case of feature selection. For tasks of learning, the quality of a learning algorithm is closely related to selecting the attribute subset, i.e. it is very important to select the most appropriate attributes or feature subset.

Approaches of selecting attribute are mostly proposed based on the efficiency of individual attributes or subsets of attributes. These Approaches can be broadly divided into two classes, the approaches based on interior information, and the approaches based on exterior information. For interior information based approaches, typically, subsets of attributes are selected based on syntactic or statistical information of the dataset. The predictability of unknown samples based on attributes or their distribution information is an example of such type. On the contrary, the exterior information based approaches usually assign weights to attributes or rank attributes based on semantics or constraints. One of the advantages of the exterior information based approaches is that it considers environmental factors and user demands, which makes the solution more precise and effective.

A review of existing research shows that the major research efforts have been focused on the internal information based approaches, although the external

---

* This work was supported by the National Nature Science Foundation of CHINA Under Grant No.61273294.

Y. Xiang et al. (Eds.): ICDKE 2012, LNCS 7696, pp. 95–102, 2012.
© Springer-Verlag Berlin Heidelberg 2012

information based approaches may be more meaningful and effective. This is due to the fact that external information covers a very diverse range, which is highly subjective, and is usually not well-defined. Consequently, it may be difficult to build a well-accepted model.

There are already quite a lot of researches of using exterior information, such as those shown in References [2–10]. Reference [5] is one of the earliest researches that proposed considering exterior information of attributes when constructing models and embedding the exterior information in forms of order of attributes into learning algorithms. Based on the results of Reference [6], research presented in Reference [5] provided a systematic description of the user preferences of attributes and attribute subsets. This description is very important both theoretically and practically for capturing user demands and designing efficient learning algorithms.

This paper focused on user demands, using set cover to calculation of Reduct (the minimal reduction), thus designed an user oriented reduction model based on the minimal set cover by seamlessly combining an order of attributes that describes user preferences. This paper is organized as follows:Section 2 gives the relating basic concepts. Section 3 gives the user oriented reduct algorithm based on the minimal cover, and illustrates the usefulness of the proposed algorithm through application of reduct construction.

2   Relating Concepts

The following concepts are closely related to this paper: information system, decision table, attribute reduction, minimum reduction, discernibility matrix, set cover, and minimal set cover, etc.

2.1   Reduction and Minimum Reduction

Information system can be described as a four-tuple (U, A, V, F), where $U = (x_1, x_2, ..., x_n)$ is the universe, $A = (a_1, a_2, ..., a_m)$ is the attributes set(U and A are both finite non-empty sets), $V = \bigcup_{a_j \in A} V_{a_j}$ (where V_{a_j} is the domain of elements in the universe with respect to attribute a_j), and $F = \{f_j | U \to V_{a_j}, j = 1, 2, ..., m\}$.

Similarly, decision table can be also expressed as a four-tuple $(U, C \cup D, V, F)$, where $U = \{x_1, x_2, ..., x_n\}$ is the universe, C is the condition attribute set and D is decision attribute set, $V = \bigcup_{a_j \in C \cup D} V_{a_j}$ (where V_{a_j} is the domain of elements in the universe with respect to attribute), and $F = \{f_j : U \to V_{a_j}, a_j \in C \cup D\}$.

Since information system is a special case of decision table, here we focused on the problems of attribute reduction with respect to decision table only.

Definition 1. [1] Given decision table $(U, C \cup D, V, F)$, for $a_j \in C \cup D$ and $x, y \in U$, if $f_j(x) = f_j(y)$, then x and y are indiscernible with respect to a_j, and

$$R_{a_j} = \{(x, y) | x, y \in U, f_j(x) = f_j(y)\} \tag{1}$$

is a discernibility relation over U induced by a_j .

Obviously, R_{a_j} is an equivalent relation over U.

$\forall B \subseteq C$, by Definition 1, the equivalent relation R_B over U induced by attribute subset B can be defined as

$$R_B = \{(x,y)|\forall a_j \in B, f_j(x) = f_j(y)\} \tag{2}$$

Definition 2. [1] Given decision table $(U, C \cup D, V, F)$, let $a \in B \subseteq C$. If

$$R_{B-\{a\}} \neq R_B \tag{3}$$

Then attribute a is an indispensable attribute in B, otherwise attribute a is a redundant attribute in B .

Definition 2 shows that the classification ability of a decision table will not be changed when deleting redundant attributes from its attributes set. Thus, redundant attribute can be deleted, but indispensible attribute cannot be deleted.

Definition 3. [1] Given decision table $(U, C \cup D, V, F)$, for $B \subset C$, if $R_B = R_C$, then B is a reduction of C .

Definition 4. [1] Given decision table $(U, C \cup D, V, F)$, for $B \subset C$, if $R_B = R_C$ and each attribute in B are indispensible, then B is a minimum reduction attribute (Reduct) of C.

By Definition 4, for $B \subseteq C$, if B is a minimum reduction of C, then $\forall b \in B$, $R_{B-\{b\}} \neq R_C$. Notice that, in general, for a given decision table, there may be more than one attribute reduction or minimal attribute reduction. In addition, finding all minimal reduction is a NP-Hard `problem`[12].

Discernibility matrix is another important concept related to this paper, which is basis of many reduction algorithms.

Definition 5. [1] Given decision table $(U, C \cup D, V, F)$, where $U = \{x_1, x_2, ..., x_n\}$, $C = \{a_1, a_2, ..., a_m\}$, and $D = \{d\}$. Then $M = (m_{ij})_{n \times n}$, where

$$m_{ij} = \begin{cases} \{a_k | a_k \in C, f_k(x_i) \neq f_k(x_j)\} & D(x_i) \neq D(x_j) \\ \emptyset & D(x_i) = D(x_j) \end{cases} \quad i, j = 1, 2, ..., n$$

is called the discernibility matrix and m_{ij} is called the discernibility element. In general, the computational complexity of discernibility matrix is $O\left(n^2 \times m\right)$. Usually, discernibility matrix M is expressed in the form of a set

$$M = \{m_{ij}|m_{ij} \neq \emptyset, i, j = 1, 2, ..., n\}$$

and can be reduced by absorption law Absorb(M):

For all $m, m' \in M$, if $m' \subseteq m$ and $m' \neq \emptyset$, then $M = M - \{m\}$ (4)

2.2   Set Cover and the Minimum Set Cover

Set cover and the minimal set cover are other group concepts related to this paper.

Definition 6. Given a set T , let $\boldsymbol{C} = \{C_1, C_2, ..., C_m\}$ be a non-empty subsets family of T , and $\cup_{C_i \in \boldsymbol{C}} C_i = T$, then $\boldsymbol{C}$ is called a set cover of T.

According to Definition 6, the following theorem holds.

Theorem 1. Let $\boldsymbol{C}$ be a set cover of T, for any $C_i \in \boldsymbol{C}$, if $C_i \subseteq \cup_{C_j \in (\boldsymbol{C} - \{C_i\})} C_j$, then $\boldsymbol{C} - \{C_i\}$ is still a set cover of T.

Definition 7. Given a set T, let $\boldsymbol{C} = \{C_1, C_2, ..., C_m\}$ be a subsets family of T, and $\cup_{C_i \in \boldsymbol{C}} C_i = T$. If for any $C_i \in \boldsymbol{C}$, $\cup_{C_j \in (\boldsymbol{C} - \{C_i\})} C_j \neq T$, then $\boldsymbol{C}$ is called the minimal set cover of T.

We need to notice that the minimal set cover exists for any T , however, there could be more than one minimal set cover.

Example 1. Let $T = \{a, b, c, d, e, f\}$, $\boldsymbol{C} = \{C_1, C_2, C_3, C_4, C_5\}$, where $C_1 = \{a, b\}$, $C_2 = \{a, c\}$, $C_3 = \{a, c, d, f\}$, $C_4 = \{b, d\}$, and $C_5 = \{b, e, f\}$. It easily to see that $\boldsymbol{C}$ is a set cover of T, while the subsets $\{C_3, C_5\}$ and $\{C_2, C_4, C_5\}$ of $\boldsymbol{C}$ are both the minimal set covers of T .

2.3   Attribute Reduction and Set Cover

In this section, we described the relationship between attribute reduction and set cover. Due to limited space, here we assumed that the decision table is consistent and $D = \{d\}$. Conclusions for inconsistent decision tables will be introduced in our later works.

Definition 8. Given decision table $(U, C \cup D, V, F)$, where $U = \{x_1, x_2, ..., x_n\}$, $D = \{d\}$ and $C = \{a_1, a_2, ..., a_m\}$. Let $M = \{\alpha_k | \alpha_k \neq \emptyset, k \leq n^2\}$ be the discernibility matrix of the given decision table after using the absorption law (4), then based on the following rules:

$$X_\alpha (a_k) = \begin{cases} 1 & if\ a_k \in \alpha \\ 0 & if\ a_k \notin \alpha \end{cases} \tag{5}$$

discernibility matrix $M = \{\alpha_k | \alpha_k \neq \emptyset, k \leq n^2\}$ can be expressed as the following discernibility table (T, C), shown in Table1, where $T = \{X_{\alpha_k} | \alpha_k \in M\}$

By the definition of discernibility matrix, it can be easily understood that notation X_{α_k} in Table1 represents the set of all sample pairs of U that can be distinguished by discernibility element α_k , i.e.

$$X_{\alpha_k} = \{(x_i, x_j) | x_i, x_j \in U \text{ and } \exists a_t \in \alpha_k, \text{ such that } f_t(x_i) \neq f_t(x_j)\} \tag{6}$$

In addition, $\cup_{\alpha \in M} X_\alpha = U$, $X_\alpha(a_k) = 0$ means that $a_k \notin \alpha$ and $X_\alpha(a_k) = 1$ means that $a_k \in \alpha$. That is, for any $(x_i, x_j) \in X_\alpha$,when $X_\alpha(a_k) = 1$, we have $a_k(x_i) \neq a_k(x_j)$. In other words, a_k can distinguish any sample pairs in X_α.

Table 1. discernibility table (T, C)

a_1	... a_m
X_{α_1} $X_{\alpha_1}(a_1)$ ... $X_{\alpha_1}(a_m)$	
X_{α_2} $X_{\alpha_2}(a_1)$ ... $X_{\alpha_2}(a_m)$	
... ...	

Theorem 2. Let $T = \{X_\alpha | \alpha \in M\}$, $C_{a_i} = \{X_\alpha | X_\alpha(a_i) = 1, \alpha \in M, a_i \in C\}$, then $C = \{C_{a_i} | a_i \in C\}$ is a set cover of T.

Proof: It is straightforward.

Based on the discussion above, the problem of calculating the attribute reduction of decision table can be transformed into the problem of calculating a set cover of set T, and then turns the problem of calculating the minimal attribute reduction of a decision table into the problem of calculating the minimal set cover of set T.

2.4   User Preferences and Their Description

User preferences of attributes can be described qualitatively and quantitatively. Quantitative descriptions require assigning weights for each attributes, while qualitative descriptions require arranging the order of attributes. However, no matter how we describe user preferences, qualitatively or quantitatively, it is essentially about an order of the significance of attributes. Similar as in Reference [12], here, we use the complete order of attribute to describe user preferences of attributes, and use the lexicographic order (from left to right) rule to decide the quality of the selected attributes subset.

3   Algorithm and Example

In this section, we gave a user oriented reduct algorithm based on the minimal set cover, and gave an example to illustrate the usefulness of the proposed algorithm through application of reduct construction.

3.1   User-Oriented Reduct Algorithm Based on the Minimal Set Cover

Given a consistent decision table $(U, C \cup D, V, F)$, where $U = \{x_1, x_2, ..., x_n\}$, $C = \{a_1, a_2, ..., a_m\}$, and $D = \{d\}$ .User preferences are describes as a complete order of attributes: $a_{i_1} \geq a_{i_2} \geq ... \geq a_{i_m}$. Let M be the discernibility matrix of decision table $(U, C \cup D, V, F)$, $T = \{X_\alpha | \alpha \in M\}$, and C be the set cover of T.

According to the above assumption, user-oriented reduction algorithm based on the minimal set cover is designed as follows.

User-Oriented Reduction Algorithm Based on Minimal Set Cover
Input: The discernibility matrix M of a decision table.
Output: A minimal attribute reduction (Reduct) R.

(1) Construct an order of attributes over C .
(2) $M = Absorb(M)$.
(3) Construct the discernibility table (T,C) of decision table :
    (3.1) $T = \{X_\alpha | \alpha \in M\}$;
    (3.2) For $i = 1, 2, ..., m$, $\alpha \in M$, if $a_i \in \alpha$, then $X_\alpha(a_i) = 1$; otherwise, $X_\alpha(a_i) = 0$.
    (4) $R = \emptyset$, $C = \emptyset$, $T = T$.
    (5) Compute $C_{a_i} = \{X_\alpha | X_\alpha(a_i) = 1, \alpha \in M\}$ based on (T,C) for $i = 1, 2, ..., m$.
(6) If $T \neq \emptyset$, selecte attribute a in the current order of attributes from left to right. If $C_a \cap T \neq \emptyset$, let $C = C \cup \{C_a\}$ and continue to (7); otherwise, let $C = C, R = R, T = T$, delete a from the current order of attributes, and return to (6).
(7) If $C_b \not\subset \cup_{C \in C-\{C_b\}} C$ for any $C_b \in C$, let $R = R \cup \{a\}$, $T = T - \{C_a\}$, delete a from the current order of attributes, and return to (6); otherwise, let $C = C - \{C_a\}$, $R = R$, $T = T$, delete a from the current order of attributes, and return to (6).
(8) Update C and R by selecting attributes from left to right until no attribute exists in the order of attributes.

Example 2. Decision table $(U, C \cup D, V, F)$ is shown in Table 2, where $U = \{x_1, x_2, ..., x_{18}\}$, $C = \{a_1, a_2, ..., a_5\}$ and $D = \{d\}$.

For this example, according to Rough Sets theory, decision table $(U, C \cup D, V, F)$ has five Reducts: $\{a_1, a_4\}, \{a_3, a_4\}, \{a_1, a_2, a_5\}, \{a_4, a_5\}$ and $\{a_3, a_5\}$. Since calculating all Reducts of a decision table is NP-hard problem, thus, the general solution is usually to calculate only one Reduct based on some heuristic algorithm. However, according to our algorithm given in this section, the following calculation shows that we can calculate the Reduct of the decision table based on user preference, instead of a random Reduct.

In this example, suppose user preference with respect to attributes is described as: $a_1 \geq a_2 \geq a_3 \geq a_4 \geq a_5$. The discernibility matrix of the decision table is : $M = \{a_1a_2a_3a_5, a_1a_3a_4, a_2a_3a_4a_5, a_2a_3a_4, a_1a_2a_3a_4a_5, a_2a_4a_5, a_3a_4a_5, a_1a_2a_3a_4, a_4a_5, a_1a_3a_5\}$. After using absorption law (4),
$M = \{a_1a_3a_4, a_2a_3a_4, a_4a_5, a_1a_3a_5\}$. Let $\alpha_1 = a_1a_3a_4$, $\alpha_2 = a_2a_3a_4$, $\alpha_3 = a_4a_5$, $\alpha_4 = a_1a_3a_5$, then $M = \{\alpha_1, \alpha_2, \alpha_3, \alpha_4\}$. Let $T = \{X_{\alpha_1}, X_{\alpha_2}, X_{\alpha_3}, X_{\alpha_4}\}$, then (T, C) can be constructed as Table 3:
And $C_{a_1} = \{X_{\alpha_1}, X_{\alpha_4}\}$, $C_{a_2} = \{X_{\alpha_2}\}$, $C_{a_3} = \{X_{\alpha_1}, X_{\alpha_2}, X_{\alpha_4}\}$, $C_{a_4} = \{X_{\alpha_1}, X_{\alpha_2}, X_{\alpha_3}\}$, $C_{a_5} = \{X_{\alpha_3}, X_{\alpha_4}\}$.
For C_{a_1}, since $C_{a_1} \neq \emptyset$, let $C = \{C_{a_1}\}$. Since $C_{a_1} \not\subset \cup_{C \in C-\{C_{a_1}\}} C$, therefore $R = \{a_1\}$, $T = T - C_{a_1} = \{X_{\alpha_2}, X_{\alpha_3}\}$. Since $T \neq \emptyset$, selecte a_2. Since $C_{a_2} \cap T = \{X_{\alpha_2}\} \neq \emptyset$, let $C = \{C_{a_1}, C_{a_2}\}$. Since $C_{a_1} \not\subset \cup_{C \in C-\{C_{a_1}\}} C$ and $C_{a_2} \not\subset$

Table 2. Decision Table

	a_1	a_2	a_3	a_4	a_5	d
x_1	3	1	0	1	0	0
x_2	4	2	2	1	1	1
x_3	3	2	0	2	1	0
x_4	4	1	0	2	0	0
x_5	4	4	1	3	1	0
x_6	4	3	1	3	1	0
x_7	3	3	0	3	0	0
x_8	4	3	1	2	0	0
x_9	4	2	1	2	0	0
x_{10}	4	4	0	4	0	0
x_{11}	4	2	0	4	0	0
x_{12}	4	3	0	4	0	0
x_{13}	3	3	0	3	1	0
x_{14}	3	2	0	2	1	0
x_{15}	4	1	2	1	1	1
x_{16}	4	2	2	2	0	0
x_{17}	4	1	2	2	0	0
x_{18}	4	4	1	4	0	0

Table 3. Discernibility Talbe (T, C) for Decision Table 2

	a_1	a_2	a_3	a_4	a_5
X_{α_1}	1	0	2	1	0
X_{α_2}	0	1	1	1	0
X_{α_3}	0	0	0	1	1
X_{α_4}	1	0	1	0	1

$\cup_{C \in C - \{C_{a_2}\}} C$, let $R = \{a_1, a_2\}$, $T = T - \{C_{a_2}\}$. Since $T = \{X_{\alpha_3}\} \neq \emptyset$, selecte a_3. Since $C_{a_3} \cap T = \emptyset$, let $C = \{C_{a_1}, C_{a_2}\}$, $R = \{a_1, a_2\}$, and $T = T$. Since $T = \{X_{\alpha_3}\} \neq \emptyset$, selecte a_4. Since $C_{a_4} \cap T \neq \emptyset$, let $C = \{C_{a_1}, C_{a_2}, C_{a_4}\}$. Since $C_{a_2} \subset \cup_{C \in C - \{C_{a_2}\}} C$, selecte $C = \{C_{a_1}, C_{a_2}\}$, $R = \{a_1, a_2\}$ and $T = T$. Since $T = \{X_{\alpha_3}\} \neq \emptyset$, selecte a_5. Since $C_{a_5} \cap T \neq \emptyset$, let $C = \{C_{a_1}, C_{a_2}, C_{a_5}\}$. Since $C_{a_1} \not\subset \cup_{C \in C - \{C_{a_1}\}} C$, $C_{a_2} \not\subset \cup_{C \in C - \{C_{a_2}\}} C$ and $C_{a_5} \not\subset \cup_{C \in C - \{C_{a_5}\}} C$, therefore $R = \{a_1, a_2, a_5\}$.

Compare to the other Reducts of the given decision table: $\{a_1, a_4\}, \{a_3, a_4\}$, $\{a_4, a_5\}, \{a_3, a_5\}$, $R = \{a_1, a_2, a_5\}$ is the optimized result that satisfies user preference.

Similarly, suppose the user preference with respect to attributes is described as: $a_3 \geq a_1 \geq a_2 \geq a_4 \geq a_5$, according to our algorithm, Reduct $R = \{a_3, a_4\}$.

Obviously, compare to the other Reducts of decision table: $\{a_1, a_4\}, \{a_1, a_2, a_5\}$, $\{a_4, a_5\}, \{a_3, a_5\}$, $R = \{a_3, a_4\}$ is also the optimized result that satisfies user preference.

4 Conclusions

In order to avoid an over-simplified assumption that all attributes are equally important, we proposed an attribute selection algorithm based on the user preference of attributes, which is more reasonable and practical.

References

1. Pawlak, Z.: Rough Sets. International Journal of Computer Science 11(5), 341–356 (1982)
2. Wang, J., Wang, J.: Reduction algorithms on discernibility matrix: the ordered attributes method. Computer Science and Technology 16(6), 489–504 (2001)
3. Yao, Y., Zhao, Y., Wang, J., Han, S.: A Model of User-Oriented Reduct Construction for Machine Learning. In: Peters, J.F., Skowron, A. (eds.) Transactions on Rough Sets VIII. LNCS, vol. 5084, pp. 332–351. Springer, Heidelberg (2008)
4. Yao, Y.Y., Chen, Y.H., Yang, X.D.: A measurement-theoretic foundation for rule interestingness evaluation. In: Proceedings of Workshop on Foundations and New Direction in Data Mining (IEEE International Conference on Data Mining), pp. 221–227 (2003)
5. Ziarko, W.: Rough set approaches for discovering rules and attribute dependencies. In: Klaosgen, W., Zytkow, J.M. (eds.) Handbook of Data Mining and Knowledge Discovery, Oxford, pp. 328–339 (2002)
6. Zhao, K., Wang, J.: A reduction algorithm meeting users requirements. Journal of Computer Science and Technology 17(5), 578–593 (2002)
7. Han, S., Wang, J.: Reduct and attribute order. Journal of Computer Science and Technology 19(4), 429–449 (2004)
8. Yao, Y., Zhao, Y., Wang, J., Han, S.: A Model of Machine Learning Based on User Preference of Attributes. In: Greco, S., Hata, Y., Hirano, S., Inuiguchi, M., Miyamoto, S., Nguyen, H.S., Słowiński, R. (eds.) RSCTC 2006. LNCS (LNAI), vol. 4259, pp. 587–596. Springer, Heidelberg (2006)
9. Zhao, M., Han, S., Wang, J.: Tree expressions for information systems. Journal of Computer Science and Technology 22(2), 297–307 (2007)
10. Liang, H., Wang, J., Yao, Y.Y.: User-oriented features selection for Machine Learning. Computer Journal 50(4), 421–434 (2007)

Determining Pattern Similarity
in a Medical Recommender System

Maytiyanin Komkhao[1], Jie Lu[2], and Lichen Zhang[3]

[1] Chair of Computer Engineering, Fernuniversität in Hagen, Germany
maytiyanin.komkhao@fernuni-hagen.de
[2] School of Software, Faculty of Engineering and Information Technology,
University of Technology Sydney, P.O. Box 123, Broadway, NSW 2007, Australia
jie.lu@uts.edu.au
[3] School of Information Engineering, Guangdong University of Technology,
100, Waihuan Xi Road, Panyu District, Guangzhou, P.R. China
lczhang@sei.ecnu.edu.cn

Abstract. As recommender systems have proven their effectiveness in other areas, it is aimed to transfer this approach for use in medicine. Particularly, the diagnoses of physicians made in rural hospitals of developing countries, in remote areas or in situations of uncertainty are to be complemented by machine recommendations drawing on large bases of expert knowledge in order to reduce the risk to patients. Recommendation is mainly based on finding known patterns similar to a case under consideration. To search for such patterns in rather large databases, a weighted similarity distance is employed, which is specially derived for medical knowledge. For collaborative filtering an incremental algorithm, called W-InCF, is used working with the Mahalanobis distance and fuzzy membership. W-InCF consists of a learning phase, in which a cluster model of patients' medical history is constructed incrementally, and a prediction phase, in which the medical pattern of each patient considered is compared with the model to determine the most similar cluster. Fuzzy sets are employed to cope with possible confusion of decision making on overlapping clusters. The degrees of membership to these fuzzy sets is expressed by a weighted Mahalanobis radial basis function, and the weights are derived from risk factors identified by experts. The algorithm is validated using data on cephalopelvic disproportion.

1 Introduction

During the past two decades, the proportion of child births carried out with Caesarean section continuously increased worldwide [1, 2]. According to several studies, the common indications for Caesarean sections are dystocia, fetal distress, breech presentation and repeated Caesarean sections [1, 3]. For dystocia it has been proposed to restrict Caesarean deliveries to cases of true cephalopelvic disproportion, with symptoms such as advanced cervical dilation and adequate uterine contractions combined with molding and arrest of the fetal head [4]. At Bhumibol Adulyadej Hospital in Thailand, for instance, 30% of the deliveries are

Y. Xiang et al. (Eds.): ICDKE 2012, LNCS 7696, pp. 103–114, 2012.
© Springer-Verlag Berlin Heidelberg 2012

by Caesarean section, and indication for it from cephalopelvic disproportion is between 5% and 7% [3, 5]. In the Sisaket Hospital, the rate of Caesarean sections increased from 32.7% in 2006 to 35.7% in 2010 [2].

According to The Royal Thai College of Obstetricians and Gynecologists, there are three criteria to describe the need for Caesarean section due to cephalopelvic disproportion, viz. (1) cervical dilatation of at least 4 cm and an effacement of at least 80% at the time of diagnosis, (2) regular uterine contractions for at least 2 hours before the time of decision making, and (3) abnormal partograph such as protraction disorders, arrest disorders or second-stage disorders [1, 3, 5]. These criteria determine a delivery route in the intrapartum period (during labour and delivery), but their detection may lead to hazards in Caesarean delivery. Therefore, radiographic pelvimetry is performed in these cases. Unfortunately, measuring the pelvic dimensions to diagnose cephalopelvic disproportion and predicting labour outcome remains of limited value [6].

To cope with diseases it is best to detect their symptoms as early as possible [7]. This, however, is difficult in remote areas, such as the rural areas of Thailand, where medical specialists and facilities are scarce and insufficient. Therefore, to support general practitioners in diagnostics and to reduce the risk of hazardous complications, e.g. cephalopelvic disproportion as considered in this paper, it would be beneficial if physicians could detect diseases before their onset and, then, transfer patients from insufficient hospitals to well-prepared ones [8, 9].

Recommender systems have proven useful for many decades in information retrieval from large databases. The most common objective to use a recommender system is, however, to make a recommendation of yet unrated items to an interested user based on his/her previous preferences [10–15]. A recommender system can suggest to the user the item(s) with the highest estimated rating by employing many different methods from machine learning [12, 16] and approximation theory [17] or by various heuristics [11]. So far, particularly for e-commerce a wide range of recommendation techniques has been developed [10, 14, 15] and deployed successfully. Therefore, it stands to reason to employ recommender systems to solve the medical problems mentioned above.

In recent years, some studies on employing collaborative techniques of recommender systems in medical care [7] were carried out. Some of them draw an analogy between recommendation in terms of commercial selection and medical prediction [7, 18, 19]. Collaborative filtering requires user profiles to identify user preferences in order to make recommendations [7, 11]. To transfer the recommender systems' methodology to medical applications, we draw on the analogy identified in [7, 18, 19] as follows: (i) patients are identified with users, (ii) vectors (called patterns) containing data of medical histories and physical examinations are identified with user profiles, (iii) for both users and patients a notion of similarity is employed, and (iv) patient diagnoses are identified with user ratings. In case of a delivery, the diagnostic result does not range over several possibilities, but can only be that Caesarean section is necessary due to cephalopelvic disproportion or a normal delivery can take place.

Based on the InCF algorithm [20] developed previously, with W-InCF an incremental collaborative filtering algorithm for personalised diagnosis of diseases will be devised in this paper. W-InCF consists of a learning phase, in which a cluster model of a large number of patients' medical history is constructed incrementally, and a prediction phase, in which the medical pattern of each patient under consideration is compared with the model to determine the most similar cluster. Fuzzy sets are employed to cope with possible confusion of decision making on overlapping clusters. Owing to experience gained with InCF, the degrees of membership to these fuzzy sets are not expressed in terms of an ordinary distance such as the Euclidian one, but by the Mahalonobis distance [21], here based on weighted Mahalanobis radial basis functions, in order to improve prediction accuracy and to avoid the scalability problem encountered in model creation of incremental learning. The weights are derived from risk factors identified by experts.

The remainder of this paper is organised as follows. Section 2 introduces medical recommender systems. In Section 3 traditional clustering algorithms employed to create models with model-based collaborative filtering are discussed. Decision surfaces of radial basis functions are introduced in Section 4. The proposed algorithm is then detailed in Section 5. A case study of a medical recommender systems is conducted in Section 6 giving rise to an empirical validation of the method. Finally, a conclusion is drawn and topics for future work are indicated in Section 7.

2   Medical Recommender Systems

For already some decades, the development of information systems to predict the risk of individual diseases is a topic of intensive research [7, 22, 23]. The main goal of developing such computer-aided methods is to assist physicians in making decisions without consulting specialists directly [17, 24]. Recently, there were some studies employing collaborative techniques of recommender systems in medical care [7, 22]. Their leitmotif is to advise a consulting patient based on the medical records of patients with similar indications [7, 22, 23]. Reasons to employ collaborative filtering techniques in searching medical databases are, first, to maximise effectiveness and quality of medical care. Then, prediction should not only be accurate, but a recommender system should also be able to help physicians in defining appropriate treatments [19], and to predict in a personalised way to any patient his or her risk both with respect to his or her disease [7] and to undesirable outcomes of possible treatments [18].

In [7] a collaborative filtering method for personalised diagnosis of diseases by combining the memory-based and the model-based approach was presented. The method aims to predict the diseases a patient may contract in the future based on his or her medical record. To this end, it calculates values of similarity between the patient's data and patterns taken from a medical database employing International Classification of Diseases codes (ICD-9-CM) from [25], and predicts the patient's disease as that of the closest match found in the database.

3   Clustering Algorithms

For setting up models in model-based collaborative filtering, clustering is an intermediate step. The clusters generated by clustering algorithms are used for further analyses and prediction purposes [14]. Clustering has successfully been used in several exploratory pattern analyses, in data mining, machine learning and in pattern classifications [26]. The effect of clustering is that users are grouped in such a way that the values of user characteristics within the same cluster have high similarity to one another, but are very dissimilar to the characteristics in other clusters [27]. There are several clustering algorithms employed for model-based collaborative filtering such as K-nearest neighbours (K-NN), hierarchical, density-based and K-Means clustering [14, 28].

In our experimental comparison presented below, K-Means and K-NN are used as part of model creations, as they are the simplest methods for pattern classification based on similarity measurement (e.g. using the Euclidean distance) to compute distances between users.

4   Radial Basis Functions

Radial basis function networks are one type of artificial neural networks. The basis functions' values are computed using a distance measure between input patterns and model clusters which characterise the signal functions at hidden neurons [29]. As signal function at a hidden neuron commonly a Gaussian function is used [29, 30]. Gaussian radial basis functions are employed in [31] to fuzzify values of input patterns into membership values with respect to a similarity distance as in the following equation:

$$\mathbf{mem}(\mathbf{p}, \mathbf{W}) = \exp\left(-\frac{1}{2\sigma_i^2} \parallel \mathbf{p} - \mathbf{W} \parallel^2\right)$$

where $\parallel \cdot \parallel$ represents the Euclidean distance used to calculate the similarity between a pattern $\mathbf{p}$ and the model $\mathbf{W}$, σ_i is the standard deviation at the ith cluster whose spread expressed by a Gaussian radial basis function is shown for two and three dimensions in Figure 1 (a) and (b), respectively.

Based on [31], Gaussian radial basis functions can be further generalised by using the Mahalanobis distance, i.e. by introducing a covariance matrix into distance calculation [21, 29]:

$$\mathrm{dist}_M(j, s) = [(\mathbf{x}_j - \mathbf{x}_s)^\mathbf{T} \mathbf{K}^{-1}(\mathbf{x}_j - \mathbf{x}_s)]^{\frac{1}{2}} \tag{1}$$

Let $\mathbf{x}_j = [x_{1,j}, \ldots, x_{n,j}]^\mathbf{T}, j = 1, \cdots, N$, be characterised by a vector of $N > 0$ attributes, and let $\bar{\mathbf{x}} = \frac{1}{N}\sum_{j=1}^{N} \mathbf{x}_j$. Then, the covariance matrix [21, 29, 32] in (1) is $\mathbf{K} = \frac{1}{N-1}\sum_{j=1}^{N}(\mathbf{x}_j - \bar{\mathbf{x}})^\mathbf{T}(\mathbf{x}_j - \bar{\mathbf{x}})$ and, correspondingly, the Mahalanobis radial basis function [29, 30] is:

$$\mathbf{mem}(\mathbf{p}, \mathbf{W}) = \exp\left(-\frac{1}{2}(\mathbf{p} - \mathbf{W})^\mathbf{T} \mathbf{K}^{-1}(\mathbf{p} - \mathbf{W})\right)$$

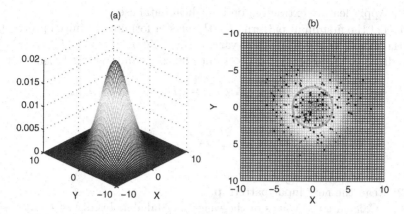

Fig. 1. Three-dimensional Gaussian radial basis function (a) and projection of a cluster of 200 samples with mean (0,0) into two dimensions (b) with boundary for membership decision marked by circle

5   Weighted Incremental Collaborative Filtering Algorithm

Based on the analogy between commercial and medical applications as outlined above, the algorithm W-InCF to be developed is to create a model in form of a cluster set from medical history data (instead as from user-rating matrices in the commercial domain), with each cluster representing a group of similar medical patterns. It uses a weighted Mahalanobis distance and weighted Mahalanobis radial basis functions to determine that a certain cluster, called the winning cluster, is the best match with an input pattern considered. Matching is defined by the degree of fuzzy membership expressed in terms of the similarity distance. The incremental learning algorithm compares input patterns joining the system with known clusters. It either associates an input pattern with a cluster, the winning cluster, already existing in the model and updates the cluster's parameters accordingly, or it includes the pattern into the model as a new cluster. The W-InCF algorithm has two main phases, viz. the *learning phase* and the *prediction phase*. Furthermore, the initialisation phase is utilised for preprocessing the dataset if it is complex. In this paper we assume, however, that the dataset was extracted by experts and does not require preprocessing.

5.1   Learning Algorithm in W-InCF

Learning from history is represented here by creating a model. This is performed incrementally processing input patterns one by one in relation to a series of model prototypes. The final model arises as result of this prototyping process. The steps of W-InCF's learning algorithm are presented in detail as follows.

Step 0: Apply feature extraction on a medical database.

Step 1: Let the first input pattern **p** be the cluster forming the initial prototype of the model **W**. Set the initial variables as follows: a counter $\mathbf{C}_{(i,new)} = 1$, the distance threshold $0 < d_{th} < 1$ and the covariance matrix $\mathbf{K}_{initial}$ as:

$$\mathbf{K}_{initial} = \sigma \Gamma_n$$

where $\Gamma_n = \begin{bmatrix} 1 & 0 & \cdots & 0 \\ 0 & 1 & \cdots & 0 \\ \vdots & \vdots & \ddots & \vdots \\ 0 & 0 & \cdots & 1 \end{bmatrix}$ and $0 < \sigma < 1$.

Step 2: Read the next input pattern **p**.

Step 3: : Calculate the values of the weighted Mahalanobis distance ($\mathbf{dist}_{M_w}$) between **p** and the clusters in **W** using the non-singular covariance matrix. The weights w are derived from the risk factors (for more details cp. Section 6.1). Here, $\sigma\Gamma$ is added to **K**

$$\mathbf{K}_{new} = \mathbf{K}_{old} + \sigma \Gamma_n$$

in order to prevent the problem that the matrix becomes singular before the proper distance is calculated:

$$\mathbf{dist}_{M_w}(\mathbf{p}, \mathbf{W}) = [w(\mathbf{p} - \mathbf{W})^{\mathsf{T}} \mathbf{K}^{-1} w (\mathbf{p} - \mathbf{W})]^{\frac{1}{2}} \qquad (2)$$

Step 4: Calculate the value of **p**'s membership to each cluster using a weighted Mahalanobis radial basis function:

$$\mathbf{mem}(\mathbf{p}, \mathbf{W}) = \mathbf{exp}\left(-\frac{1}{2}w(\mathbf{p} - \mathbf{W})^{\mathsf{T}} \mathbf{K}^{-1} w(\mathbf{p} - \mathbf{W})\right) \qquad (3)$$

Step 5: Select the winning cluster as the one for which the maximum membership value identified by the fuzzy OR operator (i.e. max operator) as applied to the components of **mem** is assumed [31]:

$$\mathtt{winner} = \mathbf{argmax}_i(mem_i)$$

$$\mathtt{winner} = mem_1 \vee mem_2 \vee \ldots \vee mem_n$$

Step 6: If the measured distance between **p** and **winner** is higher than the distance threshold defined, then extend the model by a new cluster consisting just of **p**.

Otherwise update count (4), model prototype (5) and covariance matrix (6) by applying so-called learning rules [31, 33]:

$$\mathbf{C}_{i,new} = \mathbf{C}_{i,old} + 1 \qquad (4)$$

$$\mathbf{w}_{i,new} = (1 - \beta)\mathbf{w}_{i,old} + \beta \mathbf{p} \qquad (5)$$

with $\beta = 1/\mathbf{C}_{i,new}$, and
$$\mathbf{K}_{i,new} =$$

$$(1 - \beta)\mathbf{K}_{i,old} + \beta(1 - \beta^2)(\mathbf{p} - \mathbf{w}_{i,new})(\mathbf{p} - \mathbf{w}_{i,new})^{\mathbf{T}} \qquad (6)$$

where the subscript "new"/"old" denotes the model's prototype after/before updating, $\mathbf{C}_i$ counts the number of patterns combined into the ith cluster, $\mathbf{w}_i$ is the centre of the ith cluster, $\beta = 1/\mathbf{C}_{i,new}$ and $\mathbf{K}_i$ represents the covariance matrix at the ith cluster [31, 33].

Step 7: If there is a new input pattern $\mathbf{p}$, go to **Step 2**.

5.2   Prediction Algorithm in W-InCF

The prediction phase of W-InCF is aimed to classify the characteristics of a consulting patient $\mathbf{p}$ by associating with him or her the closest cluster in the model resulting from the learning phase. It consists of the following steps.

Step 0: Read the pattern of the consulting patient $\mathbf{p}$.

Step 1: Measure the distance between $\mathbf{p}$ and the elements of the model $\mathbf{W}$ generated in the learning phase by using a weighted Mahalanobis distance dist_{M_w}:

$$\text{dist}_{M_w}(\mathbf{p}, \mathbf{W}) = [w(\mathbf{p} - \mathbf{W})^{\mathbf{T}}\mathbf{K}^{-1}w(\mathbf{p} - \mathbf{W})]^{\frac{1}{2}} \qquad (7)$$

Step 2: Calculate the values of $\mathbf{p}$'s membership in the elements of $\mathbf{W}$ by using a weighted Mahalanobis distance dist_{M_w}:

$$\text{mem}(\mathbf{p}, \mathbf{W}) = \exp\left(-\frac{1}{2}w(\mathbf{p} - \mathbf{W})^{\mathbf{T}}\mathbf{K}^{-1}w(\mathbf{p} - \mathbf{W})\right) \qquad (8)$$

Step 3: Find the winning cluster by identifying the highest degree of membership [31]:

$$\text{winner} = \text{argmax}_i(mem_i)$$

$$\text{winner} = mem_1 \vee mem_2 \vee \ldots \vee mem_n$$

Step 4: Associate $\mathbf{p}$ with the winning cluster and assign corresponding characteristics.

Step 5: If there is a new consulting patient $\mathbf{p}$, go to **Step 0**.

6   Case Study and Experimental Validation

In this section, the proposed W-InCF algorithm is utilised in a medical recommender system with input patterns defined by medical records of pregnant women. The system aims to estimate in advance the risk incurred by normal childbirth or by delivery with Caesarean section due to cephalopelvic disproportion instead of determining a delivery route not until or during labour. This approach underlines the key idea of recommender systems, viz. to advise a consulting patient based on the medical records of similar cases.

6.1   Risk Factors Identified by Experts

The medical dataset used in this case study includes attributes from the medical history of patients (Pa), and risk factors significantly associated with Caesarean section due to cephalopelvic disproportion when analysed by multivariate logistic regression. Characterised by odds ratio (OR) and 95% confidence interval (CI) these risk factors are: age > 35 years old (OR=2.73, CI=1.56–4.80), nulliparous parity (OR=6.79, CI=4.50–10.25), maternal height < 150 cm (OR=1.90, CI=1.19–3.05), fundal height > 35 cm (OR=2.11, CI=1.46–3.03), pre-pregnancy body-mass-index (BMI) > 26 kg/m^2 (OR=3.54, CI=1.73–7.27), BMI before delivery > 26 kg/m^2 (OR=2.50, CI=1.62–3.86). These risk factors are applied as weights w in a weighted Mahalanobis distance (2,3,7 and 8).

6.2   Experimental Set-Up

To demonstrate the W-InCF algorithm's applicability to real-world datasets, we first compare it with traditional clustering algorithms such as K-Means and K-NN in recommending delivery alternatives and, then, we investigate the correctness of the recommendations by comparing them with the choices actually made.

The medical dataset used comprises 802 cases of pregnant women who delivered in a public hospital in Thailand between 1 July 2005 and 31 May 2007. It contains two equally sized groups, namely 401 women who delivered by Caesarean section due to cephalopelvic disproportion, and 401 women delivered normally during the same period. Attributes in the dataset relevant for consideration by the recommender system were selected by experts.

6.3   Evaluation Matrices

There is a vast diversity of metrics that could be used to evaluate the quality of a recommender system [34, 13]. Here, the accuracy metric [34]

$$AC = \frac{\text{number of correct recommendations}}{\text{number of recommendations}} \times 100$$

i.e. the proportion of the total number of correct recommendations (number of recommendation coinciding with the actual diagnoses) to the total number of recommendations, is utilised.

6.4   Test Data and Data Preparation

In Table 1, a selected subset for 10 patients from the entire dataset comprising 802 medical records is shown. The table contains the values of nine attributes from the medical history of patients (Pa), viz. Maternal Age, Nulliparous parity, Gravidity, Pre-pregnancy Weight, Weight, Maternal Height, Pre-pregnancy BMI, BMI before Delivery and Fundal Height.

Table 1. Example of a medical dataset (Pa denoting patient)

Pa	A	P	G	PW	W	H	PB	BD	FH
1	21	0	2	48	61.5	1.58	19.22	24.63	33
2	27	1	2	47	66	1.52	20.34	28.56	35
3	33	0	1	98	108	1.65	35.99	39.66	35
4	24	0	1	48	67	1.6	18.75	26.17	40
5	25	2	3	68	75	1.6	26.56	29.29	36
6	15	0	1	50	64	1.55	20.81	26.63	32
7	25	1	2	55	66	1.65	20.20	24.24	32
8	22	1	2	39	53	1.575	15.72	21.36	31
9	27	0	1	48	67	1.57	19.47	27.18	35
10	33	2	3	45	56	1.59	17.79	22.15	33

In order to make different datasets comparable, they need to be brought to a common scale by min-max normalisation calculated by $\frac{value-min}{max-min}$ [35]. For example, the patient 1 has age 21. With the max-min values from the medical history of the 802 patients represented in the considered dataset, her normalised maternal age is $\frac{21-14}{45-14} = 0.226$.

Table 2. Min-max values for the medical dataset

Abbreviations	Max value	Min value
A=Maternal Age	45	14
P=Nulliparous Parity	6	0
G=Gravidity	45	33
PW=Pre-pregnancy Weight	103	32
W=Weight	116	42
H=Maternal Height	183	140
PB=Pre-pregnancy BMI	40.23	13.46
BD=BMI before Delivery	44.12	17.22
FH=Fundal Height	45	24

6.5 Experimental Results

Employing the medical dataset introduced above, recommendations have been simulated to compare the performance of the proposed W-InCF algorithm with that of K-Means and K-NN clustering. The results shown in Table 3 indicate that K-Means clustering yields the lowest accuracy value of recommendation (62.84%) in comparison to K-NN (68.32%) and W-InCF (69%). This relates also to the number of correct estimations of the risk incurred to patients: with 277 correct risk estimations W-InCF outperforms K-Means (252) and K-NN (274).

A major difference between K-Means and K-NN clustering on one side and W-InCF on the other is that the latter finds the number of clusters forming a model by itself employing threshold considerations. For K-Means the number of clusters is fixed when the algorithm is invoked; similarly the number of nearest neighbours

Table 3. Accuracy and number of correct recommendations

Algorithm	%of Accuracy	Correct estimations
K-Means	62.84	252
K-NN	68.32	274
W-InCF	69	277

is fixed for K-NN. Hence, W-InCF can better adjust to given situations. K-NN could only come so close to the performance of W-InCF, because it was helped by a human appropriately selecting the number of nearest neighbours.

7   Conclusion and Future Work

A weighted incremental collaborative filtering algorithm was proposed. It is used in a medical recommender system to assist physicians in predicting — at least approximately — to pregnant women the risk of childbirth before delivery actually takes place. This approach is expected to be helpful in improving the quality of medical services in remote areas with insufficient infrastructure, such as rural regions of developing countries. The algorithm was shown to yield more accurate recommendation predictions than existing collaborative filtering techniques, since it computes a similarity distance with weights derived by experts from knowledge on medical risk factors. To show the algorithm's effectiveness, experiments were carried out utilising a medical dataset on the need for Caesarean sections due to cephalopelvic disproportion obtained from a public hospital in Thailand.

The objective of future work is to improve the accuracy of W-InCF further. To this end, the usage of rule bases derived from expert knowledge will be considered, also incorporating a list of risks ranked according to severity.

Acknowledgement. Special thanks go to Dr.-Ing. Sunantha Sodsee, lecturer in the Faculty of Information Technology, King Mongkut's University of Technology North Bangkok, and to Aunsumalin Komkhao, M.D., specialist in obstetrics and gynecology at Bhumibol Adulyadej Hospital, Thailand, for providing ideas and medical expertise.

This work was supported in part by a Mercator visiting professorship granted by Deutsche Forschungsgemeinschaft, and partly also by the National Science Foundation of China under Grant No. 61173046.

References

1. Khunpradit, S., Patumanond, J., Tawichasri, C.: Risk Indicators for Caesarean Section due to Cephalopelvic Disproportion in Lamphun Hospital. Journal of The Medical Association of Thailand 88(2), 63–68 (2005)
2. Wianwiset, W.: Risk Factors of Caesarean Delivery due to Cephalopelvic Disproportion in Nulliparous Women at Sisaket Hospital. Thai Journal of Obstetrics and Gynaecology 19, 158–164 (2011)

3. Moryadee, S., Smanchat, B., Rueangchainikhom, W., Phommart, S.: Risk Score for prediction of Caesarean Delivery due to Cephalopelvic Disproportion in Bhumibol Adulyadej Hospital. Royal Thai Air Force Medical Gazette 56(1), 20–29 (2010)

4. Spörri, S., Thoeny, H.C., Raio, L., Lachat, R., Vock, P., Schneider, H.: MR Imaging Pelvimetry: A Useful Adjunct in the Treatment of Women at Risk for Dystocia? American Journal of Roentgenology 179(1), 137–144 (2002)

5. Komkhao, A.: Risk Factors for Cesarean Delivery due to Cephalopelvic Disproportion in Bhumibol Adulyadej Hospital, Thailand. Royal Thai Air Force Medical Gazette 54(70) (2008)

6. Gong, S.: A Collaborative Filtering Recommendation Algorithm Based on User Clustering and Item Clustering. Journal of Software 5(7), 745–752 (2010)

7. Davis, D.A., Chawla, N.V., Christakis, N.A., Barabási, A.L.: Time to CARE: a collaborative engine for practical disease prediction. Data Mining and Knowledge Discovery 20(3), 388–415 (2010)

8. Surapanthapisit, P., Thitadilok, W.: Risk Factors of Caesarean Section due to Cephalopelvic Disproportion. Journal of the Medical Association of Thailand 89(4), 105–111 (2006)

9. O'Driscoll, K., Jackson, R.J.A., Gallagher, J.T.: Active Management of Labour and Cephalopelvic Disproportion. The Journal of Obstetrics and Gynaecology of the British Commonwealth 77(5), 385–389 (1970)

10. Lu, J., Shambour, Q., Xu, Y., Lin, Q., Zhang, G.: BizSeeker: A Hybrid Semantic Recommendation System for Personalized Government-to-Business e-Services. Internet Research 20(3), 342–365 (2010)

11. Adomavicius, G., Tuzhilin, A.: Towards the Next Generation of Recommender Systems: A Survey of the State-of-the-Art and Possible Extensions. IEEE Transactions on Knowledge and Data Engineering 17(6), 734–749 (2005)

12. Cornelis, C., Lu, J., Guo, X., Zhang, G.: One-and-only item recommendation with fuzzy logic techniques. Information Sciences 177(22), 4906–4921 (2007)

13. Su, X., Khoshgoftaar, T.M.: A Survey of Collaborative Filtering Techniques. In: Advances in Artificial Intelligence, pp. 1–20 (2009)

14. Burke, R.: Hybrid Recommender Systems: Survey and Experiments. User Modeling and User-Adapted Interaction 12(4), 331–370 (2002)

15. Shambour, Q., Lu, J.: A Hybrid Trust-Enhanced Collaborative Filtering Recommendation Approach for Personalized Government-to-Business e-Services. International Journal of Intelligent Systems 26(9), 814–843 (2011)

16. Roh, T.H., Oh, K.J., Han, I.: The collaborative filtering recommendation based on SOM cluster-indexing CBR. Expert Systems with Applications 25(3), 413–423 (2003)

17. Adlassnig, K.P.: Fuzzy Set Theory in Medical Diagnosis. IEEE Transactions on Systems, Man, and Cybernetics 16(2), 260–265 (1986)

18. Hassan, S., Syed, Z.: From Netflix to Heart Attacks: Collaborative Filtering in Medical Datasets. In: Proc. of the 1st ACM International Health Informatics Symposium (IHI 2010), pp. 128–134 (2010)

19. Duan, L., Street, W.N., Xu, E.: Healthcare information systems: data mining methods in the creation of a clinical recommender system. Enterprise Information Systems 5(2), 169–181 (2011)

20. Komkhao, M., Lu, J., Li, Z., Halang, W.A.: An Incremental Collaborative Filtering Algorithm for Recommender Systems. In: Proc. of the 10th International FLINS Conference on Uncertainty Modeling in Knowledge Engineering and Decision Making (FLINS 2012) (to be published)

21. Mahalanobis, P.C.: On the Generalised Distance in Statistics. Proc. of the National Institute of Sciences of India 2(1), 49–55 (1936)

22. Heckerman, D.E., Horvitz, E.J., Nathwani, B.N.: Towards Normative Expert Systems: Part I, Pathfinder Project. Methods of Information in Medicine 31(2), 90–105 (1992)

23. Folino, F., Pizzuti, C.: A Comorbidity-based Recommendation Engine for Disease Prediction. In: Proc. IEEE 23rd International Symposium on Computer-Based Medical Systems (CBMS 2010), pp. 6–12 (2010)

24. Weiss, S.M., Kulikowski, C.A., Amarel, S., Safir, A.: Model-Based Method for Computer-Aided Medical Decision-Making. Artificial Intelligence 11(1-2), 145–172 (1978)

25. Centers for Disease Control and Prevention. ICD-9-CM (International Classification of Disease, 9th revision, Clinical Modification (2007), http://www.cdc.gov/nchs/icd/icd9cm.htm

26. Jain, A.K., Murty, M.N., Flynn, P.J.: Data Clustering: A Review. ACM Computing Surveys 31(3), 264–323 (1999)

27. Han, J., Kamber, M.: Data Mining: Concepts and Techniques, 2nd edn. Morgan Kaufmann Publishers, San Francisco (2006)

28. Candillier, L., Meyer, F., Boullé, M.: Comparing State-of-the-Art Collaborative Filtering Systems. In: Perner, P. (ed.) MLDM 2007. LNCS (LNAI), vol. 4571, pp. 548–562. Springer, Heidelberg (2007)

29. Kumar, S.: Neural Networks: A classroom approach. Tata McGraw-Hill Publishing Company Limited, New Delhi (2004)

30. Tanner, R., Cruickshank, D.G.M.: RBF Based Receivers for DS-CDMA with Reduced Complexity. In: Proc. IEEE 5th International Symposium on Spread Spectrum Techniques and Applications (ISSSTA 1998), vol. 2, pp. 647-651 (1998)

31. Yen, G.G., Meesad, P.: An effective neuro-fuzzy paradigm for machinery condition health monitoring. IEEE Transactions on Systems, Man, and Cybernetics, Part B 31(4), 523–536 (2001)

32. Demster, A.P.: Covariance Selection. Biometrics 28(1), 157–175 (1972)

33. Vuskovic, M., Sijiang, D.: Classification of Prehensile EMG Patterns with Simplified Fuzzy ARTMAP. In: Proc. 2002 International Joint Conference on Neural Networks (IJCNN 2002), vol. 3, pp. 2539–2544 (2002)

34. Hernandez-del-Olmo, F., Gaudioso, E.: Evaluation of recommender systems: A new approach. Expert Systems with Applications 35(3), 790–804 (2008)

35. Jain, A., Nandakumar, K., Ross, A.: Score Normalization in Multimodal Biometric Systems. Pattern Recognition 38(12), 2270–2285 (2005)

Chinese Latent Relational Search Based on Relational Similarity

Chao Liang and Zhao Lu[*]

Dept. of Computer Science and Technology, East China Normal University,
Shanghai, China
chliang@ica.stc.sh.cn,
zlu@cs.ecnu.edu.cn

Abstract. Latent relational search is a new way of searching information in an unknown domain according to the knowledge of a known domain from the Web. By analyzing the analogous relationship between word pairs, the latent relational search engine can tell us the accurate information that we need. Given a Chinese query, {(A, B), (C, ?)}, our aim is to get D which is the answer of "?". In this paper, we propose an approach to Chinese Latent relational search for the first time. Moreover, we classify the relation mappings between two word pairs into three categories according to the number of relations and the number of target words corresponding to each relation. Our approach firstly extracts relation-representing words by using the preprocessing modular and two clustering algorithms, and then the candidate word set of D corresponding to each relation-representing word can be obtained. The proposed method achieves an MRR of 0.563, which is comparable to the existing methods.

Keywords: Web mining, information retrieval, latent relational search, relational similarity, analogical search.

1 Introduction

Latent relational search (LRS) can be used to get the knowledge of an unfamiliar domain using the analogy knowledge in a familiar domain when a user queries a Web search engine. For example, a fan of Yao Ming (a famous basketball player) is interested in sports star. He wants to get the marriage information about Lin Dan (a famous badminton player). The relation between Yao Ming and Ye Li is an important clue to get his interested information. That is, given a tuple (Yao Ming, Ye Li, Lin Dan), Xie Xingfang who is Lin Dan's wifewill be returned, as the relation between Yao Ming and Ye Li is highly similar to that between Lin Dan and Xie Xingfang.

One key technology of latent relational search is relational similarity measuring between two pairs of words, which suggest the method for ranking candidate word pairs. Till now, various relational similarity measuring methods between two word pairs A, B and C, D have been proposed (Turney et al. [5, 6], Veale et al [7], Bollegala et al [8], Cao et al [9]).

---

[*] Corresponding author.

Y. Xiang et al. (Eds.): ICDKE 2012, LNCS 7696, pp. 115–127, 2012.
© Springer-Verlag Berlin Heidelberg 2012

Another key technology of latent relational search is analogical mappings between lists of words. Combining ideas from modeling of analogy-making Structure Mapping Engine (SME) [14] and Latent Relational Analysis [5], Turney [15] realized the Latent Relation Mapping Engine (LRME) which builds analogical mappings between lists of words, using a large corpus of raw text to automatically discover the semantic relations among the words.

Kato et al. [1] explained concepts and applications of latent relational search in detail. Duc et al. [2] raised the Latent relational search, and a ranking method by employing symmetry property in relational similarity is presented by Goto et al. [3]. Cross-Language Latent Relational Search (CLRS) is put forward in Duc et al's paper [4]. However, they did not consider that the number of relations between a word pair and the number of the target word corresponding to each relation are uncertain.

The main contributions of this paper include:

(1) To our knowledge, there are less published papers related to Latent relational search of Chinese corpus. It is well known that there are some special features of Chinese in diction, syntax and discourse organization. Existing methods cannot be directly transplanted to process Chinese corpus. In this paper, we do some meaningful explorations and firstly propose an approach for Chinese latent relational search.

(2) Existing methods consider less on the diversity of relation mapping which lead to a relatively low accuracy of the result. Three kinds of relation mappings between two word pairs are first classified in this paper, which are one-to-one, one-to-many and multi-relations mapping respectively. We can get different result sets according to three kinds of relation mappings and raise the accuracy of retrieval.

(3) The suggested approach achieves a good performance both in time and space consuming. The average web access is 37.6.

This paper is organized as follows. Related works are discussed in Section 2. The detailed procedures of extracting relation-representing words and candidate target words are shown in Section 3. Section 4 presents the experimental results and Section 5 concludes this paper.

2   Related Works

Kato et al. [1] propose a latent relational search approach based on Term Co-occurrence or Lexico-Syntactic Patterns. Relations between two words are represented by bag-of-word in the Term Co-occurrence based method. The second method treats n-grams as the relation representation between two words. They query a Web search engine for terms or Lexico-Syntactic patterns which are in same sentence containing both A and B. The term or pattern set T is supposed to contain terms or patterns which express the relations between A and B. Then, they extract the candidate list of D using C and terms or patterns. Finally, they rank the candidate list and get the result D. The combination of two approaches gets a high precision. It is not enough for Chinese that they only extract the words between A and B in a sentence.

Duc et al. [2] propose a Japanese latent relational search. The proposed approach extracts word pairs from a text corpus (the Web), and represents relations between words using lexical patterns. The method of representing relations between two words enables the approach achieving both high precision and recall. However, they need to extract and train a large number of corpus and to build a super large index library. In addition, their test sets are defined in limited domains, and they didn't show precisions for other domains. Duc et al. [4] propose a Cross-Language Latent Relational Search (CLRS). A hybrid (soft/hard) lexical pattern clustering algorithm to recognize paraphrased lexical patterns across languages is put forward. Using the result of the proposed clustering algorithm, they can measure the relational similarity between two entity pairs that are in different languages and rank the result list of a CLRS query.

The approach proposed by Kato et al. [1] imposes a bias towards the frequency of a word. A high frequency word D has a higher probability of being assigned a top rank, irrespective of the semantic relation shared between (A, B) and (C, D). Goto et al. [3] propose a ranking method which uses symmetry features in relational similarity to alleviate this phenomenon. They also propose "complementary rank" to improve precision in ranking result set of a relational query.

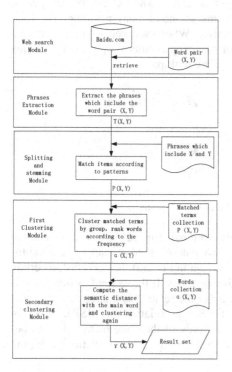

Fig. 1. The High-level Flow of the Chinese Latent relational search

Table 1. Symbols and Their Meanings

symbol	meaning
A	The first input word
B	The second input word
r	Relation-representing word
C	The third input word
D	Target word
X	The symbol denotes A or C
Y	The symbol denotes B or r
m	Punctuations or spaces
*	Any characters except m
$t_i(1 \leq i \leq n)$	A sentence containing both X and Y
T(X, Y)	Collection of t
t_{seg}	Segmented t
$T_{seg}(X, Y)$	Collection of t_{seg}
s	Stemmed t_{seg}
S (X, Y)	Collection of s
n	A noun word
v	A verb word
$\delta(X,Y)$	Collection of s
Δ	Collection of δ
q	An element in Δ
F(q)	Frequency of q
Q(X,Y)	Collection of q after clustering
α	An element in $\alpha(X,Y)$
$\alpha(X,Y)$	Sorted Q(X,Y)
θ	Correlation value of two words
β	An element in $\nabla(X,Y)$
$\nabla(X,Y)$	Collection after first clustering
R(A, B)	Relation-representing words
$\Omega(C,r)$	Collection of target word D
Θ	Collection of $\Omega(C,r)$

3   Our Approach

The high-level flow of the Chinese latent relational search is illustrated in Fig.1. Three main parts of our approach are the preprocessing modular and two clustering procedures. Symbols used in the following sections are summarized in Table 1. In this paper, we take {(Yao Ming, Ye Li), (Lin Dan, Xie Xingfang)} as an example.

3.1   Three Kinds of Relation Mapping

Given a Chinese query, {(A, B), (C, ?)}, our aim is to get all candidates of D which are the answer of "?". We call (A, B) as the example word pair, A and B are two example words, (C, D) is viewed as the target word pair where C is the third example word, and D is the target word. In this paper, a relation-representing word is used to describe the relation of a word pair.

The variety of relations and the target words is considered in the paper. For example, if A is Earth and B is Moon, the Moon is one of satellites of Earth. If we set Mars as the third example word C, then all the satellites of Mars should be returned. That is to say, the relation of the example word pair is single, while C can be mapped to many D according to this relation. We view this as one-to-many mapping. The relations between two persons are changing with time. When they were young, they were classmates and they may become couples or competitors after they grew up. In this example, the relations between the two persons are multiple.

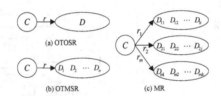

Fig. 2. Three Kinds of Relation Mapping

For a query, {(A,B), (C,?)}: If the example word pair has only one relation, and the number of target words for the relation is one, we call this kind of mapping as One-to-One mapping for Single Relation (OTOSR), shown in Fig.2(a). For OTOSR, a certain target word will be returned similar to existing methods. If the example word pair has one relation while the number of target words for the relation is many, we called this kind of mapping as One-to-Many mapping for Single Relation (OTMSR), shown in Fig.2(b). For OTMSR, we get a list of target words. If there are many relations between two example words, we call this kind of mapping as Multi-relations mapping (MR), shown in Fig.2(c).

3.2   Obtaining Relation-Representing Words

Our approach uses a preprocessing modular and two clustering procedures to get accurate relation-representing words for a word pair. The method that we use for ranking the candidate relational words is different from the others. There are two clustering procedures in our study. The first clustering separates the snippets into different groups corresponding to different lexical-patterns and determines which words should be extracted for the second clustering. The second clustering is the mainly different part from the previous works. By calculating the correlation between words, we cluster all the candidate words into different groups. The words in the same group represent the same relation. Thus we get the relation-representing words by ranking all the words in each group by frequency.

Preprocessing Modular.

There are three steps in the preprocessing modular:

Step 1. For an example word pair, extract related web pages using Baidu (a Chinese search engine). We extract the titles (as shown in Fig.3) and their contents from the returned results.

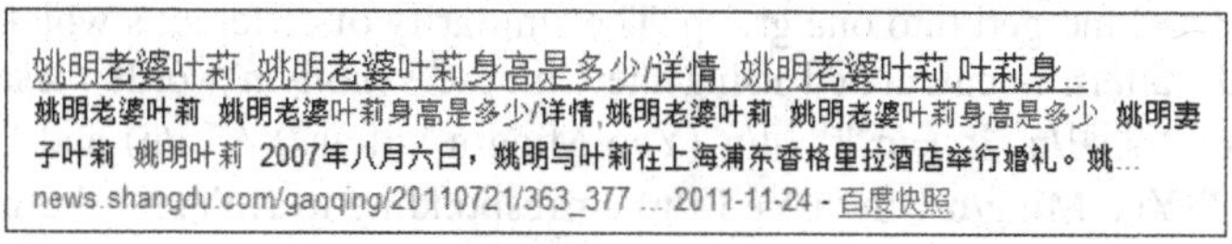
姚明老婆叶莉 姚明老婆叶莉身高是多少/详情 姚明老婆叶莉,叶莉身...
姚明老婆叶莉 姚明老婆叶莉身高是多少/详情,姚明老婆叶莉 姚明老婆叶莉身高是多少 姚明妻子叶莉 姚明叶莉 2007年八月六日，姚明与叶莉在上海浦东香格里拉酒店举行婚礼。姚...
news.shangdu.com/gaoqing/20110721/363_377 ... 2011-11-24 - 百度快照

Fig. 3. An example of a returned web page

Step 2. Collect sequence which containing both two words A and B. Considering the feature of Chinese, we extract words in the sequence containing both A and B. All words before A, between A and B and after B are extracted. That is,

$$m * A * B * m \text{ or } m * B * A * m$$

where m denotes punctuations or spaces, and * denotes any characters except m.

For example, the sequence t = "姚明老婆叶莉身高是多少" (How tall is Ye Li who is Yao Ming's wife) is collected. We mark the collection of all sequences as $T(A,B)=\{t_1,t_2,\dots t_i,\dots t_n\}$.

Step 3. Segment each sequence in T(A,B) and collect the stem for each segmented sequence. Each sequence t in $T(A, B)$ is segmented into separate words with independent meanings using a Chinese words segmentation tool ICTCLAS [10]. Each word has corresponding Part-Of-Speech tagging. We denote the collection of all segmented sequences as $T_{seg}(A, B)$. For example, "姚明/n 老婆/n 叶莉/n 身高/n 是/v 多少/r" (Yao Ming/n wife/n Ye Li/n Height/n is/v how much/r).

Considering that there are some words without semantic meanings (such as stop words and conjunctions) in each segmented sequence, we extract nouns and verbs to represent the structure and meaning of a sentence. We denote s as the stem of t_{seg}, such as "姚明/n 老婆/n 叶莉/n" (Yao Ming/n wife/n Ye Li/n). In this way, we get the collection $S(A, B)$ of all stems.

The First Clustering Procedure.

Using the preprocessing modular, the stems of the example word pair are collected. Now, the question is which words should be extracted from the collection S (A, B) to represent the relations between two words A and B. In order to find out relation-representing words accurately, 18 lexical patterns are presented in Table 2 in order to cluster all elements in S (A, B).

In Table 2, X denotes the word A, Y denotes the word B, n denotes nouns and v denotes verbs. Each term is matched to find the lexical pattern that it meets.

Table 2. 18 Lexical Patterns

nvXY	XnvY	XYnv	nXvY	nXYv	XnYv	nXY	XnY	XYn
vnXY	XvnY	XYvn	vXnY	vXYn	XvYn	vXY	XvY	XYv

We use $\delta(A, B)$ to describe the collection of all matched terms which fit the same lexical pattern, and Δ is the collection of $\delta(A, B)$. If two terms fit the same lexical pattern and there is at least one same word or synonymous word between them, they are clustered and merged into one group. The similarity of different s which meets the same lexical pattern is calculated using the Chinese synonym words thesaurus [11]. For example, "姚明/n 妻子/n 叶莉/n"(Yao Ming/n wife/n Ye Li/n) and "姚明/n 老婆/n 叶莉/n"(Yao Ming/n wife/n Ye Li/n) corresponding to XnY. Furthermore, 妻子 and 老婆 are two expressions of wife. So we can cluster two snippets into one group. Algorithm 1 is used to achieve the aim of merging all the snippets which are similar in structure and semantic into different groups.

```
Algorithm 1  The first clustering

Input: Segmented phrases collection
S(A,B):= {s₁s₂ ⋯ sₙ}, Flag := false
Output: Clustered terms Δ:= {δ₁δ₂ ⋯ δ₁₈}
For s ∈ S(A,B) do
  Switch s:
    Case s ∈ δₙ(n ∈ {1,2, ⋯ 18})
      If δₙ is null
        Add s to δₙ
      Else
        For q ∈ δₙ do
          If sim(s,q)
            F(q) := F(q) + 1
            Flag := true
            Break
          End if
        End for
        If Flag is false
          Add s to δₙ
        End if
    End if
  End switch
End for
Return Δ
```

```
Algorithm 2  The second clustering

Input: Relation-representing words
collection α(A,B), First element α₁ of
α(A,B)
Output: Relation-representing words
collection R(A,B)
For αₖ ∈ α(A,B) do
  μ:= Sim(αₖ,α₁)
  Flag:= false
  For βᵢ ∈ ∇(A,B) do
    If μ == βᵢ.μ Add αₖ to βᵢ
      Flag := true
      Break
    End IF
  End for
  IF Flag == false
    Add β to ∇(A,B)
    Add αₖ to β
  End IF
End for
For βᵢ ∈ ∇(A,B) do
  Sort(βᵢ) by F(α)(α ∈ βᵢ) in descending
  Add βᵢ[0] to R(A,B)
End for
Return R(A,B)
```

Here q is denoted as one merged element in each group $\delta(A, B)$ and $F(q)$ as the frequency of q. The terms clustered into different groups are put into one collection demonstrated as $Q(A, B)$, where each $q \in Q(A, B)$ corresponding to a frequency $F(q)$. We rank the clustered items according to $F(q)$ and extract nouns and verbs α

in each q into a word collection $\alpha(A,B)$ with their frequency $F(\alpha)$. The words in $\alpha(A,B)$ may represent different relations between A and B. Here 妻子(wife) or 老婆 (wife) will be extracted as one element in $\alpha(A,B)$.

The Second Clustering Procedure.
For each $\alpha_k \in \alpha(A,B)$, we calculate the correlation value θ of α_k and α_1 using the Chinese word similarity measure based on How-Net [12] proposed in [13]. The correlation value is calculated by using the distance between the sememes in the semantic taxonomy.

The words which have a same correlation value are clustered into the same group β_i. The clustered word collection is denoted as $\nabla(A,B) = (\beta_1\beta_2 \cdots \beta_i \cdots \beta_n)$. The second clustering algorithm is described in Algorithm 2.

In our experiment, β_1={宝宝, 女儿, 孩子, 千金,后代} ({baby,daughter,child, daughter, descendant}),β_2={妻子,老婆,夫妇 }({wife,wife,couple}),β_3={洞房,新房 }({bridal chamber, bridal chamber}) , β_4={体育,篮球}({sports,basketball})are parts of the clustering result. From this we can see that different β_i represent different relation between Yao Ming and Ye Li. β_1, β_2 and β_3 indicate that they are couple while β_4 convince that they are all have some connection with basketball sport.

For each $\beta_i \in \beta(A,B)$, we select the word with the highest frequency in each group β_i, and we get the word collection R(A,B).

3.3   Extracting Target Words

For each $r \in R(A,B)$, the word pair (C,r) is input to a Chinese search engine (such as Baidu), using the preprocessing modular and two clustering procedures as shown in Section 3.2, the target word collection will be returned. For OTOSR, the relation-representing word r is single, and the result is a certain word D. For OTMSR, the relation-representing word r is single, the result set is a one-dimensional vector $(C,r) = \{D_1, D_2, \cdots D_n\}$. For MR, there is a group of relation-representing words $(r_1, r_2 \dots r_n)$ for the example word pair, the result set is a two-dimension matrix.

$$\theta = \begin{pmatrix} \Omega(C,r_1) \\ \Omega(C,r_2) \\ \vdots \\ \Omega(C,r_n) \end{pmatrix} = \begin{pmatrix} D_{11} & D_{12} & \cdots & D_{1p} \\ D_{21} & D_{22} & \cdots & D_{2q} \\ \vdots & \vdots & \ddots & \vdots \\ D_{n1} & D_{n2} & \cdots & D_{nm} \end{pmatrix}.$$

4   Experiment Evaluations

We manually create a dataset of 25 groups of test cases to evaluate the performance of our approach referring to the test set [1]. Most relation types of 25 groups of test cases are equal while the specific test cases are newly created because of the difference between Chinese and Japanese. There are 4 word pairs in each test group. The 25 groups of test cases are separated into three parts, the first part consisting 9 groups belongs to OTOSR, the second part having 11 groups belongs to OTMSR, 5 groups containing in the third part belong to MR. $Q = \{(A, B), C)\}$ is used as a query for all test cases. The rank of a returned term is evaluated by the Mean Reciprocal Rank (MRR) [1], the percentage of target words obtained in the top k, and the average number of Web accesses.

4.1   Test Dataset

Relations of all test cases in each test group are shown in Table 3. In Table 3, the second column represents the type of word A, while the third column shows the type of word B. The relations between A and B are shown in the fourth column. There are four word pairs $\{WP_1, WP_2, WP_3, WP_4\}$ in each group. By taking any two of the four word pairs, we can get six combinations of word pairs, they are {(WP1, WP2), (WP1, WP3), (WP1, WP4), (WP2, WP3), (WP2, WP4), (WP3, WP4)} respectively. Taking the order into consideration, we obtain another six test cases {(WP2, WP1), (WP3, WP1), (WP4, WP1), (WP3, WP2), (WP4, WP2), (WP4, WP3)} in each group. In total there are 300 test cases (25 groups with 12 test cases in each group). Table 4 shows some examples of test instance which contain four words A, B, C and D in each test group.

For OTMSR, we calculate the MRR and the rank of the target word with the highest frequency. For MR, we calculate the MRR and the rank of the target word with the highest frequency for the leading relation which is the main relation of word pair.

4.2   Experiment Results

Take three rows (3th, 10th and 24th) in Table 4 as examples, for the 3th row, four words are all persons and the relation between Li Yapeng and Li Yan is single. When we put Zhao Benshan to our approach, the unique target Zhao Yufang is returned. For the 10th row, the query is {(Cangshan,Garlic,Laiyang}, where Cangshan and Laiyang are two Chinese cities. The word Garlic is a famous local product of Cangshan, and our aim is to find all famous local products of Laiyang including Pear. For the 24th row, Yao Ming and Ye Li have more than one relation, they are a couple and they are both famous basketball players serving for the national team.

We summarize some rules of classifying three kinds of relation mappings: (1) If two entities have a persistent unique relation, they belong to OTOSR; (2) For OTMSR, an entity owns different kind of entities or an entity has many specific attributions; (3) For MR, there are several relations between two entities or an entity has different roles in a specific environment.

There must be a leading relation between two entities and a leading role of an entity for MR. Moreover, we notice that the leading relation is always OTOSR from the test result, and thus we can easily find out the target word for the leading relation. In Fig.4, only the target word which ranks first is shown, so the percentage of target word which rank at the top 1 is the highest. Take the 21th group as an example, Shi Yongxin is the Buddhist abbot of Shaolin Temple, in the same time he is a monk, and Shi Yongxin appears as the Buddhist abbot of Shaolin Temple in most cases, and thus we can get a better rank of target D when using Buddhist abbot as the relation.

Table 3. Relation Types of Test Cases in Three Groups

ID	Type of A	Type of B	Relation
1	Chinese literature	Author	A is written by B
2	Religion	Founder	B is the founder of A
3	Person	Person	A is the father of B
4	Island	Country	A is an island in B
5	Person	Person	A is the brother of B
6	Country	Currency	B is the currency of B
7	Imago	Embryo	B is a young form of A
8	Company	Person	B is the CEO of A
9	Person	Role	A is the role-player of B
10	Chinese City	Special local food	B is a special local food in A
11	Country	National sport	B is a national sport of A
12	Product	Raw material	A is made from B
13	Country	Local food	B is a famous local food in A
14	Chinese Province	Snack	B is a snack in A
15	Person	Person	B is apprentice of A
16	Person	Person	B is the star broker of A
17	Animal	Animal class	B belongs to A
18	Natural satellite	Planet	A is a natural satellite of B
19	Chinese Province	Oil field	B is an oil field in A
20	Movie	Person	B is the director of A
21	Chinese Temple	Buddhist abbot	B is Buddhist abbot of A B is a monk in A
22	Country	World heritage site	A is a world heritage site in B A is a tourist attraction in B
23	Country	City	B is the capital of A B is a city of A
24	Person	Person	A is the husband of B A is a teammate of B
25	Company	Company	B is acquired by A A is a competitor of B

Table 4. Examples of Test Cases

ID	A	B	C	D
1	Luo Guanzhong	Sanguoyanyi	Wu Chengen	Xiyouji
2	Buddhism	Sakyamuni	Christianity	Jesus
3	Li Yapeng	Li Yan	Zhao Benshan	Zhao Yufang
4	Bali Island	Indonesia	Okinawa	Japan
5	Huang Jiaqiang	Huang Jiaju	Jiang Wu	Jiang Wen
6	Korea	Won	Britain	Pound
7	Butterfly	Pupa	Frog	Pollywog
8	China Mobile	Wang Jianzhou	China Unicom	Chang Xiaobing
9	Lin Daiyu	Chen Xiaoxu	Shaseng	Yan Huaili
10	Cangshan	Garlic	Laiyang	Pear
11	Korea	Muay Thai	Japan	Sumo
12	Steamed rice	Rice	Chips	Potato
13	India	Flying cake	Japan	Sushi

Table 4. (*continued*)

14	Tibet	Buttered tea	Shandong	Pancake
15	Zhao Benshan	Xiaoshenyang	Hou Yaowen	Guo Degang
16	Cai Zhuoyan	Xu Hao	Cai Shaofen	Xu Yi
17	Whale	Mammalia	Ostrich	Birds
18	Mars	Phobos	Jupiter	Io
19	Shandong	Shengli	Heilongjiang	Daqing
20	Chibi	Wu Yusen	Mei Lanfang	Chen Kaige
21	BaimaTemple	Yin Le	Shaolin Temple	Shi Yongxin
22	Egypt	Pyramid	Indonesia	Borobudur
23	France	Paris	Britain	London
24	Dan Lin	Xie Xingfang	Yao Ming	Ye Li
25	Oracle	Sun	Google	YouTube

According to the above analysis, we can make a conclusion that a high MRR can be got if the useful information is rich and there is no noise for OTOSR, or if there is an obvious target word for OTMSR. We use frequencies of relation-representing words with different ranks to show the accuracy of the extracted relation words. There are many relation-representing words extracted from the four procedures described in Section 3.1. We show the frequencies of the relation-representing words which can get the best performance when they are used with the word C to search target words. As demonstrated in Fig.4, 41 percentages of the relation-representing words which are ranked in the top 1 and about 10 percentages are ranked after the top 20.

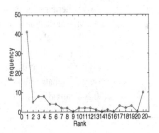

Fig. 4. The Frequencies of Relation-representing Words at Different Ranks

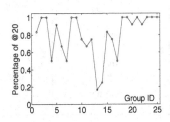

Fig. 6. Percentages of Target Words Rank Top 20 for Each Group

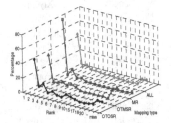

Fig. 5. The Percentages of Target Words at Different ranks for three kinds of relation mapping and ALL

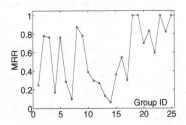

Fig. 7. MRRs of Target Word Rank Top 20 For Each Group

For the second and third parts, the experiment results are arrays or two-dimensional matrix. We calculate MRR and percentage of target words which rank before the top 20. Some result sets of OTMSR and MR examples are shown in Table 5.

Table 5. Results Examples for OTMSR and MR

Word C	Relation r	Target word 1	Target word 2	Target word 3
Sinkiang	Plant	Cotton	Flax	Grape
Rice	Make	Steamed rice	Rice cake	Rice flour
Tibetan	Special local product	Chinese caterpillar fungus	Tsampa	Saffron crocus
Zhang Yimou	Movie	Hero	Red Sorghum	Being alive
Mars	Satellite	Phobos	Deimos	
Lin Dan	Wife	Xie Xingfang		

According to relations of word pairs, we calculate the percentages of target words of different rank for the first, second and third part respectively. Then we combine the three parts together and calculate the percentage of target words at different ranks for all 25 groups, the results are shown in Fig.5. The four lines show that the percentages of the target words ranking on the first top 5 are higher than other groups. The performance of ALL is similar to OTOSR.

We calculate the percentages of the target words which rank top 20 and MRR value of target word for 25 groups of test cases, the results are shown in Fig.6 and Fig.7 respectively. From Fig.8 and 9, we can see that 2,3,8,9,18,19,21,23,24 and 25 get higher MRR values and their target words are all ranked before 20.

We also notice that MRRs of 1, 4, 6 and 7 groups are much lower, while MRRs of 2,3,5,8 and 9 groups are high. In the first group, our intention is to find out the famous island of different countries in the 4th group, but unfortunately there are a lot of noises such as the travelling advertisements. The reason why MRR of the 6th group is low is obvious: when the money is mentioned, a large group of irrelevant information such as exchange rate, policy and bond are involved in, it is hard for the engine to find the real relation that the dollar is the currency of US. For the 7th group, the corpus extracted from the web is limited which lower the accuracy. Based on the above analysis, we conclude that if the corpus has a large amount of noise or the relative phrases are little such as the seventh group, their MRRs are low.

For OTMSR, MRRs are almost low except the 18th and 19th groups. The reason is that there are many target words for OTMSR, and the number of different target words is almost the same. It is hard to find out desired items. The 19th group is a typical example of OTMSR. Shengli Oil field is located in Shandong, but there are still other oil fields in Shandong. It is noteworthy that the oil field we set is the biggest oil field in its province, so the result is also good.

Table 6. MRR and Percentage of Target Words at Different Rank

	MRR	@1	@5	@10	@20	Access
OTOSR	0.530	42.6	66.7	78.7	82.4	37.3
OTMSR	0.460	38.6	45.5	65.9	59.8	55.9
MR	0.850	78.3	98.3	98.3	98.3	74.6
ALL	**0.563**	**48.0**	**67.7**	**77.0**	**79.7**	**37.3**
CMB	0.474	40.0	57.3	61.3	62.3	40.9
CNJ	0.545	43.3	68.3	72.3	76.0	63.0

In Table 6, ALL represents the statistics of 300 test cases. CMB and CNJ are the methods proposed in [1]. We use MRR as the metric to evaluate the experiment result. Our method for OTOSR gets an MRR value of 0.530. Compared with the result of CNJ, the overall MRRs of our method is 0.563 which is higher than 0.545. On the percentage of target words at rank 1, our 48 percentage is also higher than the 43.3 percentage of CNJ method. For the other metrics, our method is higher than CNJ too.

5   Conclusion

Latent relational search plays a more and more important role in web search and artificial intelligence. In this paper we propose a method for Chinese Latent relational search based on Chinese lexical patterns for the first time. After a preprocessing procedure and two clustering procedures, the candidate word set of D can be obtained. Moreover, we classify three kinds of relation mapping between two word pairs, which are OTOSR, OTMSR and MR. Our approach achieves an MRR of 0.563, which shows its effectiveness compared with existing methods.

In this paper, we have taken both OTMSR and MR into consideration, but it is difficult to determine the kind of relation mappings automatically because of noise information and the accuracy of word similarity measurement. In the future, we will focus on the way to distinguish the three kinds of relation mapping automatically and try to raise the accuracy of our approach. Furthermore, we will expand our method from Chinese to cross-language.

Acknowledgement. This work is supported by a grant from the National High Technology Research and Development Program of China (863 Program) (No. 2011AA01A107), the grant from the Shanghai Science and Technology Foundation (No. 11511504000 and No. 11511502203).

References

1. Kato, M.P., Ohshima, H., Oyama, S., Tanak, K.: Query by analogical example: relational search using web search engine indices. In: Proc. of CIKM 2009, pp. 27–36 (2009)
2. Duc, N., Bollegala, D., Ishizuka, M.: Using Relational Similarity between Word Pairs for Latent Relational Search on the Web. In: Proc. of WI 2010, pp. 196–199 (2010)
3. Goto, T., Duc, N.T., Bollegala, D., Ishizuka, M.: Exploiting Symmetry in Relational Similarity for Ranking Relational Search Results. In: Zhang, B.-T., Orgun, M.A. (eds.) PRICAI 2010. LNCS, vol. 6230, pp. 595–600. Springer, Heidelberg (2010)
4. Duc, N., Bollegala, D., Ishizuka, M.: Cross-Language Latent Relational Search: Mapping Knowledge across Languages. In: Association for the Advancement of Artificial Intelligence, pp. 1237–1242 (2011)
5. Turney, P.D.: Similarity of semantic relations. Computational Linguistics 32(3), 379–416 (2006)
6. Turney, P.D., Littman, M.L.: Learning analogies and semantic relations. Technical Report ERB-1103, National Research Council, Institute for Information Technology (2003)

7. Bollegala, D., Matsuo, Y., Ishizuka, M.: Measuring the similarity between implicit semantic relations from the web. In: Proc. of WWW 2009, pp. 651–660. ACM (2009)
8. Veale, T.: The analogical thesaurus. In: Proc. of 15th Innovative Applications of Artificial Intelligence Conference, pp. 137–142 (2003)
9. Cao, Y.J., Lu, Z., Cao, S.M.: Relational Similarity Measure: An Approach Combining Wikipedia and WordNet. Applied Mechanics and Materials 55-57, 955–960 (2011)
10. ICTCLAS, http://ictclas.org
11. Che, W.X., Li, Z.H., Ting, L.: LTP: A Chinese Language Technology Platform. In: Proceedings of the Coling 2010:Demonstrations, Beijing, China, pp. 13–16 (2010)
12. HowNet, http://www.keenage.com/zhiwang/e_zhiwang.html
13. Liu, Q., Li, S.J.: Word Similarity Computing Based on How-net. Computational Linguistics and Chinese Language Processing 7(2), 59–76 (2002)
14. Falkenhainer, B., Forbus, K.D., Gentner, D.: The structure-mapping engine: Algorithm and examples. Artificial Intelligence 41(1), 1–63 (1989)
15. Turney, P.: The latent relation mapping engine: Algorithm and experiments. Artificial Intelligence Res. 33, 615–655 (2008)

Wikipedia Category Graph and New Intrinsic Information Content Metric for Word Semantic Relatedness Measuring

Mohamed Ali Hadj Taieb, Mohamed Ben Aouicha,
Mohamed Tmar, and Abdelmajid Ben Hamadou

MIRACL Laboratory, Sfax University, Tunisia
mohamedali.hadjtaieb@gmail.com, mohamed.benaouicha@irit.fr,
{mohamed.tmar,abdelmajid.benhamadou}@isimsf.rnu.tn

Abstract. Computing semantic relatedness is a key component of information retrieval tasks and natural processing language applications. Wikipedia provides a knowledge base for computing word relatedness with more coverage than WordNet. In this paper we use a new intrinsic information content (IC) metric with Wikipedia category graph (WCG) to measure the semantic relatedness between words. Indeed, we have developed a performed algorithm to extract the categories assigned to a given word from the WCG. Moreover, this extraction strategy is coupled with a new intrinsic information content metric based on the subgraph composed of hypernyms of a given concept. Also, we have developed a process to quantify the information content subgraph. When tested on common benchmark of similarity ratings the proposed approach shows a good correlation value compared to other computational models.

Keywords: Wikipedia, Information content, Semantic relatedness, Wikipedia category graph.

1   Introduction

Semantic relatedness (SR) measures how much two words or concepts are related using all types of relations between them [1]. Budantsky & Hirst, in their paper [2] show that semantic relatedness is more general than semantic similarity. In fact, two concepts or two words can be related but are not necessary similar like *cars* and *gasoline* cited in [3]. SR is used as a necessary pre-processing step to many Natural Language Processing (NLP) tasks, such as Word Sense Disambiguation (WSD) [4,5]. Moreover, SR constitutes one of the major stakes in the Information Retrieval (IR) [6-8] especially in some tasks like semantic indexing [9]. A powerful semantic relatedness measure influences on Semantic Information Retrieval (SIR) system. It exists in some information retrieval systems that support retrieval by *Semantic Similarity Retrieval Model* (*SSRM*) [38].

These methods are based on knowledge sources to assess the semantic relatedness degree between words and concepts. The knowledge sources can be unstructured

Y. Xiang et al. (Eds.): ICDKE 2012, LNCS 7696, pp. 128–140, 2012.
© Springer-Verlag Berlin Heidelberg 2012

documents or (semi-)structured resources such as Wikipedia, WordNet, and domain specific ontologies (e.g., the Gene Ontology). Research in [1,12,13] has shown that the accuracy of an SR method depends on the choice of the knowledge sources, without concluding an importance order between these knowledge sources.

Methods for computing SR use the semantic network features. Therefore, these methods can be classified according to path based, Information Content (IC) based, and statistical methods. Path based methods (Rada [21]; Wu and Palmer [22]; Hirst and St-Onge [18]; Leacock and Chodorow [4]) measure SR between concepts as a function of their distance in a semantic network, usually calculated using the path connecting the concepts following certain semantic links (typically is-a or known as hypernym/hyponym). IC based methods use the amount of information shared between the concerned concepts. It is usually determined by a higher level concept that subsumes both concepts in a taxonomic structure. (Resnik [26], Jiang and Conrath [23], Lin [24], Lord [14], Seco [27], Sebti [28], Pirro [25]). Statistical methods measure relatedness between words or concepts based on their distribution of contextual evidence. This can be formalized as cooccurrence statistics collected from unstructured documents or distributional concept or word vectors with features extracted from either unstructured documents [33-34] or (semi-)structured knowledge resources [10,13, 35-37].

Computing SR requires a knowledge resource about concepts or words. (Semi-)Structured knowledge sources organize explicitly the semantic knowledge about concepts and words and interlink them with semantic relations. There are some studies of SR, that include lexical resources such as WordNet Fellbaum [17], Roget's thesaurus [39], Wiktionary, and (semi-)structured encyclopedic resources such as Wikipedia. Earlier studies used WordNet such as (Hirst and St-Onge [18]; Jiang and Conrath [23]; Lin [24]; Leacock and Chodorow [4]; Resnik [26]; Seco et al. [27]; Wu and Palmer [22]). Wordnet is still a preferred knowledge source in recent works [35]. However, its effectiveness has a problem concerning its lack of coverage of specialized lexicons and domain specific concepts [1,13]). Wikipedia and Wiktionary are collaboratively maintained knowledge sources by volunteers and therefore may overcome this limitation. Wikipedia in particular, is found to have a reasonable coverage of many domains [20,36,38]). Recently, It has become increasingly popular in SR studies. Wikipedia grows exponentially and has probably become the largest collection of freely available knowledge.

Recent Wikipedia-based lexical semantic relatedness approaches have been found to outperform measures based on the WordNet graph. Recent work has shown that Wikipedia can be used as the basis of successful measures of semantic relatedness between words or text passages. Such methods stand out WikiRelate! [1], Explicit Semantic Analysis (ESA) [32], Wikipedia Link Vector Model (WLVM) [31] and WikiWalk [30].

This work exploits our novel IC metric based on hypernyms subgraph with Wikipedia categories graph as semantic taxonomic resource for measuring semantic relatedness between words. The rest of the paper is organized as follows. Section 2 focuses on the Wikipedia category system structure as semantic taxonomy. Section 3 describes the extraction categories strategy to determine the semantic relatedness between words using our novel IC metric with the Wikipedia category graph as semantic resource. Section 4 includes the detailed elaboration of our proposed metric. Section 5 includes the experiments and the evaluation to show the effectiveness of our proposed method. Concluding remarks and some future directions of our work are described in Section 6.

2   Wikipedia's Category System

In Wikipedia, at the bottom of each page all assigned categories are listed with links to the category page where an automatic index of all pages tagged with this category is shown. The number of categories has evolved from 165744 categories on 25 September 2006 to 337705 categories on March 12, 2008. For the current study, the English Wikipedia dump dated 12 March 2008 is downloaded[1] to form the category graph used as semantic resource [10].

Most of the categories are connected to a selected main category "*Contents*" that is superordinated to all other categories. Wikipedia categories and their relations do not have explicit semantics like known ontologies in computer science. The Wikipedia categorization system does not form a taxonomy like the WordNet "is a" taxonomy with a fully subsumption hierarchy, but only a thematically organized thesaurus. As an example *Computer systems* is categorized in the upper category *Technology systems* (is a) and *Computer hardware* (has part).

So the categories form a directed acyclic graph which can be taken to represent a conceptual network with unspecified semantic relations [10]. To use WCG as semantic resource for semantic relatedness computing we realize a cleanup for this network. Indeed, we start with the full categorization network consisting of 337705 nodes. We first clean the network from meta-categories used for management, e.g the categories under *Wikipedia administration*. We remove instead all those nodes whose labels contain any of the following strings: *Wikipedia, wikiproject, lists, mediawiki, template, user, portal, categories, articles, pages* and *stub*. Secondly, we browse the result graph to remove orphan nodes and we keep only the category *Contents* as root. The maximum depth of the graph passed from 291 before the cleanup to 221 for the result graph.

Moreover, in WCG a path linking two categories does not represent necessarily a semantic meaning. For example there exists a path connecting categories *video games* and *water pollution*. This property is a hard problem that decreases the results in the semantic relatedness task through the WCG. In the WCG each category is taken as a concept.

Figure 1 describes the steps followed in our system to exploit the WCG as semantic network for computing semantic relatedness between words. Indeed, firstly we must derive the WCG from a Wikipedia dump. After, using the two concerned words and the categories extraction strategy we can locate the sets of categories C_1 and C_2 assigned respectively to w_1 and w_2. The next step concerns the information content

---

[1] http://download.wikimedia.org/enwiki/20080312/
enwiki-20080312-pages-articles.xml.bz2

computing of each extracted category using its subgraph formed by its hypernyms as indicated for the category *Insects* in figure 2. In the next paragraph, we will detail the extraction strategy.

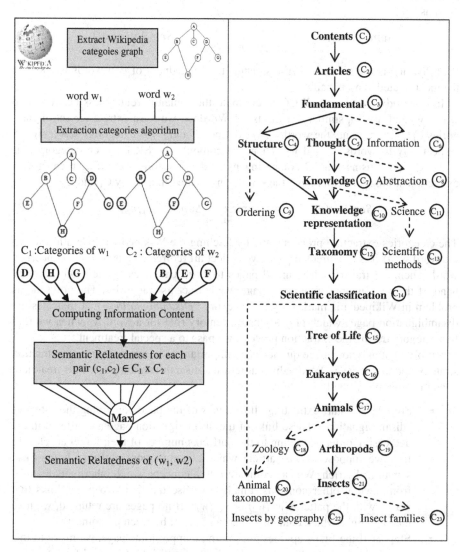

Fig. 1. Information flow for measuring semantic relatedness using the Wikipedia category graph

Fig. 2. An excerpt from Wikipedia category graph containing 23 categories. The solid arrows represent the information content subgraph of the category "*Insects*".

3   Categories Extraction Strategy

In WordNet, polysemous words may have more than one corresponding node in "is a" taxonomy, the resulting semantic relatedness of two words w_1 and w_2 can be calculated as:

$$SemRel(w_1, w_2) = \max_{(c_1,c_2) \in Syn(w_1) \times Syn(w_2)} SemRel(c_1, c_2) \qquad (1)$$

With $Syn(w_i)$ is the set of w_i synsets. Thus, the relatedness of two words is equal to the most related synsets pair.

In our study, we use the WCG to compute the semantic relatedness between two words w_1 and w_2. So, similar to synsets for Wordnet, we must extract the set of categories C_i that represents the word w_i. We define C_1 and C_2 as categories sets assigned respectively to words w_1 and w_2. Then, we compute the SR for each category pair $(c_k, c_j) \in C_1 \times C_2$ using our IC computing method. Therefore, we define a categories extraction strategy. In equation 1 the set of synsets are replaced by C_1 and C_2:

$$SemRel(w_1, w_2) = \max_{(c_1,c_2) \in C_1 \times C_2} SemRel(c_1, c_2) \qquad (2)$$

The categories extraction process starts by fetching the Wikipedia article allocated to the word w_i. If it is a redirected page, we collect all redirected pages of the concerned word. Then, we traverse all returned pages to extract their categories. On the other hand, if the page is not a redirected page, we extract its categories. The polysemous problem in Wikipedia is marked by the category "*Disambiguation*" that indicates the disambiguation pages which play a sense inventory role for a word w_i. when we find this category during the extraction process, we pass to a special treatment.

Resolving ambiguous page queries is an important task in our categories extraction strategy due to queries in Wikipedia that return a disambiguation page. This treatment contains principally the three following steps:

- **Step 1:** We start extracting all *outLinks* of the page containing the category "disambiguation". These links of the disambiguation page are ordered in the decreasing order according to the outLinks number of their target articles. In fact, we suppose that an article which contains more outLinks is the most semantically rich. We can compare it to a concept which inherits its features from several other concepts. Finally, we use the first two pages links that match with the patterns w_1 (w_2) or w_2 (w_1). If no pages are returned, we take the page links which contain w_2 and w_1 but not between parenthesis.
- **Step 2:** If the first step does not return an appropriate page, we move to this step. Indeed, using the same ordered set of outLinks extracted from the disambiguation page; we try to find links containing disambiguation tag in parenthesis.   It is enough to treat the two first turned pages to not overload the set of categories which influence negatively on the semantic relatedness computing.

- **Step 3:** If no pages are found in step2, we extract the categories from the corresponding articles of the two first links existing in the ordered set that contains the concerned word w_i.

Finally, if none of the categories are found, we take the categories of the article assigned to the first link existing in the ordered set. Once the whole of the categories is ready we calculate the IC of each pair $(c_1, c_2) \in C_1 \times C_2$. The IC calculation uses a novel metric that is detailed in the next paragraph.

4   The Information Content Metric

The IC concept was introduced for the first time by Resnik [26] following the standard argumentation of information theory. In Some previous works, was obtained the IC through <u>statistical analysis of corpora</u>, from where probabilities of concepts occurring are inferred. Other authors feel that the <u>taxonomic semantic network</u> can also be used as a statistical resource with no need for external ones. Their methods of obtaining IC values rest on the assumption that the taxonomic structure is organized in a meaningful and principled way. Following the standard argumentation of information theory [43], the IC of a concept c can be quantified as negative log likelihood: -log p(c). Notice that quantifying information content in this way makes intuitive sense in this setting: as probability increases, informativeness decreases, so the more abstract a concept is, the lower its information content is.

4.1   The Previous IC Methods

In this paragraph we present some previous IC methods like:

- The conventional way of measuring the IC of word senses is to combine the knowledge of their hierarchical structure from the semantic network with the statistics of their actual usage in a large corpus.

  The IC value is then calculated by negative log likelihood formula as follow:

$$IC(c) = -\log(p(c)) \tag{3}$$

Where c is a concept and p is the probability of encountering c in a given corpus. If sense-tagged text is available, frequency counts of concepts can be attained directly, since each concept will be associated with a unique sense. If sense tagged text is not available, it will be necessary to adopt an alternative counting scheme. Resnik [21] suggests counting the number of occurrences of a word type in a corpus, and then dividing that count by the number of different concepts/senses associated with that word. This value is then assigned to each concept. Resnik showed that semantic similarity depends on the amount of information that two concepts have in common, this shared information is given by the *Most Specific Common Abstraction* (MSCA) that subsumes both concepts.

Other works use only the taxonomy structure without making recourse to the external corpora.

- (Nuno Seco et al., 2004), in [27] they present a completely IC intrinsic measurement which is connected only to the hierarchical structure of WordNet. This minimizes the complexity treatment of a corpus in order to extract the probabilities from the concepts. The computation equation is the following:

$$IC(c) = 1 - \frac{Log(hypo(c) + 1)}{Log\ (max)} \tag{4}$$

Where *hypo(c)* is a function which returns the hyponyms number of a given concept and *max* is a constant which represents the maximum number of concepts.

- (Sebti et al., 2008) in [28] they present a new approach for measuring semantic similarity between words via concepts. Their proposed measure is a hybrid system based on using a new IC metric with the WordNet hierarchical structure. This method is based on the number of direct hyponyms of each concept pertaining to the initial way of the root until the target concept.

4.2   Our IC Metric

In this study, we present a novel IC metric that is completely derived from our works on WordNet [29, 40]. Indeed, in the "is a" hierarchical structure, a subordinate concept inherits the basic features from the superordinate concept and adds its own specific features to form its meaning. Thus, a concept is an accumulation of the propagated information from a distant ancestor to another less distant by adding specificities to each descendant. Therefore, a concept depends strongly on its direct parents and ancestors. Direct and indirect hypernym relations of a concept c from a subgraph which will take part in its IC quantification. The contribution of a concept pertaining to the hypernyms subgraph of a target concept depends on its depth. Figure 2 presents an example of hypernyms subgraph for the concept *"Insects"*. Indeed, this subgraph is formed by the category set $\{C_1, C_2, C_3, C_4, C_5, C_7, C_{10}, C_{12}, C_{14}, C_{15}, C_{16}, C_{17}, C_{19}, C_{21}\}$ (subgraph formed by solid arrows in figure 2).

In order to quantify the hypernyms subgraph of a given concept (for example IC(*Insects*)= 314.2565) we will present these notations:

Hyper(c): the set of direct hypernyms of the concept c. For example, $Hyper(C_{10})=\{C_4, C_7\}$.

Hypo(c): the number of concepts subsumed by the concept c. For example, $Hypo(C_7)=277508$ and $Hypo(C_{21})=552$ (in WCG).

SubGraph(c): set of all concepts pertaining to hypernyms subgraph modeling the IC of the concept c. For example subgraph(C_{21})= $\{C_1, C_2, C_3, C_4, C_5, C_7, C_{10}, C_{12}, C_{14}, C_{15}, C_{16}, C_{17}, C_{19}, C_{21}\}$.

Depth(c): the maximal depth of the concept c in the WCG taxonomy. For example, Depth(C_{21})=12.

AverageDepth (c): the average depth of the hypernyms subgraph of the concept c. It is computed as follows:

$$AverageDepth(c) = \frac{1}{|SubGraph(c)|} \times \sum_{c' \in SubGraph(c)} Depth(c') \qquad (5)$$

Where c' is a concept.

To compute the *IC (Categ)* where *Categ* is a category. $\forall$ $c \in SubGraph(Categ)$, we calculate a score:

$$Score(c) = \left(\sum_{c' \in Hyper(c)} \frac{Depth(c')}{Hypo(c')} \right) \times Hypo(c) \qquad (6)$$

Indeed, for each category $c' \in Hyper(c)$ we calculate a term as follows: $\frac{Hypo(c)}{Hypo(c')} \times$ $Depth(c')$ (term). *Score(c)* represents the contribution of each concept pertaining to *subgraph(Categ)* on *IC(Categ)*. Finally, we calculate the total IC of the concept *Categ* as follows:

$$IC(Categ) = \left(\sum_{c \in SubGraph(Con)} Score(c) \right) \times AverageDepth(Categ) \qquad (7)$$

As presented in the quantification process, the hyponyme number and the maximal depth of each concept are the important taxonomy properties used in our metric. Indeed, they indicate semantic richness for each concept pertaining to the semantic network. The average depth of the *subgraph(c)* gives information about the vertical distribution of *subgraph(c)*. When this value is large, it indicates an important features enrichment. This method is adapted to an "is a" taxonomy formed basically by hyponym/hypernym relations. But, the WCG cannot be taken as an "is a" taxonomy because it is not based only on hypernym/hyponym relations. In the experiment part we discuss the solution that we found to use this IC metric with the WCG as semantic knowledge.

5   Experiments and Evaluation

The Wikipedia based measure used in this article is implemented based on JWPL[2], a high-performance Java-based Wikipedia API. JWPL operates on an optimized database that is created from the database dumps available from the Wikimedia foundation. This allows for fast access to Wikipedia articles, categories, links, redirects, etc. A more detailed description of JWPL can be found in [19].

---

[2] http://www.ukp.tu-darmstadt.de/software

Following the literature on semantic similarity, we evaluate the performance by taking the Pearson product moment correlation coefficient r between the similarity scores and the corresponding human judgments. We perform an evaluation by computing semantic relatedness on three commonly used datasets, namely Miller & Charles' list of 30 noun pairs (M&C) [41] and the 65 word synonymy list for Rubenstein & Goodenough (R&G) [42] and Finkelstein (F) [6] dataset composed of 353 noun pairs. We use the Lin formula [24] coupled with our IC metric as follow:

$$Sim(c_1, c_2) = \frac{2 \times IC(\text{MSCA})}{IC(c_1) + IC(c_2)} \tag{8}$$

Then, we use the maximum function to extract the semantic similarity degree between these words:

$$Sim(w_1, w_2) = \max_{c_1 \neq c_2, (c_1, c_2) \in C1 \times C2} Sim(c_1, c_2) \tag{9}$$

Table 1. Results on correlation with human judgments of relatedness measures

M&C	R&G	F
0.40	0.34	0.38

Table 1 reports the scores obtained by computing semantic relatedness using formula (9). Considering that the experiment on benchmark datasets revealed a performance far lower than expected, we sought the problem in our semantic network (WCG). Indeed, many unrelated pairs received a score higher than expected, because of coarse grained over connected categories in the WCG. In fact, the WCG does not contain only is-a relations. So, a path which links two categories does not mean a strong semantically relation, for example we can find a path connecting the two categories *video games* and *food*. Therefore we chose to limit our search to a chosen depth when browsing the WCG. After an empirical study, we found that limiting the search improves the results. Indeed, the best maximum depth is 4. So, the subgraph formed by hypernyms is limited to the depth 4 and the function *hypo* detailed in our IC metric is limited to the same value. The analysis of results found with the value 4 shows that the problem of higher scores for unrelated pairs is resolved but another problem is appeared concerning the median values. Therefore, we chose to correct these values by computing semantic relatedness using the depth 5. In fact, when a computing value with depth 4   is inferior to a threshold (0.1 in our case), it will be replaced by the novel value found with the depth 5 if it exceeds 0.1. An excellent amelioration was noticed as indicated in table 2:

Table 2. Results on correlation with human judgments of relatedness measures after fixing depth limited search

M&C	R&G	F
0.73	0.65	0.61

In next experiments, we choose to compare the IC methods based on the taxonomy structure with our measure. Therefore, we use the IC-based formulas (Res: Resnik 1995 [26], Lin 1998 [24], and JC: Jiang and Conrath 1997 [23]).

Table 3. The coefficients correlation between human similarity judgments of the Finkelstein dataset and the suggested similarity measures

WCG								
Seco, 2004			Sebti, 2008			Our metric		
Res	Lin	JC	Res	Lin	JC	Res	Lin	JC
0.45	0.51	0.21	0.39	0.42	0.46	0.41	**0.61**	0.35
WordNet								
Seco, 2004			Sebti, 2008			Our metric		
Res	Lin	JC	Res	Lin	JC	Res	Lin	JC
0.32	0.38	0.35	0.30	0.34	0.33	0.45	0.58	0.41

Table 3 shows that our IC metric used with Lin formula and WCG as semantic resource outperforms all other measures using IC methods Seco [27] and Sebti [28]. Indeed, the result 0.61 exceeds the best result found with WCG for other methods (0.51, Seco and Lin formula). It allows us to have a profit of 0.10.

In order to show the effectiveness of our categories extraction strategy, we compared it to the strategy followed by Ponzetto [11]. In fact, the results presented in their paper [11] are 0.47 (M&C), 0.52 (R&G) and 0.49 (F) which proves the good performance of our extraction strategy. Moreover, the comparison with the WordNet shows an important advance for the WCG semantic network.

To improve the correlation value 0.61 found with Finkelstein dataset we chose to add a third set $C_{1,2}$ to sets C_1 and C_2 that contain the extracted categories from respectively word w_1 and w_2. The set $C_{1,2}$ contains the categories of the page (If it exists) which its title matches with the patterns "$w_1\ w_2$" , "$w_2\ w_1$", "$redirects(w_1)\ w_2$", "w_2

Table 4. Performance of semantic relatedness measures

Measure	Correlation with manual judgments	Reference
WordNet	0.33-0.35	[2]
Roget's thesaurus	0.55	[39]
LSA[3]	0.56	[44]
WikiRelate !	0.19-0.48	[1]
ESA	0.72	[32]
WLVM	0.69	[31]
Our method	**0.69**	

---

[3] LSA accessible plateform via http://lsa.colorado.edu/

redirects(w₁)", "*redirects(w₂) w₁*" and "*w₁ redirects(w₂)*". In Wikipedia a redirect link may provide information about synonyms, spelling variations, related terms and abbreviations. Afterwards, we apply the formula 9 on the sets $(C_1, C_{1,2})$ and $(C_2, C_{1,2})$ and take the maximum value as the semantic relatedness between w_1 and w_2. This idea leads to a remarkable improvement showed in the table 4.

The correlation 0.69 shown in table 4 can be compared directly to the results of other measures exploiting the same knowledge base (Wikipedia) and other semantic resources (WordNet and Roget's thesaurus). It is only slightly lower than the most accurate method ESA.

6   Conclusion and Future Work

This paper has demonstrated that performing our novel IC metric and a strategy for categories extraction over Wikipedia categories graph is a feasible and potentially fruitful means of computing semantic relatedness for words. Our Wikipedia-based relatedness measure proved to be competitive with other studies centered on Wikipedia features.

In future work, we will concentrate to make a thorough analysis of the WCG as an ontological source and compare it to the articles graph based on the hyperlink structure of Wikipedia. Moreover, we think about using the Wikipedia page content coupled with the category graph to study their contribution on semantic relatedness task.

References

1. Strube, M., Ponzetto, S.: WikiRelate! Computing semantic relatedness using Wikipedia. In: Proceedings of the 21st National Conference on Artificial Intelligence, AAAI (2006)
2. Budanitsky, A., Hirst, G.: Evaluating WordNet-based measures of semantic distance. Computational Linguistics 32(1), 13–47 (2006)
3. Resnik, P.: Semantic similarity in a taxonomy: An information-based measure and its application to problems of ambiguity in natural language. Journal of Artificial Intelligence Research 11, 95–130 (1999)
4. Leacock, C., Chodorow, M.: Combining local context and WordNet similarity for word sense identification. In: Fellbaum, C. (ed.) WordNet. An Electronic Lexical Database, ch. 11, pp. 265–283 (1998)
5. Han, X., Zhao, J.: Structural semantic relatedness: a knowledge-based method to named entity disambiguation. In: The 48th Annual Meeting of the Association for Computational Linguistics (2010)
6. Finkelstein, L., Gabrilovich, E., Matias, Y., Rivlin, E., Solan, Z., Wolfman, G., Ruppin, E.: Placing search in context: the concept revisited. ACM Transactions on Information Systems 20(1), 116–131 (2002)
7. Gurevych, I., Müller, C., Zesch, T.: What to be? – electronic career guidance based on semantic relatedness. In: Proceedings of ACL, pp. 1032–1039. Association for Computational Linguistics, Prague (2007)

8. Baziz, M., Boughanem, M., Aussenac-Gilles, N.: Evaluating a Conceptual Indexing Method by Utilizing WordNet. In: Peters, C., Gey, F.C., Gonzalo, J., Müller, H., Jones, G.J.F., Kluck, M., Magnini, B., de Rijke, M., Giampiccolo, D. (eds.) CLEF 2005. LNCS, vol. 4022, pp. 238–246. Springer, Heidelberg (2006)

9. Zargayouna, H.: Contexte et sémantique pour une indexation de documents semi-structurés. In: ACM COnférence en Recherche Information et Applications, CORIA 2004 (2004)

10. Zesch, T., Gurevych, I.: Analysis of the Wikipedia Category Graph for NLP Applications. In: Proceedings of the TextGraphs-2 Workshop, NAACL-HLT (2007)

11. Ponzetto, S.P., Strube, M.: Knowledge Derived From Wikipedia For Computing Semantic Relatedness. Journal of Artificial Intelligence Research 30, 181–212 (2007)

12. Zesch, T., Gurevych, I.: Wisdom of crowds versus wisdom of linguists: measuring the semantic relatedness of words. Journal of Natural Language Engineering 16, 25–59 (2010)

13. Zhang, Z., Gentile, A., Xia, L., Iria, J., Chapman, S.: A random graph walk based approach to compute semantic relatedness using knowledge from Wikipedia. In: Proceedings of LREC 2010 (2010)

14. Lord, P., Stevens, R., Brass, A., Goble, C.: Investigating semantic similarity measures across the Gene Ontology: the relationship between sequence and annotation. Bioinformatics 19(10), 1275–1283 (2003)

15. Patwardhan, S., Pedersen, T.: Using WordNet based context vectors to estimate the semantic relatedness of concepts. In: Proceedings of the EACL 2006 Workshop Making Sense of Sense, Italy (2006)

16. Völkel, M., Krötzsch, M., Vrandecic, D., Haller, H., Studer, R.: Semantic Wikipedia. In: Proceedings of the 15th International Conference on World Wide Web, Edinburgh, Scotland (2006)

17. Fellbaum, C.: WordNet: An Electronic Lexical Database. MIT Press, Cambridge (1998)

18. Hirst, G., St-Onge, D.: Lexical chains as representation of context for the detection and correction malapropisms. In: Fellbaum, C. (ed.) WordNet: An Electronic Lexical Database and Some of Its Applications, Cambridge, pp. 305–332 (1998)

19. Zesch, T., Müller, C., Gurevych, I.: Extracting lexical semantic knowledge from Wikipedia and Wiktionary. In: Proceedings of the Conference on Language Resources and Evaluation (LREC), Marrakech, Morocco (2008)

20. Zesch, T., Gurevych, I., Mühlhäuser, M.: Analyzing and Accessing Wikipedia as a Lexical Semantic Resource. In: Biannual Conference of the Society for Computational Linguistics and Language Technology, pp. 213–221 (2007)

21. Rada, R., Mili, H., Bicknell, E., Blettner, M.: Development and application of a metric on semantic nets. IEEE Transactions on Systems, Man and Cybernetics 19(1), 17–30 (1989)

22. Wu, Z., Palmer, M.: Verbs semantics and lexical selection. In: Proceedings of the 32nd Annual Meeting on Association for Computational Linguistics, pp. 133–138 (1994)

23. Jiang, J., Conrath, D.: Semantic similarity based on corpus statistics and lexical taxonomy. In: Proceedings of the International Conference on Research in Computational Linguistics, pp. 19–33 (1997)

24. Lin, D.: An information-theoretic definition of similarity. In: Proceedings of the Fifteenth International Conference on Machine Learning, pp. 296–304 (1998)

25. Pirro, G.: A semantic similarity metric combining features and intrinsic information content. Data and Knowledge Engineering 68(11), 1289–1308 (2009)

26. Resnik, P.: Using information content to evaluate semantic similarity in a taxonomy. In: Proceedings of IJCAI 1995, pp. 448–453 (1995)

27. Seco, N., Hayes, T.: An intrinsic information content metric for semantic similarity in WordNet. In: Proceedings of the 16th European Conference on Artificial Intelligence (2004)
28. Sebti, A., Barfrouch, A.A.: A new word sense similarity measure in WordNet. In: Proceedings of the International Multiconference on Computer Science and Information Technologie, Poland (2008)
29. Hadj Taieb, M., Ben Aouicha, M., Tmar, M., Ben Hamadou, A.: New Information Content Metric and Nominalization Relation_for a new WordNet-based method to measure the semantic relatedness. In: 10th IEEE International Conference on Cybernetic Intelligent Systems, University of East London (2011)
30. Yeh, E., Ramage, D., Manning, C., Agirre, E., Soroa, A.: WikiWalk: Random walks on Wikipedia for Semantic Relatedness. In: ACL Workshop"TextGraphs-4: Graph-based Methods for Natural Language Processing (2009)
31. Milne, D.: Computing Semantic Relatedness using Wikipedia Link Structure. In: Proc. of NZ CSRSC 2007 (2007)
32. Gabrilovich, E., Markovitch, S.: Computing Semantic Relatedness using Wikipedia-based Explicit Semantic Analysis. In: Proceedings of the 20th International Joint Conference on Artificial Intelligence (IJCAI), Hyderabad, India (January 2007)
33. Harrington, B.: A semantic network approach to measuring relatedness. In: Proceedings of COLING 2010 (2010)
34. Wojtinnek, P., Pulman, S.: Semantic relatedness from automatically generated semantic networks. In: Proceedings of the Ninth International Conference on Computational Semantics, IWCS 2011 (2011)
35. Agirre, E., Alfonseca, E., Hall, K., Kravalova, J., Pasca, M., Soroa, A.: A Study on Similarity and Relatedness Using Distributional and WordNet based Approaches. In: Proceedings of NAACL 2009 (2009)
36. Halavais, A.: An Analysis of Topical Coverage of Wikipedia. Journal of Computer-Mediated Communication 13(2) (2008)
37. Gouws, S., Rooyen, G., Engelbrecht, H.: Measuring conceptual similarity by spreading activation over Wikipedia's hyperlink structure. In: Proceedings of the 2nd Workshop on The People's Web Meets NLP: Collaboratively Constructed Semantic Resources (2010)
38. Varelas, G., Voutsakis, E., Raftopoulou, P., Petrakis, E., Milios, E.: Semantic similarity methods in WordNet and their application to information retrieval on the web. In: 7th ACM Intern. Workshop on Web Information and Data Management (WIDM 2005), Bremen, Germany (2005)
39. Jarmasz, M.: Roget's thesaurus as a lexical resource for natural language processsing. Master's thesis, University of Ottawa (2003)
40. Hadj Taieb, M., Ben Aouicha, M., Tmar, M., Ben Hamadou, A.: New WordNet-based semantic relatedness measurement using new information content metric and k-means clustering algorithm. In: Global WordNet Conference, Matsue, Japan (2012)
41. Miller, G.A., Charles, W.G.: Contextual correlates of semantic similarity. Language and Cognitive Processes 6(1), 1–28 (1991)
42. Rubenstein, H., Goodenough, J.: Contextual correlates of synonymy. Communications of the ACM 8(10), 627–633
43. Ross, S.: A first Course in Probability. Macmillan (1976)
44. Deerwester, S., Dumais, S., Furnas, G., Landauer, T., Harshman, R.: Indexing by latent semantic analysis. JASIS 41(6) (1990)

Nautilus: A Generic Framework for Crawling Deep Web

Jianyu Zhao[1,2] and Peng Wang[1,2]

[1] School of Computer Science and Engineering, Nanjing, China
[2] College of Software Engineering, Nanjing, China
pwang@seu.edu.cn

Abstract. This paper presents Nautilus, which is a generic framework for crawling deep Web. We provide an abstraction of deep Web crawling process and mechanism of integrating heterogeneous business modules. A Federal Decentralized Architecture is proposed to ensemble advantages of existed P2P networking architectures. We also present effective policies to schedule crawling tasks. Experimental results show our scheduling policies have good performance on load-balance and overall throughput.

Keywords: Deep Web, Crawler.

1 Introduction

Deep Web usually provides high quality and strong authority domain-specific information like products, books or movies for people. However, traditional crawlers are difficult to crawl and index deep Web databases, because that deep Web data can only be accessed via query forms but URLs. Beside, different deep websites have different query forms and their query results are also heterogeneous in structure. It also increases the difficulty of crawling deep Web.

Although there are some works discussing key issues of crawling deep Web in specific domains [1-5], there is no work to address how to integrate current techniques and feasible crawling methods for designing a generic deep Web crawler framework. This framework should be domain-independent and can handle large-scale deep Web data. This paper presents a generic deep Web crawler framework called Nautilus, which has following features: (1) Providing with complete infrastructure for crawling, like asynchronous networking facility, distributed controlling and storage system API support. (2) It is highly extensible for all modules and users can even add and distribute self-defined modules. (3) It is highly customizable by providing the Nemo description script to organize module for different crawling tasks. (4) It is highly scalable by providing federal decentralization architecture, which has high efficiency and load-balance property. (5) It has high availability, then all crawling tasks can be submitted on the fly without stopping existed running tasks.

2 Related Work

Crawling Web data is a classical topic. In recent years, researchers mainly focus on crawling policy[3][6][7], politeness and freshness[8][9]. However, to the best of our

Y. Xiang et al. (Eds.): ICDKE 2012, LNCS 7696, pp. 141–151, 2012.
© Springer-Verlag Berlin Heidelberg 2012

knowledge, although there are some crawler architectures, but none of them is focus on crawling deep Web.

SPHINX[10] is a crawler whose crawling policy is extensible by creating various text classifiers and crawling rules. Heritrix[11] provides abstraction of web crawling work flows to make modules for different crawling phases highly extensible, but not feasible for distributed crawling. Mercator[12] employs a central server as frontier to coordinate other crawlers and make crawler nodes scalable. However, its frontier stores information on hard drive, which can become a bottleneck when number of crawlers increases. UbiCrawler[13] is a decentralized crawler system providing improved consistent hashing function that satisfies balance property when scheduling tasks. However, its balance property is based on the assumption that documents need to be crawled in different hosts are of same amount, which is not satisfied by deep Web. These crawlers are not designed for crawling deep Web.

Luciano Barbosa et.al[3][4] presented useful works on crawling deep Web data sources. They implemented necessary components for seeking web forms and classified them by domains. An abstraction of data source crawling work flows is also presented. Other works mainly focus on keyword selection strategies. Siphon++[5] is a high efficient query selection method and provides architecture for retrieving data hidden behind deep Web. Alexandros Ntoulus et. al.[14] describes detailed strategies on selecting query, retrieving result pages and extracting data items. These works achieved good results on domains they focused on, but didn't provide a uniform crawler framework to make their methods scalable and reusable.

3   Nautilus Framework

3.1   System Architecture

Due to diversity and complexity of deep Web, crawling tasks for different hosts are heterogeneous in query submission and data extraction. In other words, every crawling task is intrinsically domain-specific. To make our framework more extensible, we need a domain-level abstraction for crawling. Thus we employ classic domain-driven design architecture to make existing modules more reusable. The system architecture is showed in Fig. 1.

Nautilus framework has four main components:

a. Domain Entity: Including task information, URL, forms and web documents. This component provides factory methods and prototypes for creating them.
b. Domain Logic: Including modules like downloaders, filters, extractors and classifiers, etc.
c. Nemo Description Loader: A component loads Nemo description, and integrate related modules to generate task prototype.
d. Infrastructure: Providing basic components such as asynchronous networking, multi-threading and task scheduling facilities.

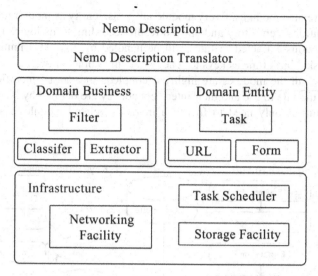

Fig. 1. Layered Architecture of Nautilus

Although deep Web crawling task is complex, no matter what it does such as finding data source, submitting query or updating particular page, it must experience some of following phases:

    a.   Preparation Phase: Determining keyword to be submitted.

    b.   Execution Phase: Downloading document of search results.

    c.   Post-Processing Phase: Filtering out error page, extracting features like links, forms or keywords, and classifying them according to task information.

    d.   Generation Phase: Generating new tasks from information extracted by previous phase. For instance, generate new tasks that submit keywords extracted from search results.

    e.   Persistence Phase: Store documents downloaded in execution phase and features generated in Post-Processing Phase.

Crawling task doesn't have to experience all of them or strictly following the order above, we'll see that Nemo Description will make customizing new task very convenient. In this way, if all steps of a crawling process can be classified in either of above phases, it can be abstracted as a crawling task.

Modules in different phases may have more or less dependencies to others. For example, result wrapper, error page filter and keyword filter all need to access result page retrieved by query submitter. When task itself is complex, those dependencies will make modules closely coupling together.

Noticing that every module may use some information previously retrieve in the same task, we employed classic blackboard architectural model. Each module retrieves and stores information in task entity, making it a repository.

Fig. 2 shows the Nautilus work flow on crawling deep Web searchable form, submitting keyword to form retrieved, extracting search results and storing them in database. All modules' names are stored like memo in task entity. A loader is responsible to instantiate related modules. Every module takes task entity as input, retrieve related resource in entities' repository and append result according to its logic. Tasks generated from previous extracted features will be handled by Task Distribution Facility, which take tasks' birth time as keys to schedule them to other crawlers.

In this way, all the modules are highly decoupled, and can be modified independently. What module to use and their inter-dependency are defined by Nemo Description, thus Nautilus only need to focus on invoking related modules and executing tasks.

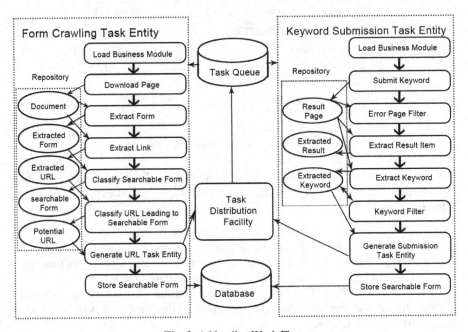

Fig. 2. A Nautilus Work Flow

3.2   Nemo Description

Due to complexity of deep Web crawling task, crawling data sources and different deep Web employ different set of modules and orders. Thus, we need a way to integrate related modules easily. Although our framework is implemented in Python with uniform interfaces, it is still not a good idea to require users to customize their tasks by writing Python code. First, since Nautilus provides plenty of modules for crawling deep Web, users may just want to describe what they need instead of writing code. Second, a convenient way for creating task is important in debugging and testing new modules. More important, asking users to write Python code may ruin uniform standard provided by Nautilus, which may affect existed modules' correctness. By these motivations, we present Nemo description, a markup language derived from XML to describe task information to Nautilus. Nemo description has eight different tags and five attributes. Their relationship can be described as follow:

Nemo = {Initialization, Task}

Initialization = {Executor, Initilize, Generate}

Task = {Parameter, Executor, Generate, name}

Executor = {module, Load, Result}

Generate = {prototype, Load}

Initialize = {module, name, Load}

Parameter = {Input}

Input = {name, type, default}

Load = {name}

Fig. 3. Elements and attributes of Nemo description

```
<Nemo>
  <Initialization>
     <Executor module="TextURLReader">
         <Load>seeds.txt</Load>
         <Result>seeds</Result>
     </Executor>
     <Generate prototype="URLTask">
         <Load>seeds</Load>
     </Generate>
  </Initialization>
  <Task name="URLTask">
     <Parameter>
         <Input name="URL" type="object" />
         <Input name="priority" type="object" default="birthtime" />
     </Parameter>
     <Executor module="HttpDowloader">
         <Load>URL</Load>
         <Result>Document</Result>
     </Executor>
     <Executor module="DuplicateDocumentFilter">
         <Load>Document</Load>
         <Load>URL</Load>
     </Executor>
     <Executor module="URLExtractor">
         <Load>Document</Load>
         <Result>urlset</Result>
     </Executor>
     <Executor module="DuplicateURLFilter">
         <Load>urlset</Load>
     </Executor>
     <Executor module="IPFilter" name="ipfilter1">
         <Load>urlset</Load>
     </Executor>
     <Generate prototype="URLTask">
         <Load>urlset</Load>
     </Generate>
     <Executor module="DBHTMLDumper">
         <Load>Document</Load>
     </Executor>
  </Task>
</Nemo>
```

Fig. 4. A Nemo description example

All identifiers beginning with capital letter are tags, the others are attributes. Tags in Nemo description can be classified in two categories: Entity and Action. Entity tags, including <Task>, <Executor> and <Parameter>, describe entities that can be instantiated in Nautilus, carrying key information of crawling. For example, <Task> tells Nautilus what modules to use in every phase and in what order to invoke them. The others are action tags, acting as glue, describe relationship among entities. For instance, <Generate> tells Nautilus what prototype and extracted information to integrate for generating new tasks.

A Nemo Description Loader will load XML file and translate it into task entities, then pass them to Task Distribution Facility for scheduling.

4   Control Policy

To increasing efficiency and throughput of Nautilus, we use multiple machines to execute tasks simultaneously. Since nodes will execute tasks independently, communicate with each other only when scheduling new tasks, P2P networking architecture is preferred. To make system work properly, Nautilus provides a mechanism coordinating every crawler node. We implement a controlling protocol based on Chord[15] to coordinate task redistribution.

4.1   Nodes Organization

Modern P2P networks have two main architectural styles: centralized and decentralized. A classic centralized architecture uses one or more servers to monitor key information of nodes, thus organizes the whole network properly. Centralized architecture makes P2P network easy to monitor and maintain, but fails when exchanging of key information is frequent because of heavy load on center server. Performance of center server will become bottle-neck of whole P2P system. Classic decentralized P2P system is featured by Chord, which supports key mapping and updating in logarithm complexity, thus is very suitable in real-time task scheduling. Also, logical topology of such system is self-organized, thus solves the problem of system performance's dependency on particular node. However, these systems are hard to monitor and maintain.

For a distributed crawler, we want to monitor the whole system and maintain every single crawler node. Simultaneously, the system should retain the property of high throughput and load-balance. Thus we ensemble advantages of centralized and decentralized architectures, making Nautilus a semi-decentralized architecture, called Federal Decentralization Architecture.

In Nautilus, there are two types of nodes: Coordinator and Crawler. Coordinator provides facility for user to monitor and maintain the whole system. Tasks generated from seeds are distributed from Coordinator to Crawlers. Also, Coordinator responses to sporadic task pulling requests from Crawlers to maintain load-balance property of the system.

Crawlers use Chord protocol to ensure stability of the system when some other Crawlers join or leave the network. Different from standard Chord protocol, every Crawler must register itself to Coordinator. In this way, Coordinator can easily keep track of work load information of every Crawler. As Coordinator itself is in the Chord loop, this modification won't affect properties of Chord protocol. On the other hand, every Crawler has weak relationship with Coordinator when join the system or send pulling request.

Thus, Coordinator acts as a federal government. It ensures the system is maintainable while keeps every Crawler running its tasks autonomously, and simultaneously alleviates the traffic head-off when coordinating the system.

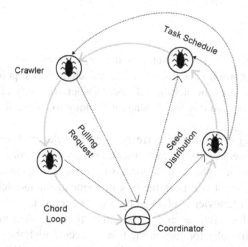

Fig. 5. Relation between Coordinator and Crawlers

4.2   Load Balancing Policy

In Nautilus, seeds are transformed into tasks and distributed to different Crawlers. Since resources related to tasks are different, numbers of new tasks generated from extracted data are different. To make the system load-balance, Nautilus employs following three task scheduling policies:

Policy 1. Conscientiousness: Once a task is retrieved from queue by a crawler, every phase in the task must be executed by this crawler. This makes fault tracing in system more convenient, and alleviates the traffic head-off when transmitting task entities containing large amount of intermediate information.

Policy 2. Pushing: Tasks generated by a Crawler will be scheduled to other Crawlers with their birth time as keys. Consistent Hashing[16] and SHA-1 guarantee these tasks will be distributed evenly in the system.

Policy 3. Pulling: If a Crawler has no task in its queue, it will pull half of tasks from queue of the Crawler who has the heaviest load at current time. Although tasks can be scheduled evenly among Crawlers, load-balance property cannot be guaranteed since tasks can be different from each other. A Crawler with easier task assignments may stay idle earlier than others, which violates load-balance property. Pulling policy requires heavy loaded Crawlers to share tasks with idle ones, making best uses of system resources.

In our implementation, Crawlers sends their load information to Coordinator sporadically. The Coordinator maintains a table to trace the load-balance condition of the system. Once the Coordinator receives load information indicating an idle Crawler, then it retrieves a Crawler with the heaviest load from load table, and asks this Crawler to send half of its tasks to the idle Crawler. This is equivalent to an idle Crawler pulling tasks from Crawler with the heaviest load. These policies guarantee load-balance property of the system.

4.3   Fault Tolerance

There are three types of errors that Nautilus may encounter: task execution error, queue information loss caused by Crawler crash, and change of topology of the network. Chord protocol ensures the stability of system when topology of the network is changed. For former two, Nautilus use redundant strategy to assure the completeness of information.

At the very beginning of each task, corresponding Crawler will record task information on hard drive. There are three cases that a task may go wrong: timeout in execution phase or persistence phase, post-processing error and Crawler crash. If the crawler encounters timeout, it will push the task in queue again and delete the backup on hard drive. In case of Crawler is blocked by remote server, task will be discarded and recorded in error log after several consecutive timeout. Post-processing error indicates the intrinsic difficulty for current modules to accomplish the task, so the task will be discarded and recorded in error log if this case happened. When a Crawler is crashed, Crawler can load the backup from hard drive and execute again after recovering. When the worst thing happened, we only have to redo one task.

Nautilus uses heap structure of Redis as task queue. Since all queue information is stored in Redis, it guarantees that even when Crawler is crashed, tasks are still retained on hard drive.

5   Experiments

We have implemented Nautilus and run it on real-world deep Web. In the experiments, we use 10 PC to organize Crawler network and an additional one to be Coordinator. These machines use 2.66GHz 2 Quad CPU and 4G memory. We select 12 websites as seeds from inner network of Southeast University and confine crawling procedure within these websites, which contains over 7000 documents.

We employ three settings in our experiment. In S-Even setting, we distribute seeds to different Crawlers evenly at the beginning, without using neither of Pushing nor Pulling policy; In S-Pushing Setting, Pulling policy is used in scheduling new tasks originally and during crawling process; S-Pulling setting uses both Pushing and Pulling policies during the process.

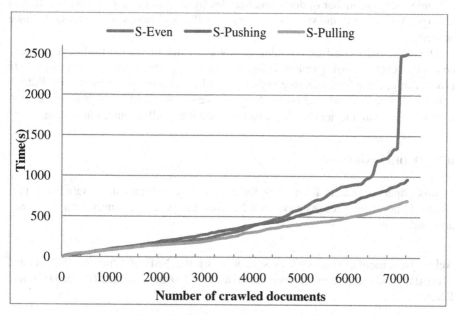

Fig. 6. Performance of different settings

Fig. 6 shows that time consumed by each setting in crawling fix number of documents from same seeds. S-Even consumed more time than others. Noticing that before 4000 documents are crawled, S-Even performed slightly better than S-Pushing.
However, when some Crawlers complete all their tasks and stay idle, throughput of
whole system goes down. Although S-Pushing and S-Pulling perform similar at the
beginning, tasks consumed more time (some big pages with full of links) make
throughput of system going down without use of pulling policy. Under S-Pulling, all
Crawlers are executing tasks at almost any time so that whole system can complete all
tasks in much shorter time.

Table 1. Number of document crawled under different settings

	S-Even	S-Pushing	S-Pulling
PC1	1821	573	728
PC2	1185	882	779
PC3	793	652	556
PC4	282	654	636
PC5	41	865	904
PC6	1623	1163	718
PC 7	542	939	737
PC 8	548	368	981
PC 9	182	528	678
PC 10	370	763	670
σ	612.08	231.23	124.96

Table 1 shows number of document crawled by each of the ten PCs under different settings. According to the standard deviation, S-Pulling obtains the best load-balance property.

The reason why consistent hashing cannot guarantee the global load-balance property is that every crawling task is different. Although pushing policy tries to distribute tasks evenly, some Crawlers received easier tasks will stay idle in short time. Pulling policy will guarantee when this case happen, idle Crawler will "pull" half of the tasks from Crawler with the heaviest load, making best use of all resources in system.

6   Conclusion

In this paper, a generic framework for crawling deep Web called Nautilus is presented. Experimental results show that Nautilus has good performance on efficiency and load-balance.

Acknowledgments. This work is supported by the NSF of China (61003156 and 61003055) and the Natural Science Foundation of Jiangsu Province (BK2009136 and BK2011335).

References

1. Jayant, M., David, K., Łucja, K., et al.: Google's Deep Web crawl. PVLDB 1(2), 1241–1252 (2008)
2. Wei, L., Xiaofeng, M., Weiyi, M.: ViDE: A Vision-Based Approach for Deep Web Data Extraction. IEEE Transactions on Knowledge and Data Engineering 22(3), 447–460 (2010)
3. Luciano, B., Juliana, F.: An adaptive crawler for locating hidden-Web entry points. In: Proceedings of the 16th International Conference on World Wide Web (2007)
4. Luciano, B., Juliana, F.: Searching for Hidden-Web Databases. In: Proceedings of WebDB (2005)
5. Karane, V., Luciano, B., Juliana, F., Altigran, S.: Siphon++: a hidden-web crawler for keyword-based interfaces. In. In: Proceedings of the 17th ACM Conference on Information and knowledge Management (2008)
6. Jon, K.: Authoritative sources in a hyperlinked environment. J. ACM 46(5), 604–632 (1999, 2001)
7. Soumen, C., Kunal, P., Mallela, S.: Accelerated focused crawling through online relevance feedback. In: Proceedings of the 11th International Conference on World Wide Web (2002)
8. Junghoo, C., Hector, G.M.: Effective page refresh policies for Web crawlers. ACM Trans. Database Syst. 28(4), 390–426 (2003)
9. Ricardo, B.Y., Carlos, C.: Balancing volume, quality and freshness in web crawling. In: Soft Computing Systems - Design, Management and Applications, Santiago, Chile (2002)
10. Robert, M., Krishna, B.: SPHINX: a framework for creating personal, site-specific Web crawlers. Computer Networks and ISDN Systems 30, 119–130 (1998)

11. Mohr, G., Kimpton, M., Stack, M., Ranitovic, I.: Introduction to Heritrix, an archival quality Web crawler. In: The 4th International Web Archiving Workshop, Bath, UK (2004)
12. Allan, H., Marc, N.: Mercator: A scalable, extensible Web crawler. World Wide Web 2(4), 219–229 (1999)
13. Boldi, P., Codenotti, B., Santini, M., Vigna, S.: UbiCrawler: a scalable fully distributed Web crawler. Softw. Pract. Exper. 34(8), 711–726 (2004)
14. Ntoulas, A., Pzerfos, P., Junghoo, C.: Downloading textual hidden web content through keyword queries. In: Proceedings of the 5th ACM/IEEE-CS Joint Conference on Digital Libraries (2005)
15. Ion, S., Robert, M., David, K., Frans Kaashoek, M., Hari, B.: Chord: A scalable peer-to-peer lookup service for internet applications. SIGCOMM Comput. Commun. Rev. 31(4), 149–160 (2001)
16. David, K., Eric, L., Tom, L., Rina, P., Matthew, L., Daniel, L.: Consistent hashing and random trees: distributed caching protocols for relieving hot spots on the World Wide Web. In: Proceedings of the Twenty-Ninth Annual ACM Symposium on Theory of Computing (1997)

Retrieving Information from Microblog Using Pattern Mining and Relevance Feedback

Cher Han Lau[1], Xiaohui Tao[2], Dian Tjondronegoro[1], and Yuefeng Li[1]

[1] Queensland University of Technology,
2 George St, Brisbane, QLD 4000
[2] University of Southern Queensland,
West Street, Darling Heights QLD 4350

Abstract. Retrieving information from Twitter is always challenging due to its large volume, inconsistent writing and noise. Most existing information retrieval (IR) and text mining methods focus on term-based approach, but suffers from the problems of terms variation such as polysemy and synonymy. This problem deteriorates when such methods are applied on Twitter due to the length limit. Over the years, people have held the hypothesis that pattern-based methods should perform better than term-based methods as it provides more context, but limited studies have been conducted to support such hypothesis especially in Twitter. This paper presents an innovative framework to address the issue of performing IR in microblog. The proposed framework discover patterns in tweets as higher level feature to assign weight for low-level features (i.e. terms) based on their distributions in higher level features. We present the experiment results based on TREC11 microblog dataset and shows that our proposed approach significantly outperforms term-based methods Okapi BM25, TF-IDF and pattern based methods, using precision, recall and F measures.

1 Introduction

Social media services such as Flickr, Youtube and Facebook has become the major user-generated media platform. In particular, Microblog has become an important tool for users to share information from personal updates, question answering [1], news [2] to general babbling [3]. Of all, Twitter achieves greatest success attracting over 200 million registered users and publishing 50 million tweets per day. While twitter has been used predominantly for sharing personal updates, it has been used for stock forecasting [4], event monitoring [5] and natural disasters [6]. Twitter also plays an important role in critical situations where reliable communication is not available such as 2009 Iranian election [7] and Mumbai terrorist attack [8].

Retrieving information from tweets is a challenge, as tweets are unstructured, ungrammatical and prone to noise. Word limit of 140 characters further causes users to employ different strategies (e.g. abbreviation, slangs, emoticon) to compress information. Huge volume of tweets delivered makes it impossible for

Y. Xiang et al. (Eds.): ICDKE 2012, LNCS 7696, pp. 152–160, 2012.
© Springer-Verlag Berlin Heidelberg 2012

humans to read and distil useful information. Therefore, a system to retrieve information effectively from Twitter is necessary.

Preliminary work in twitter retrieval exploiting its unique features includes the understanding of search type [9] and hashtags [10] to improve search quality. However, these methods are not always reliable and require extensive amount of pre-processing and computation. Other attempts include dealing with sparsity in short text [11] and using query expansion to capture more context for query, but performance of these methods is average.

Previous IR research has suggested that pattern based models using closed sequential pattern in text classification achieved better results compared with term-based approaches. However, extracting relevance features from microblogs. Firstly is the low-support problem, long patterns are more topic specific the support is relatively low. If minimum support for pattern mining is lowered, more noisy patterns will then be captured. Another issue is that sequential pattern models such as [12] are suitable for static and full length documents, but in dynamic and short documents such as tweets, the sequence will limit the possible combination that can be generated and affecting the support. Lastly, a highly frequent pattern by nature is a general and short pattern since it appears frequently. Therefore, it does not carry much unique semantics. The challenge is to use discovered patterns to evaluate features weight in the training set effectively and accurately .

This research explores topical feature discovery in Twitter from both data mining and information retrieval perspectives. An topical feature extraction algorithm from tweets using pattern mining technique is presented. The algorithm assign weight to the terms and word pairs based on the term distribution in high level feature space. Performance of the algorithm is evaluated against TREC 2011 Microblog track dataset and experiemnt results show that our method outperforms existing term-based solutions.

2 Related Work

Users have been searching information on twitter for its large amount of information and timeliness response. Users search twitter for answers, events and news development [1,9]. However, search interface provided by twitter is limited to keyword search and only ranked post by recency. Therefore, users are unable to explore the search results and may get lost and become frustrated eventually due to information overload. [13].

The main challenge in retrieving tweets is the language used in twitter. Different novel language have been developed and emerged as a standard among the users community. Users can use *username* to refer to another user, *#hashtag* to identify topical concepts and forward a tweet from another user to own followers using *retweet*. The 140 character word limit causes users to employ different strategies such as slang, emoticon and abbreviations to compress more information in tweets.

Microblogs can be considered as a different type of media based on users' information needs need [14]. While general web users search the web to locate information about facts, microblog users seek twitter for timely information (news, trending topics, events) and topical information (e.g. person, location, organisation). Users often perform search task in Twitter to answer their information.

Many existing Information Retrieval (IR) models, in particular term based model are gaining popularity for twitter search task. This is because term based models are easy to be implemented and less computational expensive. However, there are few problems exists in term based approach when being applied to microblog. Due to the length limit, there are much less words in a tweet and it does not provide sufficient contextual information as term based methods rely heavily on the statistical information. Term based model are also very sensitive to noise and affected by synonymy (multiple terms referring to same meaning) and polysemy (single term referring to multiple meanings).

Most twitter retrieval models are term-based such bag-of-words (BOW) model. Each tweet is considered as a collection of pre-processed (e.g. normalized, stemmed) weighted terms. This approach is suitable for microblog as it is reliable and does not required advanced computation. However, it is very sensitive to noise [11] due to word limit in that causes users to use different terms and abbreviations, which degrades the retrieval performance. Different novel language and standards have also emerged and becoming a standard within the community. A tweet can reference another user using @username mention, to identify topics using #hashtag, forward a tweet from another user to their own followers using retweet. Social network can be identified using following(friends) and follower(fans) relationship. Twitter also provide different meta such as time, entities and location to provide information about the tweet.

Hashtag is used to represent topics of interest (#greysanatomy), event development (#emmy) and trending issues (#carbontax). Hashtag is also used for relevance feedback and query expansion [10]. The statistics of tweets published, followers count and following-followers ratio can be used to estimate the authority of users to rank and improve the retrieval result [17].

Another problem in microblog retrieval is the understanding of user query. User queries are always short and unable to represent their information needs. For instance, query expansion is used to capture more relevant terms from the initial query [15]. Upon retrieving the results by querying, the next step is to rank the results. Since timeliness is important in Twitter, majority of the approach just choose to order the results by time in reverse order. This will only provided the latest result but no guarantee the most interesting tweet will appear in top results.

Previous studies have demonstrated that microblog retrieval performance can be improved by expanding the modifying the query and using different feature representation. Therefore, in this study we present a microblog retrieval model using higher level feature extraction using pattern mining and query expansion for the following reasons: (i) Query expansion enrich the initial query with more relevant terms, which helps to improve the search performance. (ii) Pattern mining extract high level feature with better representation of the content and the freedom of not restricted by the limitation from n-gram models and provides more context than the term level.

This section summarised key works in microblog IR. While many of them are in its early stage, but the preliminary results are promising. Some problems have been studied extensively traditional in IR field before, but the technical difficulty when applied in microblog remained a challenge due to the nature characteristic of microblogs.

3   Feature Extraction and Weighting

Twitter search is topic specific containing keywords and named entity, therefore it is important to consider both important terms and pattern feature in our algorithm. Vector Space Model (VSM) is used to represent terms feature. A tweet document d contains a set of terms where $d = \{t_1, t_2, t_3, ..., t_n\}$, the weight w of term t in d is the product of the average term frequency with proportion to the length of tweet and the logarithmic inverse document frequency, as shown in Equation 1.

Frequent Pattern Mining (FPM) is used extract closed pattern, which is a pattern with a occurrence (*support*) greater than the preset minimum support (*min_sup*). A closed pattern is the longest pattern of size n with same support of the pattern of size $n - 1$.

Let D be a tweet collection where $D = \{d_1, d_2, d_3, ..., d_n\}$, each tweet d contains terms t where $d = \{t_1, t_2, t_3, ..., t_n\}$. T denotes all the terms in the collection D. We define termset X be a set of terms from T, $coverset(X) = \{d|d \in D, X \subseteq d\}$. Its support $sup(X) = |coverset(X)|$. A termset X is called a "frequent pattern" if $sup \geq min\_sup$, a pre-defined minimum support.

A pattern $p = \{t_1, ..., t_n\}$ is an unordered list of terms, $p_2 = \{x_1, \cdots, x_i\}$ is a sub-pattern of another pattern $p_1 = \{y_1, \cdots, y_j\}$, and $p_2 \subset p_1$. With that, we can say that p_2 is a sub-pattern of p_1 and p_1 is super-pattern of p_2. A frequent pattern is defined as "*closed pattern*" if not $\exists$ any super-pattern X_1 of X such that $sup(X_1) = sup(X)$, and $P = \{CP_1, CP_2, \cdots, CP_n\}$ denotes the closed frequent pattern for all tweets.

Traditionally, terms weight are calculated based on its appearance in document and its occurrence across the document collection, to eliminate the long tail effect. This is insufficient in short text document because occurrence of each term in a document is nearly the same. Therefore, we develop equations to deploy high-level feature (pattern) over low-level feature (term) using term support based on their appearance in patterns. Patterns are extracted using *Apriori* property to reduce the search space.

$$w_{t,d} = \frac{tf_{t,d}}{|d|} \times \log(\frac{N}{df_i}) \tag{1}$$

4   Query Expansion

Query expansion is a technique to expand initial query with more related terms. It has long been suggested as an effective way to address short query and word mismatching problems in IR [18]. Query expansion techniques can be classified into two types based on the source of information into global analysis and local analysis. Global analysis utilise corpus wide statistic (e.g. co-occurrences of terms pair), and expand the results using terms pair with the highest similarity. Performance of approach are generally robust in static document collection but require considerable amount of resources when the data collection is huge, and not suitable in fast changing dataset such as tweets.

Different from global analysis, local analysis requires only some initially retrieved documents to expand the query. One well-know local analysis technique is relevance feedback, which reformulate the query based on retrieved documents relevancy. This approach achieve very good performance when sufficient correct relevance judgement is provided, however, manual effort are always required. To overcome the difficulty of manual judgement, pseudo-relevance feedback (PRF) is commonly adopted. The basic idea of PRF assumes a top k ranked result is relevant and extract expansion terms from those documents only. The benefits of using PRF is that it improves retrieval performance without external interaction [19], which is ideal for twitter retrieval since it is realistically difficult to perform multi-iteration relevance feedback performed by human. The query expansion is done using a Vector Space Model (VSM) with TF-IDF weighting. Given an initial query q, we first retrieve 100 relevant tweets and rank it by time in reverse order. The top 10 tweets are then selected as the training set Ω, and all the terms in Ω are used to expand q and form Q.

4.1   Similarity Metric

In vector space model, all queries and documents are represented as vectors in dimensional space V, where V represents all distinct terms in the collection. The similarity of documents is determined by the similarity of their content vector. This has led to three problems: (i) Low frequency terms in the collection will be assigned relatively high weight and (ii) The similarity score is low due to the absence of terms in query, and (iii) semantically related terms that does not appear in query will not be retrieved. Therefore, cosine similarity will not be used as the similarity and instead Jaccard Index will be used. Equation denotes the similarity function between a query q and a tweet d:

$$Sim(q, d) = \frac{|q \cap d|}{q \cup d} \qquad (2)$$

5   Evaluation

TREC Microblog Dataset 2011 is used to test the effectiveness of our proposed model. The dataset contains 16 millions tweets, with about 5 million English tweets, collected from January 23, 2011 to February 08, 2011. The dataset that covers wide range of topics and information superbowl, BBC staff cut and Egyptian riot. TREC 2011 provides 50 topics manually picked by human assessors of the National Institute of Standards and Technology (NIST). This dataset is reliable and stable to evaluate the model [20]. To avoid bias in experiments, all metadata and tweet specific entities (e.g. geolocations) are ignored. The documents are treated as plain text documents, pre-processed by standard stop-words list and stemmed using Porter Stemming algorithm.

Next, we develop different weighting strategies. By evaluating term supports based on their appearances in patterns. The evaluation of term supports (weights) in this paper is different from term-based approaches. For a term-based approach, the evaluation of a given term weight is based on its appearances in tweets. In this research, terms are weighted according to their appearances in discovered patterns.

5.1 Features Weighting

In order to evaluate the effect of patterns and terms, we use the following strategies to test our algorithm. RUN1 is our baseline benchmark using terms frequency without weighting.

Pattern Weighted Terms (RUN2). *Hypothesis* A term t_i is more important than t_j if t_i appears in more pattern than t_j and t_i is more important than t_j if it appears in more frequently appear pattern. The weight $w(t)$ can be calculated by aggregating the support of patterns where t appear, as below:

$$w(t) = \sum_{i=1}^{|P|} |\{p|p \in P_i, t \in p\}| \tag{3}$$

Terms Weighted Patterns (RUN3). *Hypothesis* A pattern p_i is more important than p_j if aggregated weight of $t \in p_i$ are more important than aggregated weight of $t \in p_j$. The weight $w(p)$ can be calculated by aggregating the term frequency for all terms in p,

$$w(p) = \sum_{t \in p} w(t) \tag{4}$$

Weighted Terms and Pattern (RUN4). If the hypothesis from 5.1 and 5.1 hold, term-based feature can be obtained using PWT and topical features can be extracted by pattern mining using TWP. With that, we can deduce that if a tweet is represented by both feature, it will represent both term and topic feature, therefore:

$$t_{term} = \{(t_1, tw_1), (t_2, tw_2), \cdots, (t_n, tw_n)\}$$

$$t_{pattern} = \{(p_1, pw_1), (p_2, pw_2), \cdots, (p_n, pw_n)\}$$
$$t = t_{term} \cup t_{pattern}$$

5.2 Results and Discussions

This section we will discuss our evaluation from both TREC wide results and intra-run results. The TREC wide results describe and compare the performance of our system compared to other system. Intra-run results detail the characteristics of our runs and the pros and cons.

Table 1. Performance for all relevance

RunID	MAP	R-PREC	P@30
Run1	0.0753	0.1114	0.1347
Run2	0.0486	0.0846	0.1694
Run3	0.0673	0.1191	0.2034
Run4	0.0486	0.1040	0.1973

Table 2. Performance for highly relevance

RunID	MAP	R-PREC	P@30
Run1	0.0797	0.0983	0.0374
Run2	0.0419	0.0566	0.0424
Run3	0.0646	0.0846	0.0556
Run4	0.0353	0.0513	0.0515

Table 1 and Table 2 shows the Mean Average Precision (MAP), Recall Precision (R-PREC) and the official Precision when 30 tweets are retrieved (P@30) for All Relevance (ALLREL) judgement and Highly Relevant (HIGHREL) judgement. ALLREL includes 49 topics and HIGHREL includes only 30 topics contain highly relevant tweets, on the TREC relevance scale. Topic 50 is removed from the evaluation due to insufficient relevant tweets. Table ?? shows the topics which our system did not perform well.

The highest MAP score in RUN1 is 1.00 for topic MB018 - *"William and Kate fax save-the date"*, where MB040 - *"Beck attacks Piven"* topped RUN2 and RUN3 with MAP score of 0.25 and MB012 - *"Assange Nobel peace nomination"* scored the highest with 0.30 in RUN4. In overall, RUN1 with terms frequency only performs the best and performance of RUN2 – Weighted Terms (PWT) performance is the worst. Weighted Pattern (TWP) is acceptable however it does not improve the performance of PWT as we expected. The reason behind why PWT performance is worst might be caused by the amplification effect of the original terms only (TO) approach.

In P@30 measurement, WTP performs similarly to PWT, and both significantly outperformed both term-based approach. The highest precision score in RUN1 is 0.67 for topic MB020 - *"Taco Bell filling lawsuit"*, and topic MB009 - *"Toyota Recall"* achieved best result in RUN2, RUN3 and RUN4 with precision score 0.73.

6   Conclusion and Future Work

This paper presented a feature extraction and query epxnaion to address problem in microblog retrieval. The work presented in this paper investigated four different settings to evaluate the effectiveness of term-based and pattern-based feature, for use in microblogs retrieval. We addressed the short user query problem by using pseudo-relevance feedback to expand initial query and apply different weights for different features. A similarity metric is recommended to consider only the terms appear in query, to prevent query result to be affected by non-existed terms. While the retrieval performance are still far from ideal when compared with performance of traditional IR in full length document, our work has definitely shed some light in microblogs retrieval field.

In our approach, we considered pattern mining as a key technique to extract topical feature in a natural way. Important terms are always together to indicate importance. In addition, we considered different weighting scheme to experiment the validity of our hypothesis and the results agree with our hypothesis that topical features is good for microblogs.

The future research direction of microblog is exciting and vibrant. Network analysis and trend detection models that exploit various twitter characteristics, will be beneficial from the large volume of tweets. Data mining techniques (e.g. pattern mining, association rules) can be applied to further improve the retrieval performance. Lastly, high-level semantic feature such as sentiment analysis and entity detection can then be applied in different real-world applications, which will fully unleashed the power of microblog. In the future, we plan to include more twitter related characteristics to improve the result. Another key consideration is also whether or not we should change the algorithm to improve the quality of pseudo-relevance tweets returned. We do not intend to change the feature extraction methodology as we want to keep it as simple and straightforward as possible, however the model can be further improved to achieve higher retrieval performance.

References

1. Efron, M., Winget, M.: Questions are content: A taxonomy of questions in a microblogging environment. Proceedings of the American Society for Information Science and Technology 47(1), 1–10 (2010)
2. Kwak, H., Lee, C., Park, H., Moon, S.: What is twitter, a social network or a news media? In: Proceedings of the 19th International Conference on World Wide Web, pp. 591–600. ACM (2010)
3. Boyd, D., Golder, S., Lotan, G.: Tweet, tweet, retweet: Conversational aspects of retweeting on twitter. In: Proceedings of the 2010 43rd Hawaii International Conference on System Sciences, HICSS 2010, pp. 1–10. IEEE Computer Society Press, Washington, DC (2010)
4. Asur, S., Huberman, B.A.: Predicting the future with social media. In: 2010 IEEE/WIC/ACM International Conference on Web Intelligence and Intelligent Agent Technology, pp. 492–499. IEEE (2010)
5. Shamma, D.A., Kennedy, L., Churchill, E.F.: Tweet the debates: understanding community annotation of uncollected sources. In: WSM 2009: Proceedings of the First SIGMM Workshop on Social Media, pp. 3–10. ACM, New York (2009)
6. Sakaki, T., Okazaki, M., Matsuo, Y.: Earthquake shakes twitter users: real-time event detection by social sensors. In: WWW 2010: Proceedings of the 19th International Conference on World Wide Web, pp. 851–860. ACM, New York (2010)

7. Gaffney, D.: #iranelection: Quantifying online activism. In: Web Science Conference, Raleigh, NC, USA (April 2010)
8. Oh, O., Agrawal, M., Rao, H.: Information control and terrorism: Tracking the mumbai terrorist attack through twitter. In: Information Systems Frontiers, vol. 13, pp. 33–43 (2011), 10.1007/s10796-010-9275-8
9. Teevan, J., Ramage, D., Morris, M.R.: #twittersearch: a comparison of microblog search and web search. In: Proceedings of the Fourth ACM International Conference on Web Search and Data Mining, pp. 35–44. ACM (2011)
10. Efron, M.: Hashtag retrieval in a microblogging environment. In: International ACM SIGIR Conference on Research and Development in Information Retrieval, SIGIR 2010, pp. 787–788. ACM, New York (2010)
11. Naveed, N., Gottron, T., Kunegis, J., Alhadi, A.C.: Searching microblogs: coping with sparsity and document quality. In: Proceedings of the 20th ACM International Conference on Information and Knowledge Management, CIKM 2011, pp. 183–188. ACM, New York (2011)
12. Wu, S.-T., Li, Y., Xu, Y.: Deploying approaches for pattern refinement in text mining. In: Proceedings of the Sixth International Conference on Data Mining, ICDM 2006, pp. 1157–1161. IEEE Computer Society, Washington, DC (2006)
13. Bernstein, M., Hong, L., Kairam, S., Chi, H., Suh, B.: A torrent of tweets: Managing information overload in online social streams. In: Workshop on Microblogging: What and How Can We Learn From It? (CHI 2010) (2010)
14. Efron, M.: Information search and retrieval in microblogs. Journal of the American Society for Information Science and Technology 62(6), 996–1008 (2011)
15. Massoudi, K., Tsagkias, M., de Rijke, M., Weerkamp, W.: Incorporating query expansion and quality indicators in searching microblog posts. In: Advances in Information Retrieval, pp. 362–367 (2011)
16. Abel, F., Celik, I., Houben, G.-J., Siehndel, P.: Leveraging the Semantics of Tweets for Adaptive Faceted Search on Twitter. In: Aroyo, L., Welty, C., Alani, H., Taylor, J., Bernstein, A., Kagal, L., Noy, N., Blomqvist, E. (eds.) ISWC 2011, Part I. LNCS, vol. 7031, pp. 1–17. Springer, Heidelberg (2011)
17. Nagmoti, R., Teredesai, A., De Cock, M.: Ranking approaches for microblog search. In: 2010 IEEE/WIC/ACM International Conference on Web Intelligence and Intelligent Agent Technology (WI-IAT), pp. 153–157. IEEE (2010)
18. Cui, H., Wen, J.-R., Nie, J.-Y., Ma, W.-Y.: Probabilistic query expansion using query logs. In: Proceedings of the 11th International Conference on World Wide Web, WWW 2002, pp. 325–332. ACM, New York (2002)
19. Manning, C.D., Raghavan, P., Schütze, H.: Introduction to Information Retrieval, 1st edn. Cambridge University Press (July 2008)
20. Soboroff, I., Robertson, S.: Building a filtering test collection for trec 2002. In: 26th Annual International ACM SIGIR Conference on Research and Development in Informaion Retrieval, SIGIR 2003, pp. 243–250. ACM, New York (2003)

A Secure and Efficient Mix Network Especially Suitable for E-Voting

Kun Peng

Institute for Infocomm Research
dr.kun.peng@gmail.com

Abstract. A mix network is proposed in this paper. Its most operations are carried out in an off-line one-time initialization phase so that its on-line efficiency is very high. Although this two-phase mechanism has a limitation to parameter setting, we show that the limitation does not prevent the mix network from being employed in its main application, e-voting, with the help of a grouped shuffling mechanism. Its achievement of desired security properties is formally proved.

1 Introduction

Mix network is an anonymous communication channel widely employed in private network applications like e-voting. It consists of multiple shuffling nodes, who shuffle some encrypted messages in turn by re-ordering and re-encrypting them. The encrypted messages are repeatedly shuffled in succession by all the shuffling nodes in the mix network. If at least one shuffling node conceals his permutation, the repeatedly shuffled encrypted messages cannot be traced.

Security of a mix network depends on the underlying shuffling operations. In a shuffling protocol, ciphertexts $c_1, c_2, \ldots, c_n$ are input to a shuffling node, who outputs ciphertexts $c'_1, c'_2, \ldots, c'_n$ where $c'_i = RE(c_{\pi(i)})$ for $i = 1, 2, \ldots, n$, $\pi()$ is a random permutation and $RE()$ stands for re-encryption. To guarantee that a mix network works properly, each shuffling node in it needs to publicly prove that he does not deviate from the shuffling protocol. Each shuffling node cannot reveal his permutation in his proof of validity of shuffling. More comprehensively, the following security properties must be satisfied in mix networks.

- Correctness: if the shuffling nodes follow the shuffling protocol, the plaintexts encrypted in their output ciphertexts are a permutation of the plaintexts encrypted in the input ciphertexts.
- Public verifiability: the shuffling nodes can publicly prove that they do not deviate from the mix network.
- Soundness: a successfully verified proof by a shuffling node guarantees that the plaintexts encrypted in his output ciphertexts are a permutation of the plaintexts encrypted in his input ciphertexts.
- Privacy: no information about each shuffling node's $\pi()$ is revealed.

Y. Xiang et al. (Eds.): ICDKE 2012, LNCS 7696, pp. 161–174, 2012.
© Springer-Verlag Berlin Heidelberg 2012

Among the famous mix network schemes [1,2,12,6,11,20,14,15,19,22,10,9,18], the most recent of them [11,20,15,19,22,10,9,18] are more efficient where the scheme in [7] is an extended journal version of [6] and the scheme in [13] is a slight optimisation of [12]. In the recent mix network schemes, the shuffling protocol in [20] is very efficient. However, unlike the other shuffling protocols it only allows the shuffling node to choose his permutation from a very small fraction of all the possible permutations and is weak in privacy. The other recent mix network schemes employ the same idea: given random integers t_i for $i = 1, 2, \ldots, n$, if

$$RE(\textstyle\prod_{i=1}^{n} c_i^{t_i}) = \textstyle\prod_{i=1}^{n} c_i'^{t_i'} \tag{1}$$
$$t_1', t_2', \ldots, t_n' \text{ is a permutation of } t_1, t_2, \ldots, t_n, \tag{2}$$

then $D(c_1'), D(c_2'), \ldots, D(c_n')$ must be a permutation of $D(c_1), D(c_2), \ldots, D(c_n)$ with an overwhelmingly large probability. This idea is effective and actually will be employed in our new mix network as well. However, its usage by the recent mix network schemes is not efficient enough.

An important method used by the most recent shuffling schemes [20,15,19,22,10,9,18] to show high efficiency in their efficiency analysis is employment of small exponents. They notice that although the exponentiation computations in cryptographic operations tend to employ full-length exponents (which are usually hundreds of bits long) sometimes the exponents are not necessary to be so large. Actually in many practical applications the exponents can be much smaller (e.g. scores of bits long) but still large enough to guarantee satisfactory security. For example, $t_1, t_2, \ldots, t_n$ can be scores of bits long to guarantee that the probability for any incorrect shuffling to pass the verifications in (1) and (2), which is at most $1/t_i$, is negligible. So the recent shuffling schemes [20,15,19,22,10,18] employ many small exponents and estimate their computational cost in the terms of the number of separate exponentiations with full-length exponents. More precisely, they set the computational cost of an exponentiation with a full-length exponent as the basic unit in efficiency analysis and estimate how many basic units cost the same as their operations[1]. In this way, their efficiency advantage over the previous shuffling schemes is obviously and vividly demonstrated.

In this paper, a new mix network scheme is designed, which is especially suitable for e-voting applications. Its shuffling nodes employ a new method to prove satisfaction of Equations (1) and (2). Each shuffling node carries out most of its operations in a one-time off-line initialization phase, while his on-line computation to prove validity of his shuffling is very efficient. This special mechanism has a limitation: the number of shuffled ciphertexts, n, must be fixed. Although this limitation may affect employment of the new mix network in other applications, e-voting, the main application of mix network, does not contradict with the limitation. We observe the paper-based traditional elections and notice that the shuffling mechanism in real-world election applications seldom includes all

---

[1] Namely, multiple exponentiations with small exponents are counted as one exponentiation with a full-length exponent, which has the same cost.

the votes in one single instance of shuffling. More precisely, there are usually multiple ballot boxes in elections and each of them shuffles the votes in it by shaking itself. Normally, there are many voting stations in real-world elections, each covering an area with a fixed number of voters, and the ballot box in every voting station has a fixed size so that the scale of each instance of shuffling is not too large. So multiple instances of shuffling, each with a fixed size, is consistent with practical elections and should be acceptable in e-voting applications.

When our mix network is applied to e-voting, every shuffling node divides the encrypted votes for him to shuffle into multiple groups with a fixed size and processes each group using a shuffling operation. In this way, although the scale of a shuffling operation is fixed, the votes can be grouped and them shuffled in groups, no matter how many votes there are. The idea of grouped shuffling was firstly proposed in [20]. However, the shuffling protocol in [20] only supports very small groups and so only achieves weak and impractical privacy. Our new mix network supports large groups and so can achieve practically strong enough privacy. Of course, if N, the number of ciphertexts to shuffle in the mix network, is known in advance, n can be set to be N to avoid the grouping mechanism in our new mix network.

The new mix network achieves the so-called SHVZK as a public coin argument defined in [9]. So its privacy is not statistically limited and stronger than that of most recent mix networks[2]. Soundness of the new mix network based on (1) and (2) is formally proved in a complete way with a precise overwhelmingly large probability depending on the concrete length of short exponents such that its parameter setting (to choose small exponents) and efficiency analysis (depending on exactly how small the small exponents are) are more formally and precisely guided than those in most recent mix networks. So it has obvious advantages over the existing mix networks in both efficiency and security. Moreover, the advantage in employing the efficiency improvement mechanisms in the recent mix networks is illustrated more formally, more precisely and in more details in the new mix network. The most important application of mix network is electronic voting, which employs a mix network to shuffle the sealed votes before they are opened. The way to build an e-voting scheme on the base of our new mix network is presented in the end of this paper.

2   Background

Some background knowledge about mix network to be used in this paper is recalled in the section.

2.1   Security Model

Privacy of mix network has been formally defined in the existing mix network schemes. In Section 2.5 of [9] (and in [11] and many other cryptographic schemes

---

[2] Zero knowledge in most recent mix networks is statistically imperfect. Such imperfect privacy is explicitly recognised in [11,10,18] and implicitly inevitable in [19,22] as explained in Appendix A.

based on ZK proof), a concept SHVZK (special honest verifier zero-knowledge) as defined in Definition 2 is used to model privacy of proof protocols in the form of a public coin argument as defined in Definition 1.

Definition 1. *(Public coin argument). An argument is public coin if the verifier's messages are chosen uniformly at random independently of the messages sent by the prover and the setup parameters.*

Definition 2. *The public coin argument (K, P, V) is called a special honest verifier zero-knowledge argument for R with setup G if there exists a probabilistic polynomial time simulator S such that for all non-uniform polynomial time adversaries A we have*

$$Pr[gk \leftarrow G(1^k); \sigma \leftarrow K(gk); (x, w, \rho) \leftarrow A(gk, \sigma);$$
$$tr \leftarrow < P(gk, \sigma, x, w), V(gk, \sigma, x, \rho) >: (gk, x, w) \in R \ and \ A(tr) = 1]$$
$$= Pr[gk \leftarrow G(1^k); \sigma \leftarrow K(gk); (x, w, \rho) \leftarrow A(gk, \sigma); \quad (3)$$
$$tr \leftarrow S(gk, \sigma, x, w) : (gk, x, w) \in R \ and \ A(tr) = 1]$$

where

- *G is a set-up algorithm and gk is the set-up information it generates;*
- *(P, V) are a pair of probabilistic polynomial time interactive algorithms representing the prover and the verifier, while they may have access to a common random string σ generated by a probabilistic polynomial time key generation algorithm K;*
- *R is a polynomial time decidable ternary relation;*
- *$tr \leftarrow < P(x), V(y) >$ stands for the public transcript produced by P and V when interacting on inputs x and y together with the randomness used by V.*

2.2   Commitment Algorithms

Two commitment algorithms are employed in [11,10,9] and will be used in our new mix network. Computations in the two commitment algorithms are performed in a large cyclic subgroup with order q in Z_p^*, where p and q are large primes and q is a factor of $p - 1$. g, $g_1, g_2, \ldots, g_n$ and h are generators of the cyclic subgroup such that $\log_h g$ and $\log_h g_l$ is secret for any l in $1\{1, 2, \ldots, n\}$.

In the first commitment algorithm, a message m in Z_q is committed to in $g^m h^r \mod p$ where r is randomly chosen from Z_q. In the second commitment algorithm, messages $m_1, m_2, \ldots, m_n$ in Z_q are committed to in $\prod_{l=1}^n g_l^{m_l} h^r \mod p$ where r is randomly chosen from Z_q. From now on in this paper, they are called the first commitment algorithm and the second commitment algorithm respectively. In [11,10,9] and earlier literature, they have been illustrated to achieve hidingness and bindingness defined as follows.

- Hidingness: given a commitment, it is difficult to find the message (or message tuple) committed to in it.
- Bindingness: it is difficult to find two different messages (or message tuples) to be committed to in the same commitment.

2.3 A Proof of Knowledge of Permutation

Although proof of knowledge of a permutation committed in shuffled ciphertexts is complex, it is illustrated in [11] that proof of knowledge of a permutation committed in the commitments of some shuffled integers by some special commitment algorithm is simpler. In Section 3 of [11], a proof primitive proves "a shuffle of known contents" by a secret permutation as follows.

- $t_1, t_2, \ldots, t_n$ are public integers in Z_q.
- $e_i = g^{t_{\pi(i)}} h^{r_i}$ for $i = 1, 2, \ldots, n$ are calculated and published by a party where $\pi()$ is a secret permutation of $\{1, 2, \ldots, n\}$ and r_i is a secret integer randomly chosen from Z_q.
- The party employs a proof technique called "proofs for iterated logarithmic multiplication" in Section 3 of [12] to prove that the integers committed in $e_1, e_2, \ldots, e_n$ is a permutation of $t_1, t_2, \ldots, t_n$ without revealing $\pi()$.

This proof protocol is denoted as $PP\ (\pi(); t_1, t_2, \ldots, t_n; e_1, e_2, \ldots, e_n)$ in this paper. It is formally proved in [11] that $PP()$ achieves SHVZK. With the proof techniques and the efficiency improving mechanisms in [12] and [11], $PP()$ costs a prover about $2n$ exponentiations.

3 The New Mix Network

As mentioned in Section 1, most of the computations of the shuffling nodes are carried out off-line in a one-time initialization phase in our new mix network. In the off-line initialization phase, each shuffling node chooses a secret permutation to be used in his shuffling in the mix network. He publishes some random integers and permutes them using his secret permutation and commits to the permitted integers in some commitments. He employs a batch proof technique to prove that all the commitments contain some permuted integers using the same permutation. In the on-line shuffling phase, each shuffling node groups the input ciphertexts to him (if their number is too large for his committed permutation) and shuffles them using his secret committed permutation. Then random challenges $t_1, t_2, \ldots, t_n$ are given to the shuffling node like in the recent shuffling schemes and he has to prove knowledge of a secret permutation to satisfy Equations (1) and (2). In his proof, he calculates linear functions of the committed integers in the initialization phase to equalize the challenges and thus obtain a commitment of the random challenges being permuted by his secret committed permutation. Finally, in every group he proves $RE(\prod_{i=1}^{n} c_i^{t_i}) = \prod_{i=1}^{n} c'^{t'_i}_i$ where $t'_1, t'_2, \ldots, t'_n$ are the integers in the commitment. The new mix network works as follows where $P_1, P_2, \ldots, P_k$ are the k shuffling nodes in the mix network.

1. Off-line one-time initialization
   (a) A trusted authority (e.g. the mix network manager) generates g, $g_1, g_2, \ldots, g_n, h$ as defined in Section 2.2. If no single party can be trusted, the parameters can be generated corporately by all the shuffling nodes in the mix network as a result taking each node's contribution into account to guarantee that $\log_h g$ and $\log_h g_l$ is secret to any shuffling node.

(b) The trusted authority chooses an ElGamal private key x in Z_q and calculates the corresponding public key $y = g^x \bmod p$. He publishes y and the encryption function $E(m) = (g^r \bmod p,\ my^r \bmod p)$ is employed for encryption and re-encryption in the mix network where r is a random integer in Z_q. He can share x among some decryption authorities (who will cooperate to decrypt the output ciphertexts of the mix network) or he needs to decrypt the output ciphertexts himself when required. If no single party can be trusted, the shuffling nodes can cooperate to build up the ElGamal encryption algorithm in a distributed way and share the private key [5,16,8] such that decryption is only feasible when an enough number of them cooperate. In this case, they need to cooperate to decrypt the output ciphertexts of the mix network when required.

(c) The mix network manager chooses a security parameter L such that $2^L < q$ and 2^{-L} is negligible.

(d) Each P_i randomly chooses $\pi_i()$, a permutation of $\{1, 2, \ldots, n\}$ as his secret permutation to be used in future applications of the mix network.

(e) Each P_i chooses and publishes random integers $a_{i,j,l}$ in Z_{2^L} for $j = 1, 2, \ldots, n$ and $l = 1, 2, \ldots, n$ with a condition that matrix M_i is non-singular modulo q where

$$M_i = \begin{pmatrix} a_{i,1,1} & a_{i,1,2} & \cdots & a_{i,1,n} \\ a_{i,2,1} & a_{i,2,2} & \cdots & a_{i,2,n} \\ \cdots & \cdots & \cdots & \cdots \\ \cdots & \cdots & \cdots & \cdots \\ a_{i,n,1} & a_{i,n,2} & \cdots & a_{i,n,n} \end{pmatrix}. \tag{4}$$

(f) Each P_i calculates and publishes

$$C_{i,j} = \prod_{l=1}^{n} g_l^{a_{i,j,\pi_i(l)}} h^{R_{i,j}} \bmod p \text{ for } j = 1, 2, \ldots, n$$

where every $R_{i,j}$ is randomly chosen from Z_q.

(g) For each P_i, random challenges $w_{i,1}, w_{i,2}, \ldots, w_{i,n}$ in Z_{2^L} are generated by some verifier(s) or as a one-way hash function of $a_{i,j,l}$ for $j = 1, 2, \ldots, n$ and $l = 1, 2, \ldots, n$.

(h) Each P_i calculates and publishes

$$C'_{i,l} = g_l^{\sum_{j=1}^{n} w_{i,j} a_{i,j,\pi_i(l)}} h^{r_{i,l}} \bmod p \text{ for } l = 1, 2, \ldots, n$$

where every $r_{i,l}$ is randomly chosen from Z_q. He proves knowledge of $z_{i,l} = \sum_{j=1}^{n} w_{i,j} a_{i,j,\pi_i(l)} \bmod q$ for $l = 1, 2, \ldots, n$, $R = \sum_{j=1}^{n} w_{i,j} R_{i,j} \bmod q$ and $r_{i,1}, r_{i,2}, \ldots, r_{i,n}$ such that

$$\prod_{j=1}^{n} C_{i,j}^{w_{i,j}} = \prod_{l=1}^{n} g_l^{z_{i,l}} h^{R} \bmod p \tag{5}$$

$$C'_{i,l} = g_l^{z_{i,l}} h^{r_{i,l}} \bmod p \text{ for } l = 1, 2, \ldots, n \tag{6}$$

using the proof protocol in Fig 1.

(i) Each P_i proves without revealing $\pi_i()$ that he knows a permutation of $\sum_{j=1}^{n} w_{i,j} a_{i,j,1}, \sum_{j=1}^{n} w_{i,j} a_{i,j,2}, \ldots, \sum_{j=1}^{n} w_{i,j} a_{i,j,n}$, which is committed to in $C'_{i,1}, C'_{i,2}, \ldots, C'_{i,n}$, using

$$PP\left(\pi_i(); \sum_{j=1}^{n} w_{i,j} a_{i,j,1}, \sum_{j=1}^{n} w_{i,j} a_{i,j,2}, \ldots, \sum_{j=1}^{n} w_{i,j} a_{i,j,n}; \right.$$
$$\left. C'_{i,1}, C'_{i,2}, \ldots, C'_{i,n}\right). \tag{7}$$

(a) The prover randomly chooses integers ζ_l for $l = 1, 2, \ldots, n$ from Z_{2^L} and γ, γ_l for $l = 1, 2, \ldots, n$ from Z_q and publishes

$$d = \prod_{l=1}^{n} g_l^{\zeta_l} h^{\gamma} \bmod p$$
$$d_l = g^{\zeta_l} h^{\gamma_l} \bmod p \text{ for } l = 1, 2, \ldots, n.$$

(b) A random challenge C in Z_q is generated by some verifier(s) or as a one-way hash function of $C_{i,1}, C_{i,2}, \ldots, C_{i,n}, C'_{i,1}, C'_{i,2}, \ldots, C'_{i,n}, d, d_1, d_2, \ldots, d_n$.

(c) The prover publishes

$$\mu_l = \zeta_i - C z_{i,l} \bmod q \text{ for } l = 1, 2, \ldots, n$$
$$\nu = \gamma - CR \bmod q$$
$$\nu_l = \gamma_l - C r_{i,l} \bmod q \text{ for } l = 1, 2, \ldots, n.$$

Anyone can verify

$$d = \prod_{l=1}^{n} g_l^{\mu_l} h^{\nu} (\prod_{j=1}^{n} C_{i,j}^{w_{i,j}})^C \bmod p$$
$$d_l = g^{\mu_l} h^{\nu_l} C'^C_{i,l} \bmod p \text{ for } l = 1, 2, \ldots, n$$

and reject the proof if either of the two equations is not satisfied.

Fig. 1. ZK Proof of Equality of Committed Integers

2. On-line shuffling

Every shuffling node P_i receives the ciphertexts shuffled by the previous shuffling node. He divides them into groups with size n if their number is larger than n and uses $\pi_i()$ to shuffle them (in the groups if they are grouped) and proves validity of his shuffling as follows.

(a) Receiving ElGamal ciphertexts $c_1, c_2, \ldots, c_N$ for him to shuffle, P_i randomly groups them into some groups with size n:

$$\text{Group } 1: \ G_1 = \{c_{1,1}, c_{1,2}, \ldots, c_{1,n}\}$$
$$\text{Group } 2: \ G_2 = \{c_{2,1}, c_{2,2}, \ldots, c_{2,n}\}$$
$$\cdots\cdots$$
$$\text{Group } \lceil N/n \rceil: \ G_{\lceil N/n \rceil} = \{c_{\lceil N/n \rceil,1}, c_{\lceil N/n \rceil,2}, \ldots, c_{\lceil N/n \rceil,n}\}.$$

(b) P_i calculates and publishes his shuffling result

$$a'_{\kappa,l} = a_{\kappa,\pi_i(l)} g^{s_{i,\kappa,l}} \bmod p$$

$$b'_{\kappa,l} = b_{\kappa,\pi_i(l)} y^{s_{i,\kappa,l}} \bmod p \text{ for } \kappa = 1,2,\ldots,\lceil N/n \rceil \text{ and } l = 1,2,\ldots,n$$

where $c_{\kappa,l} = (a_{\kappa,l}, b_{\kappa,l})$ and every $s_{i,\kappa,l}$ is randomly chosen from Z_q.

(c) Random challenges $t_{i,1}, t_{i,2}, \ldots, t_{i,n}$ in Z_{2^L} are generated by some verifier(s) or as a one-way hash function of $c'_{\kappa,l} = (a'_{\kappa,l}, b'_{\kappa,l})$ for $\kappa = 1,2,\ldots,\lceil N/n \rceil$ and $l = 1,2,\ldots,n$.

(d) P_i proves knowledge of $z'_{i,l} = \sum_{j=1}^{n} u_{i,j} a_{i,j,\pi_i(l)} \bmod q$ for $l = 1,2,\ldots,n$, $R' = \sum_{j=1}^{n} u_{i,j} R_{i,j} \bmod q$ and $S_\kappa = \prod_{l=1}^{n} z'_{i,l} s_{i,\kappa,l} \bmod q$ for $\kappa = 1,2,\ldots,\lceil N/n \rceil$ such that

$$\prod_{j=1}^{n} C_{i,j}^{u_{i,j}} = \prod_{l=1}^{n} g_l^{z'_{i,l}} h^{R'} \bmod p \tag{8}$$

$$g^{S_\kappa} \prod_{l=1}^{n} a_{\kappa,l}^{t_{i,l}} = \prod_{l=1}^{n} a'^{z'_{i,l}}_{\kappa,l} \bmod p \text{ for } \kappa = 1,2,\ldots,\lceil N/n \rceil \tag{9}$$

$$y^{S_\kappa} \prod_{l=1}^{n} b_{\kappa,l}^{t_{i,l}} = \prod_{l=1}^{n} b'^{z'_{i,l}}_{\kappa,l} \bmod p \text{ for } \kappa = 1,2,\ldots,\lceil N/n \rceil \tag{10}$$

using the proof protocol in Fig 2 where

$$(u_{i,1}, u_{i,2}, \ldots, u_{i,n}) = (t_{i,1}, t_{i,2}, \ldots, t_{i,n}) M_i^{-1}. \tag{11}$$

---

i. The prover randomly chooses integers $\zeta'_1, \zeta'_2, \ldots, \zeta'_n$ from Z_{2^L} and θ, $\theta_1, \theta_2, \ldots, \theta_{\lceil N/n \rceil}$ from Z_q and publishes

$$f = \prod_{l=1}^{n} g_l^{\zeta'_l} h^\theta \bmod p$$

$$\psi_\kappa = g^{\theta_\kappa} \prod_{l=1}^{n} a'^{\zeta'_l}_{\kappa,l} \bmod p \text{ for } \kappa = 1,2,\ldots,\lceil N/n \rceil$$

$$\phi_\kappa = y^{\theta_\kappa} \prod_{l=1}^{n} b'^{\zeta'_l}_{\kappa,l} \bmod p \text{ for } \kappa = 1,2,\ldots,\lceil N/n \rceil.$$

ii. C' in Z_q is randomly generated by some verifier(s) or as a one-way hash function of $c'_1, c'_2, \ldots, c'_n, C'_{i,1}, C'_{i,2}, \ldots, C'_{i,n}, f, \psi_1, \psi_2, \ldots, \psi_{\lceil N/n \rceil}, \phi_1, \phi_2, \ldots, \phi_{\lceil N/n \rceil}$.

iii. The prover publishes

$$\lambda_l = \zeta'_l - C' z'_{i,l} \bmod q \text{ for } l = 1,2,\ldots,n$$

$$\delta = \theta - C' R' \bmod q$$

$$\eta_\kappa = \theta_\kappa + C' S_\kappa \bmod q.$$

Anyone can verify

$$f = \prod_{l=1}^{n} g_l^{\lambda_l} h^\delta (\prod_{j=1}^{n} C_{i,j}^{u_{i,j}})^{C'} \bmod p$$

$$\psi_\kappa = g^{\eta_\kappa} \prod_{l=1}^{n} a'^{\lambda_l}_{\kappa,l} (\prod_{l=1}^{n} a_{\kappa,l}^{t_{i,l}})^{C'} \bmod p \text{ for } \kappa = 1,2,\ldots,\lceil N/n \rceil$$

$$\phi_\kappa = y^{\eta_\kappa} \prod_{l=1}^{n} b'^{\lambda_l}_{\kappa,l} (\prod_{l=1}^{n} b_{\kappa,l}^{t_{i,l}})^{C'} \bmod p \text{ for } \kappa = 1,2,\ldots,\lceil N/n \rceil$$

and reject the proof if any of the three equations is not satisfied.

Fig. 2. Combined ZK Proof of Equality of Discrete Logarithms

4 Security and Efficiency Analysis

Correctness of the new mix network is straightforward and any interested reader can follow it step by step to verify that honest shuffling nodes can successfully end their operations and pass the verifications against them. Soundness and privacy of the new mix network are formally proved in Theorem 1 and Theorem 2.

Theorem 1. *If P_i has passed the verification against him in the initialization phase with a probability larger than 2^{-L}, P_i's knowledge of $z'_{i,1}, z'_{i,2}, \ldots, z'_{i,n}, R, S_1, S_2, \ldots, \lceil N/n \rceil$ to satisfy (8), (9), (10) and (11) in the shuffling phase guarantees satisfaction of Equations (1) and (2).*

Proof: As P_i has passed the verification against him in the initialization phase with a probability larger than 2^{-L}, he must have successfully proved his knowledge of $z_{i,1}, z_{i,2}, \ldots, z_{i,n}, R, r_{i,1}, r_{i,2}, \ldots, r_{i,n}$ to satisfy (5), (6) and (7) with a probability larger than 2^{-L}. So according to bindingness of the two employed commitment algorithms P_i can calculate in polynomial time $z_{i,1}, z_{i,2}, \ldots, z_{i,n}$ and R such that

$$\prod_{j=1}^n C_{i,j}^{w_{i,j}} = \prod_{l=1}^n g_l^{z_{i,l}} h^R \bmod p \tag{12}$$

$$z_{i,l} = \sum_{j=1}^n w_{i,j} a_{i,j,\pi_i(l)} \bmod q \text{ for } l = 1, 2, \ldots, n \tag{13}$$

with a probability larger than 2^{-L} where $\pi_i()$ is a permutation of $\{1, 2, \ldots, n\}$. Note that $w_{i,1}, w_{i,2}, \ldots, w_{i,n}$ are randomly chosen from Z_{2^L}. So, for any J in $\{1, 2, \ldots, n\}$, there must exist $w_{i,1}, w_{i,2}, \ldots, w_{i,J-1}, w_{i,J+1}, w_{i,j+2}, \ldots, w_{i,n}$ in $Z_{2^L}^{n-1}$ and two different choices for $w_{i,J}$ in Z_{2^L}, denoted as $w_{i,J}$ and $w'_{i,J}$ respectively, such that P_i can calculate in polynomial time $z_{i,1}, z_{i,2}, \ldots, z_{i,n}, R$ and $\hat{z}_{i,1}, \hat{z}_{i,2}, \ldots, \hat{z}_{i,n}, \hat{R}$ respectively to satisfy

$$\prod_{j=1}^n C_{i,j}^{w_{i,j}} = \prod_{l=1}^n g_l^{z_{i,l}} h^R \bmod p \tag{14}$$

$$(\prod_{j=1}^{J-1} C_{i,j}^{w_{i,j}}) C_{i,J}^{w'_{i,J}} \prod_{j=J+1}^n C_{i,j}^{w_{i,j}} = \prod_{l=1}^n g_l^{\hat{z}_{i,l}} h^{\hat{R}} \bmod p \tag{15}$$

$$z_{i,l} = \sum_{j=1}^n w_{i,j} a_{i,j,\pi_i(l)} \bmod q \text{ for } l = 1, 2, \ldots, n \tag{16}$$

$$\hat{z}_{i,l} = (\sum_{j=1}^{J-1} w_{i,j} a_{i,j,\pi_i(l)}) w'_{i,J} a_{i,J,\pi_i(l)} \sum_{j=J+1}^n w_{i,j} a_{i,j,\pi_i(l)} \bmod q$$
$$\text{for } l = 1, 2, \ldots, n. \tag{17}$$

Otherwise, for any combination of $w_{i,1}, w_{i,2}, \ldots, w_{i,J-1}, w_{i,J+1}, w_{i,j+2}, \ldots, w_{i,n}$ in $Z_{2^L}^{n-1}$ there is at most one choice of $w_{i,J}$ among its 2^L possible choices for P_i to calculate in polynomial time $z_{i,1}, z_{i,2}, \ldots, z_{i,n}, R$ to satisfy (12) and (13), which means that the probability that P_i can calculate in polynomial time $z_{i,1}, z_{i,2}, \ldots, z_{i,n}$ and R to satisfy (12) and (13) is no larger than 2^{-L} and leads to a contradiction.

(14)-(15) and (16)-(17) respectively yield

$$C_{i,J}^{w_{i,J} - w'_{i,J}} = \prod_{l=1}^n g_l^{z_{i,l} - \hat{z}_{i,l}} h^{R - \hat{R}} \bmod p \tag{18}$$

$$z_{i,l} - \hat{z}_{i,l} = (w_{i,J} - w'_{i,J}) a_{i,J,\pi_i(l)} \bmod q. \tag{19}$$

Note that q is prime, $2^L < q$ and $w_{i,J}$ and $w'_{i,J}$ are L-bit integers. So $GCD(q, w_{i,J} - w'_{i,J}) = 1$ and $(w_{i,J} - w'_{i,J})^{-1} \bmod q$ can be calculated. So (18) and (19) imply

$$C_{i,J} = \prod_{l=1}^n g_l^{(z_{i,l} - \hat{z}_{i,l})/(w_{i,J} - w'_{i,J})} h^{(R - \hat{R})/(w_{i,J} - w'_{i,J})} \bmod p$$
$$(z_{i,l} - \hat{z}_{i,l})/(w_{i,J} - w'_{i,J}) = a_{i,J,\pi_i(l)} \bmod q.$$

So, as J can be any integer in $\{1, 2, \ldots, n\}$, P_i knows integers $z_{i,j,l} = (z_{i,l} - \hat{z}_{i,l})/(w_{i,j} - w'_{i,j}) \bmod q$ for $j = 1, 2, \ldots, n$ and $l = 1, 2, \ldots, n$ and $R_{i,j} = (R - \hat{R})/(w_{i,j} - w'_{i,j}) \bmod q$ for $j = 1, 2, \ldots, n$ such that

$$C_{i,j} = \prod_{l=1}^n g_l^{z_{i,j,l}} h^{R_{i,j}} \bmod p \text{ for } j = 1, 2, \ldots, n \tag{20}$$
$$z_{i,j,l} = a_{i,j,\pi_i(l)} \text{ for } j = 1, 2, \ldots, n \text{ and } l = 1, 2, \ldots, n. \tag{21}$$

(8) and (20) imply P_i's knowledge of $z'_{i,1}, z'_{i,2}, \ldots, z'_{i,n}, R', R_{i,1}, R_{i,2}, \ldots, R_{i,n}$ and $z_{i,j,l}$ for $j = 1, 2, \ldots, n$ and $l = 1, 2, \ldots, n$ to satisfy

$$\prod_{j=1}^n \left(\prod_{l=1}^n g_l^{z_{i,j,l}} h^{R_{i,j}}\right)^{u_{i,j}} = \prod_{l=1}^n g_l^{z'_{i,l}} h^{R'} \bmod p$$

and namely

$$\prod_{l=1}^n g_l^{\sum_{j=1}^n u_{i,j} z_{i,j,l}} h^{\sum_{j=1}^n u_{i,j} R_{i,j}} = \prod_{l=1}^n g_l^{z'_{i,l}} h^{R'} \bmod p. \tag{22}$$

According to bindingness of the second commitment algorithm, (22) implies

$$\sum_{j=1}^n u_{i,j} z_{i,j,l} = z'_{i,l} \bmod q, \tag{23}$$

while (4), (11), (21) and (23) imply

$$z'_{i,l} = \sum_{j=1}^n u_{i,j} z_{i,j,l} = \sum_{j=1}^n u_{i,j} a_{i,j,\pi_i(l)} = t_{i,\pi_i(l)} \bmod q. \tag{24}$$

Therefore, (24), (9) and (10) imply

$$g^{S_\kappa} \prod_{l=1}^n a_{\kappa,l}^{t_{i,l}} = \prod_{l=1}^n a'^{t_{i,\pi_i(l)}}_{\kappa,l} \bmod p \text{ for } \kappa = 1, 2, \ldots, \lceil N/n \rceil$$
$$y^{S_\kappa} \prod_{l=1}^n b_{\kappa,l}^{t_{i,l}} = \prod_{l=1}^n b'^{t_{i,\pi_i(l)}}_{\kappa,l} \bmod p \text{ for } \kappa = 1, 2, \ldots, \lceil N/n \rceil$$

and thus satisfaction of Equations (1) and (2).   □

The recent mix networks [11,19,22,10,9,18] have formally illustrated that satisfaction of (1) and (2) guarantees validity of a mix network with an overwhelmingly large probability when $t_1, t_2, \ldots, t_n$ (namely $t_{i,1}, t_{i,2}, \ldots, t_{i,n}$ in our mix network) are randomly chosen after the shuffled ciphertexts are published.

Theorem 2. *The new mix network achieves SHVZK.*

Proof: The ZK proof protocols in Fig 1 and Fig 2 are simple combinations of standard ZK proof of knowledge of discrete logarithm [21] and ZK proof of equality of discrete logarithms [4], which have been formally proved to achieve

SHVZK. So the two proof protocols achieve SHVZK as well. The ZK proof protocol $PP()$ has been formally proved to achieve SHVZK in [12] and [11] and so its application to our mix network achieves SHVZK.

Besides the output ciphertexts $c'_1, c'_2, \ldots, c'_n$ (which are the same as in the existing ElGamal-based mix networks and are not included in privacy analysis like in most existing mix networks due to recognised security of employed encryption algorithms) and what the three ZK proof protocols publish, the only published information in any P_i's shuffling is $a_{i,j,l}$ for $j = 1, 2, \ldots, n$ and $l = 1, 2, \ldots, n$, $C_{i,j}$ for $j = 1, 2, \ldots, n$, $w_{i,j}$ for $j = 1, 2, \ldots, n$ and $C'_{i,l}$ for $l = 1, 2, \ldots, n$. A probabilistic polynomial time simulator S can simulate those integers as follow.

1. It randomly chooses $a_{i,j,l}$ from Z_{2^L} for $j = 1, 2, \ldots, n$ and $l = 1, 2, \ldots, n$ with a condition that matrix M_i is non-singular modulo q.
2. It randomly chooses $\pi_i()$, a permutation of $\{1, 2, \ldots, n\}$.
3. It calculates $C_{i,j} = \prod_{l=1}^{n} g_l^{a_{i,j,\pi_i(l)}} h^{R_{i,j}} \bmod p$ for $j = 1, 2, \ldots, n$ where every $R_{i,j}$ is randomly chosen from Z_q.
4. It randomly chooses $w_{i,j}$ from Z_{2^L} for $j = 1, 2, \ldots, n$.
5. It calculates $C'_{i,l} = g^{\sum_{j=1}^{n} w_{i,j} a_{i,j,\pi_i(l)}} h^{r_{i,l}} \bmod p$ for $l = 1, 2, \ldots, n$ where every $r_{i,l}$ is randomly chosen from Z_q.

As those simulated integers have the same distribution in the real transcript of our mix network and in the simulation by S, Equation (3) is satisfied in terms of them. So their usage in our mix network achieves SHVZK. $\square$

Besides the re-encryption operations (which is the same in all the mix networks), computational cost of a shuffling node (in terms of exponentiation) includes

– in the off-line initialization phase, to calculate

$$C_{i,j} = \prod_{l=1}^{n} g_l^{a_{i,j,\pi_i(l)}} h^{R_{i,j}} \bmod p \text{ for } j = 1, 2, \ldots, n$$
$$C'_{i,l} = g_l^{\sum_{j=1}^{n} w_{i,j} a_{i,j,\pi_i(l)}} h^{r_{i,l}} \bmod p \text{ for } l = 1, 2, \ldots, n$$
$$d = \prod_{l=1}^{n} g_l^{\zeta_l} h^{\gamma} \bmod p$$
$$d_l = g^{\zeta_l} h^{\gamma_l} \bmod p \text{ for } l = 1, 2, \ldots, n.$$

and the $2n$ full-length exponentiations in calculating $PP(\pi_i(); \sum_{j=1}^{n} w_{i,j} a_{i,j,1}, \sum_{j=1}^{n} w_{i,j} a_{i,j,2}, \ldots, \sum_{j=1}^{n} w_{i,j} a_{i,j,n}; C'_{i,1}, C'_{i,2}, \ldots, C'_{i,n});$
– in the on-line shuffling phase, to calculate

$$f = \prod_{l=1}^{n} g_l^{\zeta'_l} h^{\theta} \bmod p$$
$$\psi_\kappa = g^{\theta_\kappa} \prod_{l=1}^{n} a'^{\zeta'_l}_{\kappa,l} \bmod p \text{ for } \kappa = 1, 2, \ldots, \lceil N/n \rceil$$
$$\phi_\kappa = y^{\theta_\kappa} \prod_{l=1}^{n} b'^{\zeta'_l}_{\kappa,l} \bmod p \text{ for } \kappa = 1, 2, \ldots, \lceil N/n \rceil.$$

Most exponents in them are not full-length integers in Z_q. More precisely, $a_{i,j,l}, w_{i,j}, \zeta_l, \zeta'_l$ are L-bit integers. According to [3], computing an exponentiation with an L-bit exponent costs $2^{W-1} + L + L/(W+1)$ multiplications and

172   K. Peng

computing a product of n exponentiations with L-bit exponents costs about $2^{W-1}(n+1)+L+nL/(W+1)$ multiplications where W is a parameter in the W-bit-sliding-window exponentiation method and is normally set as 3. So, in the off-line initialization phase a shuffling node needs $(n+1)(2^{W-1}(n+1)+L+nL/(W+1))+n(2^{W-1}(n+1)+2L+2nL/(W+1))+n(2^{W-1}+L+L/(W+1))$ multiplications and about $5n$ full-length exponentiations, which is approximately equal to

$$((n+1)(2^{W-1}(n+1)+L+nL/(W+1))+n(2^{W-1}(n+1)+2L+\log_2 n+$$
$$n(2L+\log_2 n)/(W+1))+n(2^{W-1}+L+L/(W+1)))/(2^{W-1}+|q|+|q|/(W+1))$$
$$+5n \approx 0.05n^2+5.29n$$

full-length exponentiations in cost when $L=80$ and $|q|=1024$ where $|q|$ is the bit-length of q. In the on-line shuffling phase, a shuffling node needs $(2\lceil N/n\rceil+1)(2^{W-1}(n+1)+L+nL/(W+1))$ multiplications and 3 full-length exponentiations, which is approximately equal to

$$(2\lceil N/n\rceil+1)(2^{W-1}(n+1)+L+nL/(W+1))/(2^{W-1}+|q|+|q|/(W+1))+3$$
$$\approx 0.037N+0.019n$$

full-length exponentiations in cost when $L=80$ and $|q|=1024$.

The communicational cost of a shuffling node in the off-line initialization phase of our mix network is about $n^2L+3n|p|+2n|q|$ bits. The communicational cost of a shuffling node in in the on-line shuffling phase of our mix network apart from that to publish the shuffled ciphertexts is $(2\lceil N/n\rceil+1)|p|+(n+2)|q|$ bits.

5   Comparison, Conclusion and Application

A comparison between the new mix network and the recent mix networks is given in Table 1 where F denotes the bit length of a full-length integer. Among the two similar mix network designs in [14,15], the fixed final version in [15] is included in the comparison. The not so recent mix networks like [1,2,12,6] are not included as they are not so advanced in security and efficiency. As the mix network in [13] is a slight modification of the work in [12] and [11] and the mix network in [7] is a slight modification of the work in [6], they [13,7] are not included either. The mix network in [20] only achieves weak privacy and so is not included. Like in the efficiency analysis in most mix networks, only the cost of a shuffling node in proving validity of his shuffling is estimated in Table 1 and the re-encryption operation is not taken into account as it is the same in all the mix networks employing the same encryption algorithm. Only the on-line shuffling cost is included, while the off-line initialization cost is not taken into account as it can be carried out in advance. For simplicity, we assume $N=n$ and thus the grouping mechanism is not used, while like in the efficiency analysis in most mix networks the figures are given in terms of multiples of N (the number of ciphertexts to shuffle) and their remainder modulo N is ignored. If $N>n$ and the grouping mechanism is used, our new mix network will be even more efficient although its privacy will be only complete in every group.

Table 1. Comparison of Mix Network Schemes

Mix Network	ZK	Shuffler's Computation	Communication Bits per Shuffler	Communication Rounds
[11][a]	statistically imperfect	$\approx 6N + 3N/\hat{k}$	$\approx 3FN + 4FN/\hat{k}$	7
[19]	statistically imperfect	$\approx 5.5N$	$\approx 8FN$	4
[22]	statistically imperfect	$\approx 2.3N$	$\approx 6FN$	5
[15]	statistically perfect	$\approx 3.4N$	$\approx 8FN$	3
[10]	statistically imperfect	$\approx 0.5N$	$\approx 5FN$	3
[9][b]	statistically perfect	$\approx 3\hat{m}N + 5N$	$\approx F(3\hat{m}^2 + 4\hat{n} + \hat{m})$	7
[18]	statistically imperfect	$\approx 3N$	$\approx 4FN$	4
New	statistically perfect	$\approx 0.056N$	$\approx 3FN$	3

[a] $\hat{k}$ is a parameter integer.
[b] $\hat{m}$ and $\hat{n}$ are two factors of N such that $N = \hat{m}\hat{n}$.

In summary, the new mix network proposed in this paper is very efficient and achieves strong and formally provable security. Its application to e-voting is simple. Some talliers act as the shuffling nodes and form a mix network to shuffle the encrypted votes from the voters. The talliers take turns to shuffle the encrypted votes, with each tallier's outputs being the next tallier's inputs. Every tallier randomly divides the inputs to him into groups with size n and then shuffle them in every group. The private key of the employed ElGamal encryption algorithm is shared among the talliers so that they can cooperate to decrypt the repeatedly shuffled encrypted votes to find out the election result.

References

1. Abe, M.: Mix-Networks on Permutation Networks. In: Lam, K.-Y., Okamoto, E., Xing, C. (eds.) ASIACRYPT 1999. LNCS, vol. 1716, pp. 258–273. Springer, Heidelberg (1999)
2. Abe, M., Hoshino, F.: Remarks on Mix-Network Based on Permutation Networks. In: Kim, K.-c. (ed.) PKC 2001. LNCS, vol. 1992, pp. 317–324. Springer, Heidelberg (2001)
3. Avanzi, R., Cohen, H., Doche, C., Frey, G., Lange, T., Nguyen, K., Vercauteren, F.: Handbook of Elliptic and Hyperelliptic Curve Cryptography. In: HEHCC (2005)
4. Chaum, D., Pedersen, T.: Wallet Databases with Observers. In: Brickell, E.F. (ed.) CRYPTO 1992. LNCS, vol. 740, pp. 89–105. Springer, Heidelberg (1993)
5. Feldman, P.: A practical scheme for non-interactive verifiable secret sharing. In: FOCS 1987, pp. 427–437 (1987)
6. Furukawa, J., Sako, K.: An Efficient Scheme for Proving a Shuffle. In: Kilian, J. (ed.) CRYPTO 2001. LNCS, vol. 2139, pp. 368–387. Springer, Heidelberg (2001)
7. Furukawa, J.: Efficient and verifiable shuffling and shuffle-decryption. IEICE Transactions 88-A(1), 172–188 (2005)
8. Gennaro, R., Jarecki, S., Krawczyk, H., Rabin, T.: Secure Distributed Key Generation for Discrete-Log Based Cryptosystems. In: Stern, J. (ed.) EUROCRYPT 1999. LNCS, vol. 1592, pp. 51–83. Springer, Heidelberg (1999)

9. Groth, J., Ishai, Y.: Sub-linear Zero-Knowledge Argument for Correctness of a Shuffle. In: Smart, N.P. (ed.) EUROCRYPT 2008. LNCS, vol. 4965, pp. 379–396. Springer, Heidelberg (2008)
10. Groth, J., Lu, S.: Verifiable Shuffle of Large Size Ciphertexts. In: Okamoto, T., Wang, X. (eds.) PKC 2007. LNCS, vol. 4450, pp. 377–392. Springer, Heidelberg (2007)
11. Groth, J.: A Verifiable Secret Shuffle of Homomorphic Encryptions. In: Desmedt, Y.G. (ed.) PKC 2003. LNCS, vol. 2567, pp. 145–160. Springer, Heidelberg (2002)
12. Neff, C.: A verifiable secret shuffle and its application to e-voting. In: ACM CCS 2001, pp. 116–125 (2001)
13. Neff, C.: Verifiable mixing (shuffling) of Elgamal pairs (2004), http://theory.lcs.mit.edu/~rivest/voting/papers
14. Nguyen, L., Safavi-Naini, R., Kurosawa, K.: Verifiable Shuffles: A Formal Model and a Paillier-Based Efficient Construction with Provable Security. In: Jakobsson, M., Yung, M., Zhou, J. (eds.) ACNS 2004. LNCS, vol. 3089, pp. 61–75. Springer, Heidelberg (2004)
15. Nguyen, L., Safavi-Naini, R., Kurosawa, K.: A provably secure and effcient verifiable shuffle based on a variant of the paillier cryptosystem. Journal of Universal Computer Science 11(6), 986–1010 (2005)
16. Pedersen, T.: A Threshold Cryptosystem without a Trusted Party. In: Davies, D.W. (ed.) EUROCRYPT 1991. LNCS, vol. 547, pp. 522–526. Springer, Heidelberg (1991)
17. Peng, K.: Survey, Analysis And Re-Evaluation — How Efficient And Secure A Mix Network Can Be. In: IEEE CIT 2011, pp. 249–254 (2011)
18. Peng, K., Dawson, E., Bao, F.: Modification and optimisation of a shuffling scheme: stronger security, formal analysis and higher efficiency. International Journal of Information Security 10(1), 33–47 (2011)
19. Peng, K., Boyd, C., Dawson, E.: Simple and Efficient Shuffling with Provable Correctness and ZK Privacy. In: Shoup, V. (ed.) CRYPTO 2005. LNCS, vol. 3621, pp. 188–204. Springer, Heidelberg (2005)
20. Peng, K., Boyd, C., Dawson, E., Viswanathan, K.: A Correct, Private, and Efficient Mix Network. In: Bao, F., Deng, R., Zhou, J. (eds.) PKC 2004. LNCS, vol. 2947, pp. 439–454. Springer, Heidelberg (2004)
21. Schnorr, C.: Efficient signature generation by smart cards. Journal of Cryptology 4, 161–174 (1991)
22. Wikström, D.: A Sender Verifiable Mix-Net and a New Proof of a Shuffle. In: Roy, B. (ed.) ASIACRYPT 2005. LNCS, vol. 3788, pp. 273–292. Springer, Heidelberg (2005)

A   Implicit Statistically Imperfect ZK in [19] and [22]

Although the mix network schemes in [19] and [22] do not explicitly recognise any statistical revealing of secret information, it is shown in [17] that those two mix network schemes actually employ incorrect moduli in computations to avoid statistical information revealing at the cost of failure in complete correctness. Although the damage to correctness in the two mix network schemes [19,22] may be controlled to a certain level by carefully adjusting their parameters, their failure in complete correctness cannot be completely avoided, unless the incorrect moduli in them are removed. Therefore, if complete correctness is desired, the two mix network schemes must publish monotone functions of a secret integers in Z without any modulus in their zero knowledge proofs and tolerate statistically imperfect privacy.

Power Analysis Based Reverse Engineering on the Secret Round Function of Block Ciphers

Ming Tang[1,2,*], Zhenlong Qiu[2], Weijie Li[2], Shubo Liu[1,2], and Huanguo Zhang[1,2]

[1] State Key Lab. of AIS & TC, Ministry of Education, Wuhan University,
Wuhan430072, China
[2] School of Computers, Wuhan University, Wuhan430072, China
m.tang@126.com

Abstract. Side Channel Analysis (SCA) has become a new threat to the hardware implementations of encryption algorithms. The reverse engineering has been adopted to explore the unknown part of the encryption algorithms. The existing SCAs for reverse engineering depend on the leakage models in a large extent and mainly focus on the single component of the algorithms while the other parts of the target algorithm are known. In this paper, we present a more general and feasible reverse analysis by combining the mathematical methods and the SCA methods. We use the strict avalanche criterion for the non-linear operations of block ciphers and apply the power analysis to reverse the structure parameters. We propose a new reverse analysis method to reduce the dependency on the leakage models, which can be combined with the structure cryptanalysis to reverse the internal parameters of the linear and non-linear operations. We finally achieve the reverse analysis on the unknown round function of block ciphers.

Keywords: Block ciphers, SCA, Reverse engineering, Cryptanalysis, MIBS.

1 Introduction

Most of the existing cryptanalysis methods, including both the traditional mathematic analyses [1-4] and side channel analyses [5-9], are based on the public algorithms and their specific implementations. However, there are many cryptographic algorithms whose implementation details are partly or totally unknown. These secret algorithms have been widely used in military and government. Some commercial cryptographic algorithms are unknown as well, such as A3/A8 [12] etc. Reverse engineering plays an important role on analyzing the security of the secret cryptographic algorithms.

1.1 Related Work

The existing reverse engineering methods mainly include: the mathematics-based reverse analyses [13-15] and SCA-based reverse analyses [16-21]. Invasive attack is another reverse analysis which reconfigures the logic circuits through different pairs

---

* Corresponding author.

Y. Xiang et al. (Eds.): ICDKE 2012, LNCS 7696, pp. 175–188, 2012.
© Springer-Verlag Berlin Heidelberg 2012

of input and output. However, this method needs complicated requirements and advanced techniques, so they are not discussed in this paper.

Mathematics-Based Reverse Engineering. In EUROCRYPT 2001, Alex and Shamir proposed the structure analysis on the cipher with SASAS structure [13], and succeed in recovering the unknown parameters of SPN with 3 rounds. Considering its high complexity, the structure analysis recovers the parameters of the unknown S-box after building the relationship between the input and output of S-box. Moreover, they tried to find the equality of the unknown linear operation through the collision, and can recover two and half rounds of block cipher with SPN structure. Alex improved their method in 2010 [22]. However, the complexity of the structure analysis was too high to the real algorithms with higher rounds. Borghoffutilized this method on the PRESENT-like Maya algorithm in 2011 [23] to recover the unknown S-box, whose size is only 4*4.

Another type of mathematics-based reverse analysis is to recover the secret S-box in the C2 algorithm in CRYPTO 2009 [14]. This method utilized the design defaults ofC2whereseveral sub key or plaintext do not go through the S-box.

The existing mathematical reverse analyses have demonstrated the feasibility to recover the unknown parts in cipher algorithms, while they all have several disadvantages such as high complexity, small number of rounds to be analyzed, and algorithm dependency.

SCA Based Reverse Engineering. This method is also called as SCARE (Side Channel Analysis of Reverse Engineering) [19]. The existing SCAREs are mainly conducted through the power analysis. Roman Novak firstly proposed a power analysis to recover the unknown S-box in A3/A8 algorithm[19], which is considered as the first work in SCARE. After several years, there have been more SCARE works on other algorithms atboth hardware and software levels [16-18]. In 2010, Sylvain Guilley proposed a new SCA, which is claimed to reverse any kind of algorithms [21]. These SCAREs are all based on CPA (Correlation Power Analysis)[7], which is highly dependent on the knowledge of the leakage model.

In SCARE, adversaries are assumed to know the basic structure of the algorithm. The target of SCAREis the unknown operation of algorithm. The reverse analysis could be considered to recover the parameters of the unknown operation.

In order to improve the practicability of the reverser analysis, we propose a new general reverse analysis method on block ciphers.

1.2   Our Contributions

We proposed a new reverse engineering analysis composed of two phases: structure analysis and parameter analysis.

The target of the reverse analysis proposed in this paper is the round function of block ciphers, which could be defined as the structure in Fig. 1.Based on the strict avalanche criterionof S-box and power analysis, we propose the reverse analysis to recover the structure of the round. The complexity of our reverse analysis is O(1).

We proposed a new reverse engineering method to recover the unknown round functionbased on the polar DPA technique. We found that the different spikes of DPA have different bias characteristics, which could be used to recover the secret of the algorithm. Our method utilizes the bias of DPA to efficiently reverse engineering the unknown operations within the round. The complexity of this reverse engineering is $O(k*(n-m))$ for the linear operation and $O(k*2^m)$ for the S-box, where n is the size of initial input, m is the size of input/output in the S-box, k is the number of S-boxes, n = m*k.

1.3   Organization

This paper is organized as follows: Section 2 introduces the structure of block cipher and polar DPA. Section 3 illustrates the reverse analysis both on the structure and inner operations. Section 4 gives the practical experiments of the reverse analysis. The final part is the conclusion.

2   Preliminary

2.1   Definition of Block Cipher

We choose block cipher as the target of reverse analysis. Most of the existing block ciphers have interactive structure, including: SPN, Feistel and extended Feistel structure as Fig.1.

In the common structures of block ciphers, such as Feistel and extended Feistel structure a, the round function can be viewed as the combination of non-linear and linear operations. The target of our reverse engineering analysis is to explore both S layer and P layer.

2.2   Differential Power Analysis

SCAs have drawn a lot of attention since Paul Kocher proposed the DPA [5] in 1999. The basic idea of power analysis (PA) is to reveal the secret key with the additional power leakages from the cryptographic device. The existing PAs includes SPA, DPA, CPA, MIA[5,7,26].

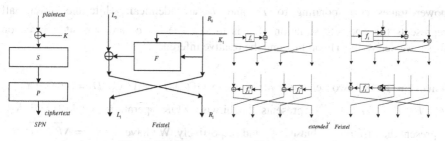

Fig. 1. Common structures of block cipher

For most of DPA attacks, the main ideas and principles originate from the model proposed by Kocher. Like other SCAs, DPA attacks are composed of two stages: data collection and statistical analysis.The differential power traces show the significant spikes when the guessed key is correct. This conclusion has been proved by Kocher [5].

DPA is based on the fact that there is a high correlation between the power dissipation and the data that is calculated in some devices. If the key is correct, spikes will arise in regions where selection function D is related to the processing data. In addition, we find that the selection function D is the most important factorin data analysis stage.

2.3   Polar DPA

Different from the traditional DPA, Polar DPA builds twoselection functions,

$$D_1 = A \wedge C_1$$
$$D_2 = A \wedge C_2 \tag{1}$$

Inequation (1), $A \wedge C$ represents the differential value of A and C, C_1, C_2 are unknown intermediates of encryption algorithm we want to know. A is a known variable which be used to partition the traces. Similarly to exploit bias signal in DPA, Polar DPA exploits the two DPA traces regarding the two selection functions to identify the value of $C_1 \wedge C_2$. We illustrate the Polar DPA in Fig.2:

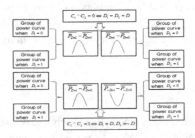

Fig. 2. The effectiveness of Polar DPA

The upper half of the Fig. 2 indicates the situation when the bias of the differential power traces corresponding to D_1 and D_2 are identical, while the lower half represents the opposite situation, that is to say, the biases are opposite. Based on these, we derive the Theorem 1 and the relative inference.

Theorem 1: For two selection functions in GF(2), $D_1 = A \wedge C_1$, $D_2 = A \wedge C_2$, A, C_1, $C_2, D_1, D_2 \in GF(2)$, $\wedge$ represents the bitwise XOR operation in GF(2), $\Delta \overline{P_1}, \Delta \overline{P_2}$ represent the differential biases of   and respectively. We have $C_1 \wedge C_2 = \Delta \overline{P_1} \wedge \Delta \overline{P_2}$.

Through polar DPA, we could get a series of differential output values, which could be used to recover the inner parameters of unknown operations in the round function.

3   The Reverse Engineering on the Round Function

3.1   Reverse Engineering on the Structure of Round Function

Based on the definition of the section 2.2,the goal of the reverse analysis of the structure of round function is to explore the size of S-boxes. Inspired by the strict avalanche criterion of S-box[24], we proposed the structure reverser analysis.

Definition 1: If $: S(X) = (f_1(X),...,f_m(X)), F_2^n \rightarrow F_2^m$ is to satisfy the strict avalanche criterion, then each output bit should change with a probability of one half whenever a single   input bit is complemented.

Our reverse analysis is based on the PA, which consists of three parts: static power, dynamic power and noise as following:

$$P_{total} = P_{dynamic} + P_{noise} + P_{static} \qquad (2)$$

$P_{dynamic}$ is the dominant part in the total power consumption, which is closely equal to the transformation of the output signals. When we input the same pair of plaintext and key, there is no transformation of the output signals in the second time and the power value is close to the sum of P_{noise} and P_{static}, which is named as P'_{total}.When we change the plaintext, we can get the $P_{dynamic}$ by subtracting P'_{total} from the total consumption P_{total}.Therefore, we utilize the dynamic power consumption to achieve the reverse analysis.

We could combine the strict avalanche criterion and the PAs to recover the size of S-boxes.

Hypothesis. From 2.1, we list the hypotheses of the round function as following:

- S-boxes are complied with the strict avalanche criterion.
- There are only S layer and P layer in the round function.
- The input size of S-box is known, which is numbered as m.
- The input size of a round equals to the output size and is numbered as n, k is the number of S-boxes in one layer.
- Each S-box is satisfied with the strict avalanche criterion.
- Regardless of the bit location, the power consumption forany bit transformation is approximatelythe same, which is denotedas P_{1bit}.

Algorithm 1. Based on the strict avalanche criterion, half of the output of S-box would be changed when one-bit of S-box input changed, which generated the transformation power consumption of $P_{1bit} * m/2$. Then if there are two-bit changed, it could generate at least $1 + m/2$ changing bits. That's the reason why we need to alter at most $1+m/2$ bits to guarantee all bits of S-box changed.   The steps of **Algorithm 1** are listed as following:

Step1： Guess the size of S-box, which is defined as gm .

Step2： Change the first bit of S-box input, and the power consumption of transformation is represented as P_{d1} .

Step3： Change $1+gm/2$ input bits of S-box from high to low order, and power consumption of transformation is denoted as P_{d2} . If P_{d2}/P_{d1} is not equal to 2, the guess is fail, otherwise, the flow goes to Step4.

Step4： Change $gm+1$ input bits of S-box from high to low order, and the dynamic power consumption is P_{d3} . If P_{d3}/P_{d1} is close to 3, the guess is succeed, otherwise, the guess fails and the flow is back to Step1 to find another guessed size of S-box.

Complexity of Algorithm 1. We have analyzed the complexity of **Algorithm 1**. It is necessary to make (m-1) times of guess and (2m-1) times of power samples to acquire the correct size of S-box. The complexity of the structure reverse analysis is O(1).

3.2   Reverse Engineering on the Parameters of Inner Operations

Combing the structure analysis and the polar DPA, we propose the reverse analysis to recover the P operation, furthermore, to acquire the parameters of S-box with polar DPA. The details of the block cipher are given in Fig. 3. We suppose that the layer P is a surjection operation.

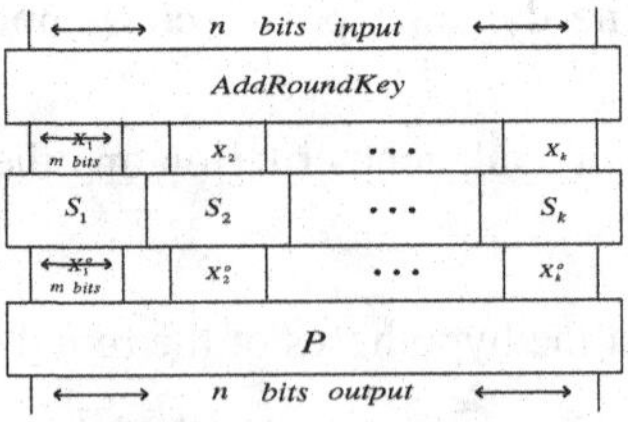

Fig. 3. The detailed structure of round function

The Reverse Engineering of Layer P. If the layer P's size of input and output is n, P could be represented as $n*n$ matrix with 0/1 elements. The reverse engineering of P equals to get the matrix, and P could be represented as the following equation:

$$Y = A \bullet X^o = \begin{bmatrix} a_{11} & a_{12} & \cdots & a_{1n} \\ a_{21} & a_{22} & \cdots & a_{2n} \\ \cdots & \cdots & \cdots & \cdots \\ a_{n1} & a_{n2} & \cdots & a_{nn} \end{bmatrix} \bullet (x_1^o, x_2^o, ..., x_n^o)^T$$

Y is a vector with n dimension, and to recover layer p means to extract the matrix A. In order to decrease the complexity, we could divide the A into several sub-blocks based on the column and X based on the row. We could get the following equation:

$$Y = \left[A_1 \mid A_2 \mid ... \mid A_k \right] \bullet (X_1^{\ o} \mid X_2^{\ o} \mid ... \mid X_k^{\ o})^T$$

Where:
$$A_i = \begin{bmatrix} a_{1((i-1)m+1)} & \cdots & a_{1(im)} \\ \cdots & \cdots & \cdots \\ a_{n((i-1)m+1)} & \cdots & a_{n(im)} \end{bmatrix}, \quad X_i^{\ o} = \begin{bmatrix} x_{(i-1)m+1}^{\ o} \\ \cdots \\ x_{im}^{\ o} \end{bmatrix}, \quad i = 1,...,k.$$

A_i could be represented as an n*m matrix with 0/1 elements, where A could be acquired by solving each A_i. As introduced in 3.1, we could get the size of S-box as m. If we set the input of the ith S-box as constant which is denoted as X_i, others are random, we could acquire several different output vector Y of layer p through several pairs of input sequences. We define the jth output vector as $Y_{i,j}$, and choose a pair of output $(Y_{i,0}, Y_{i,1})$ to analyze. For a pair of inputs have the same byte as X_i, the corresponding output of S-box should be the same and the differential of these outputs is 0. We could get the following equation:

$$A_i^{-1} \cdot Y_{i,0} \wedge A_i^{-1} \cdot Y_{i,1} = 0 \Leftrightarrow A_i^{-1} \cdot (Y_{i,0} \wedge Y_{i,1}) = 0 \tag{3}$$

A_i^{-1} could be represented as the n*m matrix with 0/1 elements, $Y_{i,0} \wedge Y_{i,1}$ is an n-dimensional vector which is named as ΔY_i . With the characters of the matrix rank, as for the matrix A_{m*n} and B_{n*s} , if $A_{m*n} * B_{n*s} = 0$ $(m < n)$ we could get $r(A_{m*n}) + r(B_{n*s}) \leq n$, where $A_{m*n} * B_{n*s} = 0$ represent the rank of A_{m*n} and B_{n*s} respectively. If A_{m*n} is full rank, $r(A_{m*n}) = m$ and $r(B_{n*s}) \leq n - m$. As a result, we only need to find (n-m) groups of linear independent vectors ΔY_i , and could solve the corresponding matrix A_i^{-1}.

To repeat the previous steps, we could get the each $A_i^{-1} (i = 1,2,...,k)$, and acquire the complete matrix A^{-1}. For the layer P is a surjection operation, we could acquire A through A^{-1} and recover the P operation.

We can recover the value of ΔY_i through the polar DPA and reverse the layer P by **Algorithm 2**.The steps of **Algorithm 2** are given below and we use the same notations in the above analysis.

Step1: To acquire (n-m) group of ΔY_i through (n-m) times polar DPA.

Step2: Solve the linear equations to get A_i^{-1}.

Step3: Repeat Step1 and Step2 k times to get all $A_i^{-1} (i = 1,2,...,k)$.

Step4: Acquire the complete matrix A_i^{-1} and reverse layer P .

Analyzing the complexity, it needs (n-m) times of the polar DPA to solve A_i^{-1} , and furthermore to acquire the matrix A after k times computation. The total complexity is $O(k*(n-m))$.

The Reverse Engineering of S-box. To choose a pair of input for the ith S-box, named as X_1 and X_2 , the corresponding differential output of P could be represented as:

$$P(S_i(X_1) \wedge S_i(X_2)) = \delta \tag{4}$$

Furthermore, we could get the differential values of $S_i(X_1)$ and $S_i(X_2)$, and build the following equations through exhaustive search of S-box:

$$S_i(X_0) \wedge S_i(X_1) = \delta_1$$
$$S_i(X_0) \wedge S_i(X_2) = \delta_2$$
$$......$$
$$S_i(X_0) \wedge S_i(X_{2^m-1}) = \delta_{2^m-1} \tag{5}$$

We could exhaust 2^m groups of S-box value, and certificate the correct S-box through one time encryption. If every S-box of one layer is distinguish, we should compute k times to recover the parameters of all different S-boxes, and the complexity is $O(k*2^m)$.

If only S-box is unknown in the algorithm, with the same idea, we also could achieve the reverse analysis on S-box. In order to solve the equations (5), we can also use polar DPA to get δ_i and the specific algorithm is given below, named **Algorithm 3.**

Step1: Execute polar DPA to get 2^m-1 groups of δ_i .

Step2: Exhaust 2^m groups of S-box valueand certificate the correctness through one time encryption

Step3: Repeat Step1 and Step2 to get all S_i $(i=1,2,...,k)$.

Step4: Reverse S layer with $S = \{S_1, S_2,...,S_k\}$.

One time of reverse analysis needs 2^m polar DPA and 2^m exhaustive searches, and the complexity to recover the all S-boxes in one layer is $O(k*2^{m+1})$, when there are different S-boxes in one S layer.

4   Experiments and Analysis

In order to verify the effectiveness of the reverse analysis, we conduct the experiments on MIBS algorithm [25] in sequential implementation, which is supposed to have the unknown round function. Our experiments are based on the simulation platform, which include Design Compiler, Modelsim, and Synopsys PrimePower.

4.1   Experiments of Structure Reverse Engineering

Firstly, we introduce the implementation of MIBS algorithm, whose S-boxes are implemented with LUTs. We use the structure reverse analysis illustrated in 3.1 to acquire the size of S-box.

We attacked the first round function of MIBS with chosen plaintext analysis, which uses the static key and chooses different plaintexts to control the input bit of the S-box in the first round from high bit to low bit. Complying with the method in 3.1, it is needed 3 groups of dynamic power consumption to verify different guessed size of S-box. We define $Cbits_i (i = 1, 2, 3)$ to represent the number of changed bits in the ith group of dynamic power consumption. Part of guessed-size schemes of S-box are listed in Table 1.

Table 1. Someguessed-size schemesof S-box

Guessed size of Sbox	$Cbits_1$	$Cbits_2$	$Cbits_3$
2*2	1	2	3
4*4	1	3	5
8*8	1	5	9

We use the PrimePower to collect power samples. As introduced in 3.1, we get the P'_{total} with a pair of same plaintexts. When we change the plaintext, we can get the dynamic power consumption by subtracting P'_{total} from the total consumption. The curves of the dynamic power consumption for the above schemes are illustrated in Fig. 4.

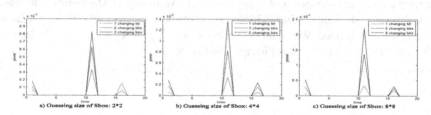

Fig. 4. Dynamic power for different guessed sizes of S-box

For one guessed size of S-box, it needs three times of power sampling. We use P_{d1}, P_{d2} and P_{d3} to represent the dynamic power of the first sampling, second and third one respectively. The ratios of the dynamic power are concluded in Table2.

Table 2. The Ratio of Dynamic Power for Different Guessedsizeof S-box

Guessed size of S-box	P_{d2}/P_{d1}	P_{d3}/P_{d1}	True/False
2*2	1.825031394	2.124703805	F
4*4	2.124703805	3.192990743	T
8*8	3.192990743	5.084137233	F

Illustration: Based on the Algorithm 1, if the guessed size of S-box is correct, the values of P_{d2}/P_{d1} and P_{d3}/P_{d1} are close to 2 and 3 respectively. Therefore, we could find the correct size of S-box is 4*4 inTable2. The result is correct according to the algorithm MIBS.

4.2   Experiments of Reverse Engineering on Inner Operations

According to the structure of MIBS algorithm, the Mixing layer and Permutation layer can be combined and regarded as the P layer. The parameters of S layer and P layer are both unknown. If the input of S-box in the second round could be named as X, we could get the equation (6).

$$X = P(S(Z)) \wedge R_0 \wedge K_2 \tag{6}$$

- Z : the input of S-box in the first round;
- R_0 : the right part of plaintext;
- K_2 : the sub-key in the second round.

The equation (6) is satisfied the policy of the polar DPA, we could recover the parameters of P. In polar DPA, we need to do two DPA experiments to get one bit differential value. For each DPA, could set the key and the left of plaintext L_0 to be static, and choose the right of plaintext R_0 randomly. R_0 is the partition part of the polar DPA. We have got the size of S-box as 4*4 in section 4.1. According to **Algorithm 2,** for each DPA, Z is set as the value of 0x31234567 and 0x39abcdef respectively, where the input of the first S-box is fixed. We could get the corresponding DPA curves of the highest bit of Z with 10000 power curves as illustrated in Fig. 5.

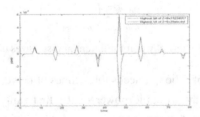

Fig. 5. DPA curve of the highest bit

From Fig.5, we can see that the polarity of two DPA curves is opposite and the correlation between two curves is -0.985464567, so the differential value between corresponding bit should be 1. For each bit, we repeat the above process and we can get the differential value of each bit, which is illustrated in Table 3.

Table 3. The differential valueofeachbit

Differential value	1001111101000110011101101101000100(0x9f4676c4)

According to Table 3, for a pair of Z(0x31234567 , 0x39abcdef), the differential value after layer S and layer P is 0x9f4676c4. In order to verify the differential value, we execute the encryption of MIBS for the pair of Z,the differential value of the outputs will be 0x9f4676c4.We can learn that the differential value of our experiment is correct. As the input of the first S-box has been fixed in the Z, thus we could get the equation (7).

$$P_1^{-1}(0x9f4676c4) = 0 \qquad (7)$$

Repeating the previous steps, we could get a series of linear equations. To solve the P_1^{-1}, it is needed 28 groups of linear independent equations. And the other 7 pair of $P_i^{-1}(i = 2, \cdots, 8)$ could be also recovered with the same method. We could recover P with P^{-1}, and as the introduction in section 3.2, we can get the differential output of S-box and build the equations as (7) so as to recover the parameter of S-box.

When there is only S-box unknown, for example MIBS-like algorithm, We can hold the 0th, 2th, 3th, 4th, 7th bits of Z as nibble Y, other bits are random. According to the MIBS algorithm, we can get the following equation.

$$X_{[4]} = S(Y) \wedge R_{0[4]} \wedge K_{2[4]} \qquad (8)$$

- $X_{[4]}$ is the 4th nibble of the second round;
- $R_{0[4]}$ is the 4th nibble input of R_0 ;
- $K_{2[4]}$ is the 4th nibble input of K_2 .

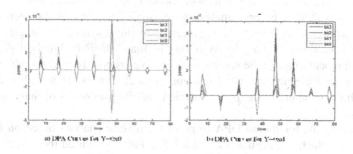

a) DPA Curves for Y=0x0   b) DPA Curves for Y=0xd

Fig. 6.DPA curves for Y=0x0 and Y=0xd

The equation (8) is satisfied the policy of the polar DPA and we can use **Algorithm 3** to reverse the parameters of S-box. For example, we can set Y as 0x0 and 0xd respectively and $R_{0[4]}$ will be used as partition part. We execute DPA twice, therefore, we can get the one-bit differential value of $S(0x0) \wedge S(0xd)$.

The correlations of each bit in the differential power curves of Y=0x0 and Y=0xd are listed in Table 4.

Table 4. Thecorrelationof DPA curves

bit3	bit2	bit1	bit0
0.388760987180	0.939511072952	-0.638112502011	0.887657305118

From the result of Table 4, we could get $S(0x0) \wedge S(0xd) = 0x2$, which corresponds the correct differential value for $S(0x0) = 0x4$, and $S(0xd) = 0x6$. Repeating the previous steps, we could get the differential value of S-box as Table 5.

Table 5. The Differential valueof S-box in MIBS

Y	1	2	3	4	5	6	7	8
$S(0x0) \wedge S(Y)$	b	7	c	9	e	8	4	f
Y	9	a	b	c	d	e	f	
$S(0x0) \wedge S(Y)$	1	3	a	6	2	5	d	

We could recover the parameters of S-box after exhausting search of $S(0x0)$ and verifying the correctness of the parameter by one time encryption.. The results proof that the reverse analysis proposed in this paper could recover the unknown round function of the block ciphers.

5   Conclusion

The unknown parts of a block cipher's secret algorithms could make a cryptanalysis more difficult. In order to check if a block cipher meets the security requirement, it is necessary to evaluate it by cryptanalysis especially by the reverse engineering analysis. The existing SCAs for reverse engineering mainly focus on the single unknown non-linear operation. The complexity is very high and might be highly dependent on the leakage model to fulfill the reverse analysis. We proposed a new reverse engineering analysis on the unknown round function of block ciphers. This method could recover both the structure of the round function and the parameters of inner operations efficiently.

We improve the traditional DPA to build the reverse analysis based on the polar power curve, which is named as the polar DPA. Firstly, we used the strict avalanche criterion to recover the size of S-box. Secondly, we acquired the parameters of nonlinear and linear operations in the round function through combination of the polar

DPA and the structure analysis. The complexity of the structure reverse analysis is $O(1)$, and the complexity of inner reverse method is $O(k*(n-m))$ for the linear operation and $O(k*2^m)$ for the non-linear operation, where n is the size of input, m is the size of input/output in the S-box, k is the number of S-boxes, n=m*k.

To improve the effectiveness of our reverse analysis, we conduct experiments on MIBS algorithm to recover the unknown rounds. The results of experiments have shown the feasibility and effectiveness of the reverse analysis, which could be regarded as a generic, reverse engineering method for most of the block ciphers, and an important evaluation for the secret block ciphers.

Acknowledgements. This work was sponsored by National Natural Science Foundation of China(Grant Nos. 60970116, 60970115,61202386, 61003267).

References

1. Matsui, M.: Linear Cryptanalysis Method for DES Cipher. In: Helleseth, T. (ed.) EUROCRYPT 1993. LNCS, vol. 765, pp. 386–397. Springer, Heidelberg (1994)
2. Biham, E., Shamir, A.: Differential Cryptanalysis of DES-like Cryptosystems. In: Menezes, A., Vanstone, S.A. (eds.) CRYPTO 1990. LNCS, vol. 537, pp. 2–21. Springer, Heidelberg (1991)
3. Biham, E., Shamir, A.: Differential Cryptanalysis of the Data Encryption Standard. Springer, London (1993) ISBN: 0-387-97930-1
4. Courtois, N.T., Pieprzyk, J.: Cryptanalysis of Block Ciphers with Overdefined Systems of Equations. In: Zheng, Y. (ed.) ASIACRYPT 2002. LNCS, vol. 2501, pp. 267–287. Springer, Heidelberg (2002)
5. Kocher, P., Jaffe, J., Jun, B.: Differential Power Analysis. In: Wiener, M. (ed.) CRYPTO 1999. LNCS, vol. 1666, pp. 388–397. Springer, Heidelberg (1999)
6. Kocher, P.C.: Timing Attacks on Implementations of Diffie-Hellman, RSA, DSS, and Other Systems. In: Koblitz, N. (ed.) CRYPTO 1996. LNCS, vol. 1109, pp. 104–113. Springer, Heidelberg (1996)
7. Brier, E., Clavier, C., Olivier, F.: Correlation Power Analysis with a Leakage Model. In: Joye, M., Quisquater, J.-J. (eds.) CHES 2004. LNCS, vol. 3156, pp. 16–29. Springer, Heidelberg (2004)
8. Biham, E., Shamir, A.: Differential Fault Analysis of Secret Key Cryptosystems. In: Kaliski Jr., B.S. (ed.) CRYPTO 1997. LNCS, vol. 1294, pp. 513–525. Springer, Heidelberg (1997)
9. Quisquater, J.-J., Samyde, D.: ElectroMagnetic Analysis (EMA): Measures and Counter-Measures for Smart Cards. In: Attali, S., Jensen, T. (eds.) E-smart 2001. LNCS, vol. 2140, pp. 200–210. Springer, Heidelberg (2001)
10. http://www.schneier.com/paper-twofish-paper.html
11. http://www.encryptfiles.net/encryption/algorithm/mars.php
12. http://jya.com//gsm061088.htm
13. Biryukov, A., Shamir, A.: Structural Cryptanalysis of SASAS. In: Pfitzmann, B. (ed.) EUROCRYPT 2001. LNCS, vol. 2045, pp. 394–405. Springer, Heidelberg (2001)
14. Borghoff, J., Knudsen, L.R., Leander, G., Matusiewicz, K.: Cryptanalysis of C2. In: Halevi, S. (ed.) CRYPTO 2009. LNCS, vol. 5677, pp. 250–266. Springer, Heidelberg (2009)

15. Borghoff, J., Knudsen, L.R., Leander, G., Thomsen, S.S.: Cryptanalysis of PRESENT-like ciphers with secret S-boxes. In: Joux, A. (ed.) FSE 2011. LNCS, vol. 6733, pp. 270–289. Springer, Heidelberg (2011)
16. Novak, R.: Side-Channel Attack on Substitution Blocks. In: Zhou, J., Yung, M., Han, Y. (eds.) ACNS 2003. LNCS, vol. 2846, pp. 307–318. Springer, Heidelberg (2003)
17. Daudigny, R., Ledig, H., Muller, F., Valette, F.: SCARE of the DES. In: Ioannidis, J., Keromytis, A.D., Yung, M. (eds.) ACNS 2005. LNCS, vol. 3531, pp. 393–406. Springer, Heidelberg (2005)
18. Clavier, C.: An Improved SCARE Cryptanalysis Against a Secret A3/A8 GSM Algorithm. In: McDaniel, P., Gupta, S.K. (eds.) ICISS 2007. LNCS, vol. 4812, pp. 143–155. Springer, Heidelberg (2007)
19. Novak, R.: Side-channel Based Reverse Engineering of Secret Algorithms. In: Proceedings of the Twelfth International Electrotechnical and Computer Science Conference (ERK 2003), September 25-26, pp. 445–448. IEEE (2003)
20. Réal, D., Dubois, V., Guilloux, A.-M., Valette, F., Drissi, M.: SCARE of an Unknown Hardware Feistel Implementation. In: Grimaud, G., Standaert, F.-X. (eds.) CARDIS 2008. LNCS, vol. 5189, pp. 218–227. Springer, Heidelberg (2008)
21. Guilley, S., Sauvage, L., Micolod, J., Réal, D., Valette, F.: Defeating Any Secret Cryptography with SCARE Attacks. In: Abdalla, M., Barreto, P.S.L.M. (eds.) LATINCRYPT 2010. LNCS, vol. 6212, pp. 273–293. Springer, Heidelberg (2010)
22. Biryukovand, A., Shamir, A.: Structural Cryptanalysis of SASAS. Journal of Cryptology 23, 505–518 (2010)
23. Borghoff, J., Knudsen, L.R., Leander, G., Thomsen, S.S.: Cryptanalysis of PRESENT-like ciphers with secret S-boxes. In: Joux, A. (ed.) FSE 2011. LNCS, vol. 6733, pp. 270–289. Springer, Heidelberg (2011)
24. Webster, A.F., Tavares, S.E.: On the Design of S-boxes. In: Williams, H.C. (ed.) CRYPTO 1985. LNCS, vol. 218, pp. 523–534. Springer, Heidelberg (1986)
25. Izadi, M., Sadeghiyan, B., Sadeghian, S.S., Khanooki, H.A.: MIBS: A New Lightweight Block Cipher. In: Garay, J.A., Miyaji, A., Otsuka, A. (eds.) CANS 2009. LNCS, vol. 5888, pp. 334–348. Springer, Heidelberg (2009)
26. Gierlichs, B., Batina, L., Tuyls, P., Preneel, B.: Mutual Information Analysis. In: Oswald, E., Rohatgi, P. (eds.) CHES 2008. LNCS, vol. 5154, pp. 426–442. Springer, Heidelberg (2008)

PEVS: A Secure Electronic Voting Scheme Using Polling Booths

Md. Abdul Based, Joe-Kai Tsay, and Stig Fr. Mjølsnes

Department of Telematics,
Norwegian University of Science and Technology,
Trondheim, Norway
{based,joe.k.tsay,sfm}@item.ntnu.no

Abstract. We present a Polling booth based Electronic Voting Scheme (PEVS) that allows eligible voters to cast their ballots inside polling booths. The ballot cast by a voter is inalterable and non-reusable. The scheme ensures vote-privacy since there is no link between the voter and the keys used for voting. A voter computer inside the booth performs the cryptographic task to construct the ballot to provide receipt-freeness. The scheme is coercion-resistant and modeled to fend off forced-abstention attacks, simulation attacks or randomization attacks. In addition, the scheme is both voter and universal verifiable. We formally analyze soundness (the eligibility of the voter, inalterability and non-reusability of the ballot), vote-privacy, receipt-freeness, and coercion-resistance in PEVS using the ProVerif tool. The analysis shows that PEVS satisfies these required properties. PEVS is the first polling booth based electronic voting scheme that satisfies all the requirements listed.

1 Introduction

Trusted voting schemes are fundamental requirements to the democratic societies. Government leaders must be elected in a proper way so that people can trust them. Often, paper-based voting schemes have some serious flaws which leave space for corruption and irregularities. This problem accelerates the need of secure electronic voting schemes.

Electronic voting has become a challenging research topic in recent years. Constructing a cryptographic protocol for secure electronic voting is rather challenging due to the complex security requirements. Among others, this includes eligibility of the voter, vote-privacy, receipt-freeness, coercion-resistance, and verifiability. Vote-privacy, receipt-freeness, and coercion-resistance are the privacy requirements [1] of a secure electronic voting scheme. Receipt-freeness means a voter cannot convince the coercer how the ballot was cast. A coercer should not be able to force a voter to abstain from voting or to cast the ballot for a particular candidate or in a particular way. This is only possible if the coercer is not able to trace whether a voter has cast a ballot or not, and how the ballot is cast. This property is known as coercion-resistance [2,3].

Y. Xiang et al. (Eds.): ICDKE 2012, LNCS 7696, pp. 189–205, 2012.
© Springer-Verlag Berlin Heidelberg 2012

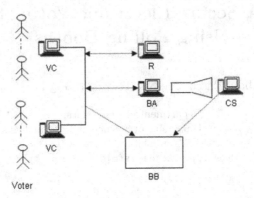

Voter

Fig. 1. PEVS. Here, $VC = Voter\ Computer, R = Registrar, BA = Ballot\ Acquirer, BB = Bulletin\ Board, and\ CS = Counting\ Servers.$

1.1   Our Contributions

We distinguish between categories of electronic voting in terms of control of people and terminals. In a remote electronic voting scheme a voter can cast a ballot from any place. However, there is no cryptographic way to defend a voter from physical coercion in such voting. Considering this, we choose the second category where a voter casts the ballot inside a polling booth (also known as election booth). Then cryptographic mechanisms are used inside the booth to achieve receipt-freeness and coercion-resistance. We name our scheme Polling booth based Electronic Voting Scheme (PEVS).

Fig. 1 shows an overview of PEVS's structure. In PEVS the voter can generate any number of key pairs using the voter computer inside the booth. Each pair has a private key and a corresponding public key. The voter gets the public keys signed by a registrar in a blind signature scheme. This ensures that there is no link between the voter and the keys, and satisfies the vote-privacy requirement. Using one of these keys, the voter computer performs the cryptographic tasks to construct the ballot, so the voter cannot prove to anyone how the ballot is cast. This satisfies the receipt-freeness requirement. In order to fend off forced-abstention attacks,[1] the voter gives the coercer the number of unused key pairs requested by the coercer before the voter enters the polling booth. The coercer cannot perform a simulation attack[2] or a randomization attack[3] [2,5] since the voter casts the ballot with the fresh keys only inside the booth. Thus PEVS is coercion-resistant.

---

[1] In a forced-abstention attack the attacker coerces a voter by demanding that the voter refrains from voting [2].

[2] In a simulation attack the attacker coerces a voter by demanding that the voter divulges his private keys so that the attacker can simulate the voter on his behalf [2].

[3] In a randomization attack the attacker coerces a voter by demanding that the voter submits randomly composed balloting material to nullify his choice with a large probability [2].

The ballots are constructed and distributed as encrypted shares to multiple counting servers. The counting servers can verify the ballots individually using a non-interactive zero knowledge protocol [6]. However, a threshold number of honest counting servers jointly count the ballots and publish the tally. We refer to [6] for details of the ballot construction and counting.

In order to achieve verifiability PEVS uses a bulletin board. The content of the bulletin board is public, so anyone can verify it. In PEVS the voters verify the keys signed and published on the bulletin board by the counting servers, this indicates that their ballots have been counted since the keys were associated with the ballots by the voters using the voter computer. This satisfies the voter verifiability[4] requirement. The counting servers also publish the ballots and the tally. Any observer can verify that the tally corresponds to the published ballots. Thus PEVS is both voter verifiable and universal verifiable[5].

We formally analyze vote-privacy, receipt-freeness, and coercion-resistance of PEVS. The ProVerif tool [7] is used to perform the analysis. We also verify soundness (eligibility of the voter, inalterability and non-reusability of the ballot) of PEVS in ProVerif. To the best of our knowledge we believe that PEVS is the first polling booth based electronic voting scheme that satisfies all these required properties.

1.2 Related Work

The 'FOO92' protocol [8] is based on a blind signature scheme and is analyzed by Nielsen et al. [9] as well as Delaune et al. [1] who both show that the protocol is not receipt-free. PEVS, which is receipt-free, also uses a blind signature technique in order to get signed keys for the voter from the registrar.

Receipt-freeness is introduced by Benaloh and Tuinstra in [14]. Lee et al. describe receipt-freeness in mix-net based voting protocols in [15]. Delaune et al. provide formal definitions of vote-privacy, receipt-freeness and coercion-resistance in [1] applied to different voting schemes [8,15,17]. Their definition of coercion-resistance is not suitable for automatic verification. Okamoto presents a voting scheme in [17] with an aim to be coercion-resistant. However, a flaw was found due to the lack of formal definitions and proofs of receipt-freeness and coercion-resistance in [14]. Helios [16] is a web-based open-audit voting scheme. Though Helios provides verifiability it is not receipt free. A paper-based voting system is presented by Rivest in [12].

Civitas is a remote electronic voting system implemented by Clarkson et al. [18] and based on the voting scheme published by Juels et al. [3]. A remote voting scheme can never be completely coercion-resistant if the coercer is able to see how the voter is casting the ballot. In the same way paper-based voting schemes are not coercion-resistant if there is options for postal voting. However, Civitas shows some sort of coercion-resistance under the assumption that all the talliers are honest. The idea is, Civitas allows a voter to cheat the coercer with

---

[4] A voter can verify that the ballot cast by that voter is really counted [13].
[5] The published tally is the sum of all ballots [13].

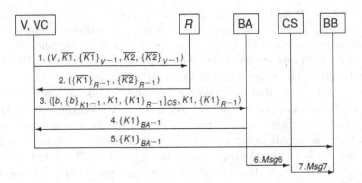

Fig. 2. The message sequence diagram of PEVS. Here, $V = Voter$, $VC = Voter$ $Computer$, $R = Registrar$, $BA = Ballot\ Acquirer$, $CS = Counting\ Servers$, and $BB = $ Bulletin Board. $Msg6 = (\{[b, \{b\}_{K1-1}, K1, \{K1\}_{R-1}]_{CS}\}_{BA-1})$ and $Msg7 = (b, \{b\}_{CS-1}, T, \{K1\}_{CS-1})$.

fake credentials. Then any ballot cast by the coercer with the fake credentials are silently dropped by the counting servers. In comparison, PEVS uses polling booths, which are controlled environments where physical coercion is not possible. Furthermore, PEVS requires only a threshold number of counting servers to act honestly.

Backes et al. [5] provide a formal definition that can be used for automatic verification of coercion-resistance for remote electronic voting schemes. We adopt their definition of coercion-resistance to polling booth based voting schemes and verify coercion-resistance of PEVS in ProVerif. In addition, we analyze vote-privacy and receipt-freeness using the definitions in [1].

We refer to [6] regarding the ballot construction in a secret sharing scheme and counting of ballots. We refer to the non-interactive zero-knowledge protocol [19] to verify the ballot by the counting servers. Two verifiable electronic voting schemes are presented in [10] and [11]. To our knowledge, these schemes are not yet formally analyzed and coercion-resistance is not addressed explicitly.

There exists quite a few analyses of voting protocols using (variants of) the applied pi calculus [21], e.g. [1,5,13]. This has the advantage that the analyses may be conducted automatically with the ProVerif [7] tool. We also apply ProVerif to automatically verify certain properties of PEVS.

1.3 Outline of the Paper

In Section 2 the voting scheme is presented as a message sequence diagram. A brief overview of ProVerif's language and the analysis of PEVS is given in Section 3. The conclusions and future plans are presented in Section 4.

2 PEVS Electronic Voting Scheme

The message sequence diagram of PEVS is shown in Fig. 2. We have voters, Voter Computers (VC), a Ballot Acquirer (BA), a Registrar (R), a Bulletin

Board (BB), and a set of Counting Servers (CS) in PEVS. The polling booths in which the voters cast their ballots are controlled by the election officials or independent authorities. A voter is not allowed to interact with other voters or the attackers inside a booth. Though multiple voters can sequentially cast their ballots in the same polling booth, only one voter is allowed inside the booth at a specific time.

The voter and the voter computer are represented as a single entity in Fig. 2. The voter performs all the operations (for example, encryption, decryption, and digital signature) using the voter computer. The registrar, the voter computer, and a threshold number of counting servers are assumed to be fully trusted in our voting scheme. The bulletin board can be treated as a centralized server, and the voter computer and the counting servers communicate with the bulletin board over the Internet. The counting servers perform the same role. However, these are different parties and the communication between them is done over authenticated and encrypted channels. Other communications between different parties are done over the Internet. We do not consider availability issues in this paper.

The following notations are used in our voting scheme:

K^{-1} is a private key and K is the corresponding public key.
$\overline{K}$ is the blinded copy of K.
$\{m\}_{K^{-1}}$ is the signature of the message m under the key K^{-1}.
$[m]_K$ is the encryption of the plain text m under the key K.

In practice, voter authentication could be done by using a smartcard, e.g., smartcard with local biometric identification. Inside the booth the voter then generates two fresh key pairs ($K1, K1^{-1}$ and $K2, K2^{-1}$) using the VC. Actually, the voter can generate an unbounded number of keys according to the request of the coercer in a forced-abstention attack, i.e. if the coercer requests n key pairs from the voter, then he typically generates $n + 1$. The voter sends 1. ($V, \overline{K1}, \{\overline{K1}\}_{V^{-1}}, \overline{K2}, \{\overline{K2}\}_{V^{-1}}$) to the registrar (First message in Fig. 2) using the VC. Here, $\overline{K1}$ is the blinded copy of $K1$ and $\overline{K2}$ is the blinded copy of $K2$, V is the public key of the voter. The blinded keys ($\{\overline{K1}\}$ and $\{\overline{K2}\}$) are signed with the private key of the voter V^{-1}.

The registrar has a list of public keys of the eligible voters. After receiving the message 1. ($V, \overline{K1}, \{\overline{K1}\}_{V^{-1}}, \overline{K2}, \{\overline{K2}\}_{V^{-1}}$), the registrar verifies the signature of the voter. Then the registrar signs the blinded keys ($\overline{K1}, \overline{K2}$) with the private key R^{-1} and sends the signed blinded keys to the voter. The message sent from the registrar to the voter is the second message 2. ($\{\overline{K1}\}_{R^{-1}}, \{\overline{K2}\}_{R^{-1}}$) in Fig. 2. The voter verifies the signature of the registrar, then unblinds the message and gets two signed public keys ($\{K1\}_{R^{-1}}, \{K2\}_{R^{-1}}$). The voter uses one key for voting and the other key to fend off forced-abstention attacks.

The voter chooses to vote for a particular candidate and the voter computer generates the ballot b from the vote. The ballot is constructed as encrypted shares for the counting servers. For the detail of the ballot construction we refer to [6]. The voter signs the ballot b using the VC with the private key $K1^{-1}$, adds $K1$ and the signature $\{K1\}_{R^{-1}}$ to the ballot, and encrypts the message with the public key of the Counting Servers (CS). The VC then adds the key $K1$ and the signature $\{K1\}_{R^{-1}}$ again with this message. The VC sends this signed and encrypted message to the ballot acquirer. This message is shown as 3. $([b, \{b\}_{K1^{-1}}, K1, \{K1\}_{R^{-1}}]_{CS}, K1, \{K1\}_{R^{-1}})$ in Fig. 2. In this case the voter can use $\{K2\}_{R^{-1}}$ against forced-abstention attacks. The voter computer is trusted and will construct only one ballot for each voter. The registrar declines the initiation of the protocol by the same voter to generate more than one ballot since the registrar maintains the list of the public keys of the eligible voters.

After receiving 3. $([b, \{b\}_{K1^{-1}}, K1, \{K1\}_{R^{-1}}]_{CS}, K1, \{K1\}_{R^{-1}})$, the ballot acquirer parses the message and verifies the signature of the registrar on the key $K1$. The ballot acquirer also maintains a list of the keys and verifies the freshness of the key $K1$. Then the ballot acquirer signs the key and sends the signature on this key $\{K1\}_{BA^{-1}}$ to the voter (Fourth message in Fig. 2). After receiving this the voter publishes it on the bulletin board (Fifth message in Fig. 2) using the voter computer. The ballot acquirer then signs the encrypted message $([b, \{b\}_{K1^{-1}}, K1, \{K1\}_{R^{-1}}]_{CS})$ received from the voter with its private key BA^{-1}, and sends it to the counting servers. This message is shown as $Msg6$. $(\{[b, \{b\}_{K1^{-1}}, K1, \{K1\}_{R^{-1}}]_{CS}\}_{BA^{-1}})$ in Fig. 2. The counting servers only accept ballots signed by the ballot acquirer.

Each of the counting servers first decrypts the message ($Msg6$) received from the ballot acquirer. Then each counting server verifies the signature of the registrar on the key $K1$ ($\{K1\}_{R^{-1}}$) and the signature of the voter on the ballot ($\{b\}_{K1^{-1}}$). After the verifications, the counting servers, of which a threshold number are honest, jointly sign and publish the ballots, then count the ballots and publish the tally. The threshold number of counting servers also sign the key $K1$ and publish the signature $\{K1\}_{CS^{-1}}$ on the bulletin board (BB). The message sent by these counting servers to the BB is shown as $Msg7$. $(b, \{b\}_{CS^{-1}}, T, \{K1\}_{CS^{-1}})$ in Fig. 2. Here, T is the tally of the counted ballots.

The ballot is sent as encrypted shares, so the dishonest counting servers do not get complete information about the individual ballot, though the threshold number of counting servers together reach a result that they agree upon. The counting servers can verify the validity of the ballot using the non-interactive zero knowledge protocol presented in [6].

The content of the bulletin board is public and used to provide voter verifiability and universal verifiability. The voter receives the signature $\{K1\}_{BA^{-1}}$ on the key $K1$ from the ballot acquirer. This signature ensures that the ballot acquirer has received the ballot. Then this signature is published on the bulletin board by the voter using the VC. On the bulletin board the counting servers also publish the signature $\{K1\}_{CS^{-1}}$ on the key $K1$ signed by these servers and the voter can easily verify this. Since the threshold number of counting servers publishes the same signature, the dishonest counting servers cannot cheat without detection. The signature $\{K2\}_{R^{-1}}$ on the key $K2$ is normally not used for voting and not published on the bulletin board. This key is only used when the voter needs to fend off the forced-abstention attacks. In that case the voter casts the ballot using the signature $\{K1\}_{R^{-1}}$ and gives the coercer the signature $\{K2\}_{R^{-1}}$.

Any observer can verify that the number of signatures published by the counting servers is equal to or less than the number of signatures published by the voters. The reason for this is that the counting servers may discard some invalid ballots after ballot verification. The counting servers may maintain a list of these signatures of the discarded ballots for future claims. The valid ballots are published on the bulletin board, so the observer can verify that the tally is the outcome of the ballots published on the bulletin board.

3   Formal Analysis of PEVS

In the following, we give a brief overview of the input language of the tool ProVerif [7], present formal definitions of security properties of PEVS, and then we present the results of our analysis. The ProVerif tool is an automatic cryptographic protocol verifier tool developed by Blanchet et al. [7] and available on the web [7]. This tool can prove properties of security protocols with respect to the so-called *Dolev-Yao* model and supports a wide range of cryptographic primitives including asymmetric encryption, digital signatures, blind signatures, and non-interactive zero-knowledge proofs. The tool is capable of proving reachability properties, correspondence assertions, and observational equivalences. ProVerif analyzes protocols with respect to an unbounded number of sessions and an unbounded message space, and tries to reconstruct attack when a property cannot be proved. However, although ProVerif proofs are sound with respect to the Dolev-Yao model, ProVerif may fail to prove a property that indeed holds, i.e. Proverif is not complete. We use these properties to verify the security properties of our voting scheme. The 'FOO92' protocol, Civitas, and the protocol by Juels et al. have already been analyzed with Proverif.

3.1   Overview of ProVerif's Language

ProVerif's input language is a variant of the applied pi-calculus, which is a formal language introduced in [21] for reasoning about concurrent processes. We give a overview of ProVerif's language, which should suffice to understand our formalization of PEVS and the properties we prove using ProVerif.

Terms are built from *names* $a, b, c, m, n, \ldots$, *variables* $x, y, z, \ldots$, and a set Σ of *function symbols* that are applied to terms. Function symbols (each with an arity) typically represent cryptographic primitives and the equivalences that hold on terms are described by an *equational theory* E. A function symbol with arity 0 is a constant. The function symbols are divided in *constructors* f and *destructors* g which are related via equations in E. For two terms M, N we write $M =_E N$ for equality modulo (the equations in) E. And $\{M_1/x_1, \ldots, M_l/x_l\}$ denotes the substitution of $x_1, \ldots, x_l$ by, respectively, $M_1, \ldots, M_l$. The language is strongly typed; any term n has one of the (user-defined) types t, written $n : t$.

Processes are built according to the grammar in Fig. 3 (where u is a meta variable that may represent a name or a variable). The null process does nothing.

$$
\begin{array}{ll}
P, Q ::= & \text{plain processes} \\
\mathbf{0} & \text{null process} \\
P \mid Q & \text{parallel composition} \\
!P & \text{replication} \\
\text{new } n : t; P & \text{name restriction} \\
\text{in}(u, x : t); P & \text{message input} \\
\text{out}(u, N); P & \text{message output} \\
\text{if } M = N \text{ then } P \text{ else } Q & \text{conditional} \\
\text{let } x = M \text{ in } P & \text{term evaluation}
\end{array}
$$

Fig. 3. ProVerif process grammar

$P \mid Q$ represents the parallel execution of P and Q, while $!P$ behaves like an unbounded number of concurrently running copies of P. The name restriction new $n : t; P$ generates a fresh name n of type t and then behaves like P. The process out$(u, N); P$ sends out term N on channel u and then behaves like P, while in$(u, x : t); P$ receives a term of type t on channel u before it behaves like P. The process if $M = N$ then P else Q behaves like P in case $M =_E N$, otherwise it behaves like Q. And let $x = M$ in P behaves like $P\{M/x\}$.

We denote by $fn(R), bn(R), fv(R), bv(R)$, respectively, the sets of free names, bound names, free variables and bound variables of R, where R is an extended process or a term. An extended process A is *closed* if $fv(A) = \emptyset$.

A *context* $C[.]$ is a process with a hole. An *evaluation context* is a context where the hole is not under a replication, a conditional, an input or an output. Context $C[.]$ *closes* process A if $C[A]$ is closed.

The operational semantics is defined by *structural equivalence* ($\equiv$), *internal reduction*($\rightarrow$), and *observational equivalence* ($\approx$). Structural equivalence is an equivalence relation that defines when syntactically different processes represent identical processes, *e.g.* it is $(P|Q)|\mathbf{0} \equiv P|(Q|\mathbf{0}) \equiv P|Q \equiv Q|P$, and $P|\text{new } a; Q \equiv \text{new } a; (P|Q)$ if $a \notin fn(P)$. Internal reduction determines the ways a process progresses, *e.g.* out$(c, M); P \mid \text{in}(c, x); Q \rightarrow P \mid Q\{M/x\}$ describes how the message M is sent and received on channel c, and let $x = D$ in P else $Q \rightarrow P\{M/x\}$ if D evaluates to M. Observational equivalence expresses the equivalence of processes with respect to their observable behavior, *i.e.*, intuitively, if processes P and Q are observational equivalent, $P \approx Q$, then no attacker (evaluation context) can distinguish whether he is interacting with P or with Q. Observational equivalence is crucial to the formalization of privacy properties of voting schemes. However, ProVerif can generally not prove observational equivalence of processes. But Proverif can prove observational equivalence relations for *biprocesses*, which are processes that have the same structure and only differ in the choice of certain terms. And this ability to prove observational equivalence of biprocesses is fortunately sufficient for our purposes.

For details on Proverif and its language we refer to [7] and to the ProVerif user manual that ships with the tool.

The free variables that are not controlled by the attacker are declared as private. For asymmetric encryption we declare type *pkey* as public key and *skey* as private key. For digital signatures we declare type *sskey* as private signing key and *spkey* as public signing key.

Correspondence assertions [20] are used to capture relationships between events. We annotate processes with events to reason about correspondence assertions. In order to capture one-to-one relationship we use injective correspondence in our modeling.

In ProVerif the public communication channels are controlled by the attacker. We assume the Dolev-Yao abstraction and therefore assume that the cryptographic primitives work properly, and the coercer only controls the public channels. The coercer can see, intercept and insert messages on the public channels, and if the coercer has the relevant keys only then he can encrypt, decrypt, and sign messages with these keys.

3.2 Modeling PEVS

We follow the general definition of [1] in order to formalize voting protocols in the language of ProVerif.

Definition 1 (Voting Process [1]). *A voting process is a closed plain process of the form*

$$VP \equiv \nu \tilde{n}.(V\sigma_1 | \dots | V\sigma_n | A_1 | \dots | A_m)$$

where $V\sigma_i$ represent the voter processes, the A_j represent the different election authorities and the $\tilde{n}$ are channel names. It is also supposed that v, which lies in the domain of σ_i, is a variable which refers to the value of the vote and that, at some moment, the outcome of the vote is made public. In addition, an evaluation context S is defined as VP but has a hole instead of two of the $V\sigma_i$.

Now we describe the modeling of PEVS in ProVerif. First we consider the cryptographic primitives that are used in PEVS: a public-key encryption scheme, a digital signature scheme, and a blind digital signature scheme consisting of a digital signature and a blinding scheme. We model these primitives by the following equational theory.

$$\mathsf{adec}(\mathsf{aenc}(m, \mathsf{pk}(k)), k) = m$$
$$\mathsf{checksign}(\mathsf{sign}(m, k), \mathsf{spk}(k)) = m$$
$$\mathsf{checksignkey}(\mathsf{signkey}(m, k), \mathsf{spk}(k)) = m$$
$$\mathsf{unblind}(\mathsf{sign}(\mathsf{blind}(m, r), k), r) = \mathsf{sign}(m, k)$$

This theory and the types that are used for modeling PEVS are defined in Fig. 4. Furthermore, we formalize processes for PEVS's honest voter, and registrar, ballot acquirer and counting server in ProVerif's language in, respectively, Fig. 5 and Fig. 6. The overall election process, given in Fig. 7, consists essentially of executing all these processes in parallel. W.l.o.g. we consider the case where the coercer in a forced-abstention attack asks for at most one key from the coerced voter, i.e., the voter generates only two key pairs in the voting booth (recall that in an actual implementation the voter can generate as many keys in the voting booth as he/she wishes). Note that we model the set of counting servers as a single honest process; in our formal analysis we do not focus on the secure multiparty computation counting scheme.

3.3 The Security Properties

Soundness of PEVS. *Eligibility* is the property that ensures that only the legitimate voters are allowed to cast their ballots in a voting scheme. The ballot cast by an eligible voter should not be altered; this property is known as *inalterability*. In addition, every voter should be allowed to vote only once. This requirement is called *non-reuseability*. Backes et al. [5] summarize these properties under the notion *soundness* of an election scheme. We use the correspondence assertions techniques [7,20] presented in [5] to verify soundness (eligibility, inalterability, and non-reuseability) in PEVS using the ProVerif tool.

We annotate four events to reason about correspondence assertions. These are: Voterkey(key), CvoterKey(key), Beginvote(key,ballot), and Endvote(ballot). The event VoterKey(key) marks the start of the blind signature scheme for signed key generation of an honest voter and the event Cvoterkey(key) marks the start of the blind signature scheme for signed key generation of a corrupted voter. The event Beginvote(key,ballot) records the start of the voting phase for an honest voter who casts the ballot with the key, while corrupted voters cast ballots without asserting any event. The event Endvote(ballot) indicates the start of tallying by the counting server. We have used two key pairs by the voter in the description and in the formal analysis as an example.

We model eligibility and inalterability by requiring that every counted ballot matches a ballot cast by an eligible voter. Non-reuseability is modeled by requiring that the matching between the events Endvote(ballot) and Beginvote(key,ballot) is injective [5]. Each Beginvote(key,ballot) event is preceded by a distinct Voterkey(key) and the event Voterkey(key) and Cvoterkey(key) depend on distinct keys. We check this automatically with ProVerif. In our scheme only the eligible voters get their keys signed by the registrar and the signed keys are used for voting by the eligible voters.

Vote-Privacy, Receipt-Freeness, and Coercion-Resistance. The privacy properties in a voting scheme are vote-privacy, receipt-freeness, and coercion-resistance. The property vote-privacy states that it is not possible to reveal for which candidate the voter casts the ballot. The formalization of this property says that no party receives information that allows to distinguish one situation from another one in which two voters swap their ballots [1] (the ballots contain their votes for particular candidates). We use the following definition of vote-privacy:

Definition 2 (Vote-privacy [1]). *A voting scheme respects vote-privacy if*

$$S[\,Voter_A\{a/_v\}\,|\,Voter_B\{b/_v\}] \approx S[\,Voter_A\{b/_v\}\,|\,Voter_B\{a/_v\}]$$

for all possible ballots a and b.

Here, S is an evaluation context. Intuitively, if an intruder cannot detect if arbitrary honest voters $Voter_A$ and $Voter_B$ swap their ballots, then in general he cannot know anything about how $Voter_A$ and $Voter_B$ cast the ballot.

Receipt-freeness says that a voter does not obtain any information (receipt) which can be used later to prove to another party how the ballot was cast. The voter may voluntarily reveal additional information to the coercer to sell his vote. However, the receipt-freeness property does not allow the voter to convince the coercer with such a proof that the ballot was cast in a particular way. We use the following formal definition for receipt-freeness [1]:

Definition 3 (Receipt-freeness [1]). *A voting scheme respects receipt-freeness if there exists a closed plain process V' such that*

- $V'^{\backslash out(c1)} \approx Voter_A\{a/v\}$, *and*
- $S[Voter_A\{c/v\}^{c1} \,|\, Voter_B\{a/v\}] \approx S[V' \,|\, Voter_B\{c/v\}]$

for all possible ballots a and c.

The context S in the second equivalence includes those authorities that are assumed to be honest. The process V' is the process in which $Voter_A$ casts the ballot for candidate a but communicates with the coercer on channel $c1$ to convince that the ballot is cast for candidate c. Intuitively, $V'^{\backslash out(c1)}$ behaves like V' but hides the outputs on channel $c1$. Since the ballot is constructed by the voter computer inside the polling booth the coercer cannot learn whether the ballot is cast for candidate a or for candidate c. The process $Voter_A\{c/v\}^{c1}$ is a voter process that communicates with the coercer on channel $c1$ and fully cooperates with the coercer to cast a ballot for candidate c.

Coercion-resistance of remote electronic voting schemes that is suitable for automated verification is defined by Backes et al. [5]. They automatically verify that the protocol by Juels et al. [2] satisfies their notion of coercion-resistance. The protocol allows the voter to provide fake credentials to the coercer. The coercer may later either casts a ballot using these fake credentials or just abstains from voting, i.e., in particular, the protocol allows voting with fake credentials. However, the ballots cast with the fake credentials are silently dropped by the talliers. Backes et al. model this in ProVerif using an extractor process. The behaviour of the extractor is determined by the actions of the coercer. If the coercer abstains from voting (with fake credentials), then the extractor does nothing. When the coercer casts a ballot with the fake credentials then the extractor adjusts the tally by removing the ballot cast by the coercer.

In comparison to the protocol of [2], the voters in PEVS cast their ballots inside a polling booth. This limits the capacity of the coercer to cast a ballot using the fake key. The voters freshly generate the keys inside the booth and give the alternative keys to the coercer based on the type of attack that needs to be fended off. In order to defend against forced-abstention attacks, the voter casts the ballot with one key pair and gives the second key pair to the coercer. In order to fend off randomization attacks or simulation attacks, the voter gives the coercer the key pair used for casting the ballot. Even though the coercer now has the keys, the coercer cannot cast any ballot with these keys since fresh keys generated inside the booth are needed to vote each time. Considering this, we derive from [5] the following definition of coercion-resistance for polling booth based voting schemes. We do not use the definition of [1] since it is not suitable for automatic verification as it quantifies over an infinite set of contexts.

Definition 4 (Coercion-resistance). *A polling booth based voting scheme respects coercion-resistance if*

- $S[Voter_A{}^{coerced(c1)}\,|\,Voter_B\{a/v\}] \approx S[Voter_A{}^{cheat(c1)}\{a/v\}\,|\,Voter_B{}^{abs}]$, *and*
- $S[Voter_A{}^{coerced(c1,c2)}\{?/v\}|E\{a/v\}^{(c2)}] \approx S[Voter_A{}^{cheat(c1,c2)}\{a/v\}|E\{?/v\}^{(c2)}]$

If we consider the first bullet point, on both sides the number of messages exchanged is equal. The ballot of $Voter_A$ is compensated by the additional voter $Voter_B$. The process $Voter_A{}^{coerced(c1)}$ models the behaviour of a coerced voter. The coerced voter gets the signed keys from the registrar and gives the coercer his keys on the channel $c1$. The coerced voter can give any key pair to the coercer and does not cast any ballot. However, the coercer cannot cast any ballot with this key pair. On the right hand side, the process $Voter_A{}^{cheat(c1)}\{a/v\}$ models the behaviour of a voter who casts a ballot using one key pair and gives the coercer the other key pair on the channel $c1$ trying to convince the coercer that the ballot was cast as requested. The coercer cannot distinguish which key pair was used by the voter to cast the ballot. The process $Voter_B{}^{abs}$ models the behaviour of a voter who just abstains from voting.

Now we consider the second bullet point, the number of messages exchanged on both sides is equal. The ballot of the coerced voter $Voter_A$ is compensated by the extractor process E. The extractor process E behaves according to the behaviour of the coerced voter. On the left hand side, the coerced voter $Voter_A{}^{coerced(c1,c2)}\{?/v\}$ may cast *any* ballot for a particular candidate according to the choice of the coercer. Then the coerced voter publishes the ballot to the extractor on channel $c2$ and to the coercer on channel $c1$. The extractor $E\{a/v\}^{(c2)}$ casts the ballot according to the choice of the coerced voter. On the right hand side, the $Voter_A{}^{cheat(c1,c2)}\{a/v\}$ models the behaviour of a voter who casts a ballot according to his own choice and tries to convince the coercer that the ballot was cast as the coercer wanted. This voter publishes the ballot to the extractor as the coercer wanted on channel $c2$. The extractor process $E\{?/v\}^{(c2)}$ then casts the ballot accordingly. We assume that the extractor is honest. There is a communication between the extractor and the counting servers so that the tally does not include the ballot cast by the coerced voter (on the left side) and by the extractor (on the right side). The threshold number of counting servers publish the keys that the coercer will try to find on the bulletin board and count only the valid ballots. The dishonest counting servers will not be able to leak any information to the coercer. The detail about how the extractor works needs further work. Note that, in comparison to the extractor defined by Backes et al. [5], this extractor does not only extract/discard unwanted ballots from the tally, but also casts ballots if needed by a coerced voter. However, the definition of [5] cannot be applied to polling booth based voting schemes where coercers cannot cast ballots with fake keys. Furthermore, we note that the definition of coerion-resistance in[1] applies to polling both based voting schemes and does without an extractor process. But again, it is not suitable for automatic verification.

3.4 Formal Security Analysis

Soundness. We first analyze the soundness property (eligibility of the voter, inalterability and non-reuseability of the ballot) as presented by Backets et al. in [5]. In order to do this analysis in the ProVerif tool, we annotate the processes that are shown in Fig. 4–7. The analysis succeeds and the result shows that PEVS guarantees soundness (eligibility of the voter, inalterability and non-reuseability of the ballot) for an unbounded number of honest voters and corrupted partic-ipants. In order to send certain messages only once between the voter and the registrar, we use nonce handshakes [5] in ProVerif.

```
free c:channel. (*public channel*)
free privCh:channel [private]. (*private channel for key distribution*)
type spkey. (*public key for signature verification*)
type sskey. (*private key for signature*) type skey. (*private key for decryption*)
type pkey. (*public key for encryption*) type nonce. type rand.
fun pk(skey):pkey. fun aenc(bitstring,pkey):bitstring.
reduc forall m:bitstring, k:skey; adec(aenc(m,pk(k)),k) =m.
fun spk(sskey):spkey. fun sign(bitstring,sskey):bitstring.
reduc forall m:bitstring, k: sskey; checksign(sign(m,k),spk(k))=m.
fun signkey(spkey,sskey):bitstring. reduc forall m:spkey, k: sskey;
checksignkey(signkey(m,k),spk(k))=m.
fun blind(spkey,rand):bitstring. reduc forall m:spkey, r:rand; unblind(blind(m,r),r)=m.
free b:bitstring [private]. (*b is ballot*) free n1:bitstring. free n2:bitstring.
event Endvote(bitstring). event Beginvote(spkey,bitstring).
event Voterkey(spkey,spkey). event Cvoterkey(spkey,spkey).
```

Fig. 4. Declaration of free variables, events, types, and functions

The free variables, events, types, and functions used in ProVerif are shown in Fig. 4. Fig. 5 models the activities of an honest voter. The voter generates fresh key pairs, blinds the public keys, sends the blinded keys to the registrar, and gets signed keys from the registrar after unblinding them. Then the voter casts the ballot using the fresh signed keys. We assume the first key pair is normally used for voting though the voter can use any of the key pair. The event voterkey(key) marks the start of the blind signature scheme for signed key generation of the voter and the event beginvote(key,ballot) records the start of the voting phase for the voter.

The event cvoterkey(key) marks the key generation phase of the corrupted voter. The corrupted voters cast ballots without asserting any event. The reg-istrar process, the processes for the ballot acquirer and the counting server are shown in Fig. 6. The event endvote(ballot) in the counting server process (Count-ingServer) indicates the tallying by the counting server. The main process is shown in Fig. 7. We execute the following query in ProVerif:

```
let Voter(skv:sskey,pkr:spkey,pcs:pkey,pba:pkey) =
    new r1:rand; new r2:rand; new nv:nonce; new sv1:sskey; (*private key of k1*)
    let k1=spk(sv1) in (*the voting key*) let blindedkey1=blind(k1,r1) in
    new sv2:sskey; let k2=spk(sv2) in let blindedkey2=blind(k2,r2) in
    event Voterkey(k1,k2);
    out(c,(n1,nv,blindedkey1,sign(blindedkey1,skv),blindedkey2,
    sign(blindedkey2,skv))); in(c,(=n2,=nv,m1:bitstring,m2:bitstring));
    let key1=checksign(m1,pkr) in let key2=checksign(m2,pkr) in
    if key1=blindedkey1 then let signedkey1=unblind(m1,r1) in
    if key2=blindedkey2 then let signedkey2=unblind(m2,r2) in
    out(c,(k1,signedkey1));
    let msg1=(b,sign(b,sv1)) in (*b is ballot*)
    let b1=(aenc((msg1,k1,signedkey1),pcs),k1,signedkey1) in
    event Beginvote(k1,b); out(c,b1).
```

Fig. 5. Voter process

```
let Registrar(skr:sskey) =
    in(privCh,(pkv:spkey)); in(c,(=n1,nv:nonce,m1:bitstring,m2:bitstring));
    out(c,(n2,nv,sign(checksign(m1,pkv),skr),sign(checksign(m2,pkv),skr))).

let BallotAcquirer(pkr:spkey,sba:skey,ssba:sskey) =
    in(c,b2:bitstring); let (b1:bitstring,k:spkey,pubv:bitstring) = b2 in
    if checksignkey(pubv,pkr)=k then out(c,signkey(k,ssba));
    let b3=sign(b1,ssba) in let ballot=(b1,b3) in out(c,ballot).

let CountingServer(scs:skey,pkr:spkey,sscs:sskey,pkba:spkey) =
    in(c,ballot:bitstring); let (b1:bitstring,b3:bitstring)=ballot in
    if checksign(b3,pkba)=b1 then let (m1:bitstring,k:spkey,pubv:bitstring)
    =adec(b1,scs) in
    if checksignkey(pubv,pkr)=k then let (b:bitstring,signedb:bitstring) = m1 in
    if checksign(signedb,k)=b then out(c,(b,signkey(k,sscs)));
    event Endvote(b).
```

Fig. 6. Processes for the registrar, the ballot acquirer and the counting server

```
process
        new skr:sskey; let pkr=spk(skr) in new sba:skey; let pba=pk(sba) in
        new scs:skey; let pcs=pk(scs) in new skv:sskey; let pkv=spk(skv) in
        new ssba:sskey; let pkba=spk(ssba) in new sscs:sskey; let pkcs=spk(sscs) in
        out(privCh,(pkcs,pkba,pcs,pba,pkr));
        ((out(privCh,pkv) ) | (!Voter(skv,pkr,pcs,pba)) |
        (!CorruptedVoter(skv,pkr,pcs,pba)) | (!Registrar(skr))
        | (!BallotAcquirer(pkr,sba,ssba)) | (!CountingServer(scs,pkr,sscs,pkba)))
```

Fig. 7. The main process

query x:bitstring,y1:spkey,y2:spkey; inj-event(Endvote(x))==>
((inj-event(Beginvote(y1,x))==>inj-event(Voterkey(y1,y2))) |
inj-event(Cvoterkey(y1,y2))).

Vote-Privacy, Receipt-Freeness, and Coercion-Resistance

Vote-privacy. We verify that PEVS satisfies the property given in Definition 2 with ProVerif. The declarations of channels, free variables, events, types, and functions are the same as in Fig. 4 with the addition of two free variables (private) for representing the ballots of two voters. These are $b1$ and $b2$, where $b1$ is the ballot of $Voter_A$ and $b2$ is the ballot for $Voter_B$. We model two processes for these two voters where the public values are same in both processes. The differences are only in the private values.

Receipt-freeness. We verify that PEVS satisfies the property given in Definition 3 with ProVerif. The first equivalence can be seen informally by considering V' (Fig. 8) without the instructions "out(c1,...)", and comparing it with $Voter_A\{a/_v\}$ visually [1]. These two processes are same. The process for $Voter_A\{a/_v\}$ is equal to the process shown in Fig. 5. For the second bullet point, we model one process for $Voter_A\{c/_v\}^{c1}$, and one process for V'. The process for $Voter_B$ is equal to the process shown in Fig. 5.

Coercion-resistance We verify that PEVS satisfies the property given in Definition 4 with ProVerif. The declarations of channels, free variables, events, types, and functions are the same as in Fig. 4 with the addition of the private channels $c1$ and $c2$. The $c1$ channel is used by the coerced voter to publish the secret values to the coercer and $c2$ is used for the communication between the coerced voter and the extractor. In $Voter_A{}^{cheat(c1)}\{a/_v\}$, the voter gives the key pair to

```
let CorruptedVoter(skv:sskey,pkr:spkey,pcs:pkey,pba:pkey) =
    new nv:nonce; new r1:rand; new r2:rand; new sv1:sskey; new sv2:sskey;
    let k1=spk(sv1) in let blindedkey1=blind(k1,r1) in
    let k2=spk(sv2) let blindedkey2=blind(k2,r2) in
    out(c,(n1,nv,blindedkey1,sign(blindedkey1,skv),blindedkey2,
    sign(blindedkey2,skv))); in(c,(=n2,=nv,m1:bitstring,m2:bitstring));
    let key1=checksign(m1,pkr) in let key2=checksign(m2,pkr) in
    if key1=blindedkey1 then let signedkey1=unblind(m1,r1) in
    if key2=blindedkey2 then let signedkey2=unblind(m2,r2) in
    out(c,choice[(k1,signedkey1),(k2,signedkey2)]);
    out(c1,choice[(k1,signedkey1),(k2,signedkey2)]);
    let msg=(b,choice[(sign(b,sv1)),sign(b,sv2)]) in
    let b1=(aenc((msg,choice[(k1,signedkey1),(k2,signedkey2)]),pcs),
    choice[(k1,signedkey1),(k2,signedkey2)]) in out(c,b1); out(c1,b1).
```

Fig. 8. The process for V'

the coercer on $c1$ after voting to obstract simulation attacks and randomization attacks. Since the key pair is freshly generated the attacker cannot mount such attacks using this key pair. Even the coercer cannot detect which key pair was used to cast the ballots by the voter. The process for $Voter_B\{a/v\}$ is the same as the process in Fig. 5 and the process for $Voter_B{}^{abs}$ is similar to the process $Voter_A{}^{coerced(c1)}$ (without the communication with the coercer on channel $c1$).

For the second bullet point, we model processes for $Voter_A{}^{coerced(c1,c2)}\{?/v\}$ and the extractor. In $Voter_A{}^{coerced(c1,c2)}\{?/v\}$, the voter casts the ballot according to the choice of the coercer, then publishes it on channel $c1$ to the coercer and on channel $c2$ to the extractor. The extractor receives the ballot on channel $c2$ and then casts the ballot accordingly. The process $Voter_A{}^{cheat(c1,c2)}\{a/v\}$ is the same as V'.

4   Conclusions

This paper has presented a polling booth based electronic voting scheme (PEVS). We have used the tool ProVerif to formally verify that PEVS satisfies soundness, vote-privacy, receipt-freeness, and coercion-resistance. Furthermore, we have shown that a voter can verify that his ballot is counted (by verifying the signatures of the counting servers on the bulletin board) and that the scheme is also universally verifiable (since any observer can verify the tally corresponds to the published ballots). Automated verification of these two properties will be done in future. Moreover, we intend to verify by hand that PEVS also satisfies the notion of coercion-resistance as given in [1] and plan to implement PEVS.

References

1. Delaune, S., Kremer, S., Ryan, M.D.: Verifying Privacy-Type Properties of Electronic Voting Protocols. Research Report LSV-08-01, Laboratorie Specification et Verification, ENS Cachan, France (2008)
2. Juels, A., Catalano, D., Jakobsson, M.: Coercion-Resistant Electronic Elections. Cryptology ePrint Archive, Report 2002/165 (2002)
3. Juels, A., Catalano, D., Jakobsson, M.: Coercion-resistant Electronic Elections. In: WPES 2005: Proceedings of the 2005 ACM Workshop on Privacy in the Electronic Society, pp. 61–70. ACM, New York (2005), http://www.rsa.com/rsalabs/node.asp?id=2860
4. Based, M. A., Mjølsnes, S.F.: A Secure Internet Voting Scheme. In: Xiang, Y., Cuzzocrea, A., Hobbs, M., Zhou, W. (eds.) ICA3PP 2011, Part II. LNCS, vol. 7017, pp. 141–152. Springer, Heidelberg (2011)
5. Backes, M., Hritcu, C., Maffei, M.: Automated Verification of Remote Electronic Voting Protocols in the Applied Pi-Calculus. In: CSF 2008: Proceedings of the 21st IEEE Computer Security Foundations Symposium, Washington, USA, pp. 195–209 (2008)
6. Based, M.A., Mjølsnes, S.F.: A Non-Interactive Zero Knowledge Proof Protocol in an Internet Voting Scheme. In: Proceedings of the the 2nd Norwegian Information Security Conference (NISK 2009), pp. 148–160. Tapir Akademisk Forlag (2009) ISBN: 978-82-519-2492-4

7. Blanchet, B., Cheval, V., Allamigeon, X., Smyth, B.: ProVerif: Cryptographic Protocol Verifier in the Formal Model, http://www.proverif.ens.fr/ (visited, March 2012)
8. Fujioka, A., Okamoto, T., Ohta, K.: A Practical Secret Voting Scheme for Large Scale Elections. In: Zheng, Y., Seberry, J. (eds.) AUSCRYPT 1992. LNCS, vol. 718, pp. 244–251. Springer, Heidelberg (1993)
9. Nielsen, C.R., Andersen, E.H., Nielson, H.R.: Static Analysis of a Voting Protocol. In: Proc. IFIP World Conference in IT Tools, pp. 21-30 (1996)
10. Sandler, D., Derr, K., Wallach, D.S.: Votebox. A Tamper-Evident, Verifiable Electronic Voting System. In: Proceedings of the 17th Conference on Security Symposium (SS 2008), pp. 349–364. USENIX Association, Berkeley (2008)
11. Benaloh, J.: Simple Verifiable Elections. In: Proceedings of the USENIX/ACCURATE Electronic Voting Technology Workshop (2006)
12. Rivest, R.L.: The ThreeBallot Voting System, http://people.csail.mit.edu/rivest/Rivest-TheThreeBallotVotingSystem.pdf (accessed on August 18, 2012)
13. Kremer, S., Ryan, M.D.: Analysis of an Electronic Voting Protocol in the Applied Pi Calculus. In: Sagiv, M. (ed.) ESOP 2005. LNCS, vol. 3444, pp. 186–200. Springer, Heidelberg (2005)
14. Benaloh, J., Tuinstra, D.: Receipt-Free Secret-Ballot Elections (extended abstract). In: Proc. 26th Annual Symposium on Theory of Computing (STOC 1994), pp. 544–553. ACM Press (1994)
15. Lee, B., Boyd, C., Dawson, E., Kim, K., Yang, J., Yoo, S.: Providing Receipt-Freeness in Mixnet-Based Voting Protocols. In: Lim, J.-I., Lee, D.-H. (eds.) ICISC 2003. LNCS, vol. 2971, pp. 245–258. Springer, Heidelberg (2004)
16. Adida, B.: Helios: Web-based Open-Audit Voting. In: Proceedings of the Seventeenth Usenix Security Symposium, pp. 335-348. USENIX Association (2008)
17. Okamoto, T.: An Electronic Voting Scheme. In: Terashima, N., et al. (eds.) IFIP World Congress, pp. 21–30. Chapman & Hall Publications, London (1996)
18. Clarkson, M.R., Chong, S., Myers, A.C.: Civitas: Toward a Secure Voting System. In: S&P 2008: Proceedings of the 2008 IEEE Symposium on Security and Privacy, pp. 354–368. IEEE Computer Society Press, Los Alamitos (2008)
19. Based, M. A., Mjølsnes, S.F.: Universally Composable NIZK Protocol in an Internet Voting Scheme. In: Cuellar, J., Lopez, J., Barthe, G., Pretschner, A. (eds.) STM 2010. LNCS, vol. 6710, pp. 147–162. Springer, Heidelberg (2011)
20. Woo, T.Y.C., Lam, S.S.: A Semantic Model for Authentication Protocols. In: Proceedings IEEE Symposium on Research in Security and Privacy, Oakland, California, pp. 178-194 (May 1993)
21. Abadi, M., Fournet, C.: Mobile Values, New Names, and Secure Communication. In: Proceedings of the 28th ACM SIGPLAN-SIGACT Symposium on Principles of Programming Languages (POPL 2001), pp. 104-115. ACM Press, New York (2001)

Certificate-Based Key-Insulated Signature*

Haiting Du[1], Jiguo Li[1], Yichen Zhang[1], Tao Li[1], and Yuexin Zhang[2]

[1] College of Computer and Information Engineering,
Hohai University, Nanjing, China
lijiguo@hhu.edu.cn
[2] School of Mathematics and Computer Science,
Fujian Normal University, Fuzhou, China

Abstract. To reduce the influence of key exposure, we introduce key-insulated into certificate-based cryptography and formalize the notion and security model of the certificate-based key-insulated signature scheme. We then present a certificate-based key-insulated signature scheme, which is proven to be existentially unforgeable against adaptive chosen message attacks in the random oracle model.

Keywords: Certificate-based signature, Key-insulated, Random oracle model.

1 Introduction

In 1984, Shamir [1] introduced the concept of identity-based cryptography (IBC), which eliminates the need for certificates in traditional public key cryptography. Since the user's private key is generated by a trusted third party, the key escrow problem is inherent in IBC. Moreover, the users' private key must be sent by secure channel. In Asiacrypt 2003, Al-Riyami and Paterson [2] proposed a new paradigm called certificateless public key cryptography (CL-PKC). CL-PKC also needs a trusted third party which is called key generation center (KGC). The KGC only generates a user's partial private key, a user computes his full private key by combining his partial private key and a secret key chosen by himself, thus the key escrow problem in IBC can be overcome through this way. Huang et al. [3-4] pointed out that some certificateless signature schemes were easily suffered from key replacement attack.

In parallel to CL-PKC, Gentry [5] introduced the notion of certificate-based encryption (CBE) in Eurocrypt 2003. A CBE scheme combines a public key encryption scheme and an identity-based encryption scheme while preserving their features. Each user generates his own public/private key pair and then requests

* This work is supported by the National Natural Science Foundation of China (61272542, 61103183, 61103184), the Fundamental Research Funds for the Central Universities (2009B21114, 2010B07114), the Six Talent Peaks Program of Jiangsu Province of China (2009182) and Program for New Century Excellent Talents in Hohai University.

Y. Xiang et al. (Eds.): ICDKE 2012, LNCS 7696, pp. 206–220, 2012.
© Springer-Verlag Berlin Heidelberg 2012

a certificate from the CA. Unlike traditional PKC, the certificate in CBE is implicitly used as a part of the user's private key for decryption. Although the CA knows the certificate of a user, it does not have the user's private key, it cannot decrypt any ciphertexts. So key escrow problem doesn't exist in CBE, and it also simplifies certificate management and eliminates third-party query in traditional PKC. Certificate-based cryptography overcomes the inherent defects in PKI and identity-based cryptography, which is the effective mechanism to construct an efficient public key infrastructure requiring fewer infrastructures. Following Gentry's idea, Kang et al. [6] proposed the security notion of certificate-based signature and two concrete certificate-based signature schemes. Unfortunately, Li et al. [7] showed that one of their schemes was insecure against key replacement attack. They refined the security model of certificate-based signature and proposed a new efficient certificate-based signature scheme. Furthermore, Wu et al. [8] provided elaborated security models of certificate-based signature and proposed a generic construction of certificate-based signature from certificateless signature. Liu et al. [9] proposed two new certificate-based signature schemes with new features and advantages. However, Zhang [10] showed that their certificate-based signature scheme without pairings was insecure. Li et al. [11] proposed a certificate-based signature secure against key replacement attacks in the standard model. Recently, Li et al. [12] proposed an efficient short certificate-based signature scheme, which makes it possess strong applicability in situations with limited bandwidth and power-constrained devices. Furthermore, they [13] defined an enhanced security model for certificate-based signcryption and proposed a new certificate-based signcryption scheme. However, with the rapid development of computer and communication technology, more and more cryptography algorithms are applied to insecure environments such as mobile devices, so the exposure of secret key is inevitable. Once the secret key has been exposed, the security of system will be massively or entirely lost. In certificate-based cryptography, if an adversary obtains the secret key and the certificate from a user, he can successfully forge a signature of the user.

To reduce the influence of key exposure, Anderson [14] presented forward-secure signature in 1997. But forward-security can not insure the security of secret key after the key exposure happened. In Eurocrypt'02, Dodis et al. [15] proposed a new notion of key-insulation. The lifetime of a system is divided into discrete time periods. The key-insulated mechanism uses key evolution method, updating the user key periodically, which is an effective method to alleviate compromise on key exposure. In this model, all cryptographic computations are done on the insecure device. A physically-secure but computationally-limited device named the helper is used to send the update key to user. A helper key is stored in the helper, and a user key is kept by the user. The public key remains unchanged throughout the lifetime, while temporary secret keys are updated periodically at the beginning of each period. The user obtains from the helper an update key for the current period. Combining this update key with the temporary secret key for the previous period, he can derive the temporary secret key for the current period. In a (l, N)-key-insulated mechanism, an adversary who compromises the insecure device and obtains keys for up to l time periods is unable to violate the security of the cryptosystem for any of the remaining $N - l$ periods.

Dodis et al. [16] proposed a strong key-insulated signature scheme in 2003. Following this work, many schemes have been constructed. Zhou et al. [17] applied the key-insulation mechanism to IBS to minimize the damage caused by key exposure in IBS, but the scheme does not satisfy the strong key-insulated security. Weng et al. [18, 19] described an IBKIS scheme with secure key-updates and an IBKIS scheme without random oracles. Wan et al. [20] extended the key-insulation mechanism to certificateless cryptography and proposed a certificateless key-insulated signature in standard model.

Our contribution. In this paper, we first extend the key-insulated mechanism to certificate-based cryptography and formalize the definition and security model for certificate-based key-insulated signature (CBKIS). Furthermore, we propose a certificate-based key-insulated signature scheme. We also provide a rigorous security proof against adaptive chosen message attacks in the random oracle model. The security of our scheme is based on the computational Diffie-Hellman (CDH) hard problem assumption.

Organization. The rest of the paper is organized as follows. Section 2 gives some definitions and security model of CBKIS. In Section 3, we propose a certificate-based key-insulated signature scheme. We provide the security proof in Section 4. In Section 5, we analyze the performance of the proposed CBKIS scheme. Finally, we conclude the paper in Section 6.

2   Security Model of the Certificate-Based Key-Insulated Signature

2.1   Bilinear Maps and Related Complexity Assumption

Let G_1 be an additive group of prime order p and G_2 be a multiplicative group of the same order. Let P denote a generator of G_1 and $e : G_1 \times G_1 \to G_2$ be a bilinear mapping with the following properties:

- Bilinear: $e(aP, bQ) = e(P, Q)^{ab}$ for all $P, Q \in G_1, a, b \in Z_p^*$.
- Non-degenerate: There exists $P, Q \in G_1$ such that $e(P, Q) \neq 1$.
- Computable: There exists an efficient algorithm to compute $e(P, Q)$ for all $P, Q \in G_1$.

Definition 1. Computational Diffie-Hellman (CDH) Problem.

Given (P, aP, bP) where $a, b \in Z_q^*$, compute abP. The advantage of an algorithm $\mathcal{A}$ in solving the CDH problem in G_1 is defined to be $Succ_{A,G_1}^{CDH} = \Pr[\mathcal{A}(P, aP, bP) = abP \,|\, a, b \in Z_q^*]$.

The CDH assumption states that for every probabilistic polynomial-time algorithm A, $Succ_{A,G_1}^{CDH}$ is negligible.

2.2   Outline of Certificate-Based Key-Insulated Signature

For completeness, we provide a formal definition of certificate-based key-insulated signature scheme (based on [7,11-13,15,16]). A certificate-based key-insulated signature scheme is defined by eight algorithms: **Setup, UserKeyGen, Cert-Gen, SetInitialKey, UpdH, UpdS, Sign**, and **Verify**. The description of each algorithm is as follows.

Setup: This algorithm takes as input a security parameter 1^k and a total number of periods N, returns the certifier's master secret key msk and system public parameters $params$.

UserKeyGen: This algorithm takes $params$ as input. It returns a public key PK and a secret key SK.

CertGen: This algorithm takes master secret key msk, $params$, the identity ID of a user and its public key PK_{ID} as input. It returns the user's certificate $Cert_{ID}$.

SetInitialKey: This algorithm takes $params$, the identity ID of the user, the user's certificate $Cert_{ID}$ and secret key SK as input. It returns the user's initial temporary secret key $TSK_{ID,0}$ and helper key HK_{ID}.

UpdH: This algorithm takes $params$, the identity ID of the user, helper key HK_{ID}, two period indices t and t' as input. It returns an update key $UK_{ID,t,t'}$.

UpdS: This algorithm takes $params$, the identity ID of the user, two period indices t and t', a temporary secret key $TSK_{ID,t'}$ and an update key $UK_{ID,t,t'}$ as input. It returns the temporary secret key $TSK_{ID,t}$.

Sign: This algorithm takes $params$, the identity ID of the user, a message m, the user's certificate $Cert_{ID}$, a period index t and a temporary secret key $TSK_{ID,t}$ as input. It returns the signature (t,σ).

Verify: This algorithm takes a message m, the signature pair (t,σ), $params$, the user's identity ID and its public key PK_{ID} as input. It returns 0 or 1. With output value 1, we say that σ is a valid signature of the message m, otherwise invalid.

The **Setup** and **CertGen** algorithms are performed by the certifier. The user himself performs **UserKeyGen, SetInitialKey, UpdS** and **Sign** algorithms. The **UpdH** algorithm is perfomed by the helpers.

2.3   Security Model

Similar to the certificate-based signature scheme [7, 11-13], we discuss two kinds of adversary for a certificate-based key-insulated signature scheme. The Type I adversary A_I can obtain a valid signature under the public key which may be replaced by himself, with the restriction that he can supply the corresponding secret key. The second kind of Type II adversary A_{II}, who has the master secret key, wishes to generate a valid signature under the public key without the knowledge of the corresponding secret key. Type II adversary A_{II} mainly simulates a malicious certifier who is able to produce certificate but is not allowed to replace the target user's public key.

Inspired by the idea [15, 16], a certificate-based key-insulated signature should satisfy the security notions of key-insulation and strong key-insulation. The description of each security notion is as follows.

Basic Key Insulation We model the above attacks by defining appropriate oracles to which the adversary is given access. We consider a game between challenge B and adversary $A \in \{A_I, A_{II}\}$ as follows.

UserKeyGen Query: B maintains a list $L = (ID_i, SK_{ID_i}, PK_{ID_i}, f_i)$ which is initially empty. If ID_i does not appear in L, B selects a random number $s_{ID_i} \in Z_q^*$ as the secret key of ID_i, compute $(SK_{ID_i}, PK_{ID_i}) = (s_{ID_i}, s_{ID_i}P)$ and add $(ID_i, SK_{ID_i}, PK_{ID_i}, 0)$ into L. Otherwise, PK_{ID_i} is returned to A.

PKReplace Query: On input a user's identity ID and public key PK'_{ID}, B checks the list L. If ID has already been created, B replaces the user's original public key PK_{ID} with PK'_{ID} which is chosen by himself. B change (ID, SK_{ID}, PK_{ID}) into $(ID, \perp, PK'_{ID})$ in list L. Otherwise, B adds $(ID_i, \perp, PK'_{ID_i})$ into the list L.

Corruption Query: On input a user's identity ID_i, B checks whether $(ID_i, SK_{ID_i}, PK_{ID_i}, f_i)$ has already been defined in the list L. If $(ID_i, SK_{ID_i}, PK_{ID_i}, f_i)$ has already been defined and $f_i = 1$, B refuses to answer the query. If $(ID_i, SK_{ID_i}, PK_{ID_i}, f_i)$ has been defined and $f_i = 0$, B returns SK_i to A_I. Otherwise, B selects a random number $s_{ID_i} \in Z_q^*$? computes $(SK_{ID_i}, PK_{ID_i}) = (s_{ID_i}, s_{ID_i}P)$ hen B adds $(ID_i, SK_{ID_i}, PK_{ID_i}, 0)$ into the list L and returns $SK_{ID_i} = s_{ID_i}$ to A_I.

Certification Query: On input a user's identity ID and public key PK_{ID}, B runs the algorithm **CertGen** and returns the certificate $Cert_{ID}$.

Temporary Secret Key Query: On input a user's identity ID and a period index t, B runs the algorithm **UpdS** and returns $TSK_{ID,t}$.

Sign Query: On input a pair $< ID, t, m >$, B runs the algorithm **Sign** and returns the signature (t, σ).

Game2-1

Setup: The challenger B runs the algorithm **Setup**, returns $params$ and mpk to the adversary A_I and keeps msk secret.

Queries: A_I can adaptively submit the six queries defined above.

Forge: Finally, A_I outputs a message m^* and a signature (t^*, σ^*) corresponding to a target identity ID^* and a public key PK_{ID}^*. The adversary wins the game if

- Verify $(param, (t^*, \sigma^*), m^*, ID^*, PK^*) = 1$.
- ID^* has never been submitted to the **Certification Query**.
- $< ID^*, t^* >$ has never been submitted to the **Temporary Secret Key Query**.

- (ID^*, m^*) has never been submitted to the **Sign Query**.
- Assume A_I makes **Temporary Secret Key Query** for q_t, then $q_t \leq l, t \in \{1, \ldots, N\}$
- If A_I has replaced PK with PK', he can not ask for a **Temporary Secret Key Query** and **Sign Query**.

The success probability of adaptively chosen message and chosen identity adversary A_I wins the above games is defined as $Succ_{A_I}$.

Definition 2. We say a certificate-based key-insulated signature scheme is secure against a chosen message adversary A_I, if A_I runs in polynomial time t, makes at most q queries and $Succ_{A_I}$ is negligible.

Game2-2

Setup: The challenger B runs the algorithm **Setup**, returns $params$, mpk and msk to the adversary A_{II}.

Queries: A_{II} can adaptively submit **UserKeyGen Query**, **Corruption Query**, **Temporary Secret Key Query** and **Sign Query**, all queries are defined above. Here, A_{II} has obtained the master secret key, namely, he can calculate any user's certificate by himself. So A_{II} need not submit any **Certification Query**. A_{II} cannot submit public key replacement query.

Forge: Finally, A_{II} outputs a message m^* and a signature (t^*, σ^*) corresponding to a target identity ID^* and a public key PK_{ID}^*. The adversary wins the game if

- Verify $(param, (t^*, \sigma^*), m^*, ID^*, PK^*) = 1$.
- ID^* has never been submitted to the **Corruption Query**.
- $< ID^*, t^* >$ has never been submitted to the **Temporary Secret Key Query**.
- (ID^*, m^*) has never been submitted to the **Sign Query**.
- Assume A_{II} makes **Temporary Secret Key Query** for q_t on ID^*, then $q_t \leq l, t \in \{1, \ldots, N\}$.

The success probability of adaptively chosen message and chosen identity adversary A_{II} wins the above games is defined as $Succ_{A_{II}}$.

Definition 3. We say a certificate-based key-insulated signature scheme is secure against a chosen message adversary A_{II}, if A_{II} runs in polynomial time t, makes at most q queries and $Succ_{A_{II}}$ is negligible.

Strong key insulation We consider a game between challenge B and adversary $A \in \{A'_I, A'_{II}\}$ as follows.

Game2-3

Setup: The challenger B runs the algorithm **Setup**, returns $params$ and mpk to the adversary A'_I and keeps msk secret.

Queries: A'_I can adaptively submit the **UserKeyGen, PKReplace Query, Certification Query** and **Sign Query** queries defined above. In addition, A'_I can submit **HelperKey Query**. But A'_I cannot submit **Temporary Secret Key Query** for any period. The **HelperKey Query** is defined as follows.

HelperKey Query: On input a user's identity ID, B maintains a list a list E^{list} as $(ID_i, h_{ID_i}, T_{ID_i})$ and checks whether ID_i exsists in E^{list}. If not, B selects a random number $h_{ID_i} \in Z_q^*$ and adds $(ID_i, h_{ID_i}, T_{ID_i})$ into E^{list}. At last, B returns the helper key h_{ID_i} to A'_I.

Forge: Finally, A'_I outputs a message m^* and a signature (t^*, σ^*) corresponding to a target identity ID^* and a public key PK^*_{ID}. The adversary wins the game if

- Verify $(param, (t^*, \sigma^*), m^*, ID^*, PK^*)=1$.
- ID^* has never been submitted to the **Certification Query**.
- (ID^*, m^*) has never been submitted to the **Sign Query**.
- If A'_I has replaced PK with PK', he can not ask for a **Sign Query**.

The success probability of adaptively chosen message and chosen identity adversary A'_I wins the above games is defined as $Succ_{A'_I}$.

Definition 4. We say a certificate-based key-insulated signature scheme is strong key-insulated secure against a chosen message adversary A'_I, if A'_I runs in polynomial time t, makes at most q queries and $Succ_{A'_I}$ is negligible.

Game2-4

Setup: The challenger B runs the algorithm **Setup**, returns $params, mpk$ and msk to the adversary A'_{II}.

Queries: A'_{II} can adaptively submit the **UserKeyGen, Corruption Query** and **Sign Query** queries defined above. In addition, A'_{II} can submit **HelperKey Query**.

HelperKey Query: The same as Game 2-3.

Forge: Finally, A'_{II} outputs a message m^* and a signature (t^*, σ^*) corresponding to a target identity ID^* and a public key PK^*_{ID}. The adversary wins the game if

- Verify$(param, (t^*, \sigma^*), m^*, ID^*, PK^*)=1$.
- ID^* has never been submitted to the **Corruption Query**.
- (ID^*, m^*) has never been submitted to the **Sign Query**.

The success probability of adaptively chosen message and chosen identity adversary A'_{II} wins the above games is defined as $Succ_{A'_{II}}$.

Definition 5. We say a certificate-based key-insulated signature scheme is strong key-insulated secure against a chosen message adversary A'_{II}, if A'_{II} runs in polynomial time t, makes at most q queries and $Succ_{A'_{II}}$ is negligible.

3   Our Certificate-Based Key-Insulated Signature Scheme

In the following, we propose a certificate-based key-insulated scheme, the detail steps are shown as follows:

Setup: Given a security parameter k, the algorithm works as follows:

1. Let G_1, G_2 be groups of a prime order q in which there exists a bilinear pairing map $e : G_1 \times G_1 \to G_2$.
2. Select a random number $s \in Z_p^*$ and a random element $P \in G_1$. Let the master secret key $msk = s$, and the master public key $mpk = sP$.
3. Choose four cryptographic hash functions $H_0 : \{0,1\}^* \times G_1 \to G_1$, $H_1 : \{0,1\}^* \times G_1 \times G_1 \to G_1$, $H_2 : \{0,1\}^* \times G_1 \times \{0,1\}^* \to G_1$, $H_3 : \{0,1\}^* \times \{0,1\}^* \times \{0,1\}^* \times G_1 \to G_1$.

The system parameters are $params =< G_1, G_2, e, p, P, mpk, H_0, H_1, H_2, H_3 >$.

UserKeyGen: Given $params$, select a random number $s_{ID} \in Z_p^*$ as the user private key SK_{ID} and compute $PK_{ID} = s_{ID}P$ as the user public key.

CertGen: Given $params$, master secret key s, user public key PK_{ID} and user identity $ID \in \{0,1\}^*$, compute $Q_{ID} = H_0(ID, PK_{ID})$ and the certificate $Cert_{ID} = sQ_{ID}$.

SetInitialKey: For a given identity ID, user ID selects a random number $HK_{ID} \in Z_P^*$, computes $T_{ID} = HK_{ID}P$, $U_{ID} = H_1(ID, PK_{ID}, T_{ID})$, $W_0 = H_2(ID, T_{ID}, 0)$, $S_{ID,0} = s_{ID}U_{ID} + HK_{ID}W_0$. Set initial key $TSK_{ID,0} = (S_{ID,0}, T_{ID})$. Output $TSK_{ID,0}$ and helper key HK_{ID}. User sents HK_{ID} to helper and deletes HK_{ID} from user.

UpdH: Given $params$, two period indices t,t', user identity ID and helper key HK_{ID}, computes $W_t = H_2(ID, T_{ID}, t)$, $W_{t'} = H_2(ID, T_{ID}, t')$, then defines and returns the update key as $UK_{ID,t,t'} = HK_{ID}(W_t - W_{t'})$.

UpdS: Given a period index t', an update key $UK_{ID,t,t'}$ and a temporary secret key $TSK_{ID,t'} = (S_{ID,t'}, T_{ID})$, the temporary secret key for user ID in period t can be computed as $S_{ID,t} = S_{ID,t'} + UK_{ID,t,t'} = s_{ID}U_{ID} + HK_{ID}W_{t'} + HK_{ID}(W_t - W_{t'}) = s_{ID}U_{ID} + HK_{ID}W_t$, so the temporary secret key in period t is $TSK_{ID,t} = (S_{ID,t}, T_{ID})$. Then output $TSK_{ID,t}$ and delete $TSK_{ID,t'}$ and $UK_{ID,t,t'}$ from user.

Sign: Given $params$, user identity ID, a temporary secret key $TSK_{ID,t} = (S_{ID,t}, T_{ID})$ in period t, a certificate $Cert_{ID}$ and a message $m \in \{0,1\}^*$, the algorithm works as follows:

- Choose $r \in Z_p^*$, compute $R = rp$, $P_m = H_3(t, ID, m, R)$, $V = Cert_{ID} + S_{ID,t} + rP_m$.
- The signature is $\sigma = (R, V, T_{ID})$.

Verify: Given $params$, user public key PK_{ID} and message/signature pair (m, σ). Compute $P_m = H_3(t, ID, m, R)$, $U_{ID} = H_1(ID, PK_{ID}, T_{ID})$, $W_t =$

$H_2(ID, T_{ID}, t)$. This algorithm outputs true if $e(P, V) = e(Q_{ID}, mpk)e(PK_{ID}, U_{ID}) \, e(T_{ID}, W_t)e(R, P_m)$. Otherwise it outputs false.

Correctness

It is easy to see that the proposed signature scheme is correct. If a signature $\sigma = (R, V, T_{ID})$ is valid, then it can pass the verification equation. Because $e(P, V)$

$$= e(P, Cert_{ID} + S_{ID,t} + rP_m)$$
$$= e(P, Cert_{ID})e(P, S_{ID,t})e(P, rP_m)$$
$$= e(mpk, Q_{ID})e(P, s_{ID}U_{ID} + HK_{ID}W_t)e(R, P_m)$$
$$= e(mpk, Q_{ID})e(P, s_{ID}U_{ID})e(P, HK_{ID}W_t)e(R, P_m)$$
$$= e(mpk, Q_{ID})e(PK_{ID}, U_{ID})e(T_{ID}, W_t)e(R, P_m).$$

4   Security Analysis

Theorem 1. In the random oracle model, if there is a Type I chosen message adversary A_I which can submit at most q_R queries wins **Game2-1** defined in Section 2.3 with a probability ε, then there exists an algorithm B which can solve the CDH problem with a probability $\varepsilon' \geq \frac{e}{q_R+1}\varepsilon$ in polynomial time.

Proof. Let (P, aP, bP) be a random instance of the CDH problem taken as input by B where $P_1 = aP, P_2 = bP$. Its goal is to output abP. In the proof, we regard the hash functions as the random oracles. Algorithm B will simulate the oracles and interact with the adversary A_I as follows:

Setup: B sets the master public key $mpk = aP = P_1$? P_1 is the input of CDH problem. B sends mpk to A_I.

UserKeyGen: B maintains a list $L = (ID_i, SK_{ID_i}, PK_{ID_i}, f_i)$ which is initially empty. If ID_i does not appear in L, B selects a random number $s_{ID_i} \in Z_q^*$ as the secret key of ID_i, compute $(SK_{ID_i}, PK_{ID_i}) = (s_{ID_i}, s_{ID_i}P)$ and add $(ID_i, SK_{ID_i}, PK_{ID_i}, 0)$ into L. Otherwise, PK_{ID_i} is returned to A_I.

H_0 **Query:** On input $< ID_i, PK_{ID_i} >$, B selects a random number $coin_i \in \{0, 1\}$ such that $\Pr[coin = 1] = \delta$ where the value of δ will be determined later.

1. If $coin_i = 0$, B chooses a random number $c_i \in Z_q^*$ and sets $H_0(ID_i, PK_{ID_i}) = h_{0,i} = c_iP$.
2. Else $coin_i = 1$, B chooses a random number $c_i \in Z_q^*$ and sets $H_0(ID_i, PK_{ID_i}) = h_{0,i} = c_iP + P_2$, where P_2 is another input of CDH problem.

In both cases, B will add $(< ID_i, PK_{ID_i} >, coin_i, c_i, h_{0,i})$ into $H_0 - list$ and return $h_{0,i}$ to A_I.

H_1 **Query:** On input $< ID_i, PK_{ID_i}, T_{ID_i} >$, B selects a random number $d_i \in Z_q^*$ and sets $H_1(ID_i, PK_{ID_i}, T_{ID_i}) = h_{1,i} = d_iP$. Then B adds $(< ID_i, PK_{ID_i}, T_{ID_i} >, d_i, h_{1,i})$ into $H_1 - list$ and returns $h_{1,i}$ to A_I.

H_2 **Query:** On input $< ID_i, T_{ID_i}, t >$,B selects a random number $\lambda_i \in Z_q^*$ and sets $H_2(ID_i, T_{ID_i}, t) = h_{2,i} = \lambda_i P$. Then B adds $(< ID_i, T_{ID_i}, t >, \lambda_i, h_{2,i})$into $H_2 - list$ and returns $h_{2,i}$ to A_I.

H_3 **Query:** On input $< t, ID, m, R >$,B selects a random number $\beta_i \in Z_q^*$ and sets $H_3(t, ID, m, R) = h_{3,i} = \beta_i P$. Then B adds $(< t, ID, m, R >, \beta_i, h_{3,i})$ into $H_3 - list$ and returns $h_{3,i}$ to A_I.

Corruption Query: On input a user's identity ID_i, B checks whether $(ID_i, SK_{ID_i}, PK_{ID_i}, f_i)$ has already been defined in the list L. If $(ID_i, SK_{ID_i}, PK_{ID_i}, f_i)$ has already been defined and $f_i = 1$, B refuses to answer the query. If $(ID_i, SK_{ID_i}, PK_{ID_i}, f_i)$ has been defined and $f_i = 0$, B returns SK_i to A_I. Otherwise, B selects a random number $s_{ID_i} \in Z_q^*$, computes $(SK_{ID_i}, PK_{ID_i}) = (s_{ID_i}, s_{ID_i}P)$ then B adds $(ID_i, SK_{ID_i}, PK_{ID_i}, 0)$ into the list L and returns $SK_{ID_i} = s_{ID_i}$ to A_I.

PKReplace Query: On input a user's identity ID_i and public key PK'_{ID_i}, B scans the list L to check whether ID_i has been defined. If so, B sets $PK_{ID_i} = PK'_{ID_i}$ and $x_{ID_i} = \perp$, updates the list L as $(ID_i, \perp, PK'_i, 1)$. Otherwise, B adds $(ID_i, \perp, PK'_i, 1)$ into the list L.

Certification Query: On a certificate query ID_i, B first checks the list L to obtain this user's public key PK_{ID_i}, If $f_i = 1$, it showed that this user's public key PK_{ID_i} has been replaced. In this case,B rejects to respond. Otherwise,$f_i = 0$ and B checks $H_0 - list$.

1. If $coin_i = 0$, which means $Q_{ID_i} = H_0(ID_i, PK_{ID_i}) = c_i P$,B returns the certificate $Cert_{ID_i} = c_i P_1$.
2. Otherwise,B aborts.

Temporary Secret Key Query: On input a user's identity ID_i,B maintains a list a list E^{list} as $(ID_i, h_{ID_i}, T_{ID_i})$ and checks whether ID_i exsists in E^{list}. If not, B selects a random number $h_{ID_i} \in Z_q^*$ and sets $T_{ID_i} = h_{ID_i} P_1$. Then, B will add $(ID_i, h_{ID_i}, T_{ID_i})$ to E^{list}. Next B checks whether $(< ID_i, T_{ID_i}, t >, \cdot, \cdot)$ exsists in H_2-list. If it does,B obtains $h_{2,i}$. Otherwise, B selects a random number$\lambda_i \in Z_q^*$ and computes$H_2(ID_i, T_{ID_i}, t) = h_{2,i} = \lambda_i P$. B adds $(< ID_i, T_{ID_i}, t >, \lambda_i, h_{2,i})$ to $H_2 - list$. Finally,B computes $S_{ID_i,t} = s_{ID_i} U_{ID_i} + \lambda_i h_{ID_i} P_1$ and returns $TSK_{ID_i,t} = (S_{ID_i,t}, T_{ID_i})$ to A_I.

Sign Query: On input a signing query $< ID_j, t, m_i >$,B checks $H_0 - list$ to obtain $(< ID_j, PK_{ID_j} >, c_i, coin_j)$. If $coin_j = 0$,B can generate the certificate $Cert_{ID_j}$ and temporary secret key and use $(Cert_{ID_j}, TSK_{ID_j,t})$ to sign the message m_i. Otherwise, $coin_j = 1$ and $H_1(ID_j, PK_{ID_j}) = c_j P + P_2$,B selects a random number $r_i \in Z_q^*$ and sets $R_i = r_i P - P_1$.

1. Firstly, he checks whether ID_j exists in $E^{list}, H_1 - list, H_2 - list, H_3 - list$. If not, he computes $T_{ID_j} = h_{ID_j} P_1, H_1(ID_j, PK_{ID_j}, T_{ID_j}) = d_i P, H_2 (ID_j, T_{ID_j}, t) = \lambda_i P, H_3(t, ID_j, m_i, R_i) = \beta_i P + P_2$ and adds to lists. Otherwise, B must rechoose the numbers until there is no collision.

2. Secondly, he computes $V_i = c_i P_1 + s_{ID_j} U_{ID_j} + \lambda_i h_{ID_j} P_1 + \beta_i R_i + r_i P_2$ and outputs $(t, (R_i, V_i, T_{ID_j}))$ as the signature.

Correctness $e(V_i, P)$

$= e(c_i P_1 + s_{ID_j} U_{ID_j} + \lambda_i h_{ID_j} P_1 + \beta_i R_i + r_i P_2, P)$

$= e(c_i P_1 + abP + s_{ID_j} U_{ID_j} + \lambda_i h_{ID_j} P_1 + \beta_i R_i + r_i P_2 - abP, P)$

$= e(a(c_i P + P_2) + s_{ID_j} H_1(ID_j, PK_{ID_j}, T_{ID_j}) + (r_i - a)H_3(t, ID_j, m_i, R_i) + \lambda_i h_{ID_j} P_1, P)$

$= e(mpk, Q_{ID_j})e(H_1(ID_j, PK_{ID_j}, T_{ID_j}), PK_{ID_j})e(H_3(t, ID_j, m_i, R_i), R_i)$
$e(H_2(ID_j, T_{ID_j}, t), T_{ID_j})$

At last, A_I outputs a valid forgery $(t^*, \sigma^*) = (t^*, (R^*, V^*, T_{ID}^*))$ on message m^* with respect to (ID^*, PK_{ID}^*). We assume that $(< ID^*, PK_{ID^*} >, coin^*, c^*, h_0^*)$, $(< ID^*, PK_{ID^*}, T_{ID^*} >, d^*, h_1^*), (< ID^*, T_{ID^*}, PK_{ID^*}, t^* >, \lambda^*,$ $h_2^*), (< t, ID^*, M^*, R^* >, \beta^*, h_3^*), (ID^*, h_{ID^*}, T_{ID^*})$ have been in $H_0 - list, H_1 - list, H_2 - list, H_3 - list$ and E^{list} respectively. If σ^* is a valid signature of the message m^*, then $V^* = aH_0(ID^*, PK_{ID^*}) + d^* PK_{ID^*} + \lambda^* T_{ID^*} + \beta^* R^*$.

1. If $coin_i = 1, H_0(ID^*, PK_{ID^*}) = c^* P + P_2$. Therefore, B can compute $abP = V^* - (c^* P_1 + d^* PK_{ID^*} + \lambda^* T_{ID^*} + \beta^* R^*)$.
2. Otherwise, B fails to solve this instance of CDH problem.

According to the simulation, B can compute the value of abP if and only if all the following events happen:

Event. E_1 : B does not fail during the simulation.

Event. E_2 : A_I outputs a valid forgery on period t^*.

Event. E_3 : In the forgery output by A_I, $coin^* = 1$.

Therefore, the probability that B can solve this instance of CDH problem is $\varepsilon' = \Pr[E_1 \wedge E_2 \wedge E_3] = \Pr[E_1]\Pr[E_2|E_1]\Pr[E_3|E_1 \wedge E_2]$. In addition, all the simulation can be done in polynomial time.

From the simulation, we have $\Pr[E_1] \geq (1-\delta)^{q_R}, \Pr[E_2|E_1] = \varepsilon$, $\Pr[E_3|E_1 \wedge E_2] = \delta$, so $\varepsilon' \geq \delta(1-\delta)^{q_R}\varepsilon$. Let $\delta = \frac{1}{q_R+1}$, then $\varepsilon' \geq \frac{e}{q_R+1}\varepsilon$, where e is the base of natural logarithm.

Theorem 2. In the random oracle model, if there is a Type II chosen message adversary A_{II} which can submit at most q_R queries wins **Game2-2** defined in Section 2.3 with a probability ε, then there exists an algorithm B which can solve the CDH problem with a probability $\varepsilon' \geq \frac{e}{q_R}\varepsilon$ in polynomial time.

Proof. Let (P, aP, bP) be a random instance of the CDH problem taken as input by B where $P_1 = aP, P_2 = bP$. Its goal is to output abP. In the proof, we regard the hash functions as the random oracles. Algorithm B will simulate the oracles and interact with the adversary A_{II} as follows:

Setup: B selects a random number $s \in Z_p^*$, sets the master secret key $msk = s$ and public key $mpk = sP$. B sends mpk and msk to A_{II}.

UserKeyGen: On a new **UserKeyGen Query** ID_i,B acts as following. Suppose there are up to q' UserKeyGen queries, B will choose a random number $\pi \in \{1,2,\cdots,q'\}$.

1. ID_i is the πth query, B sets $SK_{ID_i} = \perp$ and $PK_{ID_i} = P_1$. Here, the symbol $\perp$ means B doesn't know the corresponding value.
2. Otherwise, B chooses a random number $s_{ID_i} \in Z_q^*$ and sets (SK_{ID_i}, PK_{ID_i}) $= (s_{ID_i}, s_{ID_i}P)$.

In both cases, B adds $(ID_i, SK_{ID_i}, PK_{ID_i})$ into the list L and returns PK_{ID_i} to A_{II}.

H_0 **Query:** On input $< ID_i, PK_{ID_i} >$,B selects a random number $c_i \in Z_q^*$ and sets $H_0(ID_i, PK_{ID_i}) = h_{0,i} = c_iP$,$B$ adds $(< ID_i, PK_{ID_i} >, c_i, h_{0,i})$ to $H_0 - list$ and returns $h_{0,i}$ to A_{II}.

H_1 **Query:** On input $< ID_i, PK_{ID_i}, T_{ID_i} >$, B selects a random number $d_i \in Z_q^*$ and sets $H_1(ID_i, PK_{ID_i}, T_{ID_i}) = h_{1,i} = d_iP + P_2$. Then B adds $(< ID_i, PK_{ID_i}, T_{ID_i} >, d_i, h_{1,i})$ into $H_1 - list$ and returns $h_{1,i}$ to A_{II}.

H_2 **Query:** On input $< ID_i, T_{ID_i}, t >$,B selects a random number $\lambda_i \in Z_q^*$ and sets $H_2(ID_i, T_{ID_i}, t) = h_{2,i} = \lambda_iP$. Then B adds $(< ID_i, T_{ID_i}, t >, \lambda_i, h_{2,i})$ into $H_2 - list$ and returns $h_{2,i}$ to A_{II}.

H_3 **Query:** On input $< t, ID, m, R >$, B selects a random number $\beta_i \in Z_q^*$ and sets $H_3(t, ID, m, R) = h_{3,i} = \beta_iP$. Then B adds $(< t, ID, m, R >, \beta_i, h_{3,i})$ into $H_3 - list$ and returns $h_{3,i}$ to A_{II}.

Corruption Query: On input a user's identity ID_i,B will check the list L and return SK_{ID_i} to A_{II}. If $SK_{ID_i} = \perp$, B fails to checks the list L.

Temporary Signing Key Query: On input a user's identity ID_i,B can compute as follows:

1. B maintains a list a list E^{list} as $(ID_i, h_{ID_i}, T_{ID_i})$ and checks whether ID_i exsists in E^{list}. If not,B selects a random number $h_{ID_i} \in Z_q^*$ and sets $T_{ID_i} = h_{ID_i}P_1$. Then,B will add $(ID_i, h_{ID_i}, T_{ID_i})$ to E^{list}.
2. B checks whether $(< ID_i, PK_{ID_i}, T_{ID_i} >, \cdot, \cdot)$?exsists in $H_1 - list$? If it does,B obtains $h_{1,i}$. Otherwise, B selects a random number $d_i \in Z_q^*$ and computes $H_1(ID_i, PK_{ID_i}, T_{ID_i}) = h_{1,i} = d_iP$. B adds $(< ID_i, PK_{ID_i}, T_{ID_i} >, d_i, h_{1,i})$ to $H_1 - list$?
3. B checks whether $(< ID_i, T_{ID_i}, t >, \cdot, \cdot)$ exsists in $H_2 - list$. If it does,B obtains $h_{2,i}$. Otherwise, B selects a random number $\lambda_i \in Z_q^*$ and computes $H_2(ID_i, T_{ID_i}, t) = h_{2,i} = \lambda_iP$. B adds $(< ID_i, T_{ID_i}, t >, \lambda_i, h_{2,i})$ to H_2-list.
4. B computes $S_{ID_i,t} = d_iPK_{ID_i} + \lambda_ih_{ID_i}P_1$ and returns $TSK_{ID_i,t} = (S_{ID_i,t}, T_{ID_i})$ to A_{II}.

Sign Query: On input a signing query $< ID_j, t, m >$,B first checks the list L.

1. If $SK_{ID_j} = \perp$,B will select a random number $r_i \in Z_q^*$ and set $R_i = r_iP$.Then, he checks whether ID_j exists in $E^{list}, H_1 - list, H_2 - list,$

$H_3 - list$. If not, he computes $T_{ID_j} = h_{ID_j}P_1, H_1(ID_j, PK_{ID_j}, T_{ID_j}) = d_iP, H_2(ID_j, T_{ID_j}, PK_{ID_j}, t) = \lambda_iP, H_3(t, ID_j, m_i, R_i) = \beta_iP$ and adds to lists. Otherwise, B must rechoose the numbers until there is no collision. B computes $V_i = Cert_{ID_i} + d_iPK_{ID_i} + \lambda_ih_iP_1 + \beta_iR_i$ and outputs the signature $(t, (R_i, V_i, T_{ID_i}))$.

Correctness $e(V_i, P)$
$= e(Cert_{ID_j} + d_iPK_{ID_j} + \lambda_ih_{ID_j}P_1 + \beta_iR_i, P)$
$= e(Cert_{ID_j} + SK_{ID_j}(d_i)P + \lambda_ih_{ID_j}P_1 + \beta_iR_i, P)$
$= e(Cert_{ID_j}, P)e(SK_{ID_j}(d_i)P, P)e(\lambda_ih_{ID_j}P_1, P)e(\beta_iR_i, P)$
$= e(mpk, Q_{ID_j})e(H_1(ID_j, PK_{ID_j}, T_{ID_j}), PK_{ID_j})e(H_2(ID_j, T_{ID_j}, t), T_{ID_j})$
$e(H_3(t, ID_j, m_i, R_i), R_i)$

2. Otherwise, he can use $S_{ID_j,t}$ and $Cert_{ID_j}$ to generate the signature on this message.

At last, A_{II} outputs a valid forgery $(t^*, \sigma^*) = (t^*, (R^*, V^*, T_{ID}^*))$ on message m^* with respect to (ID^*, PK_{ID}^*). We assume that $(< ID^*, PK_{ID^*} >, coin^*, c^*, h_0^*)$, $(< ID^*, PK_{ID^*}, T_{ID^*} >, d^*, h_1^*), (< ID^*, T_{ID^*}, PK_{ID^*}, t^* >, \lambda^*, h_2^*)$, $(< t, ID^*, M^*, R^* >, \beta^*, h_3^*), (ID^*, h_{ID^*}, T_{ID^*})$ have been in $H_0 - list$, $H_1 - list$, $H_2 - list$, $H_3 - list$ and E^{list} respectively. If σ^* is a valid signature of the message m^*, then $V^* = sc^*P + SK_{ID^*}(d^*P + P_2) + \lambda^*T_{ID^*} + \beta^*R^*$.

1. If $PK_{ID^*} = P_1, SK_{ID^*} = a$. Therefore, B can compute $abP = V^* - (sc^*P + d^*P_1 + \lambda^*T_{ID^*} + \beta^*R^*)$.
2. Otherwise, B fails to solve this instance of CDH problem.

According to the simulation, B can compute the value of abP if and only if all the following events happen:

Event. E_1 : B does not fail during the simulation.

Event. E_2 : A_{II} outputs a valid forgery on period t^*.

Event. E_3 : In the forgery output by A_{II}, $PK_{ID^*} = P_1$.
Therefore, the probability that B can solve this instance of CDH problem is $\varepsilon' = \Pr[E_1 \wedge E_2 \wedge E_3] = \Pr[E_1]\Pr[E_2|E_1]\Pr[E_3|E_1 \wedge E_2]$. In addition, all the simulation can be done in polynomial time.
From the simulation, we have $\Pr[E_1] \geq (1-\frac{1}{q'})^{q_R}, \Pr[E_2|E_1] = \varepsilon$, $\Pr[E_3|E_1 \wedge E_2] = \frac{1}{q'}$, where $1 \neq q' \leq q_R$, q' denotes the number of queries submitted to the oracle **UserKeyGen**. So $\varepsilon' \geq \frac{1}{q'}(1-\frac{1}{q'})^{q_R}\varepsilon \geq \frac{e}{q_R}\varepsilon$, where e is the base of natural logarithm.

Theorem 3. In the random oracle model, if there is a Type I chosen message adversary A'_I which can submit at most q_R queries wins **Game2-3** defined in Section 2.3 with a probability ε, then there exists an algorithm B which can solve the CDH problem with a probability $\varepsilon' \geq \frac{e}{q_R+1}\varepsilon$ in polynomial time.

Theorem 4. In the random oracle model, if there is a Type II chosen message adversary A'_{II} which can submit at most q_R queries wins **Game2-4** defined in

Section 2.3 with a probability ε, then there exists an algorithm B which can solve the CDH problem with a probability $\varepsilon' \geq \frac{e}{q_R}\varepsilon$ in polynomial time.

Due to the space limitation, the proof of theorem 3,4 refers to those of theorem 1,2 respectively.

5 Performance Analysis

In this section, we will analyze the proposed scheme from computation efficiency and signature length and summarize the result in Table 1. We denote by E the exponentiation in G_1, P the bilinear pairing operation, $|G_1|$ the bit length of an element in group G_1. In verification phase, $e(Q_{ID}, mpk)$ and $e(PK_{ID}, U_{ID})$ are pre-computable.

Table 1. Performance analysis

Scheme	Signature Length	Signature Generation	Verification
Our scheme	$3|G_1|$	$2E$	$3P$

6 Conclusion

It is meaningful to research on certificate-based key-insulated signature schemes. In this paper, we propose the formal definition and security model of certificate-based key-insulated signatures. Besides, we construct a certificate-based key-insulated signature scheme from bilinear maps. Under the computational Diffie-Hellman assumption, we prove the scheme is existentially unforgeable against adaptive chosen message attacks in the random oracle model. In addition, performance of the scheme is analyzed. There exist most certificate-based signature schemes that are secure in the random oracle model, but for which any implementation of the random oracle results in insecure schemes. We construct certificate-based key-insulated signatures without random oracle, which is the future work of our paper.

Acknowledgments. We would like to thank anonymous referees for their helpful comments and suggestions.

References

1. Shamir, A.: Identity-Based Cryptosystems and Signature Schemes. In: Blakely, G.R., Chaum, D. (eds.) CRYPTO 1984. LNCS, vol. 196, pp. 47–53. Springer, Heidelberg (1985)
2. Al-Riyami, S.S., Paterson, K.G.: Certificateless Public Key Cryptography. In: Laih, C.-S. (ed.) ASIACRYPT 2003. LNCS, vol. 2894, pp. 452–473. Springer, Heidelberg (2003)

3. Huang, X., Susilo, W., Mu, Y., Zhang, F.: On the Security of Certificateless Signature Schemes from Asiacrypt 2003. In: Desmedt, Y.G., Wang, H., Mu, Y., Li, Y. (eds.) CANS 2005. LNCS, vol. 3810, pp. 13–25. Springer, Heidelberg (2005)
4. Li, J.G., Huang, X.Y., Mu, Y., Wu, W.: Cryptanalysis and Improvement of an Efficient Certificateless Signature Scheme. Journal of Communications and Networks 10(1), 10–17 (2008)
5. Gentry, C.: Certificate-Based Encryption and the Certificate Revocation Problem. In: Biham, E. (ed.) EUROCRYPT 2003. LNCS, vol. 2656, pp. 272–293. Springer, Heidelberg (2003)
6. Kang, B.G., Park, J.H., Hahn, S.G.: A Certificate-Based Signature Scheme. In: Okamoto, T. (ed.) CT-RSA 2004. LNCS, vol. 2964, pp. 99–111. Springer, Heidelberg (2004)
7. Li, J., Huang, X., Mu, Y., Susilo, W., Wu, Q.: Certificate-Based Signature: Security Model and Efficient Construction. In: López, J., Samarati, P., Ferrer, J.L. (eds.) EuroPKI 2007. LNCS, vol. 4582, pp. 110–125. Springer, Heidelberg (2007)
8. Wu, W., Mu, Y., Susilo, W., Huang, X.Y.: Certificate-Based Signatures Revisited. Journal of Universal Computer Science 15(8), 1659–1684 (2009)
9. Liu, J.K., Baek, J., Susilo, W., Zhou, J.: Certificate-Based Signature Schemes without Pairings or Random Oracles. In: Wu, T.-C., Lei, C.-L., Rijmen, V., Lee, D.-T. (eds.) ISC 2008. LNCS, vol. 5222, pp. 285–297. Springer, Heidelberg (2008)
10. Zhang, J.: On the Security of a Certificate-Based Signature Scheme and Its Improvement with Pairings. In: Bao, F., Li, H., Wang, G. (eds.) ISPEC 2009. LNCS, vol. 5451, pp. 47–58. Springer, Heidelberg (2009)
11. Li, J.G., Huang, X.Y., Mu, Y., Susilo, W., Wu, Q.H.: Constructions of Certificate-Based Signature Secure against Key Replacement Attacks. Journal of Computer Security 18(3), 421–449 (2010)
12. Li, J.G., Huang, X.Y., Zhang, Y.C., Xu, L.Z.: An Efficient Short Certificate-Based Signature Scheme. Journal of Systems and Software 85(2), 314–322 (2012)
13. Li, J.G., Huang, X.Y., Hong, M.X., Zhang, Y.C.: Certificate-Based Signcryption with Enhanced Security Features. Computers and Mathematics with Applications (accepted, 2012), http://dx.doi.org/10.1016/j.camwa.2012.01.006
14. Anderson, R.: Invited Lecture. In: Proceedings of the 4th ACM Computer and Communications Security (1997)
15. Dodis, Y., Katz, J., Xu, S., Yung, M.: Key-Insulated Public Key Cryptosystems. In: Knudsen, L.R. (ed.) EUROCRYPT 2002. LNCS, vol. 2332, pp. 65–82. Springer, Heidelberg (2002)
16. Dodis, Y., Katz, J., Xu, S., Yung, M.: Strong Key-Insulated Signature Schemes. In: Desmedt, Y.G. (ed.) PKC 2003. LNCS, vol. 2567, pp. 130–144. Springer, Heidelberg (2002)
17. Zhou, Y., Cao, Z., Chai, Z.: Identity Based Key Insulated Signature. In: Chen, K., Deng, R., Lai, X., Zhou, J. (eds.) ISPEC 2006. LNCS, vol. 3903, pp. 226–234. Springer, Heidelberg (2006)
18. Weng, J., Liu, S., Chen, K., Li, X.: Identity-Based Key-Insulated Signature with Secure Key-Updates. In: Lipmaa, H., Yung, M., Lin, D. (eds.) Inscrypt 2006. LNCS, vol. 4318, pp. 13–26. Springer, Heidelberg (2006)
19. Weng, J., Chen, K.F., Liu, S.L., et al.: Identity-Based Strong Key-Insulated Signature without Random Oracles. Jounal of Software 19(6), 1555–1564 (2008)
20. Wan, Z., Lai, X., Weng, J., Liu, S., Long, Y., Hong, X.: Certificateless Key-Insulated Signature without Random Oracles. Journal of Zhejiang University Science A 10(12), 1790–1800 (2009)

The Generalized Construction and Linear Complexity of Binary Sequences with Three-Level Autocorrelation Values*

Zuling Chang and Dandan Li

Department of Mathematics,
Zhengzhou University, Zhengzhou, 450001, P.R. China

Abstract. Binary sequences with good autocorrelation and large linear complexity are needed in many applications. As an application of theory of interleaved sequences, one family of binary pseudo-random sequences is constructed. Furthermore, the autocorrelation values and linear complexity of such constructed binary sequences are derived in this paper.

Keywords: Interleaved sequences, linear complexity, autocorrelation values.

1 Introduction

Pseudo-random sequences are widely used in ranging systems, spread spectrum communication systems, multi-terminal system identification, code division multiple access communication systems, global position systems, software testing, circuit testing, computer simulation and stream ciphers. Balance property, good autocorrelation and large linear complexity are important measures of sequences which can be applied in the above domains[1,2,3].

Let $\mathbf{u} = \{u_t\}^N = \{u_0, u_1, ..., u_{N-1}\}$ is a binary sequence. $\mathbf{u}$ is said to be have optimal autocorrelation property if it satisfies one or two of the following conditions:

1) The maximal out-of-phase autocorrelation magnitude is as small as possible;
2) The number of occurrences of the maximal out-of-phase autocorrelation magnitude is as small as possible.

If $\mathbf{u}$ satisfies condition 1), then it is referred to as a sequence with the optimal autocorrelation magnitude. Furthermore, $\mathbf{u}$ is said to be a sequence with optimal autocorrelation value if it also satisfies condition 2).

To characterize binary sequences with optimal autocorrelation value, we need to introduce difference sets and almost difference sets.

---

* This work is supported by the Natural Science Foundation of China (Grant Nos. 61102093, 61174085).

Y. Xiang et al. (Eds.): ICDKE 2012, LNCS 7696, pp. 221–229, 2012.
© Springer-Verlag Berlin Heidelberg 2012

Definition 1. [11] Let $(A, +)$ be an abelian group of order v. Let C be a k-subset of A. The set C is a (v, k, λ) *difference set* (DS) in A, if $d_c(\omega) = \lambda$ for every nonzero element ω of A, where $d_c(\omega) = |C \cap (C + \omega)|$ is the difference function defined for A. The complement $\overline{C}$ of a (v, k, λ) difference set C in A is defined by $A \backslash C$ and is a $(v, v - k, v - 2k - \lambda)$ difference set.

Cyclic difference sets in $GF(2^n)^*$ with Singer parameters are those with parameters $(2^n - 1, 2^{n-1} - 1, 2^{n-2} - 1)$ for some integer $m \geq 2$ or their complements. Let D be any cyclic difference set in $GF(2^n)^*$, then the characteristic sequence of $\log_\alpha D \subset Z_{2^n-1}$ is a binary sequence with ideal autocorrelation, where α is any primitive element of $GF(2^n)$. There are many constructions of cyclic difference sets with Singer parameters. The reader is referred to [11] for details of difference sets.

Definition 2. [11] Let $(A, +)$ be an abelian group of order v. Let C be a k-subset of A. The set C is a (v, k, λ, t) *almost difference set* (ADS) in A, if $d_c(\omega)$ takes on λ altogether t times and $\lambda + 1$ altogether $v - 1 - t$ times when ω ranges over all the nonzero elements of A, where $d_c(\omega) = |C \cap (C + \omega)|$ is the difference function defined for A.

In [8], Gong etc. introduced the interleaved structure of sequence, which is indeed a good method not only for understanding a sequence structure, but also for constructing new sequences from an old sequence. We know that some binary sequences of period $2^n - 1$ (where n is composite number) with ideal autocorrelation can be represented as an interleaved structure. In [2], Cai and Ding constructed a new class of almost difference set: let m be one even number and R_2 be any $(2^{\frac{m}{2}} - 1, 2^{\frac{m-2}{2}} - 1, 2^{\frac{m-4}{2}} - 1)$ difference set in $GF(2^{\frac{m}{2}})^*$, $R_1 = \{x \in GF(2^m) | Tr_{\frac{m}{2}}^m(x) = 1\}$ and $R = \{r_1 r_2 | r_1 \in R_1, r_2 \in R_2\}$, then $\log_\alpha R$ is a almost difference set. Later, Wang gave the linear complexity of the characteristic sequences of the almost difference sets above and took the Singer difference set and GMW difference set plugged in R_2 for examples in [12]. Inspired by these interpretations, we generalize construction of Cai and Ding into a more ordinary form by the interleaved method. Furthermore, we can give a plain way to obtain the autocorrelation values and linear complexity of the new sequences.

The paper is organized as follows. In section 2, we give preliminary concepts and the related results on sequences for understanding this paper. We generalize construction of Cai and Ding and discuss the autocorrelation values and linear complexity of new binary sequences which correspond to modified construction in section 3. In section 4, we analyze autocorrelation values and linear complexity of the sequences with $n = 2m$ as the special case; moreover, we consider some results and examples as corollaries. We end this paper with some conclusions in section 5.

2   Preliminaries

The following notations will be used throughout this paper.

For positive integers n and m, let $m | n$. A trace function from $GF(2^n)$ to $GF(2^m)$ is denoted by $Tr_m^n(x)$; i.e.,

$$Tr_m^n(x) = x + x^{2^m} + \ldots + x^{2^{m(\frac{n}{m}-1)}}, \qquad x \in GF(2^n)$$

or simply as $Tr(x)$ if $m = 1$ and the context is clear.

The *linear complexity* (or *linear span*) of **u** is defined as the degree of the minimal polynomial of **u**, which we denote by $LC(\mathbf{u})$. The linear complexity of sequence is equivalent to the weight of trace representation of the sequence. The assertion was made clear in [8].

Suppose that $\mathbf{u} = \{u_t\}^N = \{u_0, u_1, ..., u_{N-1}\}$ is a binary sequence of period N. Let C be a subset of Z_N, the characteristic sequence **u** of the set C is defined as

$$u_i = \begin{cases} 1 & \text{if } i \pmod N \in C \\ 0 & \text{otherwise} \end{cases}$$

correspondingly, the set C is called *the support* or *characteristic* of **u**.

The mapping $\mathbf{u} \leftrightarrow f(x)$ is a one-to-one correspondence from sequences with period N to the trace representation of the sequence. That is, $u_i = f(\alpha^i), i = 0, 1, ...$ with period $N|(q^n - 1)$, where α is a primitive element of $GF(q)$ with $q = p^m$. Where p is prime and m is a positive integer.

Let **u** be a sequence over $GF(q)$ of period vd, where v and d are unequal to 1. We can arrange the elements of the sequence **u** into a $v \times d$ array as follows

$$A = \begin{bmatrix} u_0 & u_1 & \cdots & u_{d-1} \\ u_d & u_{d+1} & \cdots & u_{2d-1} \\ & & \cdots & \\ u_{(v-1)d} & u_{(v-1)d+1} & \cdots & u_{vd-1} \end{bmatrix}$$

If each column vector of the array above is either a phase shift of a q-ary sequence, say **a**, of period v or a zero sequence, then we say that **u** is a (v, d) *interleaved sequence* over $GF(q)$ (with respect to **a**). We also say that A is the array form of **u** and call the j-th column vector of A, A_j, the j-th column sequence of **u**.

It is known that A_j is a transpose of $L^{e_j}(\mathbf{a})$ or $(0, 0, ..., 0)$, where e_j is a nonnegative integer. Thus, we may write

$$A_j = L^{e_j}(\mathbf{a}) \quad 0 \leq j < d, \quad e_j \in Z_{q-1} \cup \{\infty\}$$

where we set $e_j = \infty$ if $A_j = (0, 0, ..., 0)$ by convention. The vector $(e_0, e_1, ..., e_{d-1})$ is said to be a *shift sequence* of **u** (with respect to **a**) and **a** is a *base sequence* of **u**. For given **a** and **e**, the interleaved sequence **u** is uniquely determined, that is, $u_{id+j} = a_{i+e_j} \ 0 \leq j < d, 0 \leq i < v$.

We extend the shift sequence **e** of **a** so that it is an m-sequence over $GF(q)$ of degree n, regarded as a $(q^m - 1, d)$ interleaved sequence where $d = \frac{q^n-1}{q^m-1}$ and $m|n$. For $k = id + j, 0 \leq j < d$ with $d \leq k < q^n - 1$, we define

$$e_k = e_{id+j} = \begin{cases} \infty & \text{if } e_j = \infty \\ e_j + i \pmod{q^m - 1} & \text{otherwise} \end{cases}$$

Proposition 1. [8] *For $\tau \not\equiv 0 \pmod d$, we define the following two sets:*

$$T_0(\tau) = \{e_{j+\tau} - e_j \pmod{q^m - 1}|e_{j+\tau} \neq \infty \text{ and } e_j \neq \infty, 0 \leq j < d\}$$

$$T_\infty(\tau) = \{j | e_{j+\tau} = \infty \text{ and } e_j = \infty, 0 \le j < d\}.$$

Then each element in Z_{q^m-1} occurs q^{n-2m} times in $T_0(\tau)$ and $|T_\infty(\tau)| = \frac{q^{n-2m}-1}{q^m-1}$ for every τ with $\tau \not\equiv 0 \pmod d$.

Proposition 2. [8] *Let n be a composite number, and m be a proper factor of n and $d = \frac{q^n-1}{q^m-1}$. Then any m-sequence over $GF(q)$ of degree n can be arranged into a $(q^m-1) \times d$ array where each column sequence is either an m-sequence over $GF(q)$ of degree m or a zero sequence for which all the m-sequences are shift equivalent. Furthermore, there are $\frac{q^{n-m}-1}{q^m-1}$ zero columns in the array.*

Assume that both v and d are arbitrary positive integers. For simplicity, we will also use the notation of the Hermitian dot product of two vectors. Let $\mathbf{a} = (a_0, a_1, \ldots, a_{v-1})$ and $\mathbf{b} = (b_0, b_1, \ldots, b_{v-1})$ be two vectors of $GF(q)^v$. That is,

$$< \mathbf{a}, \mathbf{b} > = (\chi(\mathbf{a}), \chi(\mathbf{b})) = \sum_{i=0}^{v-1} \chi(a_i - b_i) = \sum_{i=0}^{v-1} \omega^{a_i - b_i}$$

where ω is a primitive p-th root of unity. In particular, when $p = 2$,

$$< \mathbf{a}, \mathbf{b} > = \sum_{i=0}^{v-1} (-1)^{a_i - b_i}.$$

Then, if $A = (A_0, A_1, \ldots, A_{d-1})$ and $B = (B_0, B_1, \ldots, B_{d-1})$ are the array forms of $\mathbf{u}$ and $L^\tau(\mathbf{u})$, respectively. The autocorrelation of $\mathbf{u}$ can be computed by

$$C_\mathbf{u}(\tau) = \sum_{j=0}^{d-1} < A_j, B_j > .$$

3   One Generalized Construction of Binary Sequences with Three-Valued Autocorrelation

In this section, we generalize the construction of binary sequences of period $2^n - 1$ in the view of theory of interleaved structure. Besides, out-of-phase autocorrelation of generalized sequence is established and we give the linear complexity of the new constructed sequences. Let $\mathbf{u} = \{u_0, u_1, u_2, \ldots, u_{N-1}\}$ be a 2-level autocorrelation sequence of period $N = 2^n - 1$. Suppose $n = k \cdot m$, where m and k are positive numbers, which are unequal to 1.

Construction: A new binary sequence $\widehat{\mathbf{u}}$ of period $2^n - 1$ is defined by a (v, d) interleaved structure $\widehat{A} = (\widehat{A}_0, \widehat{A}_1, \ldots, \widehat{A}_{d-1})$. Where $v = 2^m - 1$, $d = \frac{2^n-1}{2^m-1}$,
(1) $\mathbf{u}$ has a (v, d) interleaved structure with 2-level autocorrelation , denoted by $A = (A_0, A_1, ..., A_{d-1})$;
(2)

$$\widehat{A}_j = \begin{cases} \mathbf{0} & \text{if } A_j = \mathbf{0} \\ \overline{A}_j & \text{if } A_j \neq \mathbf{0} \end{cases}$$

where $\mathbf{0}$ and $\overline{A}_j$ stand for zero sequence and complement sequence of the column sequence A_j, respectively.

There are $\frac{2^{n-m}-1}{2^m-1}$ zero column sequences in $\widehat{A}$ and the others are shift-equivalent sequences of period 2^m-1 with 2-level autocorrelation by proposition 2.

Firstly, we consider the autocorrelation values of the above new sequences.

Theorem 1. *Based on construction of array $\widehat{A}$, the autocorrelation values of corresponding sequence $\widehat{\mathbf{u}}$ are:*

$$C_{\widehat{\mathbf{u}}}(\tau) = \begin{cases} 2^n - 1 & \text{if } \tau = 0 \\ -1 & \text{if } \tau = 0 (\text{mod } d) \text{ and } \tau \neq 0 \\ -1 + 4 \cdot \left(\frac{2^{n-m}-2^{n-2m}}{2^m-1}\right) & \text{otherwise} \end{cases}$$

Proof. Let $A = (A_0, A_1, \ldots, A_{d-1})$ be the interleaved array of $\mathbf{u}$, $B = L^\tau(\mathbf{u}) = (B_0, B_1, \ldots, B_{d-1})$, $\widehat{A} = (\widehat{A}_0, \widehat{A}_1, \ldots, \widehat{A}_{d-1})$, $\widehat{B} = L^\tau(\widehat{\mathbf{u}}) = (\widehat{B}_0, \widehat{B}_1, \ldots, \widehat{B}_{d-1})$, and $\tau = rd+t, 0 \leq r < v, 0 \leq t < d$. Firstly, compared with interleaved structure of the original sequence $\mathbf{u}$, we find that the nonzero column sequences of the modified sequence $\widehat{\mathbf{u}}$ are just the complement sequences of the corresponding columns of $\mathbf{u}$; and the zero columns of $\widehat{\mathbf{u}}$ are identical to zero columns of $\mathbf{u}$. $C_{\widehat{\mathbf{u}}}(\tau)$ can be discussed by means of the classification of τ as follows.

case 1: $\tau = 0$, it is easy to achieve.

case 2: $\tau = 0 \pmod{d}$ and $\tau \neq 0$, then for $j = 0, 1, \ldots, d-1$, if $\widehat{A}_j = \mathbf{0}, \widehat{B}_j = \mathbf{0}$; if $\widehat{A}_j \neq \mathbf{0}, \widehat{B}_j \neq \mathbf{0}$, and at this time $\widehat{A}_j = \overline{A}_j, \widehat{B}_j = \overline{B}_j$. So we always have

$$< \widehat{A}_j, \widehat{B}_j >=< A_j, B_j >$$

and

$$C_{\widehat{\mathbf{u}}}(\tau) = C_{\mathbf{u}}(\tau) = -1.$$

case 3: $\tau \neq 0 (\text{mod } d)$, arbitrary column sequence of $\widehat{A}$ with τ-shift may be nonzero column or zero column of $\widehat{B}$. In the light of proposition 2, there is $\frac{2^{n-m}-1}{2^m-1}$ zero columns in $\widehat{A}$ or $\widehat{B}$, but the number of the case such that $< \widehat{A}_j, \widehat{B}_j >=< \mathbf{0}, \mathbf{0} >$ is $\frac{2^{n-2m}-1}{2^m-1}$ according to proposition 1. So the number of the case such that $< \widehat{A}_j, \mathbf{0} >, \widehat{A}_j \neq \mathbf{0}$ and the case such that $< \mathbf{0}, \widehat{B}_j >, \widehat{B}_j \neq \mathbf{0}$ are $2(\frac{2^{n-m}-1}{2^m-1} - \frac{2^{n-2m}-1}{2^m-1})$. If $\widehat{A}_j = \widehat{B}_j = \mathbf{0}$, then

$$< \widehat{A}_j, \widehat{B}_j >=< A_j, B_j > .$$

If $\widehat{A}_j \neq \mathbf{0}$ and $\widehat{B}_j \neq \mathbf{0}$, then

$$< \widehat{A}_j, \widehat{B}_j >=< \overline{A}_j, \overline{B}_j >=< A_j, B_j > .$$

If $\widehat{A}_j \neq \mathbf{0}$ and $\widehat{B}_j = \mathbf{0}$, then

$$< \widehat{A}_j, \widehat{B}_j >=< \overline{A}_j, \mathbf{0} >= 1 = -1 + 2 =< A_j, B_j > +2.$$

If $\widehat{A}_j = \mathbf{0}$ and $\widehat{B}_j \neq \mathbf{0}$, then

$$< \widehat{A}_j, \widehat{B}_j >=< \mathbf{0}, \overline{B}_j >= 1 = -1 + 2 =< A_j, B_j > +2.$$

Clearly we have

$$C_{\widehat{\mathbf{u}}}(\tau) = C_{\mathbf{u}}(\tau) + 2 \cdot 2(\tfrac{2^{n-m}-1}{2^m-1} - \tfrac{2^{n-2m}-1}{2^m-1})$$
$$= -1 + 2 \cdot 2(\tfrac{2^{n-m}-2^{n-2m}}{2^m-1})$$
$$= -1 + 4 \cdot (\tfrac{2^{n-m}-2^{n-2m}}{2^m-1}).$$

$\square$

Now we consider the linear complexity of such new sequences. firstly we provide the following lemma.

Lemma 1. *The weight of* $(Tr_m^n(x))^{2^m-1}$ *is* k^m*, where* $n = k \cdot m$*.*

Proof.

$$(Tr_m^n(x))^{2^m-1} = (x + x^{2^m} + \cdots + x^{2^{(k-1)m}})^{2^m-1}$$
$$= (x + x^{2^m} + \cdots + x^{2^{(k-1)m}})^{2^0+2^1+2^2+\cdots+2^{m-1}}$$
$$= \prod_{i=0}^{m-1} (x + x^{2^m} + \cdots + x^{2^{(k-1)m}})^{2^i}.$$

Each term in the expansion of $(Tr_m^n(x))^{2^m-1}$ is the multiplication of the m elements chosen from each column in the following matrix

$$J = \begin{bmatrix} x^{2^0} & x^{2^1} & \cdots & x^{2^{m-1}} \\ x^{2^m} & x^{2^{m+1}} & \cdots & x^{2^{m+m-1}} \\ & & \cdots & \\ x^{2^{(k-1)m}} & x^{2^{(k-1)m+1}} & \cdots & x^{2^{(k-1)m+m-1}} \end{bmatrix}$$

It is easy to find that the base of binary number in Z_{2^n-1} consists of all the exponents of x in the array J. In other words, any exponent of x in the expansion of $(Tr_m^n(x))^{2^m-1}$ can be represented as

$$\tau_{2^m-1}(\mathbf{t}) = 2^{t_1 m} + 2^{t_2 m+1} + 2^{t_3 m+3} + \ldots + 2^{t_m m+m-1}$$

$t_1 \in Z_k, ..., t_m \in Z_k$; that is, $\mathbf{t} = (t_1, ..., t_m) \in Z_k^m$. Thus the binary number $\tau_{2^m-1}(\mathbf{t})$ has Hamming weight $m < n$. So, $\tau_{2^m-1}(\mathbf{t}) < 2^n - 1$, for all $\mathbf{t} \in Z_k^m$. Any integer in Z_{2^n} has a unique binary representation. It follows that

$$\tau_{2^m-1}(\mathbf{t}) \not\equiv \tau_{2^m-1}(\mathbf{t}') \qquad \text{for all } \mathbf{t} \not\equiv \mathbf{t}' \in Z_k^m$$

Then all the exponents are pairwise distinct. Thus there are k^m possibilities of the exponents of x. So, the weight of $(Tr_m^n(x))^{2^m-1}$ is k^m. $\square$

Furthermore, we arrive at conclusion that the trace representation and linear complexity of the new constructed sequences.

Theorem 2. *In the construction above, if $f(x)$ is the trace representation of sequence $\mathbf{u}$. Then the trace representation of the sequence $\widehat{\mathbf{u}}$ is $F(x) = f(x) + (Tr_m^n(x))^{2^m-1}$. If $f(x)$ and $(Tr_m^n(x))^{2^m-1}$ have not the same monomial, the linear complexity of $\widehat{\mathbf{u}}$ is $LC(\mathbf{u}) + k^m$.*

Proof. Let α be a primitive element of $GF(2^n)$. Let $c_i = Tr_m^n(\alpha^i), i = 1, 2, ...$; then $\mathbf{c} \leftrightarrow Tr_m^n(x)$; in the subfield $GF(2^m)$, $\mathbf{c}$ is just the m-sequence, and $\mathbf{c}$ can be arranged a $(2^m - 1, \frac{2^n-1}{2^m-1})$ interleaved structure, denoted by $C = (C_0, C_1, ..., C_{d-1})$. For each nonzero column in the array C, all elements in $GF(2^m)^*$ occur only once. We know that if $Tr_m^n(\alpha^i) \neq 0$, then

$$(Tr_m^n(\alpha^i))^{2^m-1} = 1.$$

From the construction of our new sequences, we know that for $j = 0, 1, ..., d-1$, if $C_j = \mathbf{0}$ then $A_j = \widehat{A}_j = \mathbf{0}$; if $C_j \neq \mathbf{0}$ then $A_j \neq \mathbf{0}$ and $\widehat{A}_j \neq \mathbf{0}$. So If $Tr_m^n(\alpha^i) = 0$, then

$$\widehat{u}_i = u_i = 0 = u_i + (Tr_m^n(\alpha^i))^{2^m-1}.$$

If $Tr_m^n(\alpha^i) \neq 0$, then

$$\widehat{u}_i = u_i + 1 = u_i + (Tr_m^n(\alpha^i))^{2^m-1}.$$

Clearly we always have

$$F(\alpha^i) = \widehat{u}_i = u_i + (Tr_m^n(\alpha^i))^{2^m-1} = f(\alpha^i) + (Tr_m^n(\alpha^i))^{2^m-1},$$

so we deduce that the trace representation of the new sequence is

$$F(x) = f(x) + (Tr_m^n(x))^{2^m-1}.$$

By lemma 1, $w((Tr_m^n(x))^{2^m-1})$ is k^m. So if $f(x)$ and $(Tr_m^n(x))^{2^m-1}$ have not the same monomial, the linear complexity of $\widehat{\mathbf{u}}$ is given by $LC(\mathbf{u}) + k^m$. □

4   The Special Case $n = 2m$ and Examples

By analyzing existed results and classical examples, we find that some results and examples adapt to the special case of the theorems in section 3. Further, we show more simple proofs of existed conclusions.

At this time, we show the formula with the autocorrelation values and linear complexity of new constructed sequence immediately when $n = 2m$. The autocorrelation values of corresponding sequence $\widehat{\mathbf{u}}$ as follows:

$$C_{\widehat{\mathbf{u}}}(\tau) = \begin{cases} 2^n - 1 & if \ \tau = 0 \\ -1 & if \ \tau = 0 \pmod{d} \ and \ \tau \neq 0 \\ 3 & otherwise. \end{cases}$$

The trace representation of $\widehat{u}$ in section 3 is $F(x) = f(x) + (Tr_m^{2m}(x))^{2^m-1}$ and linear complexity of $\widehat{u}$ is $LC(\mathbf{u}) + 2^m$ if $f(x)$ and $(Tr_m^{2m}(x))^{2^m-1}$ have not the same monomial.

Now we illustrate that a new class of almost difference set by Cai and Ding in [2] caters for the construction. Furthermore, autocorrelation and linear complexity of the characteristic sequences of the almost difference set above are the special cases of new theorems in section 3. Hereafter, let $m \geq 4$ be an even positive number.

Corollary 1. [2] *Let R_2 be any $(2^{\frac{m}{2}} - 1, 2^{\frac{m-2}{2}} - 1, 2^{\frac{m-4}{2}} - 1)$ difference set in $GF(2^{\frac{m}{2}})^*$. $R_1 = \{x \in GF(2^m) | Tr_{\frac{m}{2}}^m(x) = 1\}$ and $R = \{r_1 r_2 | r_1 \in R_1, r_2 \in R_2\}$. Then the characteristic sequence of the support set $\log_\alpha R$ has the uniform out-of-phase autocorrelation $\{-1, 3\}$. R is almost difference set.*

Proof. Let α be the generator of $GF(2^{\frac{m}{2}})^*$, $v = 2^{\frac{m}{2}} - 1$, $d = \frac{2^m-1}{2^{\frac{m}{2}}-1} = 2^{\frac{m}{2}} + 1$ and $\beta = \alpha^d$ is generator of $GF(2^{\frac{m}{2}})$. $\log_\beta \overline{R_2}$ corresponds to $m-$sequence with period $2^{\frac{m}{2}} - 1$, $R_1 = \{x \in GF(2^m) | Tr_{\frac{m}{2}}^m(x) = 1\}$, let $\mathbf{b} = Tr_{\frac{m}{2}}^m(x)$ be an $m-$sequence over $GF(2^{\frac{m}{2}})$ of degree 2 with period $2^{\frac{m}{2}} - 1$. Then $\mathbf{b}$ can be arranged a $v \times d$ interleaved structure, denoted by $B = (B_0, B_1, \ldots, B_{d-1})$. In the light of proposition 2, there is only one zero column sequence in B. Arbitrary nonzero $m-$sequence B_j contains all elements in $GF(2^{\frac{m}{2}})^*$ $(0 \leq j < d)$. Because one occurs only once in every nonzero column, we regard the position of one in nonzero columns as shift sequence $\mathbf{e}$ and view zero column as ∞ of shift sequence. And we also regard the characteristic sequence of $\log_\beta \overline{R_2}$ as the base sequence $\mathbf{a}$; then $\mathbf{u}$ is a (v, d) interleaved sequence associated with $(\mathbf{a}, \mathbf{e})$. The characteristic sequence of $\log_\beta R_2$ is the complement of $\log_\beta \overline{R_2}$. Then $\widehat{u}$ is interleaved sequence associated with $(\overline{\mathbf{a}}, \mathbf{e})$. So, the characteristic sequence of the support set $\log_\alpha R$ satisfies construction in section 3. It is to easy to get the autocorrelation values by Theorem 1. And that R is almost difference set is referred to [2]. $\square$

Wang[12] studied the linear complexity of the sequences constructed in [2], but by using corollary 1 and theorem 2, we can easily deduce the same results, the only work need to do is just to prove that the trace representation $f(x)$ of basic sequence $\mathbf{u}$ and $(Tr_{\frac{m}{2}}^m(x))^{2^{\frac{m}{2}}-1}$ have not the same monomial. The details are omitted here and we just list the main results as the following corollaries.

Corollary 2. [12] *If the Singer difference sets is plugged in as R_2, the linear complexity of the characteristic sequence $\widehat{u}$ of the set $\log_\alpha R$ is $2^{\frac{m}{2}} + m$.*

Corollary 3. [12] *If the GMW difference set is plugged in as R_2, the linear complexity of the characteristic sequence $\widehat{u}$ of the set $\log_\alpha R$ is $2^{\frac{m}{2}} + (2k)^{\omega-1}m$.*

5   Conclusions

In the paper, we studied the binary ideal 2-level sequences that admitted (v, d) interleaved structure, and generalized the construction of binary sequences with three-level autocorrelation. As well, we established the linear complexity of a new family of binary sequences. Furthermore, we discussed the special case that $n = 2m$ and some existed results as corollaries.

References

1. Antweiler, M., Bomer, L.: Complex sequences over $GF(p^M)$ with a two-level autocorrelation function and a large span. IEEE Transactions on Information Theory 38, 120–130 (1982)
2. Cai, Y., Ding, C.: Binary sequences with optimal autocorrelation. Theorem Computer Science 410, 2316–2322 (2009)
3. Gong, G.: Run, component sequences and vector sequences of m-sequences over Galois fields. Acta Etectronica Sinica 35(4), 94–100 (1986)
4. Gong, G.: On q-ary sequences generated by mapping $GF(q^m)$ sequences into GF(q). Fondazione Ugo Bordoni Rome. Rep. 3B00692 (January 1992)
5. Gong, G.: Linear space decomposition of sequences over $GF(q^m)$ (August 1993)
6. Gong, G.: Theory and application of q-ary interleaved sequences. IEEE Transactions on Information Theory 41(3), 400–411 (1995)
7. Gong, G.: Q-ary cascaded GMW sequences. IEEE Transactions on Information Theory 42, 263–267 (1996)
8. Golomb, S.W., Gong, G.: Signal Design for Good Correlation-For Wireless Communication, Cryptography and Radar. Cambridge Univ. Press (2005)
9. Lidl, R., Niederreiter, H.: Finite Fields. Cambridge Univ. Press (1997)
10. Park, W.J., Komo, J.J.: it Relations hips between m-sequences over $GF(q)$ and $GF(q^m)$. IEEE Transactions on Information Theory 35(1), 183–186 (1989)
11. Singer, J.: A theorem in finite protective geometry and some application to number theorem. Transactions Amercian Mathmatics Society 43(1), 377–385 (1938)
12. Wang, Q.: The linear complexity of some binary sequences with three-level autocorrelation. IEEE Transactions on Information Theory 56, 4046–4052 (2010)

Anonymous Hierarchical Identity-Based Encryption in Prime Order Groups

Yanli Ren, Shuozhong Wang, and Xinpeng Zhang

School of Communication and Information Engineering,
Shanghai University, Shanghai 200072, China
{ryl1982,shuowang,xzhang}@shu.edu.cn

Abstract. A hierarchical identity-based encryption (HIBE) scheme is called anonymous if the ciphertext does not leak the identity of the recipient. Currently, anonymous HIBE schemes are constructed in composite order groups or achieve selective-ID security in prime order groups and the ciphertext size is linear in the maximum depth of hierarchy. We propose an anonymous HIBE scheme with constant size ciphertext, which is adaptive-ID secure without random oracles in prime order groups. Our scheme improves security and efficiency of the anonymous HIBE schemes simultaneously compare with the previous work.

1 Introduction

An identity based (ID-based) system is a public key cryptosystem where the public key can be represented as an arbitrary string such as an email address [2]. The user's private key is generated by a trusted authority, called a private key generator (PKG), which applies its master key to issue private keys to identities that request them. Shamir proposed the notion of identity based encryption (IBE) as a way to simplify public key and certificate management. Many ID-based schemes have been proposed after that, but practical ID-based encryption schemes were not found until the work of Boneh and Franklin [5].

Although having a single PKG would completely eliminate online lookup, it is undesirable for a large network because the PKG has a burdensome job. Hierarchical ID-based cryptography was first proposed in [4] and [9]. It allows a root PKG to distribute the workload by delegating private key generation and identity authentication to lower-level PKGs. Canetti et al. give the first HIBE with a selective-ID security proof without random oracles, but that is not efficient [15]. Waters described a fully secure HIBE scheme without random oracles using a method of dual system encryption [3], but the ciphertext size is linear in the maximum depth of hierarchy. Luo et al. propose a new HIBE scheme with constant size ciphertexts and short parameters, and the scheme is also fully secure without random oracles [16].

An anonymous IBE scheme means the ciphertext does not leak the identity of the recipient. In addition to its obvious privacy benefits, an anonymous IBE system can be leveraged to construct public key encryption with keyword

Y. Xiang et al. (Eds.): ICDKE 2012, LNCS 7696, pp. 230–242, 2012.
© Springer-Verlag Berlin Heidelberg 2012

search (PEKS) schemes [14]. Boyen and Waters presented the first anonymous HIBE scheme, which is selective-ID secure without random oracles [17]. The anonymous HIBE system generates secret keys of size proportional to l^2 and ciphertext of size proportional to l, where l is the maximum depth of hierarchy. Shi and Waters used composite order groups to construct an HIBE scheme where private key size is $O(l)$ and ciphertext size linear in l [7]. The scheme achieves selective-ID security based on several composite complexity assumptions. Seo et al. also used composite order groups to construct an anonymous HIBE scheme, with constant size ciphertext and linear size private keys [11]. The scheme also achieves selective-ID security without random oracles. Afterwards, several anonymous HIBE schemes constructed in composite order groups are proposed in [1], [8] and [10], respectively. These schemes have constant size ciphertext and are adaptive-ID secure without random oracles based on several non-standard complexity assumptions.

As we know, the security of composite order groups is based on the hardness of factoring the order of groups. To achieve the same security level, the order of composite order groups should be at least 1024 bits while the order of prime order groups is 160 bits. As a result, the paring on composite order groups would be very slower than the same pairing on comparable prime order groups. For example, the Tate pairing on a 1024-bit supersingular curve is roughly 50 times slower than the Tate pairing on a 170-bit MNT curve [6]. Thus, it is very meaningful to construct an anonymous HIBE schemes in prime order groups. Lee et al. constructed an anonymous HIBE scheme with constant size ciphertext in prime order groups, which is only selective-ID secure without random oracles [12]. Recently, Ducas proposed an anonymous HIBE scheme using asymmetric bilinear map in prime order groups [13], but the scheme has linear size ciphertext and private key and is only selective-ID secure without random oracles based on the asymmetric P-BDH assumption.

Currently, there is no anonymous HIBE scheme with constant size ciphertext, which is adaptive-ID secure without random oracles in prime order groups. In this paper, we present an anonymous HIBE scheme with constant size ciphertext in prime order groups. Our idea is motivated from [16], which is provably secure without random oracles but cannot provide receiver anonymity. The proposed scheme is anonymous and adaptive-ID secure without random oracles based on asymmetric D-bilinear Diffie-Hellman (DBDH) and D-linear assumption. The security proof is executed by a sequence of games using the method of dual system encryption.

2 Definitions

We review the definition of an asymmetric bilinear map and discuss the complexity assumptions on which our system is based. We also review the security model for an anonymous HIBE system.

2.1 Asymmetric Bilinear Map

Let p be a large prime number, $G, \hat{G}$ and G_T be three groups of order p, and $g, \hat{g}$ be generators of G and $\hat{G}$ respectively. $e : G \times \hat{G} \to G_T$ is an asymmetric bilinear map, which has the following properties [13]:

(1) Bilinearity: For all $u \in G, v \in \hat{G}$ and $a, b \in Z_p$, $e(u^a, v^b) = e(u, v)^{ab}$.
(2) Non-degeneracy: $e(g, \hat{g}) \neq 1$.
(3) Computability: There exists an efficient algorithm to compute $e(u, v)$, $\forall u \in G, v \in \hat{G}$.

2.2 Complexity Assumption

Our scheme is constructed based on asymmetric decisional bilinear Diffie-Hellman (DBDH) assumption [13] and asymmetric decisional linear (D-Linear) assumption [16], which are defined as follows.

Asymmetric DBDH Assumption. Let $a, b, c \in Z_p^*$ be chosen at random and $g, \hat{g}$ be generators of G and $\hat{G}$ respectively. The asymmetric DBDH assumption is that no probabilistic polynomial-time (PPT) algorithm can distinguish the tuple $[g, g^b, g^c, \hat{g}, \hat{g}^a, \hat{g}^b, e(g, \hat{g})^{abc}]$ from the tuple $[g, g^b, g^c, \hat{g}, \hat{g}^a, \hat{g}^b, T]$ with non-negligible advantage where T is a random element in G_T.

Asymmetric D-linear Assumption. Let $a, b \in Z_p^*$ be chosen at random, g, f, ν be random generators of G, and $\hat{g}, \hat{f}, \hat{\nu}$ be random generators of $\hat{G}$. The asymmetric D-Linear assumption is that no PPT algorithm can distinguish the tuple $[g, f, \nu, \hat{g}, \hat{f}, \hat{\nu}, g^a, f^b, \nu^{a+b}]$ from the tuple $[g, f, \nu, \hat{g}, \hat{f}, \hat{\nu}, g^a, f^b, T]$ with non-negligible advantage where T is a random element in G.

This assumption can also be presented that no probabilistic polynomial-time algorithm can distinguish the tuple $[g, f, \nu, \hat{g}, \hat{f}, \hat{\nu}, \hat{g}^a, \hat{f}^b, \hat{\nu}^{a+b}]$ from the tuple $[g, f, \nu, \hat{g}, \hat{f}, \hat{\nu}, \hat{g}^a, \hat{f}^b, T]$ with non-negligible advantage where T is a random element in $\hat{G}$.

2.3 Security Model

In this section, we define adaptive-ID security against an chosen plaintext attack (ANON-IND-ID-CPA) for an anonymous HIBE scheme. It is executed by the following game between an adversary A and a challenger B. We adopt the modified definition by Waters [3], which distinguishes the keys generated from the authority or from a delegation operation of the user's prefix.

Setup. The challenger B runs the Setup algorithm and gives PK to the adversary A.

The challenger also initializes a list $L = \phi$, which stores the identity and the corresponding secret keys it has created, but not given out.

Phase 1. The adversary A can make the following queries repeatedly.

Create query (ID): A submits an identity vector ID. The challenger creates a secret key SK_{ID} for that vector, but does not give it to the adversary. It instead adds (ID, SK_{ID}) to the list L and gives the attacker a reference to it.

Derive query (ID, ID'): The adversary gives the challenger two identity vectors ID and ID', where ID is a prefix of ID' and ID already exists on the list. The challenger runs the Derive algorithm to get a new secret key $SK_{ID'}$ and adds $(ID', SK_{ID'})$ to the list L.

Reveal query (ID): The adversary specifies an identity vector ID on the list L for a secret key SK_{ID}. The challenger removes the item (ID, SK_{ID}) from the list L and gives the adversary the secret key.

Challenge. A submits two challenge identity vectors (ID^0, ID^1) and two equal length messages (M_0, M_1) to B with the restriction that each identity vector ID given out in the key phase must not be a prefix of ID^0 or ID^1. The challenger randomly chooses $\beta, \gamma \in \{0, 1\}$ and sends the ciphertext $CT^* = Encrypt(PK, ID^\beta, M_\gamma)$ to A.

Phase 2. Phase 1 is repeated with the restriction that any revealed identity vector ID is not a prefix of ID^0 or ID^1.

Guess. Finally, the adversary outputs its guess $\beta', \gamma' \in \{0, 1\}$ and wins the game if $(\beta', \gamma') = (\beta, \gamma)$.

We call the adversary A in the above game an ANON-IND-ID-CPA adversary. The advantage of A is defined as $|Pr[(\beta' = \beta) \wedge (\gamma' = \gamma)] - \frac{1}{4}|$.

Definition 1. An anonymous HIBE scheme is called ANON-IND-ID-CPA secure if no probabilistic polynomial time adversary A has a non-negligible advantage in winning the ANON-IND-ID-CPA game.

3   The Proposed Anonymous HIBE Scheme

We present an anonymous HIBE scheme with constant size ciphertext in prime order groups. The scheme is adaptive-ID secure without random oracles based on DBDH and D-Linear assumptions. A detailed description of the scheme follows.

3.1   Setup

Given the security parameter λ and the maximum depth of hierarchy l, the setup algorithm first gets $[p, G, \hat{G}, G_T, g \in G, \hat{g} \in \hat{G}, e] \longleftarrow \mathcal{G}(\lambda)$. It randomly chooses $a_1, a_2, b, \alpha, \eta, \eta_1, \eta_2, \eta_3, \theta_i, \delta_i, i \in \{1, \dots, l\}$, and sets:

$$v = g^\eta, v_1 = g^{\eta_1}, v_2 = g^{\eta_2}, w = g^{\eta_3}, u_i = g^{\theta_i}, h_i = g^{\delta_i}, i \in \{1, \dots, l\},$$
$$\hat{v} = \hat{g}^\eta, \hat{v}_1 = \hat{g}^{\eta_1}, \hat{v}_2 = \hat{g}^{\eta_2}, \hat{w} = \hat{g}^{\eta_3}, \hat{u}_i = \hat{g}^{\theta_i}, \hat{h}_i = \hat{g}^{\delta_i}, i \in \{1, \dots, l\},$$
$$\tau_1 = vv_1^{a_1}, \tau_2 = vv_2^{a_2}, \tau_1^b, \tau_2^b, Y = e(g, \hat{g})^{\alpha a_1 b}.$$

The public key PK is published as

$$(Y, g, \hat{g}, g^b, \hat{g}^b, g^{a_1}, g^{a_2}, g^{ba_1}, g^{ba_2}, \tau_1, \tau_2, \tau_1^b, \tau_2^b,$$
$$v, v_1, v_2, w, u_i, h_i, i \in \{1, \dots, l\}),$$

and the master key $MK = (\hat{g}^\alpha, \hat{g}^{\alpha a_1}, \hat{v}, \hat{v}_1, \hat{v}_2, \hat{w}, \hat{u}_i, \hat{h}_i, i \in \{1, \dots, l\})$.

3.2 KeyGen

For an identity $ID = (I_1, \ldots, I_n) \in (Z_p^*)^n$, the algorithm chooses random $r_1, r_2, z_1, z_2, tag_k, tag_{n+1}, \ldots, tag_l \in Z_p^*$ and computes:

$$D_1 = \hat{g}^{\alpha a_1}\hat{v}^{r_1+r_2}, D_2 = \hat{g}^{-\alpha}\hat{v}_1^{r_1+r_2}\hat{g}^{z_1}, D_3 = (\hat{g}^b)^{-z_1},$$
$$D_4 = \hat{v}_2^{r_1+r_2}\hat{g}^{z_2}, D_5 = (\hat{g}^b)^{-z_2}, D_6 = (\hat{g}^b)^{r_2}, D_7 = (\hat{g})^{r_1},$$
$$K = (\hat{u}_1^{I_1}\hat{u}_2^{I_1 I_2} \ldots \hat{u}_n^{I_1 I_n}\hat{w}^{tag_k}\hat{h}_1\hat{h}_2^{I_2} \ldots \hat{h}_n^{I_n})^{r_1},$$
$$K_{n+1} = (\hat{u}_{n+1}^{I_1}\hat{w}^{tag_{n+1}}\hat{h}_{n+1})^{r_1}, \ldots, K_l = (\hat{u}_l^{I_1}\hat{w}^{tag_l}\hat{h}_l)^{r_1}.$$

The secret key for the identity ID is

$$SK_{ID} = (D_1, D_2, \ldots, D_7, K, K_{n+1}, \ldots, K_l, tag_k, tag_{n+1}, \ldots, tag_l).$$

3.3 Derive

Given $SK_{ID|_n} = (D_1', D_2', \ldots, D_7', K', K_{n+1}', \ldots, K_l', tag_{k'}, tag_{n+1}, \ldots, tag_l)$ for an identity $ID|_n = (I_1, \ldots, I_n) \in (Z_p^*)^n$, the algorithm generates a secret key for $ID|_{n+1} = (I_1, \ldots, I_{n+1})$ as follows.

It randomly chooses $z_1, z_2 \in Z_p^*$, and sets

$$D_1 = D_1', D_2 = D_2' \cdot \hat{g}^{z_1}, D_3 = D_3' \cdot (\hat{g}^b)^{-z_1}, D_4 = D_4' \cdot \hat{g}^{z_2},$$
$$D_5 = D_5' \cdot (\hat{g}^b)^{-z_2}, D_6 = D_6', D_7 = D_7', K = K' \cdot (K_{n+1})^{I_{n+1}},$$
$$tag_k = tag_{k'} + I_{n+1}tag_{n+1}, K_{n+2} = K_{n+2}', \ldots, K_l = K_l'.$$

The secret key for the identity $ID|_{n+1}$ is

$$SK_{ID|_{n+1}} = (D_1, D_2, \ldots, D_7, K, K_{n+2}, \ldots, K_l, tag_k, tag_{n+2}, \ldots, tag_l).$$

3.4 Encrypt

To encrypt a message M for an identity $ID = (I_1, \ldots, I_n) \in (Z_p^*)^n$, randomly choose $s_1, s_2, t, tag_c \in Z_p^*$, and compute

$$C_0 = MY^{s_2}, C_1 = (g^b)^{s_1+s_2}, C_2 = (g^{ba_1})^{s_1}, C_3 = (g^{a_1})^{s_1},$$
$$C_4 = (g^{ba_2})^{s_2}, C_5 = (g^{a_2})^{s_2}, C_6 = \tau_1^{s_1}\tau_2^{s_2}, C_7 = (\tau_1^b)^{s_1}(\tau_2^b)^{s_2}w^{-t},$$
$$E_1 = (u_1^{I_1}u_2^{I_1 I_2} \ldots u_n^{I_1 I_n}w^{tag_c}h_1h_2^{I_2} \ldots h_n^{I_n})^t, E_2 = g^t.$$

The ciphertext is $CT = (C_0, C_1, \ldots, C_7, E_1, E_2, tag_c)$.

3.5 Decrypt

To a ciphertext CT for an identity ID, the user decrypts it using the secret key SK_{ID} as follows.

$$A_1 = e(C_1, D_1)e(C_2, D_2)e(C_3, D_3)e(C_4, D_4)e(C_5, D_5),$$
$$A_2 = e(C_6, D_6)e(C_7, D_7), A_3 = A_1/A_2,$$
$$A_4 = (e(E_1, D_7)/e(E_2, K))^{1/(tag_c - tag_k)}, M = C_0/(A_3/A_4).$$

3.6   Correctness

The correctness of the proposed HIBE scheme is as follows.

$$e(C_1, D_1) = e(g, \hat{g})^{\alpha a_1 b(s_1+s_2)} e(g, \hat{v})^{b(r_1+r_2)(s_1+s_2)},$$
$$e(C_2, D_2)e(C_3, D_3) = e(g, \hat{g})^{-\alpha a_1 bs_1} e(g, \hat{v}_1)^{ba_1 s_1(r_1+r_2)},$$
$$e(C_4, D_4)e(C_5, D_5) = e(g, \hat{v}_2)^{ba_2 s_2(r_1+r_2)},$$
$$A_1 = e(g, \hat{g})^{\alpha a_1 bs_2} e(g, \hat{v})^{b(r_1+r_2)(s_1+s_2)} e(g, \hat{v}_1)^{ba_1 s_1(r_1+r_2)} e(g, \hat{v}_2)^{ba_2 s_2(r_1+r_2)}.$$
$$e(C_6, D_6) = e(v, \hat{g})^{br_2(s_1+s_2)} e(v_1, \hat{g})^{ba_1 s_1 r_2} e(v_2, \hat{g})^{ba_2 s_2 r_2},$$
$$e(C_7, D_7) = e(v, \hat{g})^{br_1(s_1+s_2)} e(v_1, \hat{g})^{ba_1 s_1 r_1} e(v_2, \hat{g})^{ba_2 s_2 r_1} e(w, \hat{g})^{-r_1 t},$$
$$A_2 = e(v, \hat{g})^{b(r_1+r_2)(s_1+s_2)} e(v_1, \hat{g})^{ba_1 s_1(r_1+r_2)} e(v_2, \hat{g})^{ba_2 s_2(r_1+r_2)} e(w, \hat{g})^{-r_1 t}.$$
$$A_3 = A_1/A_2 = e(g, \hat{g})^{\alpha a_1 bs_2} e(g, \hat{w})^{r_1 t}.$$
$$A_4 = (e(w, \hat{g})^{tr_1 tag_c}/e(g, \hat{w})^{tr_1 tag_k})^{1/(tag_c - tag_k)} = e(g, \hat{w})^{r_1 t}.$$
$$C_0/(A_3/A_4) = M e(g, \hat{g})^{\alpha a_1 bs_2}/e(g, \hat{g})^{\alpha a_1 bs_2} = M.$$

Note: The proposed HIBE scheme is anonymous based on asymmetric bilinear groups because that $(\hat{w}, \hat{u}_i, \hat{h}_i, i \in \{1, \ldots, l\})$ is secret and the adversary cannot verify the identity of the receiver through the equation $e(E_1, \hat{g}) = e(E_2, \hat{u}_1^{I_1} \hat{u}_2^{I_1 I_2} \ldots \hat{u}_n^{I_1 I_n} \hat{w}^{tag_c} \hat{h}_1 \hat{h}_2^{I_2} \ldots \hat{h}_n^{I_n})$.

4   Analysis of the Anonymous HIBE Scheme

Our anonymous HIBE scheme is adaptive-ID secure without random oracles by using asymmetry bilinear map. In order to prove security, we need to define two additional algorithms: semi-functional ciphertexts and semi-functional keys, which will not be used in the real scheme, but be used in our proof.

4.1   Semi-functional Algorithms

Semi-functional Ciphertexts. First, execute the encryption algorithm to generate a normal ciphertext $CT' = (C_0', C_1', \ldots, C_7', E_1', E_2', tag_c')$. It then randomly chooses $x \in \mathbb{Z}_p$, and sets:

$$C_0 = C_0', C_1 = C_1', C_2 = C_2', C_3 = C_3', E_1 = E_1', E_2 = E_2', tag_c = tag_c',$$
$$C_4 = C_4' \cdot g^{ba_2 x}, C_5 = C_5' \cdot g^{a_2 x}, C_6 = C_6' \cdot v_2^{a_2 x}, C_7 = C_7' \cdot v_2^{ba_2 x}.$$

The semi-functional ciphertext is $CT = (C_0, C_1, \ldots, C_7, E_1, E_2, tag_c)$.

Semi-functional Keys. It first executes the key generation algorithm to obtain a normal secret key

$$SK_{ID}' = (D_1', D_2', \ldots, D_7', K', K_{n+1}', \ldots, K_l', tag_k', tag_{n+1}', \ldots, tag_l')$$

for an identity ID. It randomly chooses $\gamma \in \mathbb{Z}_p$, and sets:

$$D_1 = D' \cdot \hat{g}^{-a_1 a_2 \gamma}, D_2 = D_2' \cdot \hat{g}^{a_2 \gamma}, D_3 = D_3', D_4 = D_4' \cdot \hat{g}^{a_1 \gamma},$$
$$D_5 = D_5', D_6 = D_6', D_7 = D_7', K = K', K_{n+1} = K_{n+1}', \ldots, K_l = K_l',$$
$$tag_k = tag_k', tag_{n+1} = tag_{n+1}', \ldots, tag_l = tag_l'.$$

The semi-functional secret key is

$$SK_{ID} = (D_1, D_2, \ldots, D_7, K, K_{n+1}, \ldots, K_l, tag_k, tag_{n+1}, \ldots, tag_l).$$

Note that the semi-functional ciphertexts and private keys cannot be generated from the public parameters because they need $v_2^{ba_2}$ and $\hat{g}^{a_1 a_2}$ respectively.

In addition, a normal secret key can decrypt a semi-functional ciphertext and a normal ciphertext can be decrypted by a semi-functional secret key correctly. However, a semi-functional secret key will fail to decrypt a semi-functional ciphertext. Here we omit the presentation of correctness due to limited space.

4.2 Security Proof

Our security proof can be constructed by a sequence of games as follows.

$Game_{Real}$: It is a real HIBE security game as described in Section 2.3.

$Game_k (0 \le k \le q)$: Assume the adversary makes q key queries. The game is like $Game_{Real}$ except that the challenge ciphertext is semi-functional and the first k secret keys are semi-functional and the rest are normal. Hence, only the challenge ciphertext is semi-functional in $Game_0$, and the challenge ciphertext and all of the keys are semi-functional in $Game_q$.

$Game_{Final}$: The game is like $Game_q$ except that the challenge ciphertext is a semi-functional encryption of a random message, not one of the messages provided by the adversary.

We will show the games are indistinguishable through three lemmas.

Lemma 1. Assume there is an algorithm $\mathcal{A}$ such that $Game_{Real}Adv_{\mathcal{A}} - Game_0 Adv_{\mathcal{A}} = \varepsilon$. Then we can construct an algorithm $\mathcal{B}$ with advantage ε in breaking the D-Linear assumption.

Proof. $\mathcal{B}$ is given a challenge vector $(g, f, \nu, \hat{g}, \hat{f}, \hat{\nu}, g^{c_1}, f^{c_2}, T)$, and then simulates $Game_{Real}$ or $Game_0$ with $\mathcal{A}$.

Setup. $\mathcal{B}$ randomly chooses $b, \alpha, \eta, \eta_1, \eta_2, \eta_3, \theta_i, \delta_i, i \in \{1, \ldots, l\}$, and sets:

$$g^b, g^{a_1} = f, g^{a_2} = \nu, g^{ba_1} = f^b, g^{ba_2} = \nu^b, \hat{g}^{a_1} = \hat{f},$$
$$v = g^\eta, v_1 = g^{\eta_1}, v_2 = g^{\eta_2}, w = g^{\eta_3}, u_i = g^{\theta_i}, h_i = g^{\delta_i}, i \in \{1, \ldots, l\},$$
$$\hat{v} = \hat{g}^\eta, \hat{v}_1 = \hat{g}^{\eta_1}, \hat{v}_2 = \hat{g}^{\eta_2}, \hat{w} = \hat{g}^{\eta_3}, \hat{u}_i = \hat{g}^{\theta_i}, \hat{h}_i = \hat{g}^{\delta_i}, i \in \{1, \ldots, l\},$$
$$\tau_1 = vv_1^{a_1} = vf^{\eta_1}, \tau_2 = vv_2^{a_2} = v\nu^{\eta_2}, \tau_1^b, \tau_2^b, Y = e(g, \hat{g})^{\alpha a_1 b} = e(f, \hat{g})^{\alpha b}.$$

$\mathcal{B}$ sends the public key PK to $\mathcal{A}$, where $PK =$

$$(Y, g, \hat{g}, g^b, \hat{g}^b, g^{a_1}, g^{a_2}, g^{ba_1}, g^{ba_2}, \tau_1, \tau_2, \tau_1^b, \tau_2^b,$$
$$v, v_1, v_2, w, u_i, h_i, i \in \{1, \ldots, l\}).$$

Phase 1. Since $\mathcal{B}$ has the actual master secret key MK, it can execute $KeyGen$ algorithm to generate a normal secret key for an identity ID.

Challenge. $\mathcal{A}$ submits two equal-length messages (M_0, M_1) and two challenge identities (ID^0, ID^1). $\mathcal{B}$ randomly chooses $\beta, \gamma \in \{0, 1\}$, and first runs $Encrypt$

(PK, ID^β, M_γ) algorithm to obtain a normal ciphertext $(C'_0, C'_1, \ldots, C'_7, E'_1, E'_2, tag_c)$, where s'_1, s'_2 be the random exponents used in creating the ciphertext. Then $\mathcal{B}$ sets:

$$C_0 = C'_0 \cdot (e(g^{c_1}, \hat{f})e(f^{c_2}, \hat{g}))^{b\alpha}, C_1 = C'_1 \cdot (g^{c_1})^b, C_2 = C'_2 \cdot (f^{c_2})^{-b},$$
$$C_3 = C'_3 \cdot (f^{c_2}), C_4 = C'_4 \cdot (T^b), C_5 = C'_5 \cdot T, C_6 = C'_6(g^{c_1})^\eta(f^{c_1})^{-\eta_1}T^{\eta_2},$$
$$C_7 = C'_7((g^{c_1})^\eta(f^{c_1})^{-\eta_1}T^{\eta_2})^b, E_1 = E'_1, E_2 = E'_2.$$

Finally $\mathcal{B}$ returns $CT = (C_0, C_1, \ldots, C_7, E_1, E_2, tag_c)$.

Phase 2. $\mathcal{A}$ adaptively issues queries as Phase 1, and $\mathcal{B}$ answers these queries in the same way as Phase 1.

Guess. $\mathcal{A}$ submits a guess $(\beta', \gamma') \in \{0,1\}$. If $T = \nu^{c_1+c_2}$, CT has the same distribution as a standard ciphertext with $s_1 = -c_2 + s'_1, s_2 = s'_2 + c_1 + c_2$ and $s_1 + s_2 = c_1 + s'_1 + s'_2$; otherwise it will be distributed identically to a semi-functional ciphertext.

$\mathcal{B}$ outputs 0 if $(\beta', \gamma') = (\beta, \gamma)$. So, B can decide whether $T = \nu^{c_1+c_2}$ or a random tuple of G using the output of $\mathcal{A}$.

Lemma 2. Suppose there exists a polynomial time algorithm $\mathcal{A}$ such that $Game_{k-1}Adv_\mathcal{A} - Game_k Adv_\mathcal{A} = \varepsilon$. Then we can construct an algorithm $\mathcal{B}$ with advantage ε in breaking D-linear assumption, where $1 \le k \le q$.

Proof. $\mathcal{B}$ is given a tuple $(g, f, \nu, \hat{g}, \hat{f}, \hat{\nu}, \hat{g}^{c_1}, \hat{f}^{c_2}, T)$, and then it simulates $Game_{k-1}$ or $Game_k$ with $\mathcal{A}$.

Setup. $\mathcal{B}$ chooses random $\alpha, a_1, a_2, \eta_1, \eta_2, \eta_3, A_i, B_i, \theta_i, \delta_i, i \in \{1, \ldots, l\}$, and sets:

$$g^b = f, \hat{g}^b = \hat{f}, g^{ba_1} = f^{a_1}, g^{ba_2} = f^{a_2}, Y = e(f, \hat{g})^{\alpha a_1},$$
$$v = \nu^{-a_1 a_2}, v_1 = \nu^{a_2}g^{\eta_1}, v_2 = \nu^{a_1}g^{\eta_2}, w = fg^{\eta_3},$$
$$\hat{v} = \hat{\nu}^{-a_1 a_2}, \hat{v}_1 = \hat{\nu}^{a_2}\hat{g}^{\eta_1}, \hat{v}_2 = \hat{\nu}^{a_1}\hat{g}^{\eta_2}, \hat{w} = \hat{f}\hat{g}^{\eta_3},$$
$$u_i = f^{-A_i}g^{\theta_i}, h_i = f^{-B_i}g^{\delta_i}, \hat{u}_i = \hat{f}^{-A_i}\hat{g}^{\theta_i}, \hat{h}_i = \hat{f}^{-B_i}\hat{g}^{\delta_i}, i \in \{1, \ldots, l\},$$
$$\tau_1 = vv_1^{a_1} = g^{\eta_1 a_1}, \tau_2 = vv_2^{a_2} = g^{\eta_2 a_2}, \tau_1^b = f^{\eta_1 a_1}, \tau_2^b = f^{\eta_2 a_2}.$$

$\mathcal{B}$ sends the public key PK to $\mathcal{A}$, where

$$PK = (Y, g, \hat{g}, g^b, \hat{g}^b, g^{a_1}, g^{a_2}, g^{ba_1}, g^{ba_2}, \tau_1, \tau_2, \tau_1^b, \tau_2^b,$$
$$v, v_1, v_2, w, u_i, h_i, i \in \{1, \ldots, l\}).$$

Phase 1. It is broken into three cases. Consider the k-th query made by $\mathcal{A}$.

Case 1: $i < k$
When i is less than k, $\mathcal{B}$ will generate a semi-functional key for the requested identity ID. Since $\mathcal{B}$ has the actual master secret key MK and $\hat{g}^{a_1}, \hat{g}^{a_2}, \hat{g}^{a_1 a_2}$, it can generate a semi-functional secret key for an identity ID.

Case 2: $i = k$
B first executes $KeyGen$ algorithm to obtain a normal secret key SK_{ID} for an identity ID with

$$(D_1', D_2', \ldots, D_7', K', K_{n+1}', \ldots, K_l', tag_k, tag_{n+1}, \ldots, tag_l), \text{ where}$$
$$tag_k = F_1(I_1) + I_2 F_2(I_1) + \ldots + I_n F_n(I_1), tag_{n+1} = F_{n+1}(I_1), \ldots,$$
$$tag_l = F_l(I_1), F_j(x) = A_j x + B_j, 1 \le j \le l.$$

Let r_1', r_2', z_1', z_2' be the random exponents used in the normal secret key generation phase above. $\mathcal{B}$ then sets:

$$D_1 = D_1' \cdot T^{-a_1 a_2}, D_2 = D_2' \cdot T^{a_2}(\hat{g}^{c_1})^{\eta_1}, D_3 = D_3' \cdot (\hat{f}^{c_2})^{\eta_1},$$
$$D_4 = D_4' \cdot T^{a_1}(\hat{g}^{c_1})^{\eta_2}, D_5 = D_5' \cdot (\hat{f}^{c_2})^{\eta_2}, D_6 = D_6' \cdot \hat{f}^{c_2},$$
$$D_7 = D_7' \cdot \hat{g}^{c_1}, K = K' \cdot (\hat{g}^{c_1})^{I_1 \theta_1 + \delta_1 + \sum_{j=2}^{n} I_j(I_1 \theta_j + \delta_j) + tag_k \eta_3},$$
$$K_{n+1} = K_{n+1}' \cdot (\hat{g}^{c_1})^{I_1 \theta_{n+1} + \delta_{n+1} + tag_{n+1} \eta_3}, \ldots, K_l = K_l' \cdot (\hat{g}^{c_1})^{I_1 \theta_l + \delta_l + tag_l \eta_3}.$$

$\mathcal{B}$ returns $SK_{ID} = (D_1, \ldots, D_7, K, K_{n+1}, \ldots, K_l, tag_k, tag_{n+1}, \ldots, tag_l)$ as the secret key for the k-th query. If $T = \hat{v}^{c_1 + c_2}$, SK_{ID} has the same distribution as a standard secret key with

$$z_1 = z_1' - \eta_1 c_2, z_2 = z_2' - \eta_2 c_2, r_1 = r_1' + c_1, r_2 = r_2' + c_2;$$

otherwise it will be distributed identically to a semi-functional secret key.

Case 3: $i > k$
When i is greater than k, $\mathcal{B}$ will generate a normal key for the requested identity ID. Since $\mathcal{B}$ has the actual master secret key MK, it can generate a normal secret key for an identity ID.

Challenge. $\mathcal{A}$ submits two equal-length messages (M_0, M_1) and two challenge identities (ID^0, ID^1). $\mathcal{B}$ randomly chooses $\beta, \gamma \in \{0, 1\}$, and runs $Encrypt$ (PK, ID^β, M_γ) algorithm to obtain a normal ciphertext $(C_0', C_1', \ldots, C_7', E_1', E_2', tag_c)$, where $tag_c = F_1(I_1) + I_2 F_2(I_1) + \ldots + I_n F_n(I_1)$, and s_1', s_2', t' be the random exponents used in creating the ciphertext. Then $\mathcal{B}$ makes the ciphertext semi-functional as follows. It chooses a random $x \in Z_p$, and sets:

$$C_0 = C_0', C_1 = C_1', C_2 = C_2', C_3 = C_3', C_4 = C_4' \cdot f^{a_2 x},$$
$$C_5 = C_5' \cdot g^{a_2 x}, C_6 = C_6' \cdot v_2^{a_2 x}, C_7 = C_7' \cdot f^{\eta_2 x a_2} v^{-a_1 a_2 x \eta_3},$$
$$E_1 = E_1' \cdot (v^{I_1 \theta_1 + \delta_1 + \sum_{j=2}^{n} I_j(I_1 \theta_j + \delta_j) + tag_c \eta_3})^{a_1 a_2 x}, E_2 = E_2' \cdot v^{a_1 a_2 x}.$$

Finally $\mathcal{B}$ returns $CT = (C_0, C_1, \ldots, C_7, E_1, E_2, tag_c)$.

Phase 2. $\mathcal{A}$ adaptively issues queries as Phase 1, and $\mathcal{B}$ answers these queries in the same way as Phase 1.

Guess. $\mathcal{A}$ submits a guess $(\beta', \gamma') \in \{0, 1\}$. If $T = \hat{v}^{c_1 + c_2}$, $\mathcal{A}$ receives a normal secret key for the k-th query and we are in **Game$_{k-1}$**, otherwise $\mathcal{A}$ receives a semi-functional secret key for the k-th query and we are in **Game$_k$**.

$\mathcal{B}$ outputs 0 if $(\beta', \gamma') = (\beta, \gamma)$. So, $\mathcal{B}$ can decide whether $T = \hat{v}^{c_1 + c_2}$ or a random tuple of G using the output of $\mathcal{A}$.

Lemma 3. Suppose there is an algorithm $\mathcal{A}$ such that $Game_q Adv_{\mathcal{A}} - Game_{Final} Adv_{\mathcal{A}} = \varepsilon$. Then we can construct an algorithm $\mathcal{B}$ with advantage ε in breaking the DBDH assumption.

Proof. At the beginning of the game, $\mathcal{B}$ is given $(g, g^{c_2}, g^{c_3}, \hat{g}, \hat{g}^{c_1}, \hat{g}^{c_2}, T)$. Then it simulates $Game_q$ or $Game_{Final}$ with $\mathcal{A}$.

Setup. $\mathcal{B}$ randomly chooses $a_1, b, \eta, \eta_1, \eta_2, \eta_3, \theta_i, \delta_i, i \in \{1, \ldots, l\}$, and sets:

$$g^b, g^{a_1}, g^{a_2} = g^{c_2}, g^{ba_1}, g^{ba_2} = (g^{c_2})^b,$$
$$v = g^\eta, v_1 = g^{\eta_1}, v_2 = g^{\eta_2}, w = g^{\eta_3}, u_i = g^{\theta_i}, h_i = g^{\delta_i}, i \in \{1, \ldots, l\},$$
$$\hat{v} = \hat{g}^\eta, \hat{v}_1 = \hat{g}^{\eta_1}, \hat{v}_2 = \hat{g}^{\eta_2}, \hat{w} = \hat{g}^{\eta_3}, \hat{u}_i = \hat{g}^{\theta_i}, \hat{h}_i = \hat{g}^{\delta_i}, i \in \{1, \ldots, l\},$$
$$\tau_1 = vv_1^{a_1}, \tau_2 = vv_2^{a_2} = vg^{c_2\eta_2}, \tau_1^b, \tau_2^b, Y = e(g^{c_2}, \hat{g}^{c_1})^{a_1 b}.$$

Note that this simulation sets $\alpha = c_1 c_2$, which is unknown for $\mathcal{B}$.
$\mathcal{B}$ sends the public key PK to $\mathcal{A}$, where

$$PK = (Y, g, \hat{g}, g^b, \hat{g}^b, g^{a_1}, g^{a_2}, g^{ba_1}, g^{ba_2}, \tau_1, \tau_2, \tau_1^b, \tau_2^b,$$
$$v, v_1, v_2, w, u_i, h_i, i \in \{1, \ldots, l\}).$$

Phase 1. When $\mathcal{A}$ submits an identity ID, $\mathcal{B}$ creates a semi-functional secret key. It randomly chooses $r_1, r_2, z_1, z_2, \gamma', tag_k, tag_{n+1}, \ldots, tag_l \in Z_p^*$, and sets:

$$D_1 = (\hat{g}^{c_2})^{-a_1\gamma'}\hat{v}^{r_1+r_2}, D_2 = (\hat{g}^{c_2})^{-\gamma'}\hat{v}_1^{r_1+r_2}\hat{g}^{z_1}, D_3 = (\hat{g}^b)^{-z_1},$$
$$D_4 = (\hat{g}^{c_1})^{a_1}\hat{g}^{a_1\gamma'}\hat{v}_2^r\hat{g}^{z_2}, D_5 = (\hat{g}^b)^{-z_2}, D_6 = (\hat{g}^b)^{r_2}, D_7 = \hat{g}^{r_1},$$
$$K = (\hat{u}_1^{I_1}\hat{u}_2^{I_1 I_2} \ldots \hat{u}_n^{I_1 I_n}\hat{w}^{tag_k}\hat{h}_1\hat{h}_2^{I_2} \ldots \hat{h}_n^{I_n})^{r_1},$$
$$K_{n+1} = (\hat{u}_{n+1}^{I_1}\hat{w}^{tag_{n+1}}\hat{h}_{n+1})^{r_1}, \ldots, K_l = (\hat{u}_l^{I_1}\hat{w}^{tag_l}\hat{h}_l)^{r_1}.$$

Challenge. $\mathcal{A}$ submits two equal-length messages (M_0, M_1) and two challenge identities (ID^0, ID^1). $\mathcal{B}$ randomly chooses $\beta, \gamma \in \{0, 1\}$, and creates a semi-functional ciphertext of M_γ or a random message associated with ID^β. It chooses $s_1, t, tag_c, x' \in Z_p^*$ and computes:

$$C_0 = M_\gamma \cdot T^{a_1 b}, C_1 = g^{s_1 b}(g^{c_3 b}), C_2 = g^{ba_1 s_1},$$
$$C_3 = g^{a_1 s_1}, C_4 = (g^{c_2})^{bx'}, C_5 = (g^{c_2})^{x'}, C_6 = \tau^{s_1}(g^{c_3})^\eta(g^{c_2})^{\eta_2 x'},$$
$$C_7 = (\tau^b)^{s_1}(g^{c_3})^{b\eta}(g^{c_2})^{\eta_2 x' b}w^{-t}, $$
$$E_1 = (u_1^{I_1}u_2^{I_1 I_2} \ldots u_n^{I_1 I_n}w^{tag_c}h_1 h_2^{I_2} \ldots h_n^{I_n})^t, E_2 = g^t.$$

Finally $\mathcal{B}$ returns $CT = (C_0, C_1, \ldots, C_7, E_1, E_2, tag_c)$.

Phase 2. $\mathcal{A}$ adaptively issues queries as Phase 1, and $\mathcal{B}$ answers these queries in the same way as Phase 1.

Guess. $\mathcal{A}$ submits a guess $(\beta', \gamma') \in \{0, 1\}$. If $T = e(g, \hat{g})^{c_1 c_2 c_3}$, CT is a semi-functional ciphertext of M_γ and we are in **Game$_q$**, otherwise CT is a semi-functional ciphertext of a random element and we are in **Game$_{Final}$**.

$\mathcal{B}$ outputs 0 if $(\beta', \gamma') = (\beta, \gamma)$. So, $\mathcal{B}$ can decide whether $T = e(g, \hat{g})^{c_1 c_2 c_3}$ or a random tuple of G_T using the output of $\mathcal{A}$.

Theorem 1. *If asymmetric D-linear and DBDH assumption hold, then our HIBE scheme achieves semantic security and receiver anonymity without random oracles.*

Proof. We conclude that the real game is indistinguishable from the final game from three Lemmas above, and the bit of w is random for the adversary. Therefore, the adversary can obtain no advantage in breaking the HIBE scheme and our scheme is semantic secure and anonymous without random oracles based on D-linear and DBDH assumption.

4.3   Comparison

In this section, we compare security and efficiency of our anonymous HIBE scheme with that of the previous ones. These schemes are all proven secure without random oracles.

In Table 1, l represents the maximum depth of hierarchy, and "sID, ID" denote "selective-ID" and "adaptive-ID" security model respectively.

From Table 1, we conclude that the scheme of [7,11,1,8,10] are constructed in composite order groups, which have very low efficiency compare with the schemes in prime order groups. Moreover, their security is proven based on some non-standard complexity assumptions. In [17,12] and [13], the anonymous HIBE schemes are only selective-ID secure though they are proposed in prime order groups. Moreover, the ciphertext size is linear in the maximum depth of hierarchy in the scheme of [17,13]. Our scheme has constant size ciphertext and achieves adaptive-ID security in prime order groups based on the DBDH and D-Linear assumption. So, the proposed scheme has better security and is more efficient than that of the previous work.

Table 1. Comparison among anonymous HIBE schemes

Scheme	Prime order groups	Complexity assumptions	Security model	Public key size	Ciphertext size	Decrypt time
[7]	no	cBDH, c3DH	sID	$O(l)$	$O(l)$	$O(l)$
[11]	no	l-wBDHI* l-cDH, BSD	sID	$O(l)$	$O(1)$	$O(1)$
[1]	no	subgroup decision for four primes	ID	$O(l)$	$O(1)$	$O(1)$
[8]	no	as [1]	ID	$O(l)$	$O(1)$	$O(1)$
[10]	no	as [1]	ID	$O(l)$	$O(1)$	$O(1)$
[17]	yes	D-linear	sID	$O(l^2)$	$O(l)$	$O(l)$
[12]	yes	l-wBDHI* l-P3DH	sID	$O(l)$	$O(1)$	$O(1)$
[13]	yes	P-BDH	sID	$O(l)$	$O(l)$	$O(l)$
Ours	yes	DBDH D-linear	ID	$O(l)$	$O(1)$	$O(1)$

5   Conclusion

We present an anonymous HIBE scheme with constant size ciphertext based on [16] using asymmetric bilinear map. The scheme is adaptive-ID secure without random oracles in prime order groups. The proposed scheme improves security and efficiency of the anonymous HIBE simultaneously compare with the previous ones.

Acknowledgement. We thank the anonymous referees for their helpful comments and suggestions. This work was supported by the Natural Science Foundation of China (61202367, 61073190, 60832010), and the Research Fund for the Doctoral Program of Higher Education of China (20113108110010).

References

1. De Caro, A., Iovino, V., Persiano, G.: Fully Secure Anonymous HIBE and Secret-Key Anonymous IBE with Short Ciphertexts. In: Joye, M., Miyaji, A., Otsuka, A. (eds.) Pairing 2010. LNCS, vol. 6487, pp. 347–366. Springer, Heidelberg (2010)
2. Shamir, A.: Identity-Based Cryptosystems and Signature Schemes. In: Blakely, G.R., Chaum, D. (eds.) CRYPTO 1984. LNCS, vol. 196, pp. 47–53. Springer, Heidelberg (1985)
3. Waters, B.: Dual System Encryption: Realizing Fully Secure IBE and HIBE under Simple Assumptions. In: Halevi, S. (ed.) CRYPTO 2009. LNCS, vol. 5677, pp. 619–636. Springer, Heidelberg (2009)
4. Gentry, C., Silverberg, A.: Hierarchical ID-Based Cryptography. In: Zheng, Y. (ed.) ASIACRYPT 2002. LNCS, vol. 2501, pp. 548–566. Springer, Heidelberg (2002)
5. Boneh, D., Franklin, M.: Identity-Based Encryption from the Weil Pairing. In: Kilian, J. (ed.) CRYPTO 2001. LNCS, vol. 2139, pp. 213–229. Springer, Heidelberg (2001)
6. Freeman, D.M.: Converting Pairing-Based Cryptosystems from Composite-Order Groups to Prime-Order Groups. In: Gilbert, H. (ed.) EUROCRYPT 2010. LNCS, vol. 6110, pp. 44–61. Springer, Heidelberg (2010)
7. Shi, E., Waters, B.: Delegating Capabilities in Predicate Encryption Systems. In: Aceto, L., Damgård, I., Goldberg, L.A., Halldórsson, M.M., Ingólfsdóttir, A., Walukiewicz, I. (eds.) ICALP 2008, Part II. LNCS, vol. 5126, pp. 560–578. Springer, Heidelberg (2008)
8. Wang, H., Xu, Q.: Anonymous HIBE Scheme Secure Against Full Adaptive-ID Attacks. Chinese Journal of Computers 34(1), 25–37 (2011)
9. Horwitz, J., Lynn, B.: Toward Hierarchical Identity-Based Encryption. In: Knudsen, L.R. (ed.) EUROCRYPT 2002. LNCS, vol. 2332, pp. 466–481. Springer, Heidelberg (2002)
10. Seo, J., Cheon, J.: Fully Secure Anonymous Hierarchical Identity-Based Encryption with Constant Size Ciphertexts. Cryptology ePrint Archive, Report 2011/021 (2011), http://eprint.iacr.org/
11. Seo, J.H., Kobayashi, T., Ohkubo, M., Suzuki, K.: Anonymous Hierarchical Identity-Based Encryption with Constant Size Ciphertexts. In: Jarecki, S., Tsudik, G. (eds.) PKC 2009. LNCS, vol. 5443, pp. 215–234. Springer, Heidelberg (2009)
12. Lee, K., Lee, D.: New Techniques for Anonymous HIBE with Short Ciphertexts in Prime Order Groups. KSII Transactions on Internet and Information Systems 4(5), 968–988 (2010)
13. Ducas, L.: Anonymity from Asymmetry: New Constructions for Anonymous HIBE. In: Pieprzyk, J. (ed.) CT-RSA 2010. LNCS, vol. 5985, pp. 148–164. Springer, Heidelberg (2010)
14. Abdalla, M., Bellare, M., Catalano, D., Kiltz, E., Kohno, T., Lange, T., Malone-Lee, J., Neven, G., Paillier, P., Shi, H.: Searchable Encryption Revisited: Consistency Properties, Relation to Anonymous IBE, and Extensions. In: Shoup, V. (ed.) CRYPTO 2005. LNCS, vol. 3621, pp. 205–222. Springer, Heidelberg (2005)

15. Canetti, R., Halevi, S., Katz, J.: A Forward-Secure Public-key Encryption Scheme. In: Biham, E. (ed.) EUROCRYPT 2003. LNCS, vol. 2656, pp. 255–271. Springer, Heidelberg (2003)

16. Luo, S., Chen, Y., Hu, J., Chen, Z.: New Fully Secure Hierarchical Identity-Based Encryption with Constant Size Ciphertexts. In: Bao, F., Weng, J. (eds.) ISPEC 2011. LNCS, vol. 6672, pp. 55–70. Springer, Heidelberg (2011)

17. Boyen, X., Waters, B.: Anonymous Hierarchical Identity-Based Encryption (Without Random Oracles). In: Dwork, C. (ed.) CRYPTO 2006. LNCS, vol. 4117, pp. 290–307. Springer, Heidelberg (2006)

Weaknesses of "Security Analysis and Enhancement for Three-Party Password-Based Authenticated Key Exchange Protocol"

Muhammad Khurram Khan[1,*] and Debiao He[2]

[1] Center of Excellence in Information Assurance, King Saud University, Saudi Arabia
mkhurram@ksu.edu.sa
[2] School of Mathematics and Statistics, Wuhan University, Wuhan, China
hedebiao@whu.edu.cn

Abstract. The three-party password-based authenticated key exchange (3PAKE) protocol allows two users to share a session key for future communication with the help of a trusted server in the public network. Recently, Zhao et al. [Zhao J., Gu D., Zhang L., Security analysis and enhancement for three-party password-based authenticated key exchange protocol, *Security Communication Networks* 2012; 5(3):273-278] proposed an efficient 3PAKE protocol using smart cards. They proved that their protocol can withstand various known attacks found in the previously published schemes. However, in this paper, we point out that their protocol is vulnerable to three kinds of attacks namely, off-line password-guessing attack, privileged insider attack and stolen smart card attack. Hence, Zhao et al.'s scheme is not recommended for practical applications.

Keywords: Key exchange, Password, Three-party, off-line password guessing attack, privileged insider attack, stolen smart card attack.

1 Introduction

Key exchange protocol is a cryptography mechanism, by which participants could generate a session key to ensure future secure communications in public communication networks. Recently, three-party password-based authenticated key exchange (3PAKE) protocols have been studied widely [1-6]. In a 3PAKE protocol, users share a password with the remote authentication server. Then the server could help the two users to authenticate each other and generate a session key using the shared passwords. In 2008, Chen et al. [7] proposed a novel 3PAKE protocol. Their protocol just needs three rounds to generate the session key. Besides, the authentication server in their scheme does not maintain security-sensitive table or database. Chen et al.'s protocol is more secure and efficient than the previous protocol. However, Zhao et al. [8] pointed out that Chen et al.'s protocol is vulnerable to the man-in-the-middle attack.

---

* Corresponding author.

Y. Xiang et al. (Eds.): ICDKE 2012, LNCS 7696, pp. 243–249, 2012.
© Springer-Verlag Berlin Heidelberg 2012

To overcome the weakness of Chen et al.'s scheme, Zhao et al.'s also proposed an improved 3PAKE protocol using smart cards. Zhao et al. claimed that their protocol could resist various attacks. Unfortunately, in this paper, we will show Zhao et al.'s protocol is vulnerable to three kinds of attacks.

The rest of this paper is organized as follows. We give a short description Zhao et al.'s scheme in Section 2. The weaknesses of Zhao et al.'s scheme are shown in Section 3. Finally, we give some conclusions in Section 4.

2   Zhao et al.'s Protocol

In this section, we will briefly review Zhao et al.'s protocol. Their protocol consists of two phases: initialization phase and authenticated key exchange phase. For convenience, notations used in the paper are listed as follows.

A, B : Two legal participants;

S : A trusted server;

ID_A, ID_B : Identities of A and B separately;

pw_A, pw_B : Passwords of A and B separately;

p, q, g : The large primes p and q with $q \mid p-1$ and a generator g of group G with the order q;

x, y : The long-term key of S, where $y = g^x \bmod p$;

$h(\cdot)$: A secure hash function;

2.1   Initialization Phase

In this phase, a user who wants to perform registration should submit his information to the server and performs the following steps:

1) A chooses his password pw_A and identity ID_A, computes $\Delta_A = g^{pw_A} \bmod p$ and sends Δ_A and ID_A to the server.

2) After receiving Δ_A and ID_A from A, S checks whether Δ_A and Δ_I are equal, where Δ_I is the representative of the participants' component of authentication information. If Δ_A and Δ_I are equal, S demands A to choose a different password.

3) S stores Δ_A and ID_A into a smart card and returns it to A.

By the similar way, B could register at the server and get a smart card containing $\Delta_B = g^{pw_B} \bmod p$ and ID_B.

2.2 Authenticated Key Exchange Phase

In this phase, A and B could authenticate each other and generate a session key with the help of S. At first, A and B computes $V_A = y^{pw_A} \bmod p$ and $V_B = y^{pw_B} \bmod p$. Then, as shown in the Fig.1, the following operations will be performed:

Round 1

A generates a random number a, computes $R_A = g^a \bmod p$, $C_{AS} = h(ID_A, ID_B, T_A, R_A, V_A)$ and $W_A = (C_{AS}, T_A, R_A, \Delta_A)$, where T_A is the current timestamp. Then A sends ID_A, ID_B and W_A to S. A also sends ID_A, T_A and R_A to B.

Round 2

Upon receiving ID_A, T_A and R_A, B generates a random number b, computes $R_B = g^b \bmod p$, $sk = R_A^b \bmod p$, $C_{BS} = h(ID_B, ID_A, T_B, R_B, V_B)$, $C_{BA} = h(T_A, R_A, R_B, sk)$ and $W_B = (C_{BS}, T_B, R_B, \Delta_B)$. Then B sends ID_B, ID_A and W_B to S. B also sends ID_B, T_B, R_B and C_{BA} to A.

Round 3

1) S checks whether T_A is valid. If T_A is not valid, S stops the session. Otherwise, S computes $V_A' = \Delta_A^x \bmod p$ and checks whether C_{AS} and $h(ID_A, ID_B, T_A, R_A, V_A')$ are equal. If they are not equal, S terminates the session. Otherwise, S computes $C_{SA} = h(C_{AS}, T_B, R_B, V_A')$ and sends it to A.

2) S checks whether T_B is valid. If T_B is not valid, S terminates the session. Otherwise, S computes $V_B' = \Delta_B^x \bmod p$ and checks whether C_{BS} and $h(ID_B, ID_A, T_B, R_B, V_B')$ are equal. If they are not equal, S terminates the session. Otherwise, S computes $C_{SB} = h(C_{BS}, T_A, R_A, V_B')$ and sends it to B.

3) A checks whether T_B is fresh. If T_B is not fresh, A terminates the session. Otherwise, A computes $sk' = R_B^a \bmod p$ and checks whether

$h(T_A, R_A, R_B, sk')$ and C_{BA} are equal. If they are not equal, A stops the session. Otherwise, A computes $C_{AB} = h(T_B, C_{BA}, sk')$ and sends it to B.

After this round, A checks if $T' - T_A$ is in a valid time period, where T' is the time A receives C_{SA}. If so, A checks whether C_{SA} and $h(C_{AS}, T_B, R_B, V_A)$ are equal. If it holds, A stops the session.

Similar, B checks if $T' - T_B$ is in a valid time period, where T' is the time B receives C_{SB}. If so, B checks whether C_{SB} and $h(C_{BS}, T_A, R_A, V_B)$ are equal. If it does not hold, B terminates the session. Otherwise, B checks whether C_{AB} and $h(T_B, C_{BA}, sk)$ are equal. If they are not equal, B terminates the session. Otherwise, B finishes the session.

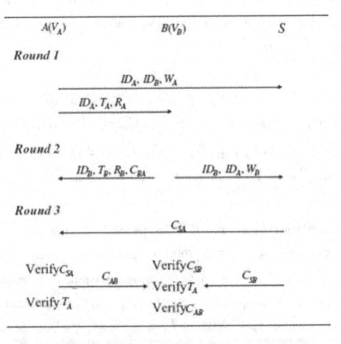

Fig. 1. Authenticated key exchange phase of Zhao et al.'s protocol

3   Cryptanalysis of Zhao et al.'s protocol

Since all the communication of messages is over public network, we could assume that an adversary $\mathscr{A}$ completely controls the communication channel among A, B and S, which means that he can perform some unwanted operations e.g. delete, insert or alter any messages transmitted over the network channel. We will demonstrate that Zhao et al.'s protocol is susceptible to off-line password guessing attack, privileged insider attack and stolen smart card attack.

3.1 Off-line Password Guessing Attack

It is well known that the user in the 3PAKE protocol is allowed to choose the password of his choice. We assume that for convenience, the user may like to choose a password that is easy to remember [12]. However, these easy-to-remember passwords are at the risk of guessing attacks since the entropy of these passwords are very limited. There are two kinds of password guessing attacks, namely online password guessing attack and offline password guessing attack, which are inherent in password-based authentication systems. In online password guessing attacks, an adversary tries to confirm the correctness of the guessed password in an online setup. While in the offline password attacks, an intruder or adversary tries to confirm the correctness of the guessed password using the intercepted message in an offline setup. Generally speaking, the off-line password attack is more dangerous since there is no need for the user or the server to participate in it.

In Ref. [8], Zhao et al. claimed that their protocol could withstand password guessing attacks. We will give a concrete off-line password guessing attacks in this subsection. Assume the adversary $\mathcal{A}$ intercepts the message $W_A = (C_{AS}, T_A, R_A, \Delta_A)$ transmitted between A and S, where $R_A = g^a \bmod p$, $C_{AS} = h(ID_A, ID_B, T_A, R_A, V_A)$ and $\Delta_A = g^{pw_A} \bmod p$. Then the adversary $\mathcal{A}$ can find the password pw_A by executing the following steps.

1) $\mathcal{A}$ guesses a password pw'_A and computes $\Delta'_A = g^{pw'_A} \bmod p$.
2) $\mathcal{A}$ checks whether the equation $\Delta'_A = \Delta_A$ holds. If the equation holds, $\mathcal{A}$ finds the valid password of the registered user. Otherwise, $\mathcal{A}$ repeats steps 1) and 2) until the valid password is matched or found.

From the aforementioned points, we proved that the adversary could get the correct password easily. Therefore, Zhao et al.'s protocol cannot withstand the off-line password guessing attack.

3.2 Privileged Insider Attack

In practical applications, many users use same passwords to access different applications or servers for their convenience e.g. email servers, online banking etc. [9]. However, if the administrator or a privileged insider $\mathcal{A}$ of the authentication server S knows the passwords of a registered user, he may misuse his password or impersonate that user by accessing his accounts, which is a very big security threat. In the initialization phase of Zhao et al.'s protocol, the user A sends his identity ID_A, the password-verifier $\Delta_A = g^{pw_A} \bmod p$ to S. Although, the password pw_A of a registered user is not directly transmitted to the authentication system, the privileged-insider or administrator of S could get the password by performing the offline password guessing attack. The detail of this attack is described in the following:

1) $\mathscr{A}$ guesses a password pw_A' and computes $\Delta_A' = g^{pw_A'} \bmod p$.

2) $\mathscr{A}$ checks whether the equation $\Delta_A' = \Delta_A$ holds. If the equation holds, $\mathscr{A}$ finds the correct password. Otherwise, $\mathscr{A}$ repeats steps 1) and 2) until the right password is found.

From the aforementioned points, we proved that the adversary could get the password correctly. Hence, Zhao et al.'s protocol is susceptible to the privileged insider attack.

3.3   Stolen Smart Card Attack

Kocher et al. [10] and Messerges et al. [11] demonstrated that the secret information stored in smart cards can be extracted by the differential power analysis attack. Then, we assume that the stored secret values Δ_A and ID_A could be extracted by an adversary $\mathscr{A}$ once the smart card of the user A was stolen by $\mathscr{A}$, where $\Delta_A = g^{pw_A} \bmod p$. The adversary $\mathscr{A}$ can find the password pw_A by executing the same steps in the above subsections. Hence, Zhao et al.'s protocol is susceptible to the stolen smart card attack.

4   Conclusion

Recently, Zhao et al. proposed an efficient 3PAKE protocol using smart cards. In this paper, we have pointed out that their protocol is vulnerable to three kinds of attacks in different scenarios. Hence, as per our security analysis Zhao et al.'s protocol is not suitable for real-world authentication applications.

Acknowledgements. This paper is supported by NPST Program by King Saud University Project Number 09-INF883-02.

References

1. Lin, C.L., Sun, H.M., Steiner, M., Hwang, T.: Three - party encrypted key exchange without server Public-keys. IEEE Communication Letters 5, 497–499 (2001)
2. Chang, C.C., Chang, Y.F.: A novel three-party encrypted key exchange protocol. Computer Standards and Interfaces 26, 471–476 (2004)

3. Lee, T.F., Hwang, T., Lin, C.L.: Enhanced three-party encrypted key exchange without server public keys. Computers & Security 23, 571–577 (2004)
4. Lee, S.W., Kim, H.S., Yoo, K.Y.: Efficient verifier-based key agreement protocol for three parties without server's public key. Applied Mathematics and Computation 167, 996–1003 (2005)
5. Guo, H., Li, Z., Mu, Y., Zhang, X.: Cryptanalysis of simple three-party key exchange protocol. Computers & Security 27(1-2), 16–21 (2008)
6. Huang, H.: A simple three-party password-based key exchange protocol. International Journal of Communication Systems 22(7), 857–862 (2009)
7. Chen, T.H., Lee, W.B., Chen, H.B.: A round- and computation-efficient three-party authenticated key exchange protocol. The Journal of Systems and Software 81, 1581–1590 (2008)
8. Zhao, J., Gu, D., Zhang, L.: Security analysis and enhancement for three-party password-based authenticated key exchange protocol. Security & Communication Networks 5(3), 273–278 (2012)
9. Hsiang, H., Shiha, W.: Improvement of the secure dynamic ID based remote user authentication next term scheme for multi-server environment. Computer Standards & Interfaces 31(6), 1118–1123 (2009)
10. Kocher, P.C., Jaffe, J., Jun, B.: Differential Power Analysis. In: Wiener, M. (ed.) CRYPTO 1999. LNCS, vol. 1666, pp. 388–397. Springer, Heidelberg (1999)
11. Messerges, T., Dabbish, E., Sloan, R.: Examining smart-card security under the threat of power analysis attacks. IEEE Transactions on Computers 51(5), 541–552 (2002)
12. Zhian, Z.: An Efficient Authentication Scheme for Telecare Medicine Information Systems. Journal of Medical Systems, Springer (2012), doi: 10.1007/s10916-012-9856-9

Author Index